WORKING IN THE ARCHIVES

Working
in the *Archives*

PRACTICAL RESEARCH METHODS
FOR RHETORIC AND COMPOSITION

ALEXIS E. RAMSEY,

WENDY B. SHARER,

BARBARA L'EPLATTENIER, AND

LISA S. MASTRANGELO

Southern Illinois University Press / Carbondale

13 12 11 10   4 3 2 1

Library of Congress Cataloging-in-Publication Data
Working in the archives : practical research methods for rhetoric and composition / [edited by] Alexis E. Ramsey ... [et al.].
        p. cm.
Includes bibliographical references and index.
ISBN-13: 978-0-8093-2950-2 (pbk. : alk. paper)
ISBN-10: 0-8093-2950-6 (pbk. : alk. paper)
1. English language—Rhetoric—Study and teaching—United States. 2. English language—Rhetoric—Research—Methodology. 3. Rhetoric—Archival resources. I. Ramsey, Alexis E., 1979–
PE1405.U6W67 2010
808'.042072—dc22   2009016638

To those who left their traces for us to find

CONTENTS

PART THREE: WORKING WITH/THROUGH ARCHIVAL MATERIAL

ACKNOWLEDGMENTS

We thank the contributors for their generosity in sharing what they have learned about archival work, as well as their willingness to revise, re-edit, check citations, and get permissions. We would also like to thank the two anonymous peer reviewers of this manuscript for their generous praise and enthusiasm; similarly, Southern Illinois University Press and Karl Kageff and his team have been marvelous to work with. We recommend the experience to everyone.

Additionally, we are grateful to our departments, our colleagues, our universities, and our families for their support throughout this three-year project. With these debts of gratitude in mind, we would each like to offer some more specific thank-yous:

Alexis. Thank you to Barb, Wendy, and Lisa whose willingness to work with me during the editing process taught me more about being a scholar than I could have imagined. I feel honored to count them as colleagues and friends. Thank you also to Shirley K Rose, Susan Curtis, and Sammie Morris, all of whom introduced me to archives, encouraged me to explore and play among the collections, and opened up this amazing avenue of research. Finally, thank you to my parents and to my husband, Francis, for their encouragement and love.

Wendy. First, thank you to Barb and Lisa for getting this project going and for being kind enough to ask me to participate. Without their inspiration and hard work, I would probably still be complaining that there needs to be a book that talks about how to do archival research in composition and rhetoric. Thanks also to Alexis, whose knowledge of archival theory and methods has made this book so much stronger. I'm also deeply indebted to my wonderful colleagues at East Carolina University—particularly Will Banks, Michelle Eble, and Catherine Smith—who have been generous with their time and energy in helping me to think about archival research and in enabling me to have some downtime from the day-to-day stresses of WPA life so that I could concentrate on this project.

The biggest thank-you, however, must go to my husband, Brent, who supports me in too many ways to list here.

Barb. This project has been as much about having fun as about work, and I thank Lisa, Alexis, and Wendy for that. Your patience, good humor, and flexibility made this a wonderful endeavor and deeply enriched my understanding of archival work; I am grateful that you are my colleagues and friends. As always, I want to thank Lisa, without whom my life would be *far* less interesting. Your friendship and your support in all things academic and personal mean more to me than I can ever tell you. I also thank my wife, Sarah, for her patience, support, and understanding throughout all of my projects.

Lisa. This project reminded me yet again why writing should never take place alone. The connections and friendships I have developed with the individual authors and the new relationships I have created with Wendy and Alexis are just one by-product of that. Their humor and depth of intellect have made them a joy to work with. The fact that Barb and I have now edited two books together and still remain friends is a testament to her patience and ability to push me further (both personally and intellectually) than I think I can go. Your ideas are what have led us to this moment. I also thank Anthony for his patience with yet another project, and Grace for reminding me that sometimes turning off the computer and baking a cake really is the most important thing in the world.

WORKING IN THE ARCHIVES

INTRODUCTION

*Alexis E. Ramsey, Wendy B. Sharer, Barbara
L'Eplattenier, and Lisa S. Mastrangelo*

> The Archive is not potentially made up of everything, as is human memory;
> and it is not the fathomless and timeless place in which nothing goes
> away that is the unconscious. The Archive is made from selected and
> consciously chosen documentation from the past and also from the mad
> fragments that no one intended to preserve and just ended up there.
> —*Carol Steedman*, Dust: The Archive and Cultural History

As historians of composition and rhetoric, each of us has spent time in various archives, at large and small institutions, in town and county archives, in attics and dusty rooms, searching for materials that might flesh out the stories and histories of modern rhetoric and composition we were presenting. For the most part, we've learned on our own how to search for documents, how to talk to archivists, how to achieve funding, and how to work with documents once we found them. Only one of us had any formal training in archival methods during graduate school—a single semester of class work researching and working in a local archive. Even with that training, our major source for information about archives was trial and error and conversation with others who have "gone before." As archival researchers, we've relied upon the generosity and advice of colleagues, mentors, and archivists to lead us to the materials that we could use. For, as Lynée Lewis Gaillet points out in her chapter in this collection, there are no books or collections of essays that teach rhetoric and composition scholars, both those new to the field and those who are experienced, the basics of archival research or how to use the archive from a rhetorical standpoint.

What does exist either addresses historical research and archival construction within a larger conversation about qualitative research methods (Connors in Kirsch and Sullivan, for example) or locates the discussion within a variety of disciplines, such as the social sciences and cultural studies.[1] Other guides to conducting archival research are focused on specific collections and how historical documents might be found and/or used in those particular collections.[2] The work these publications do is extremely important—published guides to collections, for example, have been important to many of our research projects. However, the result of their differing audiences and purposes is that these guides do not account for many of the unique contexts and situations in which archival work in rhetoric and composition gets done. Publications that do directly address methods for archival research in rhetoric and composition are few, taking the form of isolated articles in journals or chapters in edited collections that address larger themes.

One of the few texts devoted to the connection between rhetoric and composition and archival work was a special issue of *College English* in May 1999. The collection of articles, "Archivists with an Attitude," with essays by John C. Brereton, Linda Ferreira-Buckley, Steven Mailloux, and Thomas Miller and Melody Bowdon offers calls for further attention to methods of archival research, but these essays do little to offer solutions themselves (notably, this is not their purpose, but neither do they address this). Indeed, in the introduction to the issue, Brereton suggests that rhetoric and composition scholars need to "rethink and redefine the composition and rhetoric archive," highlighting "the interpretative acts needed to make sense of the archives in the first place" (575). Yet, his call for a theoretical understanding of the archive has remained largely unanswered. A notable exception to this overall silence is the Winter 2002 issue of *Rhetoric Society Quarterly*, which is dedicated to reconsidering archival methodologies, including the frameworks that influence how we devise research questions, the traditions that inform how we work with the archival sources we locate, and the means by which we might infuse archival research in rhetoric and composition with insights from feminist and cultural theory. Contributors to this important issue include Patricia Bizzell, Karlyn Kohrs Campbell, Richard Leo Enos, Susan Jarratt, Carol Mattingly, Christine Mason Sutherland, and Hui Wu.

Our hope is to extend this work and the work of scholars like Robert Connors who, in his 1992 essay "Dreams and Play: Historical Method and Methodology," encourages researchers to start with a hypothesis and then go into the archives and "play" (21–23). He calls the archive a place "where storage meets dreams, and the result is history," a claim that is hard to dispute for anyone who has had the pleasure of finding fascinating documents in a collection. But this depiction of archives and the lighthearted approach Connors recommends are likely not very helpful to the archival researcher who has never worked in an archive before or who is dependent on the finding of information to complete a thesis, an article, a book chapter, or a book, while traveling on limited means, living in a low-budget hotel, and restricted to a single week in an archive.

Connors's suggestion that researchers simply "play" might throw untrained researchers into what Carolyn Steedman calls archive fever (the physical condition of Jacques Derrida's more theoretical version). This fever is a kind of mental exhaustion brought about by the fear that, regardless of the amount of time spent in the archive, it is still not enough to give an accurate accounting of the past. As a researcher you lie

> in the bed of a cheap hotel. . . . You cannot get to sleep because you lie so narrowly, in an attempt to avoid anything that isn't shielded by sheets and pillowcase. The first sign then, is an excessive attention to the bed, an irresistible anxiety about the hundreds who have slept there before you. (17)

This anxiety broadens into the archive and the awareness of

> the myriads of the dead, who all day long, have pressed their concerns upon you. You think: these people have left me *the lot*. You think: I could hate these people; and then: I can never do these people justice; and finally: I shall never *get it done*. (17, italics in original)

This "fever" grips even the most seasoned of archival researchers, those who know their agendas and how to use finding aids, take researcher notes, and create taxonomic grids to help interpret their findings. For unseasoned researchers, such a fever is even more overwhelming—it is difficult to envision a project out of "the lot" left to you by "these people."

While we obviously find the framework Connors offers for thinking about archival work very appealing, we recognize the importance of attending to the practical aspects of archival work. Knowing how to approach a collection before going in can prevent wasting time and can maximize the researcher's experience in the archives. Knowing how and where to look and doing some homework in advance are imperative to a successful research experience. Finally, knowing how to navigate the archival space makes the archive less threatening and more manageable. We write this book, then, for the scholar new to the archive in the hope of helping prevent archive fever while at the same time enabling them to more systematically "play" in the archives.

An important note here is that we are distinguishing between *methodologies*, which Wu defines (for historians) as the theorization of the goal of research, and *methods*, which we define as techniques or ways of proceeding in gathering evidence (Kirsch and Sullivan) and working with said gathered evidence. For us, methods mean the practical application of methodologies—what occurs when we put the theory of methodologies into action and how that application is reflected in our work habits. We define methods, in part, as the answer to the question: "What do I do *next*?" or the question before that one, "*What do I do?*" The term *methods*, for us, means talking about issues related to the pragmatics of doing archival research. (Our recurring question to the authors during the writing process was, "What is the take-away of this piece for someone who has never worked in an archive before?") This collection will help scholars find, access, analyze, and compile the archival materials upon which diverse histories of rhetoric and composition might continue to be built.

We begin with two pieces that together provide a broad-stroke overview of the many issues—practical and theoretical—surrounding archival research methods in the field. Cheryl Glenn and Jessica Enoch use their archival research experiences to introduce some of the constructions around and through which archival research must proceed, demonstrating that archival research can be shaped by practices used to define and categorize materials within "the archive"; by the historical moments that influence which documents are produced, used, and ultimately preserved; by the disciplinary paradigms that influence the kinds of questions researchers tend to ask; and by researchers' cultural and intellectual position relative to the archival materials they seek to study. Gaillet's chapter complements Glenn and Enoch's contribution by providing a pragmatic overview of the steps involved in getting to the archive and to specific archival sources. Along the way, Gaillet provides sage advice on topics ranging from seeking funding for archival research to understanding rules and regulations governing archival research.

Following these introductory pieces, the collection provides more detailed discussion of both the theoretical and practical aspects of archival research methods. This discussion is organized around three themed sections:

Accessing the Archives

This section addresses methods that an archival researcher will use throughout his or her work but which figure most prominently just before or just as archival research begins. Questions taken up by chapters in this first grouping include: How do archivists process collections, and how do they make those collections accessible to researchers? What does a researcher need to understand about the construction of archives in order to locate items in them most effectively? What repository rules and standard practices can affect a researcher's access to collections? What publications and databases are available to assist in locating relevant archival materials, and how are these finding aids used? How do online archival materials enrich and complicate archival research methods? How can an archival researcher locate unique types of archival materials, such as pressed letter books and photographs?

Working with/through Archival Material

This section includes information to help archival researchers categorize, analyze, and make sense of the materials they locate in the archives. Questions addressed in this section include: What are some possible heuristics for organizing and analyzing archival materials? How can a researcher approach archival sources that are composed or organized in a way that obscures the issues of most interest to scholars in rhetoric and composition? What research methods can be used outside of the archive—observations and interviews, for example—to complement and extend research conducted within archival spaces? What external research should be done in order to understand, as fully as possible, the historical and cultural contexts of archival materials?

Creating Archives as Research Process

The final section of the collection explores methods of creating archival materials for use within a researcher's own project or for use by future archival researchers. Questions guiding the chapters in this portion of the book include: How are oral histories compiled, and how can they be used within the archives of rhetoric and composition? How can a researcher create an archives through disparate collecting practices? How can specialists in rhetoric and composition contribute to the preservation and processing of materials composed and used by leaders in the field? Through what methods can historians of rhetoric and composition further the construction of archives for the discipline?

Talking about Archival Research

Interspersed throughout these themed sections are stories of archival research as told by experienced historians of rhetoric and composition. Thanks to the work of Lori Ostergaard, these interviews provide a personalized glimpse of the struggles and successes of archival research, conveying information about research practices that these historians found beneficial and suggesting creative avenues for locating archival materials. Although Ostergaard developed her interview questions around the idea of serendipity in the archives, a consistent theme emerges: serendipity occurs because of preparation, awareness, and hard work.

Our categories and groupings, of course, are fluid: several of the individual pieces could have fit in a number of the sections, but we have located them where we thought they could best be used to generate conversations with other chapters in the section. Archival research, even when the researcher is prepared with a methods toolbox, is never a rigid process, nor should it be. Similar to the composing process itself, archival research is often recursive—subject to starts and stops, revisions and reworking, throughout the lifetime of a project. Recognizing the nonlinearity of the archival research process, we encourage you to read the selections in a nonlinear manner, to read against the organizational scheme we have imposed on these pieces, and to tease out other patterns, connections, and even complications across the chapters and sections.

We also encourage you to think about archival research as something that varies in scale and scope. While many of the pieces included in this collection explore extended archival research projects, and while the sheer size of many archives can make it seem as though archival research is synonymous with year-long, if not decades-long research projects, archives can also yield rewarding shorter-length projects. Often, shorter research projects focus on an archive's specialty and even on specific objects within that archive. In "The Platteville Papers Revisited," Kathryn Fitzgerald examines papers written by forty-four seniors at Platteville Normal School. Other chapters within the *Local Histories: Reading the Archives of Composition* collection also use similarly focused source material—college catalogs, meeting minutes, a set of letters from one student to her family—to construct their histories of composition practices within specific American colleges and universities.

Researchers at all levels of experience benefit from shorter, more focused archival projects. As part of their work in composition classes, for instance, many first-year students at East Carolina University participate in a three-week writing project that centers on archival research. After attending an orientation session in the campus library's North Carolina Collection—an archive of regional items dating back to colonial times—each student selects an object or document in the collection to research, with the ultimate goal of composing a concise reference guide for future users of the collection. These student-authored reference works provide historical context and any background information necessary to understand the significance of the item and its location in the larger collection.

Similarly, but with more advanced student-researchers in mind, professors Shirley K Rose, Susan Curtis, and Kris Bross offer a class on archival theory and methodology at Purdue University. In this class, students work with a single collection, processing the collection and developing semester-long research projects based on that collection. These smaller-scale projects, with the supervision and encouragement of experienced archival researchers, can be a wonderful way for newcomers to gain familiarity with archival principles and practices.

We hope that this book can act as a guide for both long- and short-term projects and that the pieces herein will capture the challenges, the frustrations, and, above all, the rewards of the archival research process.

Notes

1. See, for example, Philip C. Brooks, *Research in Archives*; Antoinette Burton, ed., *Archive Stories: Facts, Fictions, and the Writing of History*; John W. Creswell, *Qualitative*

Inquiry and Research Design: Choosing among Five Traditions and *Research Design: Qualitative, Quantitative, and Mixed Methods Approaches*; Norman K. Denzin and Yvonne S. Lincoln, *The SAGE Handbook of Qualitative Research*; Steven Fisher, *Archival Information (How to Find It; How to Use It)*; Patricia K. Galloway, *Practicing Ethnohistory: Mining Archives, Hearing Testimony, Constructing Narrative*; Gary McCulloch, *Documentary Research: In Education, History and the Social Sciences*; Ellen Perecman and Sara R. Curran, eds., *A Handbook for Social Science Field Research: Essays & Bibliographic Sources on Research Design and Methods*; and Anselm C. Strauss and Juliet M. Corbin, *Basics of Qualitative Research: Grounded Theory Procedures and Techniques*. Another important title is *Refiguring the Archive* by Carolyn Hamilton, Verne Harris, Michèle Pickover, and Graeme Reid, which focuses on African archives and demonstrates the degree to which thinking about archives is embracing new realities and new possibilities. Similarly, *An Archive of Feelings: Trauma, Sexuality, and Lesbian Public Cultures* by Ann Cvetkovich argues for the expansion of the use of archives and what is considered appropriate archivable materials.

2. See, for example, Meredith B. Colket and Frank Bridgers, *Guide to Genealogical Records in the National Archives*; Robert B. Matchette and Jan Danis, *Guide to Federal Records in the National Archives of the United States*; Richard S. Wright III, Nathan S. Rives, Mirjam J. Kirkham, and Saskia Schier Bunting, *Ancestors in German Archives: A Guide to Family History Sources*.

Works Cited

Brereton, John C. "Rethinking our Archives: A Beginning." *College English* 61.5 (1999): 574–76.

Brooks, Philip C. *Research in Archives*. Chicago: U of Chicago P, 1982.

Burton, Antoinette, ed. *Archive Stories: Facts, Fictions, and the Writing of History*. Durham, NC: Duke UP, 2005.

Colket, Meredith B., and Frank E. Bridgers. *Guide to Genealogical Records in the National Archives*. Washington, DC: National Archives and Records Administration, 1964.

Connors, Robert. "Dreams and Play: Historical Method and Methodology." *Methods and Methodology in Composition Research*. Ed. Gesa Kirsch and Patricia Sullivan. Carbondale: Southern Illinois UP, 1992. 15–36.

Creswell, John W. *Qualitative Inquiry and Research Design: Choosing among Five Traditions*. Thousand Oaks, CA: Sage, 1997.

———. *Research Design: Qualitative, Quantitative, and Mixed Methods Approaches*. Thousand Oaks, CA: Sage, 2002.

Cvetkovich, Ann. *An Archive of Feelings: Trauma, Sexuality, and Lesbian Public Cultures*. Durham, NC: Duke UP, 2003.

Denzin, Norman K., and Yvonna S. Lincoln, eds. *The SAGE Handbook of Qualitative Research*. Thousand Oaks, CA: Sage, 2005.

Derrida, Jacques. *Archive Fever: A Freudian Impression*. Trans. Eric Prenowitz. Chicago: U of Chicago P, 1996.

Fisher, Steven. *Archival Information (How to Find It; How to Use It)*. Westport, CT: Greenwood, 2004.

Fitzgerald, Kathyrn. "The Platteville Papers Revisited: Gender and Genre in a Normal School Writing Assignment." *Local Histories: Reading the Archives of Composition*. Ed. Patricia Donahue and Gretchen Flesher Moon. Pittsburgh, PA; U of Pittsburgh P, 2007. 115–33.

Galloway, Patricia K. *Practicing Ethnohistory: Mining Archives, Hearing Testimony, Constructing Narrative.* Lincoln: U of Nebraska P, 2006.

Hamilton, Carolyn, Verne Harris, Michèle Pickover, Graeme Reid, Razia Saleh, and Jane Taylor, eds. *Refiguring the Archive.* New York: Springer, 2002.

Kirsch, Gesa, and Patricia Sullivan, eds. *Methods and Methodology in Composition Research.* Carbondale: Southern Illinois UP, 1992.

Matchette, Robert. B., and Jan Danis. *Guide to Federal Records in the National Archives of the United States.* Washington, DC: National Archives and Records Administration, 1995.

McCulloch, Gary. *Documentary Research: In Education, History and the Social Sciences.* London: Routledge Falmer, 2004.

Perecman, Ellen, and Sara R. Curran, eds. *A Handbook for Social Science Field Research: Essays & Bibliographic Sources on Research Design and Method.* Thousand Oaks, CA: Sage, 2006.

Steedman, Carolyn. *Dust: The Archive and Cultural History.* New Brunswick, NJ: Rutgers UP, 2002.

Strauss, Anselm C., and Juliet M. Corbin. *Basics of Qualitative Research: Grounded Theory Procedures and Techniques.* Thousand Oaks, CA: Sage, 1990.

Wright, Raymond S., III, Nathan S. Rives, Mirjam J. Kirkham, and Saskia Schier Bunting. *Ancestors in German Archives: A Guide to Family History Sources.* Baltimore: Genealogical, 2004.

Wu, Hui. "Historical Studies of Rhetorical Women Here and There: Methodological Challenges to Dominant Interpretive Frameworks." *Rhetoric Society Quarterly* 32.1 (Winter 2002): 81–98.

PART ONE

General Information for Using Archives

INVIGORATING HISTORIOGRAPHIC PRACTICES IN RHETORIC AND COMPOSITION STUDIES

Cheryl Glenn and Jessica Enoch

"History" has become "histories," and histories change in response to the dominant values of institutions, cultures, and historiographers (history writers) themselves. *The* history of rhetoric and associated traditional research agendas strived for objectivity and truth, while contemporary historiographers make claims for unqualified objectivity in their reach for the "truth." Most of the scholars in our field now readily admit the impossibility of getting the story exactly right, let alone recovering an objective truth. Most of us realize that our historiographies will be subjective, given in large part to the interestedness of our research stance and our theoretical grounding. After all, each of us wants history and our view of that history to contribute to the positive value of our daily life. When history does not meet this requirement, we historiographers set to work, revisiting the archives, scouting out new ones, rewriting, and often overturning history. Histories of rhetoric and composition are a case in point.

Just a quick glimpse of some of the historical work in our field reveals how this complexity unfolds. In his 1953 dissertation, Albert R. Kitzhaber initiated disciplinary reflection by studying archived textbooks, leading the way for James A. Berlin's examination of textbooks, exams, surveys, and course and professional materials. John C. Brereton found that his research questions concerning the origins of composition studies could best be addressed by magazine articles, scholarly reports, early textbooks, teachers' testimony, student papers, writing curricula, and course instructions—documents that "were part of the common knowledge of composition teachers and administrators" (*Origins* xv).

As the proverbial dust settled on these histories, others began to question and extend the stories these historians told. In "History in the Spaces Left: African American Presence and Narratives of Composition Studies," Jacqueline Jones Royster and Jean C. Williams not only critiqued the ways in which historiographies like Brereton's, Berlin's, and Kitzhaber's "cast a shadow" on the work of African Americans inside composition studies but also expanded our professional consciousness by shedding light on the many ways such figures as Hallie Quinn Brown, Hugh M. Gloser, and Alain Locke contributed to the practice and pedagogy of composition in the university (581). Anne Ruggles Gere's "Kitchen Tables and Rented Rooms: The Extracurriculum of Composition" turned our historical gaze from the traditional classroom to alternative sites of writing and rhetorical instruction. Along with Gere, Royster, and Williams, many other historiographers continue to challenge understandings of what our history is by drawing our attention to people and places outside the traditional composition classroom: Nan Johnson's research has revealed a dazzling array of nineteenth-century parlor rhetorics; David Russell, the pedagogies for writing in academic disciplines other than English; Lucille M. Schultz, writing pedagogies for and practices of young nineteenth-century writers; and Jean Ferguson Carr, Stephen L. Carr, and Schultz, the nineteenth-century literacy textbooks used at home and at school. Such a rich bounty of archival recuperation galvanizes our field as we identify new materials or reread old ones and contextualize those materials in terms of contemporary scholarly conversations.

So far, the positive results of studies like these are at least three. First, of course, is that the results comprise a variety of versions of what the history of rhetoric and composition is and should be, implicitly arguing that there is no one history but instead many histories. Second, such studies stimulate our thinking in terms of which historical moments, people, and places merit our scholarly attention. And, third, these studies reflect the ways historiographic practice shifts in relation to the questions and imperatives of the present moment. Thomas P. Miller and Joseph G. Jones remind us of this: "Our histories are not what they were but neither are we." As motivated actions, whether showcasing traditionally valued people and practices or shedding light on the "ways that underrepresented groups have acquired and exercised the arts of rhetoric to garner historical agency," the historiographies resulting from all of these archival studies demonstrate just how rhetoric and composition history, once compiled and written, falls apart, only to be recompiled and rewritten, regularly and purposefully (Miller and Jones 436).

In this essay, we examine the historiographic trajectory of rhetoric and composition studies by interrogating the most basic elements of traditional archival practice and historiography. Our goal is to reflect on what we do in the archive and to suggest ways that we might broaden the scope of historiographic methods by identifying new places to look, new questions to ask, and new issues to consider. We pose this challenge to traditional historiographic research methods by drawing from our own and other scholars' experiences in conducting extensive archival research, much of which troubles histories of rhetoric and composition. As Cheryl researched and wrote *Rhetoric Retold* and *Unspoken*, she worked at the Newberry Library in Chicago; the Houghton Library, Cambridge, Massachusetts; the National Library of Scotland and the University of Edinburgh Library, Edinburgh, Scotland; and the Center for Southwest Studies, Albuquerque, New Mexico. To support her work in *Refiguring Rhetorical Education*, Jess researched at the Library of Congress, Washington, D.C.; the Cumberland County History Society, Carlisle, Pennsylvania; the American Antiquarian Society, Worcester, Massachusetts; and the Webb County Heritage Foundation, Laredo, Texas. Naturally, many of our assertions here arise from our experiences, our successes, our many false starts, and our innumerable failures. Nonetheless, we hope that our argument reveals how the interrogation of various features of archival research and historiographic method can create opportunities for researchers to continue to enrich contemporary understandings of researching and writing histories of our field.

The Search for Archival Materials

The formulation of the project and concomitant research agenda is most often the first step in historiography and archival research. Rarely do researchers identify an archive and hope to find a research project in it. Instead, they begin with a broad research question and then read widely and deeply until they begin to identify an outline of significance or basis of investigation for the project at hand. Once researchers have a handle on the topic, they consider the kind of archival documents that would support, extend, further, and energize the project.

From their initial sense of a topic, researchers extract questions crucial to the research plan: What materials should they now look for? What kinds of primary and archival documents will help them to answer their research question? To answer these questions, researchers must conduct a good deal of detective work: combing libraries large and small, studying catalogs, and tracing collections—all with the singular "purpose" of identifying specific kinds of archival documents, manuscripts, and personal papers.

Literary scholars traditionally search out the papers or manuscripts of an author or those financial, political, or social papers that might give new light to a literary text. Archival researchers in rhetoric and composition, however, often turn their gaze toward other kinds of documents: "actual student writings, teacher records, unprinted notes, and pedagogical materials, and ephemera that writing courses have always generated but never kept" (Connors 225). If our purpose is to study the history of university-level writing practices, these are the kinds of materials that provide insight into the practices of English 101 and its iterations. As Robert J. Connors writes, the historian's project in rhetoric and composition is "the telling of stories about the tribe that make the tribe real. [. . . W]e are telling the stories of our fathers and mothers, we are legitimating ourselves through legitimating them" (234).

But what if the scholar is curious to know about how women or marginalized groups learned or taught rhetoric and writing? How might this initial archival move *dis*enable the researcher from finding resources that would permit pursuit of this line of inquiry, that would fulfill the research purpose?

Over the course of her research for *Refiguring Rhetorical Education*, Jess asked and answered the preceding question during the process of considering how female teachers participated in the education of African American, Native American, and Chicano/a students. Jess's initial, wide-ranging reading of secondary sources concerning Chicano/a students in particular had stimulated her interest in Mexican education in Texas during the period of the Mexican Revolution (1910–20). Given that this historical moment was marked by shifting national identities, economic growth and disparity, and wartime strife, Jess deduced that educational practices must have also gained new shape during this period of change. When she began her search for what Connors identifies as field-specific archival materials (textbooks, student writing, teacher notes, and pedagogical materials), she came up with nothing. Her search seemed only to reify what Guadalupe San Miguel Jr. calls the "myth of Mexican indifference toward public education"—a myth that promotes the idea that "Mexican Americans have not really cared for education or else they have failed to appreciate its importance and benefit to their community in particular and to the society at large" (xvi).

Determined to challenge this myth, Jess returned to secondary materials again, this time purposefully reading *beyond* the myth of indifference to consider how other kinds of materials might reflect educational initiatives inside the Mexican community. Finally, she came across a 1974 article by scholar José Limón called "*El Primer Congreso Mexicanista de 1911* [The first Mexican Congress of 1911]: A Precursor to Contemporary Chicanismo." In it, Limón discusses *La Crónica* [The Chronicle], a Spanish-language newspaper, based in Laredo, Texas, that was owned and operated by the Idar family. Limón writes that the Idars—one of whom being Jovita Idar, a local Laredo teacher—used *La Crónica* to wage a campaign of "journalistic resistance" and focused on a number of local issues, one of the most prominent being the discrimination of Mexican students in Texas public schools (86).

Jess immediately looked for *La Crónica* and found that it was available on microfilm and through interlibrary loan—but in Spanish, of course. In order to translate these materials, Jess spent hour after hour working with graduate students in the Spanish department, discovering—in the process—a wealth of information concerning Mexican female teachers and students. Three of these teachers, Jovita Idar, Marta Peña, and Leonor Villegas de Magnón, used the press as an alternative site to educate Mexican students, thereby avoiding the discriminatory practices taking place in Texas public schools. Given their impressive pedagogical endeavors, these teachers quickly became the central focus of one of Jess's chapters in *Refiguring Rhetorical Education.*

It is important to note that finding these teachers and their work was contingent on letting go of the disciplinary ideal of the kinds of materials that constitute primary and archival material. If Jess had ended her search after finding no textbooks, pedagogical materials, or student papers, she would never have found *La Crónica,* let alone the teachers who taught through its pages. To imagine the historiographic possibilities attendant in the works of Idar, Peña, and Villegas, Jess had to reconsider the act of identifying historical texts in two ways. First, she had to question the traditional means of rhetorical education and consider what *other* forms teachers might use to teach or students to learn. Second, and more important, she had to rethink the language these specific students and teachers had used. Of course, in retrospect, Jess realizes that Spanish would have been the language of instruction for Idar's, Peña's, and Villegas's readers, but the traditional practice of our field (and our scholars) prompts us to think in terms of English only with regard to the documents that constitute the history of rhetoric and composition.

Simply rethinking the starting point of primary and archival research enriches the histories of rhetoric and composition with possibilities for new perspectives and voices. But alternative source materials and non-English languages are not our only means of doing so. When Cheryl was working at the Newberry Library on *Rhetoric Retold,* her goal was to locate materials that delineated expectations for ancient women and their cultural roles, materials that helped explain the cultural constraints on women's rhetorical participation—a frustrating goal, to be sure. On a lark, she turned her attention to gynecological guides from second-century AD naturalist Galen of Pergamum. Ultimately (and ironically), these guides illuminated for her the one-sex model of humanity that dominated thinking from antiquity through the Renaissance. With his structural models of the male and female reproductive organs, Galen persuaded early thinkers that women were, in essence, imperfect, undeveloped men who lacked one vital and superior characteristic: heat. Furthermore, he provided the gynecological and anatomical drawings to prove his point: "Now just as mankind is the most perfect of all animals, so within mankind the man is more perfect than the woman, and the reason for his perfection is his excess of heat, for heat is Nature's primary instrument" (2:630).

To reach an understanding of ancient perceptions of women and Mexican education, both Cheryl and Jess had to gain, in Richard Enos's words, a greater "awareness of our limited methods of research" and allow for other types of material to enrich scholarly conversations and understandings (67). As Enos argues, scholars in the field often "clin[g] to extant texts as the sole material for scholarly study" and rarely work to "'discover' new evidence" (69). Our work, then, should be to let go of our dependence on traditional texts and research materials and push ourselves to search for new kinds of evidence that might reveal different understandings of how people throughout history have learned and deployed rhetoric and writing. Thus, by questioning the first and most basic act of archival research—identifying potential resources—we can see how all scholars might redirect the field's attention in important ways.

Archival Locations

Of course, it is difficult to tease apart these moments of researching, writing, and reading, because at the same time that scholars are refining the research question and looking for sources, they are mostly likely also considering which archives to visit. After all, the physical space of the archive holds an honored and almost religious place in the scholar's mind. In "My Dream Archive," Christopher Phelps writes that the "archive is a revered place of pilgrimage. It is the Mecca of historians" (1). Phelps goes on to explain that the journey to the archive often "requires temporal and financial sacrifice, but the traveler is sustained by the prospect of discovery and the insight, the perpetual hope that the next box, the next folder, the next file, will contain the elusive find that will afford a window to the past" (1). Connors confirms Phelps's description, defining the upper-case-A Archives as "specialized kinds of libraries" containing those "rarest and most valuable of data" that usually exist in "only a single copy" (225). The Archive, then, is the place that contains what most scholars believe to be the "only *real* historical sources" (225; emphasis added).

Locating these Meccas of information is simultaneously easy and difficult. Scholars rarely know what they'll find until they arrive. And despite the fact that just getting there "can be expensive and difficult," scholars still "have to travel to the distant places where [they hope] their quarry lies" (Altick 11). Given these difficulties, many scholars begin their Archival search at rare-book libraries at large research institutions, as many in the field continue to tether their research to such sites as Harvard's archival collection of student writing, the Richard S. Beal Collection of rhetoric and composition documents (divided between the University of New Hampshire and the University of Rhode Island), the Kenneth Burke Papers at the Pennsylvania State University, and the John A. Nietz Old Schoolbook Collection at the University of Pittsburgh. These Archives, and many others, have enabled scholars working on a wide variety of historiographic projects to gather all sorts of archival materials and then rewrite the history of rhetoric and composition.

Not all archival research in rhetoric and composition begins—or ends—on a university campus or at a prestigious research library, however. With increasing regularity, many researchers in rhetoric and composition have looked beyond Connors's Archive to consider what other, lower-case-*a* archives might hold, archives that don't immediately promise insights into the practices or histories of our field. These *a* archives can range from small, local archives run by community members such as the Cumberland County Historical Society and the Webb County Heritage Foundation—archives Jess visited during her research process—to boxes of materials found in someone's office, garage, or even in a relative's attic. Wendy Sharer, for instance, opens *Vote and Voice: Women's Organizations and Political Literacy, 1915–1930* by describing how her project came into being: with the discovery of political materials in her grandmother's attic. Here, Sharer found material evidence of her grandmother's involvement in a women's club, the Y-Dames of Bethlehem, Pennsylvania. This archive was full of "records of meetings and collaborative projects that were devoted to, among other things, reforming internal affairs, studying political history, and advancing career opportunities for women" (*Vote* 2). Such a finding made Sharer realize that her "understanding of 'citizenship' and 'politics' was severely limited and, as a result, so was [her] knowledge of women's discursive practices of civic and political engagement" (3). This realization, of course, led to more archival research, more writing, and the publication of *Vote and Voice*.

Charlotte Hogg's discovery of her grandmother's unpublished writings set in motion the intellectual project on women's literacy practices that was to become *From the Garden Club: Rural Women Writing Community*. In her examination, Hogg studies "Early Paxton," a leather-bound collection of remembrances of pre-1925 Paxton, Nebraska, written by local women. One of the most prolific and talented in the group was Hogg's grandmother: "While most women who contributed to the book wrote less than ten pages . . . , my grandma wrote forty-four pages" (20). Not surprisingly, "Early Paxton" was not archived in a great research library on a university campus; it was shelved at the local library, which, years ago, Hogg's grandmother urged her eleven-year-old granddaughter to visit upon moving to Paxton. Hogg reflects,

> Shortly after my family moved to Paxton, I was restless and sulky, and my grandma encouraged me to go to the library. I borrowed her key (she was president of the library board at the time) and walked two blocks to the library, where my grandma and other women from town had contributed to "Early Paxton." I opened the book to see my grandma's pages and to see

if I recognized any other contributors. Grandma's neighbor, Elsie Lenore Holmstedt Windels, had also written a piece for this volume of remembrances. [. . .] Even at the age of eleven, I sensed how important a sense of place was to those who lived there. [. . .] That was the first time I realized that there was more to the people in Paxton than I would have guessed. And I made this discovery through the [unpublished] writings of older women in town. (28–29)

Years later, Hogg would return to this unpublished book manuscript to read it through the lens of rhetoric and composition studies. In addition to tapping "Early Paxton," she fortified her study by examining newspaper clippings, short essays, cards, letters, funeral programs, and notes that her grandmother had saved over the years in her roles as mother, grandmother, library president, Methodist-church historian, and Paxton correspondent of the *Keith County News*.

Through her research, Hogg did not visit Harvard's or Yale's archival holdings but instead found her own fascinating and important archive in the small town of Paxton. Her work and Sharer's, as well as the work of many others, compel us to look beyond the traditional university library as the only worthy Archive and consider other sites as viable for archival work.

When researchers identify nontraditional archives, they are presented with new and fascinating archival questions: Why should we see this collection of materials as an archive? What should happen to this archive and its materials? How do we recognize and respect this archive as a site not just to do research but as a site with other kinds of local, community, or familial investments? By widening the scope of the sites for our historical research, we necessarily confront new questions about and new possibilities for archival recovery, archival methods, and historiographic intervention. For when one shifts the site of analysis, other research features such as the figures, practices, and insights recovered will also shift accordingly. Thus, even when we don't have the good fortune to find archives in our relatives' attics or bureaus, there are smaller, local archives that interpellate us, calling us to value their holdings and reflect on the purpose that archive might serve. These smaller collections or serendipitous discoveries also expand our notions of what counts as a primary resource and especially of what counts as a contribution to the histories, theories, and practices of rhetoric and composition.

Agents in the Archive

As we work to identify materials and locate archives, we must also acknowledge the people who make this kind of recovery possible. So far in this essay, we have defined researchers like ourselves—scholars in rhetoric and composition—as the primary agents in the research project: We pose the research question, identify a destination archive, travel to it, and then activate the materials we locate there.

In the following section, we focus attention on the work that we do as researchers and the reflections we should make as we take up our work. In this section, we highlight the importance of the *other* agents in the archive and offer suggestions as to how we might create stronger "archival relationships" that would make archival recovery more effective, more visible, and more accessible.

Other Researchers

First among the group of other agents are the scholars in the field of rhetoric and composition whose work and collegiality enable their fellow researchers to build on their findings and ask different historiographic questions. In "Archivists: Rethinking Our Archive," Brereton writes that "historians depend on the work of their forebears, on the collecting that forms libraries and repositories great and small and on the interpretations and narratives that shape consciousnesses" (575). Where would we be if Kitzhaber had not created that extensive bibliography? How would we know where to go if Brereton himself had not mentioned the specific archives he tapped in order to compose his groundbreaking *Origins of Composition Studies*? Thus, it is the work of our forebears and our contemporaries that provides researchers with guideposts for locating materials, inspiration for working in long-established and more informal archives, and ideas for how best to employ archived materials for our own purposes.

Although it is true that we share archival information in the acknowledgments and bibliographies of our texts, scholars might also work on other ways to improve our collaboration about research methods and archival findings. In "Dialoging with *Rhetorica*," Jane Donawerth and Lisa Zimmerelli stress the importance of scholars networking with one another about the potential of an archive. For Donawerth, "networking" is the "shortest route to discovery": "Whenever I meet a feminist scholar, I ask her whether she has come across any pre-1900 women's writing on communication. Eleanor Kerkham remembered Sei Shonagon's *Pillow Book*, and there I found sections on letter writing, conversation, and preaching" (6). Donawerth's anecdote exemplifies the rich serendipity of off-the-cuff conversations that deliver the initial inspiration of a research project.

Casual revelations can be exciting, to be sure, but systematic and public networking would be even more productive for established researchers and graduate students alike. To that end, we might formalize collaboration about archival research, starting with the membership of the Special Interest Groups on Archival Work at the Conference on College Composition and Communication and ending, perhaps, with a collaborative archival database. This database could be either a specialized print or online publication in which scholars report on the archives they have visited and the work they have conducted there. Such a publication or site could be modeled on the Bedford Bibliographies, but instead of briefly annotating new scholarship, the archival bibliography could offer readers summaries of sources researchers have located in various archives and links to the Web sites of the archives themselves. This kind of database would not only enable new scholars in the field to see the range and variety of our archival work, but it would also help them to see how and where historiographic recovery gets done.

Archivist Agents

In addition to creating stronger networks in the field between researcher-agents inside rhetoric and composition, it is also important to acknowledge the archivists as vital agents in the archive. They are the ones who catalog the materials that we locate; they are the ones who decide what to preserve and how to catalog it, thereby controlling the materials we can access and the processes we take to get to them. And they are the ones who see the archive collections purposefully, as a whole, while we, too often, limit our vision to the small part of the archive we intend to use. As Sharer writes in "Disintegrating Bodies of Knowledge," it is important that scholars of rhetoric and composition not only be knowledgeable in the methods and methodologies of historical scholarship in our field but also in the work of the archivist. Sharer explains, "We cannot afford to ignore the various materials processes—acquisition, appraisal, collection management, description, indexing, preservation, oxidation, and deaccession—that affect the corpus of records on which we may be able to construct diverse and subversive narratives to challenge previous, exclusionary historical accounts of rhetoric" (124).

Sharer calls on scholars to gain a sense of the archivists' work and to establish lines of communication with them about the kinds of primary and archival materials valuable to our field. One excellent example of such a practice is the collaboration between rhetoric and composition scholars Cinthia Gannett, Kate Tirabassi, Amy Zenger, and Brereton with archivist Elizabeth Slomba. This team worked together to create the Archives on the History of Writing and Writing Instruction at the University of New Hampshire—an archival project that became "enormously valuable" for all parties involved (115). Through the process of building the archive, the four scholars in rhetoric and composition "learned a great deal about how archives are constructed and participated directly in the composition and collection of the archive itself," while Slomba "came to value a variety of artifacts related to writing pedagogy and writing program administration" (115). Of course, Gannett, Tirabassi, Zenger, Brereton, and Slomba are not the only ones who will reap the benefits of this program. This archive will enable the writing community at UNH in particular and the field more generally to gain a deep and detailed picture of writing in a specific university setting. Such collaborations can serve as models for how researchers in rhetoric and composition might work with archivists not only to preserve the important and valued documents in our field but also to widen the possibilities for archival investigation. If more scholars and archivists follow the lead of those who composed the UNH archive, we would be able to gain a much fuller sense of how writing has been taught across time and institutions (see also "Invisible Hands: Recognizing Archivists' Work to Make Records Accessible" by Sammie L. Morris and Shirley K Rose in part 2 of the current volume).

Archival Reflections

In this section, we examine what it means to see ourselves as "sources of data" that are important to the research process (Connors 227). To be sure, our interestedness and theoretical grounding mean much to the archival project in particular and the project of writing history more generally. We acknowledge that histories are always partial and always interested—*partial* in the sense that it remains incomplete with respect to the reality they presume to depict and *interested* in the sense that it is an interpretive rendering of evidence (Howard). Archival acts of reading are tethered to and in the researcher's own perceptions and prejudices as well as the theoretical frame used to approach the work. As we make these considerations about our interestedness and our theoretical grounding, though, we also explore how these two ideas prompt us to acknowledge other important agents in the act of archival recovery besides the researcher and the archivist.

Interestedness

In the field of rhetoric and composition, it has become almost commonplace for researchers to devote space in their manuscripts to revealing their standpoint and interestedness in relation to their project. Taking responsibility for how and why we might read and write as we do extends far beyond the printed page in which scholars acknowledge their positionality. This understanding of one's position inside of and approach to the final text must accompany each scholar from the initial stages of archival inquiry through the completion of the writing, steadily interanimating the multiple acts that constitute the writing process. Such statements also help the reader understand where the researcher thinks he or she stands in terms of the project and the ways that interestedness informs both the researcher's overarching research agenda and the final text.

Often, it is one's positionality that creates a fruitful, research-launching dissonance. At the outset of our historiographic projects, both of us felt dissonance in our intellectual lives, with our field of study, with received-at-the-time history. Instead of contributing a positive value to our daily life, traditional histories of rhetoric and composition offered shortcomings—shortcomings about women rhetors (Cheryl) and women teachers (Jess). As we entered the archive to engage in the act of re-reading, then, we acknowledged our interestedness and re-read documents in ways that enabled us to listen to texts in new ways. Naturally, any stance inevitably leads to our accentuating some materials and passing over others; we cannot tell everything and move in every direction. What is important is that we do our best to try to uncover the ways our positionality operates and to consider, throughout the historiographic process, how this stance channels us to write one kind of history and directs us away from other possibilities.

Theoretical Grounding

Together, with many other scholars, we have worked to "break up and dissolve those parts" of the past that conflicted with our contemporary ideologies, consciously reading the primary materials we accessed in the archive through a theoretical framework (Nietzsche 75). As we engaged in this process, we soon realized that this relationship between archival reading and theoretical grounding creates a generative tension that opens up possibilities for what we see, value, and then leverage.

Thus, when we began our respective research projects, we found that we needed to relinquish the conceptual apparatus that produced a male-only tradition of rhetoric (Cheryl) and a specific definition of rhetorical education (Jess). Not surprisingly, feminist theory enabled us (and many others) to resist traditional histories and historiographic practices at the same time that we were creating new kinds of historical inquiry and archival reading practices. Cheryl's initial, graduate-student work on Aspasia (seven pages of historical description) moved forward only after she used feminism as a way to broaden her definition of rhetoric and its practice (to include the private sphere) and her requirements for being a rhetor (to include figures whose contributions appear only in secondary sources, like Socrates)—small theoretical adjustments with rich payoffs. Jess also made use of feminist theory's calling into question overarching disciplinary narratives by critically examining the definition and history of rhetorical education. She found that when composing histories of rhetorical education, scholars often looked for moments when students learned about canonical rhetorical theorists and their respective rhetorical principles and theories. Building from feminist theory, Jess saw that if she shifted the definition of rhetorical education to the pedagogical practices that enable students to participate in cultural and civic conversations, the historical lens allowed for a much-wider range of archival texts to read and people to study.

For the two of us, feminist theory made it possible to adopt different kinds of reading practices in the archives. Although every scholar will not and should not use feminist theory as a primary theoretical impulse, it is vital to note the ways in which any theoretical frame we choose—like our positionality—both enhances and limits our work. For example, Carol Mattingly warns in "Telling

Evidence" that the feminist perspective scholars bring to the archives can lead them to focus on only certain kinds of historical women, overlooking the rhetorical work of women who now seem socially conservative (103). As a way to address Mattingly's concern, scholars of every theoretical stripe must continually place their archival reading in conversation with their theoretical disposition, forging a reciprocal process that permits theory to speak to archival finds and archival findings to push against, open up, question, extend, constrict, or even disregard the theoretical frame altogether. In other words, the reading and the theory should inform each other.

More Agents in the Archive

Finally, in addition to reflecting one's positionality in terms of the project as well as one's theoretical approach, we must consciously acknowledge those who, beyond the researcher and archivist, might be affected by our scholarly conversation. When Royster sets out her afrafeminist methodological approach in *Traces of a Stream*, she explains that her approach should prompt a paradigm shift in the ways in which scholars conceive of both their subjects and their audiences. According to Royster, scholars should develop more discerning understandings of "*who* the primary and secondary audiences are and *who*, even, the *agents* of research and scholarship include" (*Traces* 274). In other words, researchers must keep in mind the members of the community they are writing about: "Whatever the knowledge accrued, it [sh]ould be both presented and represented with this community, and at least its potential for participation and response, in mind" (274). To enact such a methodological approach towards both subjects and audiences, researchers must take up "four sites of critical regard: careful analysis, acknowledgement to passionate attachments, attention to ethical action, and commitment to social responsibility" (279).

Royster is not alone in this perception. Researchers using various methodologies are expected to and should strive to account for how their own positionalities and ways of asking, seeing, interpreting, speaking, and writing might affect their research subjects and their communities. Increasingly, rhetoric and composition scholars like Royster are identifying agencies and audiences and then "operating ethnographically" as a means to tell their stories (Royster, *Traces* 282). When Cheryl, for instance, embarked on the research that would become *Unspoken: A Rhetoric of Silence*, she spent several weeks working in the Center for Southwest Research, an archive located in Zimmerman Library, on the University of New Mexico campus. Her purpose was to uncover materials that illuminated the widely touted figure of the "silent Indian." Cheryl soon discovered that in order to make sense of the archival materials and sociolinguistic research, she needed to speak with Native people herself, asking for their comments on the materials she had uncovered. During a series of interviews and meetings, Cheryl realized that all the Native people knew about the stereotype and welcomed the opportunity to get the story straight—to speak for themselves (never for *all* Native people) on tape, in person, over the telephone, or through e-mail. And when Cheryl shared her word-for-word transcripts with them, they sometimes improved it, talking to researchers and research, speaking for themselves.

This kind of communication with and consideration of communities about whom we might research is vitally important to historiographic writing. As Royster explains, "the goal is better practices so that we can exchange perspectives, negotiate meaning, and create understanding with the intent of being in a good position to cooperate," benefit, and understand the people who are "*subject matter* but not *subjects*" ("When the First Voice" 38, 32; emphasis added).

Even with this goal in mind, the dialogic ethnography that Cheryl undertook (and many other researchers in our field continue to employ) remains first and foremost a genre involving the art of interpretation. It is not an exact science and carries with it many of the same tensions of historiography: the task of connecting the "real" and the discourse. Therefore, even the most collaborative and dialogic ethnography or archival inquiry, even the most ethically admirable, is an intervention into a world that has been lived and narrated by the person who has experienced it and then is once again recorded, interpreted, and circulated by the researcher. In other words, historiographers, like ethnographers, concentrate on connecting the experiences of *someone* to the representation of those experiences by *someone else*. Thus, the issue is not so much *why* we approach various groups of people or archival collections but *how* we work to understand and honor their perspective, their experience. The *goal* of accurate interpretation is never enough. When we engage in research, we need to know what our self-interest is, how that interest might enrich our disciplinary field as it affects others (perhaps even bridging the gap between academia and other communities), and resolve to participate in a reciprocal cross-boundary exchange, in which we talk *with* and listen *to* Others, whether they are speaking to us in person or via archival materials.

Invigorating Our Histories through Archival Reflection

As we hope we have demonstrated, it is essential that we reflect critically on the work we do in the archive and how we represent that work in our historiographies. Each new generation (and half generation) of rhetoric and composition scholars from Kitzhaber and Berlin to Gere and Johnson extends our understanding of archival recovery by producing a version of history that in turn prompts new questions and concerns about the historiographic process and product.

Our analysis here aims to help scholars continue to consider how we might open up even more possibilities for archival recovery. A concerted attention to choices of archival documents and locations should enable us to enrich our sense of the kind of "texts" that can contribute to our historical understandings as well as the places where these "texts" might be found. A greater consciousness of the agents in the archive should prompt us to initiate better networks among scholars and to collaborate with archivists as a means to broaden our historiographic vision and deepen our knowledge of what an archive is and can be. And, finally, a consistent reflection on who we are as researchers should call us to think more critically about our interestedness in our research agendas, our choice of theoretical frames, and our attention to and regard for the *other* agents in the archive—our historical subjects. Thus, this analysis of our archival work has indeed brought into focus many important issues and concerns.

We conclude here with one final point. As we highlight the importance of the theoretical lens we use to complement our research process, we do not mean to say that "anything goes" in terms of reading primary and archival documents and writing our histories. Although no single historiography can be the "correct" one, although new archives and archival materials are recovered every year by every generation of scholars, all responsible archival research and the resulting historiography must be based on facts, research, and primary materials. Even as we work on that axis we refer to as "history," an axis pitted by the skeptical probings of postmodern and poststructural critiques, we continue to place real value in historical knowledge, in understanding research methods, in reading promiscuously, in contextualizing our research; in short, in doing our homework. Linda Ferreira-Buckley admonishes us to do just that: "Years ago, our histories were undertheorized; today I fear they are underresearched" (28).

As we hope our discussion indicates, rhetoric and composition scholars can continue to probe our research practices and articulate our histories. After all, historiographers want to make truth claims. We care whether a given account is genuinely credible and probable, because what is ultimately at stake is not only constructing a "usable past" that speaks to present concerns but also treating that past ethically while getting it right (as far as doing so is possible). In the process, rhetoric and composition scholars might well rediscover some treasures among the written, visual, or material artifacts that our subjects have left behind. More important, though, if we consciously and carefully activate the materials in the archives, we might discover ways in which to address the present scholarly moment meaningfully and announce the near future insightfully.

Works Cited

Altick, Richard D. *The Scholar Adventurers.* 1950. New York: Free, 1966.

Berlin, James A. *Rhetoric and Reality: Writing Instruction in American Colleges 1900–1985.* Carbondale: Southern Illinois UP, 1987.

———. *Writing Instruction in Nineteenth-Century American Colleges*. Carbondale: Southern Illinois UP, 1984.

Brereton, John C., ed. *The Origins of Composition Studies in the American College, 1875–1925*. Pittsburgh: U of Pittsburgh P, 1995.

———. "Rethinking Our Archive: A Beginning." *College English* 61.5 (1999): 574–76.

Carr, Jean Ferguson, Stephen L. Carr, and Lucille M. Schultz. *Archives of Instruction: Nineteenth-Century Rhetorics, Readers, and Composition Books in the United States*. Carbondale: Southern Illinois UP, 2005.

Connors, Robert J. "Dreams and Play: Historical Method and Methodology." *Selected Essays of Robert J. Connors*. Ed. Lisa Ede and Andrea Lunsford. Boston: Bedford, 2003. 221–35.

Donawerth, Jane, and Lisa Zimmerelli. "Dialoguing with *Rhetorica*." *Peitho* 8.1 (2003): 4–6.

Enoch, Jessica. *Refiguring Rhetorical Education: Women Teaching African American, Native American, and Chicano/a Students, 1865–1911*. Carbondale: Southern Illinois UP, 2008.

Enos, Richard Leo. "The Archeology of Women in Rhetoric: Rhetorical Sequencing as a Research Method for Historical Scholarship." *Rhetoric Society Quarterly* 32.1 (2002): 65–79.

Ferreira-Buckley, Linda. "Serving Time in the Archives." *Rhetoric Review* 16.1 (Fall 1997): 26–28.

Galen of Pergamum. *On the Usefulness of the Parts of the Body*. Trans. Margaret Tallmadge May. 2 vols. Ithaca, NY: Cornell UP, 1968.

Gannett, Cinthia, Elizabeth Slomba, Kate Tirabassi, Amy Zenger, and John C. Brereton. "'It Might Come in Handy.' Composing a Writing Archive at the University of New Hampshire: A Collaboration between the Dimond Library and the Writing-across-the-Curriculum/Connors Writing Center, 2001–2003." *Centers for Learning: Writing Centers and Libraries*. Ed. James Elmborg and Sheril Hook. Chicago: Association of College and Research Libraries, 2005. 115–37.

Gere, Anne Ruggles. "Kitchen Tables and Rented Rooms: The Extracurriculum of Composition." *College Composition and Communication* 45.1 (1994): 75–107.

Glenn, Cheryl. *Rhetoric Retold: Regendering the Tradition from Antiquity through the Renaissance*. Carbondale: Southern Illinois UP, 1997.

———. *Unspoken: A Rhetoric of Silence*. Carbondale: Southern Illinois UP, 2004.

Hogg, Charlotte. *From the Garden Club: Rural Women Writing Community*. Lincoln: U of Nebraska P, 2006.

Howard, Jean. "Towards a Postmodern, Politically Committed, Historical Practice." *Uses of History: Marxism, Postmodernism, and the Renaissance*. Ed. Francis Backer, Peter Hulme, and Margaret Iverson. Manchester, Eng.: Manchester UP, 1991. 108–9.

Johnson, Nan. *Gender and Rhetorical Space, 1866–1910*. Carbondale: Southern Illinois UP, 2002.

Kitzhaber, Albert R. *Rhetoric in American Colleges, 1850–1900*. Intro. John T. Gage. Dallas: Southern Methodist UP, 1990.

Limón, José. "*El Primer Congreso Mexicanista de 1911*: A Precursor to Contemporary Chicanismo." *Aztlán* 5.1–2 (1974): 85–117.

Mattingly, Carol. "Telling Evidence: Rethinking What Counts in Rhetoric." *Rhetoric Society Quarterly* 32.1 (2002): 99–108.

Miller, Thomas P., and Joseph G. Jones. "Review: Working Out Our History." *College English* 67.4 (Mar. 2005): 421–39.

Nietzsche, Friedrich. "On the Uses and Disadvantages of History for Life." *Untimely Meditations*. Trans. R. J. Hollingdale. Cambridge: Cambridge UP, 1983. 57–123.

Phelps, Christopher. "My Dream Archive." *Chronicle of Higher Education* 53.18 (2007): 1.

Royster, Jacqueline Jones. *Traces of a Stream: Literacy and Social Change among African American Women*. Pittsburgh, PA: U of Pittsburgh P, 2000.

———. "When the First Voice You Hear Is Not Your Own." *College Composition and Communication* 47.1 (Feb. 1996): 29–40.

Royster, Jacqueline Jones, and Jean C. Williams. "History in the Spaces Left: African American Presence and Narratives of Composition Studies." *College Composition and Communication* 50.4 (1999): 563–84.

Russell, David. *Writing in the Academic Disciplines: A Curricular History*. 2nd ed. Carbondale: Southern Illinois UP, 2002.

San Miguel, Guadalupe, Jr. *"Let Them All Take Heed": Mexican Americans and the Campaign for Educational Equality in Texas, 1910–1981*. Austin: U of Texas P, 1987.

Schultz, Lucille M. *The Young Composers: Composition's Beginnings in Nineteenth-Century Schools*. Carbondale: Southern Illinois UP, 1999.

Sharer, Wendy. "Disintegrating Bodies of Knowledge: Historical Material and Revisionary Histories of Rhetoric." *Rhetorical Bodies*. Ed. Jack Selzer and Sharon Crowley. Madison: U of Wisconsin P, 1999. 120–42.

———. *Vote and Voice: Women's Organizations and Political Literacy, 1915–1930*. Carbondale: Southern Illinois UP, 2004.

ARCHIVAL SURVIVAL:
NAVIGATING HISTORICAL RESEARCH

Lynée Lewis Gaillet

> Because history is told by the victors. Everything else falls away. With
> pharaohs, they chipped out the names of those who had come before
> and destroyed their temples and statues. It was every ruler's greatest fear,
> because they knew if there was nothing to remind people they had lived,
> they would be forgotten. Not only forgotten, erased. . . . When we have
> truth, we have a chance at understanding. Through understanding, we
> can reach freedom. When the truth is hidden, we are all wounded.
>
> —*Tucker Malarkey*, Resurrection

Tucker Malarkey's words from the novel *Resurrection* set the stage for this chapter.
Historians of rhetorical practices examine archives in an effort to seek nuanced,
complicated tales—ones moored to their own times and cultural exigencies. Our
adoption of recovery and revision methodologies often leads us to reexamine traditional "truths"; this important work depends on a plurality of research methods
and the willingness of the researcher to carefully (re)consider venues and genres
for disseminating our work. Kathleen A. Welsch tells us that

> historians in rhetoric and composition are more than storytellers who invite
> listeners to sit at separate fires to learn separate tales of the past. They are
> also teachers. It is the historian's responsibility to teach us a variety of ways
> to read the past, to engage in historical debate, to position narratives in
> relation to each other so as to gain critical perspective, to draw conclusions
> on and consider implications of opposing historical projects, and to create
> constructive tension that moves us forward in our inquiry. (122)

But how do we prepare ourselves to be not only researchers but also effective, scholarly storytellers? As researchers and teachers of the history of rhetoric and composition, the projects we undertake, assign, and direct (including theses and dissertations) adopt a range of methodologies—most of which are not empirical in nature. We must acknowledge that mastering qualitative research methodologies and methods is a messier task (with far fewer definitive resources) than acquiring quantitative research skills. However, in trying to understand historical/archival research methods and methodologies—and in trying to collate published scholarship with my own experiences and research practices—I've come to realize how little codified information on archival research that we, as a profession, offer new scholars. We don't have many treatises addressing the how-to of archival research, and, as a result, many of us visit archives initially equipped with little training in procedures for investigating primary works and few tools for analyzing what we might find in those repositories. In an effort to bridge this gap, in 2007 I designed a new graduate-level research methodologies course for my institution. In preparation, I begged my friends and colleagues who teach history of rhetoric courses from across the country to share their teaching theories and assignments with me; I reviewed all the recent literature I could find addressing pedagogy and research methodologies in rhetoric/composition (plenty of scholarship based on the investigation of primary documents surfaced but disappointingly little advice specifically delineating steps for conducting archival research within rhet/comp studies); and I searched frantically for a current, full-length textbook addressing rhet/comp research methods—none to be had. In this chapter, then, I share information concerning archival research that I gleaned from designing and teaching the revised methodologies course and offer a few suggestions for scholars who are interested in visiting the archives.

Archival Research (Re)Defined

Sometimes, archival research involves following a Nancy Drew–like trail of clues that culminates in the rare, intriguing, "holy grail" find at the conclusion of the search—but not often. I've only had that experience once or twice in my professional life. In 1990, as I was researching educator George Jardine in Glasgow, Scotland, I came upon a decrepit and flimsy box housing 136 letters tied together with a faded red ribbon—letters written by Jardine over the course of his life. These letters held the genus of Jardine's teaching theories and pedagogy. I had found the mother lode—at least in this phase of my search for Jardine artifacts. I've had other "ah-hah!" moments involving archival finds that changed the trajectory of my research, but for the most part, archival research is somewhat tedious, involves following trails that fork, branch, or dissipate and rarely involves holy grail discoveries.

The *Glossary of Library and Internet Terms* defines *archive* as a "repository hold-ing documents or other material, usually those of historical and/or rare value. Also referred to as Special Collections" (Fowler). Most disciplines agree the word *history* involves the study of the past and that the term *archives* includes nonreplaceable, valuable items, but in the field of rhetoric/composition, defining *rhetorical history* while determining what legitimately constitutes *archives* is often complicated. James J. Murphy breaks down the term *rhetorical history* into its constituent parts; he defines *history* as "the reconstruction of important human questions from the recorded answers of the past" (187) and *rhetoric* as the study of means for future discourse" (188). On the other end of the spectrum, Robert Connors romantically tells us that the "[a]rchive is where storage meets dreams, and the result is his-tory" (17). The murkiness of determining and defining historical/archival research within the field is reflected in rhet/comp historians' definitions of key terms. I interpret the term *archives* broadly to include a wide range of artifacts and docu-ments, such as (unpublished and published) letters, diaries and journals, student notes, committee reports, documents and wills, newspaper articles, university calendars/handbooks/catalogs, various editions of manuscripts and print docu-ments (books, pamphlets, essays, etc.), memos, course materials, online sources, audiotapes, videotapes, and even "archeological" fragments and finds.

Thomas P. Miller and Melody Bowdon highlight the difficulty in doing and evaluating historical research when the field's scholars interpret basic terms such as *archive* and *rhetoric* differently: "Methods are a means to an end, and before we can discuss methods or purposes, we need to be clear about what the object of study is" (591). If defining what exactly constitutes the field is unclear, then, of course, discerning a single method of research becomes improbable. Recognizing the shift in the nature of rhetorical study described by Miller and Bowdon, Linda Ferreira-Buckley calls for continued education in traditional methodology: "[F]ar from being incompatible with a progressive politics, [traditional methodology] is in fact the best agent of change" (582). She states that what "is most required to look at [historical] materials and to recover others is scholarly training." In an honest lamentation, she suggests that

> our students—and some of us—are underprepared in the specialized re-search techniques necessary to revisionist histories. Theoretical sophistica-tion does not obviate the need for practical training. We lack the tools of the historians' trade; familiar with only the most obvious granting agencies, we cannot secure the money needed to carry out research agendas that are both deep and broad. There are exceptions, of course, but they are too few. I urge all progressive historians to master traditional and emerging research methodologies—tools crucial to revising traditional accounts of history. (582)

I agree with Ferreira-Buckley. Regardless of the object of archival study, training in the basic tenets of primary research is necessary for anyone interested in this research method. This chapter, then, offers basic instructions and some guidelines for visiting manuscript libraries and analyzing the materials found there.

Practical Training for the Historian

How do we, as historians and teachers of research skills, answer Ferreira-Buckley's call? What are the methodologies and tools that we ourselves must master and hand down to our students? Much of the published scholarship addressing rhetoric/composition archival research fails to outline the "steps" necessary to follow when researching archives—an omission, in part, giving rise to this collection. In my class, the students and I began wading through journal articles, Web sites, books, and the class text (Kirsch and Sullivan's now-dated 1992 *Methods and Methodology in Composition Research*), seeking concrete methods and clear-cut advice addressing the complexities of conducting historical research. We had specific questions about the guidelines that define both individual and pluralistic research methods. For the most part, we were disappointed in our search for a pedagogical plan—one that blends methodology with method—either overtly intended for historical/archival research or a method that could easily be adapted for this kind of research. Many rhetoric/composition scholars address methodology (in fascinating depth), but method is often project-specific or glossed over. Robert Connor's chapter in *Methods and Methodology* provides a good point of departure, particularly the discussion of what he terms "the three primary parts to traditional historical analysis: external criticism, internal criticism, and synthesis of materials" (25), but as Connors aptly reminds us, "History is not, and never has been, systematic or scientific" (31). James Murphy's "Conducting Research in the History of Rhetoric: An Open Letter to a Future Historian of Rhetoric," in Olson and Taylor's *Publishing in Rhetoric and Composition*, includes a list of strategies or "Pragmatics for the Historian of Rhetoric" (189–94). Embedded in this list is the genus of archival methods for the historiographer. We were getting closer in our search for a codified discussion of tools and steps associated with examining archives and artifacts, but I quickly realized that if I wanted a list of guidelines, steps, and tools for analyzing primary documents, I was going to have to create it for myself. The next two sections enumerate and describe pragmatic tasks and skills archivists need to consider.

Visiting Manuscript Libraries

The following projects and heuristics will help familiarize newcomers with some of the components of historical/archival research. Keep in mind that these prompts are not equal in weight. The first two, for example, are designed as an introduction to archival research. The remainder are designed for researchers who have selected a site or archive to visit. Embedded within the assignments is advice for conducting research, along with typical guidelines and requirements often associated with this research method. I offer these heuristics simply as an introduction to archival research and as an aid for gaining access and funding to visit archival collections. I have formatted the list in the form of assignments.

1. To get a sense of manuscript or primary-document research, visit any collection of primary materials or archives housed nearby. Try to find intriguing documents to peruse, but don't worry if the collection seems a bit far afield of your interests. Research the collection, noting the kinds of documents included, the organization and cataloguing of the materials, how to gain access to the collection, and rules for examining and copying the documents. Unfortunately, many scholars visit archival collections for the first time when they have limited time/resources and have traveled great distances (not always under the best conditions) to reach the research site. A field trip to a local archive will help in anticipating not only the conditions of conducting research but also the problems and concerns that may be difficult to address far away from home and your local support network.

2. Select a site to visit or a collection to examine, and conduct preliminary investigation online relevant to the research topic. Become familiar with the online catalog of archival holdings housed in the facility you wish to visit; in addition to university libraries, check out public libraries, newspapers, and government agencies for information about local events, figures, and news stories from the historical period you're researching. To save time and money (especially if traveling great distances), find as much information as possible online. Catalog and annotate findings.

3. Find possible funding sources to support your research and defray the expense of traveling to manuscript sites. Collect all guidelines, necessary forms, and sample grant applications if available. Look for funding from businesses, academic and government agencies, collection holders (schools, libraries, and individuals who want to make their collections available to scholars), and special-interest groups or foundations interested in specific work (AAUW, unions, county historical societies). Make hard copies or an electronic portfolio of findings.

4. Practice writing different sections of the grant application. Some agencies provide grant-writing counselors. A grant application typically includes a narrative explaining the project and methodology, a justification or need analysis for the research, a literature review, a plan for disseminating the findings (including a target audience for the work), a budget, and your résumé. Follow the guidelines to the letter, including all—but only—the requested materials.

5. Plan an itinerary and budget (required for most grant applications) for visiting an archive outside of your geographical region. Obviously, you will need to find travel options and prices, local accommodations near the investigation site,

and dining choices. Remember to account for transportation (bus, taxi, rail, car rental) from house to site and back again. Other (perhaps unexpected) costs might include technology fees, admissions to special and museum collections—and, in some countries, a pocket full of change for admission to public restrooms! Investigate photocopying limitations and fees, which for many researchers are a significant part of the budget. Some institutions charge as much as a dollar per page; others limit copies to a specific number per day. Some collections do not allow photographing of artifacts, so check what the restrictions, if any, are in force at the collection site.

6. Make a list of and obtain necessary documents. Don't leave home without a reference letter vouching for your institutional affiliation and the validity of the research project from both your department chair and research advisors. These letters can be invaluable in helping you gain admission to libraries and collections (sometimes at a reduced fee), securing temporary library cards and privileges (such as photocopying, parking, and lockers), and finding lodging and access to faculty dining in some instances (a necessary perk when conducting research in isolated, remote, and/or expensive areas). To the actual research site, take a driver's license or other photo identification, school identification, school library cards, passport, and other officially issued documentation. Manuscript librarians are often more willing to help if they understand the project, so be ready to provide a written project description—the narrative information necessary for grant applications—and if you've received a grant, be sure to inform the librarian, letting him or her know that you are "sanctioned."

7. Make a list of equipment needed onsite: laptop, cables, wireless cards, adaptors for electrical current and outlets (plugs), pencils, pens, and paper for those collection sites that don't allow or accommodate electronic notetaking, essential books and research guides (only those unavailable at the site) necessary for understanding the documents you're examining, and a sturdy bag (preferably with compartments for protecting documents).

8. Before visiting any archive, contact the manuscript librarian or curator of the archives to arrange specific times to visit the collection or collections. A collection may be loaned out to another library or researcher, relocated for housekeeping purposes, or stowed somewhere else for safekeeping. I planned to visit an east-coast collection a full year after Hurricane Hugo had threatened the area. Although unaffected by the storm, the library's manuscripts, which had been boxed and stored inland for safekeeping, were still unavailable. The library had taken advantage of the opportunity to remodel. I'm glad I called.

9. Become familiar ahead of time with the rules and regulations of the facility. Check out the institution's Web site for information, if available, or ask the librarian in advance for a copy of the facility's rules of usage. Because documents are often

irreplaceable, manuscript libraries are often quite strict about what is taken into the reading room and the handling of documents. To optimize your visit and to ensure access to documents, plan ahead. There are some general, practical rules for best preserving the documents and avoiding disturbing other researchers:

- Know what items are forbidden: no permanent markers (pens, ballpoints, Sharpies, or highlighters)—only pencils allowed; no food and drink in the reading rooms; no backpacks, computer bags, or coats (to prevent theft and control what is brought into the space); no bulky notebooks or binders, only loose paper or laptops for taking notes; no cell phones or pagers, so that you don't disturb other researchers. Lockers may be available for storing your personal possessions.
- Wash your hands before handling documents. Touch archival materials as little as possible; some libraries require you to wear cotton gloves.
- Don't hold materials while reading. Instead, place materials squarely in the middle of the reading desk so edges don't get crumpled or stained.
- Use provided foam wedges to support documents and to help best position the materials for reading and paperweights, if provided and necessary, for positioning unwieldy documents.

Examining Archival Data

Once scholars have prepared for the physical tasks of traveling to manuscript repositories and handling primary documents, methods of evaluating and reporting discovered data become paramount. Vickie Tolar Collins's "The Speaker Respoken: Material Rhetoric as Feminist Methodology" presents both a method and "a methodology based on the concept of material rhetoric that can help scholars avoid problems of appropriation, anachronism, and decontextualization as we reclaim women's historical texts and support the epistemological worth of women's ordinary experience, particularly as revealed in their narratives" (546) and offers a good template for constructing a general historical/archival research method. Collins's "material method" closely examines primarily published documents and adopts a rhetorical approach to interpretation that is easily generalizable to historiographical practices. Adopting, borrowing, modifying, and expanding Collins's "method" to include a more inclusive definition of archival artifacts and blending her method with the advice and guidelines offered by Connors, Murphy, and many feminist historians, I attempt below to list and define some of the steps often associated with evaluating archival materials. The following tasks and questions (the sequence is not prescribed) concern examining data, not necessarily the initial discovery of archival materials:

1. Determine the research questions. When approaching an archive, what do you think or hope you will find? Remember, you may have to refine, redefine, and sometimes abandon hypotheses along the way, depending on the contents of the archive, the inability to corroborate data, conflicting reports, and the like.

2. Provide a physical description of the document or artifact. Describe the paper, watermarks, binding, print or handwriting, marginalia. Photocopy or transcribe the title page and table of contents as they appear; photograph other artifacts. Keeping in mind that you may not be able to revisit the archive, make notes about contents (preface, chapter titles, afterword, appendixes). Be sure to note any cataloguing information that may be pertinent when referring to or citing an archive, that is, manuscript-collection titles and numbers, other artifacts housed within the same collection, distinguishing marks of anonymous writings such as individual student notes.

3. Categorize the findings. What are the venue and genre of the works you are examining? If the item is not a published, printed, or taped document, what are the options for describing it?

4. Couch both archival materials and your analyses/stories within political, social, economic, educational, religious, or institutional histories of the time. Consult multiple secondary sources, related or competing primary sources, other disciplines or venues, and historical accounts in order to "locate" your materials within contemporary exigencies.

5. Ask yourself how best to corroborate your assumptions and claims. How can you substantiate the story you tell? What other sources or archives might you consult to add credence and validity to your narrative?

6. Locate your subject within contemporary rhetorical artifacts and events, such as publications, conversations, public events, and/or performances. Consult a wide range of both secondary sources and contemporary primary sources. What is the rhetorical significance of your subject/object of study?

7. Ascertain the motives inherent in the materials studied. What is their nature, and who commissioned their creation? Are the materials personal, didactic, written for hire, government sponsored?

8. Carefully analyze the original audience for the artifact, both intended and secondary.

9. Investigate the contemporary reception of the work. If published, what are the production and sales records? If the artifact was intended to promote rhetorical engagement, did it? How? Where? When? Under what circumstances?

10. Research the subsequent reputation of the materials. If the materials were initially influential, when, under what circumstances, and to what degree did that influence wane? Did future generations appropriate the materials in ways

not originally intended? Did these materials spawn other publications, practices, and similar products or theories?

11. Decide how to tell your story. What is your stance? Who is the audience? How will you organize and disseminate the findings?

I've offered very practical advice for visiting manuscript libraries and considering what you find there, but in qualitative research, there remains another important element to consider: the "presence" of the archivist. Determining your role as a researcher and articulating it to readers—essentially learning to become the scholarly storyteller—are shifting, more abstract tasks to master.

It's Personal: The Role of the Researcher

Recovery and revision historiographical theory in rhet/comp argues that the researcher becomes a part of the project—a participant whose *ethos* is evident is his or her research. In qualitative research, the relationship between researcher and subject is often problematic and needs to be addressed. The researcher's interests, prejudices, selection of subject matter, research questions, and biases inform and guide the research, and the researcher should inform readers of these factors up front. Carol Berkenkotter's 1989 proclamation is still valid (and still goes unrecognized by many present-day researchers): "[W]hen we articulate our models of knowing and discuss our differences in good faith, it becomes much easier" to expand traditional notions of quantitative and qualitative research and "to engage in 'multimodal approaches'" and pluralistic research methods. To illustrate, in my research of historical figures and teaching practices (both secular and religious), I bring a humanist interest in mooring figures to their individual cultural times, a historian's interest in texts and archival research, and a rhetoricians' interest in persuasion, rhetorical engagement, and influence. I wish to see neglected or misrepresented figures (both male and female) recovered and, in some cases, their reputations revisited. In that vein, I also wish to see these figures' works made widely available. I want our predecessors viewed culturally, within the framework and exigencies of their times, not subsequent generation's. Finally, I am a "rhetorical activist" in that I want neglected writings included in contemporary histories of the rhetorical tradition. Being honest about my personal goals, research lens, and preconceived research agenda helps me, along with readers, both define the scope of my research and reflect critically on my methodological choices.

I believe storytelling—with a purpose, based on painstaking research, tied to a particular cultural moment, making clear the teller's prejudices—is the real task of the historian, regardless of the negative connotations often associated in academia with storytelling. Although many historians have looked to the past to understand the present, that goal is not universally embraced and has recently fallen out of favor in the wake of charges of "presentism." Connors tells us "In fact, history is narrative, and every attempt to create a system to give that narrative a predictive meaning is fraught with peril" (31). So if our primary task is not to research the past to see what those events tell us about the future, then with what are we left? Unearthing and interpreting facts, layering stories of rhetorical engagement, bringing to light multiple histories and perspectives that reveal the complexities inherent in humanistic study, weaving facts and research into persuasive narratives. Interesting and exciting work! The researcher becomes a filter and a lens—an integral and recognizable component of archival research.

Omissions and Conclusions

Although I've not covered "management issues" in this chapter, methods for organizing and codifying research findings is a recurring problem for experienced and new scholars alike. Methods of storage, coding, and retrieval that work well for one research project are not necessarily generalizable or appropriate for managing another. Connors explains in his 1992 discussion of "synthesis of archival research" that the "questions involved in *writing* history are stylistic, presentational, small-scale"; yet, these questions, raised so long ago, are still asked—and often go unanswered. These queries, as posed by Connors, include how we should organize data, which quotes do we include or discard, should we present data thematically or chronologically, how much background information should we provide (29). Often the answers to these seemingly "small-scale" issues send us back to the archives or force us to reexamine our original research hypotheses, as Connors himself admits. If the management answers were predictable, prescribed, easy, then we wouldn't need to keep asking the questions. We wouldn't have a need fifteen years later for this collection. With the advent of digital records and research methods, the list of unanswered management questions continues to morph and swell.

Miller and Bowdon remind us that not all archives are easily accessible and that "archival work requires the research skills to locate holdings and the finances to visit them." They complicate the discussion of access by raising issues of Internet research: "The Web offers unprecedented access to archival materials—to those with the requisite technological resources and institutional affiliations, which are not insignificant requirements" (595). As manuscript libraries make their holdings available online, historians must adapt their research methods. Archival retrieval no longer only entails tracking down the location of desired artifacts, applying for travel grants, and spending long days taking copious notes in cold, musty library basements. While many of us who crave the physical search for primary documents bemoan the loss of hands-on examination of artifacts, we realize that historical research is expensive and difficult—especially for beginning scholars or those working at institutions with limited research budgets. However, the move from tangible examination of materials to virtual document handling toys with one of the fundamental truths of historical research: "Search is play." As Connors explains, "archival reading is . . . a kind of directed ramble, something like an August mushroom hunt" (23)—an activity that naturally defies codification. If we agree that historical research constitutes a form of detective work, then how must the search shift when the trail begins, and in many cases ends, online? How does the historian's line of inquiry accommodate online searches? What questions can and can't be answered solely through online research? And perhaps most important, in what ways must we shift our method/methodological processes when researching historical documents/issues online? These questions will surely push to the foreground of historical research as more documents and library holdings become digitally available.

In these pages, I have not addressed legal matters or issues of ethics connected to archival research. I hope other scholars more knowledgeable than I will tackle the legal and moral complexities often associated with investigating manuscript collections. Also, issues of validity and credibility are always a concern for the archivist, particularly when examining unpublished works. Methods of corroboration and procedures for testing reliability need to be codified. Perhaps most important, as Nan Johnson and Barb L'Eplattenier often suggest, we must come to the realization that historical research is exciting, that layered storytelling is interesting, compelling, and engaging. Much work remains to be done, particularly in terms of method, but this collection presents a wide-open door, inviting the next generation of historians/archivists to come on in.

Works Cited

Berkenkotter, Carol. "The Legacy of Positivism in Empirical Composition Research." *Journal of Advanced Composition* 9 (1989): 69–82. <http://www.jacweb.org/Archived_volumes/Text_articles/V9_Berkenkotter.htm>.

Collins, Vickie Tolar. "The Speaker Respoken: Material Rhetoric as Feminist Methodology." *College English* 61 (May 1999): 545–73.

Connors, Robert. "Dreams and Play: Historical Method and Methodology." *Methods and Methodology in Composition Research*. Ed. Gesa Kirsch and Patricia Sullivan. Carbondale: Southern Illinois UP, 1992. 15–36.

Ferreira-Buckley, Linda. "Rescuing the Archives from Foucault." *College English* 61 (May 1999): 577–83.

Fowler, Charlotte. "Archive." *Glossary of Library and Internet Terms*. U of South Dakota. 09 Jan. 2001. 1 Sept. 2008 <http://www.usd.edu/library/instruction/glossary.shtml>.

Hill, Michael R. *Qualitative Research Methods #31: Archival Strategies and Techniques*. Thousand Oaks, CA: Sage, 1999.

Kirsch, Gesa E., and Patricia A. Sullivan, eds. *Methods and Methodology in Composition Research*. Carbondale: Southern Illinois UP, 1992.

Malarkey, Tucker. *Resurrection*. New York: Riverhead, 2006.

Miller, Thomas P, and Melody Bowdon. "A Rhetorical Stance on the Archives of Civic Action." *College English* 61 (May 1999): 591–98.

Murphy, James J. "Conducting Research in the History of Rhetoric: An Open Letter to a Future Historian of Rhetoric." *Publishing in Rhetoric and Composition.* Ed. Gary A. Olson and Todd W. Taylor. Albany: State U of New York P, 1997. 187–95.

Welsch, Kathleen A. Review. "History as Complex Storytelling." *CCC* 50.1 (1998): 116–22.

Useful Web Sources about Archives

Abraham, Terry. *Repositories of Primary Sources.* May 2009 <http://www.uidaho.edu/special-collections/Other.Repositories.html>.

Barratt, Nick. *Archival Research Techniques and Skills.* 2002. <http://www.arts-scheme.co.uk/>.

Find Databases by Title and Category. New York University Libraries. Oct. 2008. <http://library.nyu.edu/cgi-bin/bobst/databases.pl?query=HUMANITIES>.

Research. U.S. National Archives and Record Administration. <http://www.archives.gov/research/index.html>.

World's Libraries Connected, The. OCLC, Online Computer Library Center. 2009. <http://www.oclc.org/global/default.htm>.

OPEN TO THE POSSIBILITIES: SEVEN TALES OF SERENDIPITY IN THE ARCHIVES

Lori Ostergaard

> It . . . helps to have serendipity on your side, but that, of course,
> is not something one can arrange purposefully, although I
> am convinced one can be open to the possibility.
> —*Gesa E. Kirsch, "Walking in the Footsteps of a Historical Subject"*

Interspersed among the chapters of this collection investigating the more pragmatic side of archival research are several short interchapters that explore the role chance can sometimes play in our methods. These seven narratives are included here to illustrate the balance between serendipity and process—the unpredictable interplay between accident and intention—that often characterizes archival research.

The interchapters were drafted out of interviews I conducted with practiced archival researchers—Lindal Buchanan, David Gold, Peter Mortensen, Jessica Enoch, Kathryn Fitzgerald, Kenneth Lindblom, and Lynée Lewis Gaillet. While I provide a short introduction to each interchapter, the narratives that follow are told in the researchers' own words.

In addition to imparting some practical advice to new archival researchers, each interchapter demonstrates what can happen when you have "serendipity on your side" in the archives, bears witness to these researchers' love of working with primary source material, and affirms just how important research in the archives is to the future of rhetoric/composition. While I asked each of these scholars to discuss their more serendipitous moments in the archives, most of them also underscored the importance of a systematic and ethical approach to research. And they all acknowledged that accidental discoveries in the archives must be accompanied by the wisdom to recognize the significance of those discoveries, for, as Louis Pasteur reminds us, "[C]hance favors only the prepared mind."

Work Cited

Kirsch, Gesa E. "Walking in the Footsteps of a Historical Subject." *Peitho: Newsletter of the Coalition of Women Scholars in the History of Rhetoric and Composition* 9.1 (Fall 2004). <http://cwshrc.org/wp-content/uploads/2008/03/peitho9_1.htm>.

INTERVIEW: DAVID GOLD—
ON KEEPING A BEGINNER'S MIND

David Gold is the author of *Rhetoric at the Margins: Revising the History of Writing Instruction in American Colleges, 1873–1947* (2008). His recent essay in the edited collection *Research as a Lived Process* (2008), "The Accidental Archivist: Embracing Chance and Confusion in Historical Scholarship," examines the role of serendipity in archival research. For this interview, Gold's responses probe the paradoxical nature of research in the archives: Archival scholars must possess both a "beginner's mind" that will allow them to be open to accidental discoveries and the expert knowledge necessary to recognize the significance of their discoveries.

I do research on the history of rhetorical education, particularly looking to how marginalized communities and constituencies—African Americans, women, rural and working-class students—have been trained to read, write, and speak and how they have made use of their training in public forums. I conduct my research in libraries, archives, and attics and make use of any relevant source material I can find: catalogs, yearbooks, literary journals, newspapers, diaries, student essays, letters, class notes, crush notes, census records, board of regents reports, recipes, receipts, photographs, oral histories, magazine advertisements, napkin scrawls, gossip, and Google searches. I try to immerse myself in the era and region I am studying, so I often find myself reading contemporary newspapers, magazines, and biographies even when they do not directly speak to the scholarly material at hand.

Within the archives, I can't say there has been one serendipitous moment that stands above all. Rather, there has been a series of smaller ones that have kept me going, convinced me I was on the right track, or set me off in another direction. For me, the golden moments are when a new piece of evidence answers a question raised by an old one. For example, wondering what it must have been like for a young rural student to attend Texas Woman's University, then overhearing the librarians discussing the student who was so impressed by the luxury of hot chocolate she wrote about it in her diary. Or picking up a popular autobiography of a 102-year-old African American man for background information on black life in the early-twentieth-century south and discovering he grew up not far from the black liberal-arts college I had been studying.

I'm currently researching a history of public women's colleges in the South. While skimming through Florida State College for Women yearbooks, I came across a wonderful pair of photos: one shows the school's "most modern girl," decked out in flight gear in the cockpit of a bi-wing plane. The other depicts the school's "old fashioned girl," standing demurely in a white full-length dress in the lush garden of a grand plantation home. It's a perfectly antebellum scene—except for the student's hair, which is cut in a decidedly modern bob. Perhaps "traditional" at FSCW, circa 1935, was a more flexible term than we might expect. I'm still trying to figure it out. But I keep returning to those pictures.

One of the few things I recall from high-school chemistry is my teacher's insistence that there are no accidents in science; Alexander Fleming, she told us, discovered penicillin only because he knew what he was looking for. Historical scholarship—any scholarship really—is not dissimilar. We "strike gold," I think, by having a strong sense of what we *should* find—and allowing ourselves to be equally surprised whether our expectations are confirmed or confounded.

When I began working on rhetorical education at black colleges, I was surprised to discover that the classical tradition persisted at these schools far longer than our general histories suggested they should have. I knew this was something worth exploring further. When I discovered that several black liberal-arts colleges in Texas used a relatively progressive rhetoric textbook and taught oratory in freshman composition, I knew these were leads worth following. By themselves, they were only small pieces of data—a few lines in a college catalogue—but they suggested other possible riches to come.

Keeping ourselves open to accidental discoveries is difficult. It is crucial to keep a beginner's mind. The more we know about a topic, the easier it is for our expectations to guide our interpretations. When I began researching Texas Woman's University, I was surprised to find that women were being trained in a different way than I had expected, given what I had read about rhetorical training at private women's colleges. But was TWU representative of public women's colleges or simply one point on a continuum of possibilities? Now that I am working on a research project on a group of public women's colleges in the South, I have to be careful not to let my new hypothesis about these schools, based on TWU, cloud my judgment. To counter this tendency, I might pick up a primary-source document and take a long series of notes without making commentary, just absorbing the information. Or I will make it a point to highlight in my notes evidence that is contrary to my working hypothesis. I also read a lot of detective fiction; a standard conceit is the grizzled veteran who always notes the importance of not jumping too quickly to a conclusion based on limited or even overwhelming evidence, lest one ignore clues that don't fit one's theory. I know there is great pressure to write, to publish, to get the dissertation done, but it's tremendously valuable to just sit on the floor amidst a pile of materials for a few days and simply read.

INTERVIEW: PETER MORTENSEN—"I HAD A HUNCH"

Peter Mortensen is coauthor of *Imagining Rhetoric: Composing Women of the Early United States*, and his historical scholarship has appeared in *College English, Rhetoric Society Quarterly*, and *Rhetoric Review*. Mortensen is currently working on a book project, tentatively titled *Manufacturing Illiteracy in the United States*, and in the narrative that follows, he discusses how serendipity has played a role in his research for that book.

My main project—one I've been working on for quite some time now—teases out the ironies inherent in prose representations of illiteracy around the turn of the twentieth century. The irony that most intrigues me is this: In the 1890s and into the early twentieth century, the consumption of print (newspapers, magazines, and books) grew precipitously. This growth was driven as much by new print and distribution technologies as it was by widespread schooling, at least for whites, in the latter half of the nineteenth century. Popular in the prose consumed by metropolitan readers were narratives about rural America and, specifically, southern Appalachia. And recurrent in these narratives was the theme of "illiterate backwardness," the root of mountain people's inability to become modern.

Now, at the same time they were learning about southern Appalachians' illiteracy, metropolitans were beneficiaries of natural resources that were being extracted with abandon from the region—in many cases, stolen from mountain people whom metropolitans had been convinced were incapable stewards of the natural wealth on their land. Of particular interest to me is the emergence of the pulp, paper, and printing industries in the mountain south. In the early twentieth century, pulp and paper mills often consumed timber at an unsustainable rate and frequently produced toxic effluent that damaged downstream landscapes throughout the mountains—all in the name of feeding metropolitans' insatiable appetite for print.

My archive for this project is vast and varied. I make use of old books (some moldering away in open stacks, others in special collections) and magazines and newspapers (many available on microfilm, some now available digitally), along with government documents (prepared by the census, commerce, education, and labor bureaucracies) that reside in select library collections. I've also made use of formal archival holdings of personal papers (e.g., the papers of Cora Wilson Stewart, an anti-illiteracy crusader from Kentucky; and those of Reuben Robertson, a paper-company executive who lived and worked in western North Carolina).

For some time, my project had focused on the impact of the Champion Paper mill in Canton, North Carolina. I argued (as had others) that downstream pollution generated by the mill had suppressed economic development along the Pigeon River into Tennessee. In my judgment, the suppression of economic development had resulted in demonstrably lower literacy rates in the counties through which the dirty water flowed on its way toward Knoxville. After reading an article from the project a few years ago, a colleague suggested that I was missing an important angle. He asked, "What about the workers in the Canton mill? Didn't they have opportunities to become literate that they would not have had without an industrial presence in their town?" Good question. As I sought to answer it, I traveled to western North Carolina to do some archival work on personnel at the Canton mill. That effort, pleasant as it was, didn't produce any startling insights.

But, at roughly the same time, I was spending some time reading through old (1910–30) issues of *Publishers' Weekly,* searching for statistics on the escalating consumption of books. Bound volumes of *PW* are bulky, so I did my reading in the bowels of the stacks in the main library at Illinois. That's where I "struck gold" (though it was hard to see it in the dim light). What I discovered was an article on what was purported to be the world's largest printing plant, soon to open in Kingsport, Tennessee. The plant was part of a "vertically integrated" operation that ran from timber harvesting in the mountains, through a pulp and paper mill in Kingsport, into a nearby printery, and then a bindery and huge distribution warehouse. All the resources to make books—and make them cheaply—were locally at hand, from the trees in the forest to the cotton (for the books' cloth covers) in the field. Trouble was, the only laborers available were supposedly illiterate "mountaineers." The *PW* article speculated that mountain people were trainable and marveled at the prospect that one day they might be able to read something of the "Niagara of print" that they were manufacturing for consumption in the nation's great cities.

Discovery of this article has led to hours of research on the birth of Kingsport as a model industrial city in the 1910s. So much of what I'm reading worries about how mountain people's supposed illiteracy might hold back the city's economic growth. So anxious were the city fathers that they apparently paid good money to Columbia University to develop a school curriculum to address the situation. In a next step, with research assistance from Patrick Berry, I discovered that the

Columbia curriculum was actually a version of the system put in place in Gary, Indiana, for children of steel-mill workers there.

I knew I had struck gold because of the condescending way the *PW* article characterized the mountain residents of east Tennessee. I had a hunch that the attitude expressed in the article (which, as it turns out, was actually a condensed version of a piece that first ran in the *New York Times*) was indicative of an anxiety about mountain people and illiteracy that I would find expressed with greater intensity in private papers and unpublished documents related to the establishment of Kingsport.

I relish the fruits of accidental discoveries and have made more than one by pursuing answers to little questions that were unaddressed in the primary and scholarly materials I read. That said, I'm aware that I may not be able to share every answer I find. Today, scholarly publishers generally have a preference for shorter rather than longer monographs, so I'm always asking myself questions like these: Does this new material from the archive *change* my argument? Is it better evidence for a point I'm making, or does what I've found simply complement evidence that I've already offered up? I try to apply these filters only after I've given myself a chance to evaluate where a lead might take me. Here it must be said that having tenure is of special value. I feel a bit more freedom to pursue leads than I did before having the security of tenure. Time spent pursuing what turns out to be a dead-end clue may in some sense be wasted—but without career-ending consequences.

PART TWO

Accessing the Archives

INVISIBLE HANDS: RECOGNIZING ARCHIVISTS' WORK TO MAKE RECORDS ACCESSIBLE

Sammie L. Morris and Shirley K Rose

Seasoned researchers know that it's a good idea to contact an archive before visiting to do research. This ensures that needed collections will be available onsite during the actual visit to the archives and allows the researcher to begin a conversation with the archivist about any additional relevant resources available. Starting such a conversation (the "reference interview") with the archivist in advance helps make a visit to the archives more efficient and fruitful. This reference role of archivists is generally understood, if not fully exploited, by most archival researchers.

For many researchers, however, the archivist's processing of collections, which includes all work done by the archivist to make a collection available to researchers, remains a mystery. The researcher may understand, for example, that certain preservation steps are taken with collections after they are received by the archives, but other steps are not always evident. We believe that if archival researchers know how to recognize the outcomes of archivists' processing and understand the principles behind processing decisions, they will have a better understanding of the archival materials they study.

Understanding archival theory and principles and knowing the best practices derived from them will help researchers anticipate potential problems and assess the potential usefulness of the archival materials they consult. It is especially important for researchers to know how to work with a repository's archivist if the materials they wish to examine are not yet processed. As an archivist (Sammie) and a researcher (Shirley) who worked together on a recent project, we've come to believe that if archival researchers can be better equipped to recognize the outcomes of archival practice, they can better interpret the materials they study and become better researchers. Our purpose here is to help researchers recognize and understand the work of the archivist's "invisible hands." Using the processing of the James Berlin Papers,[1] a collection of documents created by rhetorician James Berlin during his academic career as a case study, we explain how the two primary principles governing archival work—provenance and original order—inform archival-processing practices from selection through description.

We begin by describing the context for processing the James Berlin Papers, along with the goals of the processing project and its outcomes. Decisions made during the collection processing are explained as they relate to making it physically and intellectually accessible to researchers. We also hope to illustrate the importance to researchers of learning more about the reasoning behind archivists' decision making and about how to recognize the ways a collection changes after passing through the archivist's invisible hands. Researchers who understand what has guided archival decisions will be better prepared to ask the right questions about a collection and how it has been altered from the time it was acquired by the archives. With answers to these questions, researchers can feel more confident in drawing conclusions from a collection that may be used as evidence in their scholarly endeavors. We hope to spark a dialogue between our readers and the archivists with whom they work that will ultimately lead to better access to and research use of archival collections.

Background of the Project

The Office of the Provost at Purdue University supports a fellowship program, the Faculty Program of Study in a Second Discipline, that offers faculty an opportunity to extend their scholarship through study in a separate field by providing released time for engaging in study on the West Lafayette, Indiana, campus. As an English department faculty member, Shirley won a fellowship for spring 2006 for one semester's study of archival practice under Sammie's direction as the Purdue University archivist in order to develop practical experience to complement an understanding of archival theory. As an archival researcher in the humanities, Shirley had published essays based on the examination of archival materials related to rhetoric and composition and essays on theoretical issues related to records management and administration of writing programs. She had also taught two graduate seminars on documentation strategies for writing programs. Although she developed some knowledge of archival theory through informal study, she had not had an opportunity to study the theory in a systematic way or to develop hands-on experience in archival processing, applying theoretical principles in specific, concrete contexts.

Shirley had three primary objectives for her program of study: to develop sound practices in archival processing, such as accessioning, preservation, arrangement, and description; to enhance her theoretical understanding of principles and issues in archival practice; and to develop interdisciplinary connections between archival theory and rhetorical theory by working to articulate a theory of the archives as rhetorical practice. Although the Society of American Archivists has recognized the relevance of theory in areas such as sociology, philosophy, political science, law, accounting, anthropology, and economics, as well as science and the arts, the relevance of rhetorical theory to archival practices has not been explicitly recognized by the professional archivist community. Yet, because rhetorical theory addresses the creation, interpretation, and use of documents in specific contexts, it promises to be especially useful to archival practitioners.

As the Purdue University archivist, Sammie's role in the fellowship project was to provide advice and guidance to Shirley in processing a specific collection, the James Berlin Papers. This included explanation of archives accessioning practices, including the legal transfer of the collection to the archival repository, along with guidelines for arranging, preserving, and describing the papers according to archival theory and principles. Sammie and Shirley met twice a week over the course of the semester to answer questions relating to the project. Sammie provided guidance on ordering the correct types of preservation supplies and on creating the finding aid[2] (archival inventory) describing the contents of the papers. Although the primary goal of the project was to allow Shirley to gain hands-on experience processing archival materials, Sammie also benefited from the project by gaining a better understanding of the viewpoint of the researcher. Our essay is an outcome of those discussions.

The James Berlin Papers

Shirley chose to process the James Berlin Papers for her fellowship project, which had been placed in her custody by Berlin's widow several years earlier. We will use Shirley's work on the project, under Sammie's supervision, as an example of the need for researchers to have an understanding of archivists' practices.

As most of our readers will know, James Berlin was an important scholar of the history of rhetoric and composition and a leading theorist of cultural studies composition pedagogies. He was a member of the English Department at Purdue University when he died suddenly of a heart attack in February 1994. The Berlin Papers comprise seven cubic feet of materials from Berlin's academic career, including teaching materials, research materials, and collegial correspondence dated from 1978 through 1994, with the bulk of the materials dating from Berlin's work at Purdue from 1986 to 1994.

Understanding Provenance

To understand the materials in any archival collection, researchers must know as much as possible about their provenance, the chain of custody of the materials, including what happened to them (and when) from the time they were originally created up to the point of being accessioned or added to the archival repository. This will allow the researcher to evaluate the authenticity and integrity of the materials as evidence.

For example, knowing that the materials in the James Berlin Papers were placed in Shirley's custody in 1998 by Sandy Berlin, the widow of James Berlin, helps an archival researcher to establish their authenticity as reliable documents created by Berlin. Knowing they are the contents of the file cabinets in Berlin's faculty office on campus at the time of his unexpected death will help a researcher understand why most of the materials date from 1986 or later. More specifically, knowing that some of the teaching materials were removed from Berlin's office files and later returned by faculty colleagues who took over his classes within a few days of his death will help a researcher understand why a few folders are organized differently from the others.

General information about the provenance of a collection is usually included in the public finding aid for a collection; but often the archivist or other staff will have access to additional, more specific information and will be able to give a more detailed account of the collection's history. Many archival repositories maintain a "collection file" for each collection, in which, along with other relevant information, they include a more detailed account of the collection's provenance—specifically, who among the staff has worked on the collection. There is even a good chance that the archives staff member with whom a researcher consults will have been involved in acquiring the materials or will have contributed to some or all of the processing for the collection and will be able to give a firsthand account of some of its history. As Frank G. Burke notes, in some cases, "the curator becomes the ultimate finding aid" (55).

In some cases, a researcher can also contribute to identifying the provenance of a collection by clarifying the relationships of previous owners of the collection. For example, sometimes a repository has records of a collection being donated by a particular person but does not know that person's relationship to the original creator[3] of the collection. In these instances, a researcher who is familiar with the background and family relationships of the creator of the collection can help clarify who the donor was and his or her relationship to the creator.

Researchers rely on the ability to draw conclusions about a person's life by examining the papers of that person. Items found in the person's papers are assumed to have been owned by the person and kept for some reason. These items can be used as evidence in learning about what types of subjects were important to the person and can sometimes reveal information about a person's interests that may not appear in secondary sources such as biographies or encyclopedia entries. For these reasons, it is crucial that the papers of one individual or organization never be intermingled with those created by another person or organization, even if the subjects within the papers are similar. This principle of provenance is one of the two most significant theories guiding archives work and has its roots in the beginnings of the archives profession.

During the French Revolution (1789–99), there was a large increase in the creation and use of records. The French, recognizing that records such as land deeds were critical to protecting the rights of the public, sought to preserve the evidence contained in their records. They felt that the public had the right to examine the records produced and kept by their government. As a result, formal archival practice was established. The principle of provenance, or *"respect des fonds"* in French, was an outgrowth of the French Revolution and literally means "respect for the group." This principle is fundamental to contemporary archives work and exists to protect the integrity and authenticity of archival records as evidence by retaining the nature of the relationship that exists among records by the same creator. Although the principle of provenance was a result of the French Revolution, archivists generally did not begin applying the principle to their work until the second half of the nineteenth century (Posner). The impact of the French Revolution on the archives profession cannot be overstated, because out of it came the principle that the public had the right to access the records of its government. This increased governmental accountability to the people.

Understanding Original Order

The second foundational principle informing an archivist's work is the principle of respect for "original order," which refers to the original creator's arrangement of the materials. Like provenance, it is a principle that guides all professional archives work, and it exists for a similar reason: to document the relationships among the records themselves. Original order is also important because the arrangement of a collection can sometimes reveal things about the person or organization that created and used the records.

Archivists take care to determine and maintain the original order to the extent possible given their responsibilities both to preserve the materials from deterioration and to make them accessible to researchers. Archivists do not impose their own organizational principles upon materials that are already organized but rather devote their efforts to identifying and clarifying the organizational principles followed by the creator, recognizing that the arrangement itself may be of interest and significance to researchers. For archival researchers interested in rhetorical issues, original order may be of even greater interest than for other researchers because it can reflect the original context or rhetorical situation of the materials. It is critically important, then, for researchers to know whether original order has been maintained in the materials they examine.

For example, as was evident from the materials themselves and confirmed by colleagues who worked closely with him, Berlin's professional papers—those related to his teaching, research, and faculty service—were organized into file folders that were titled by subject and filed in alphabetical order. When Shirley developed the plan for arranging the papers, Berlin's existing file order was maintained to the extent possible. Understanding how what was "possible" was determined can serve as a useful example for researchers unfamiliar with archival arrangement. Detailed information regarding how a collection's arrangement may have changed after being processed is typically not included in a publicly accessible finding aid, and researchers may wish to consult the archivist for these types of specifics.

It's perhaps self-evident that researchers from different disciplines come to archives with different kinds of questions and therefore need different kinds of information about the collections there. Rhetoric and composition researchers are no different. Because of their interest in discursive genres, rhetoric and composition researchers are likely to want more information about archival document types and forms. Because of their interest in rhetorical contexts, they are likely to have extensive and specific questions about the provenance of records and be especially interested in the form in which records were originally created and the purpose for which they were created. They will also want as much information as possible about the history of how a collection has evolved from the time of the original creation of its contents up through processing decisions made by the archivists in whose custody the collection resides.

As any student of rhetoric is well aware, a knowledge of the rhetorical situation, or the context and events that gave rise to discourse, is critical to understanding that discourse. Researchers examining materials in a collection will draw inferences about the intellectual relationships among the materials from their physical relationships to each other. Materials in files organized alphabetically by subject will have a different relationship to one another than materials in files placed in chronological order. For example, Berlin arranged his folders containing copies of typescripts by academic colleagues alphabetically by the author's last name. He could have chosen other organizational methods—he might have ordered them by date of his receipt of them, or he might have organized them according to the subject of the manuscripts. One can imagine reasons either of these alternative orders might have been useful to Berlin as the original creator of the files, but the fact that he ordered them alphabetically by author's names tells us something about how he anticipated possibly consulting them at a future date, which in itself reflects Berlin's conceptual organization of intellectual content of the files: Relationships among authors are more salient than relationships among subjects.

Because respect for the original order of archival materials is a fundamental principle of archival practice, determining whether and to what extent original order has been altered is one of the archivist's highest priorities in working with a collection. Determining the original order is a kind of educated guesswork based on the archivist's knowledge of the creator's life and activities and the circumstances of creation of the materials. This determination enables the archivist to make good decisions about appropriate arrangement and description and to make good judgments about refiling materials that appear to be misfiled or removing materials that have no relevance to the life of the creator of the records. *Original order* is sometimes more a concept represented in an intellectual model of the collection (through the collection's finding aid) than it is a description based on actual physical proximity. Thus, it is more important to "know" the original order of materials than to actually physically keep materials in their original order.

For the researcher, understanding this about the archivist's work will be critically important to knowing what conjectures can safely be drawn about the relationships among materials. Furthermore, the researcher should consult the archivist to learn what he or she can about the rationale for the arrangement of collection materials. In addition to the public finding aid, the archivist may also have access to the original container list created when the collection was accessioned and other accessioning and processing notes that will reveal the order the collection was in when it was received by the archives.

Determining who may have used the files and altered their original order after they left the creator's custody is not always an easy task, particularly when papers are kept by a family over an extended period of time or custodianship has changed between the time the creator organized the files and the time they were acquired by the archival repository. In some cases, even the archivist will not be aware of how original order has been compromised prior to the materials arriving at the archives. A separate, but equally interesting, problem is the collection that arrives with no original order at all. The collection may have been organized in the past, but perhaps when the materials were packed, they were jumbled together and switched around in order to make them fit better into boxes. Or worse, perhaps the creator had no discernable arrangement scheme—perhaps the creator knew how to locate his or her own files, but the system was indecipherable for anyone else. In the interest of making the collection accessible, archivists will sometimes have to make choices about arranging these types of collections. When this happens, archivists rely on their training to guide them into arranging the collection in a way that is most likely to reflect the creator's own view of the relationships among materials. For this task, the archivist must "reconstruct" original order through researching the life and activities of the creator prior to establishing an arrangement scheme. Most archivists will already have researched the creator anyway in order to better understand the materials in the collection during processing or description.

Because significance can often be attributed to the order of materials, it is critically important that when researchers use archival collections, they maintain the order in which they find materials even if they cannot identify an ordering principle or the original order appears to have been disrupted. Otherwise, the next person who consults the materials—who may well be the researcher himself or herself, back for a second look—will be misled. If a researcher believes materials have been disarranged, he should call it to the attention of the archivist, who will be able to make an informed judgment about the order.

Archival Preservation Principles

While archival preservation materials and techniques vary, some practices are standard; a researcher might, in fact, be able to recognize whether or not a collection has been processed by noting the preservation measures that have been taken. Although techniques and materials change with improvements in technology and accelerated aging tests, archivists' decisions about appropriate preservation steps are informed by two general principles: chemical and physical damage to materials should be prevented, stopped, or slowed where possible without undermining the integrity of the records' content and form; and, to the extent possible, preservation steps should serve to make materials more accessible to researchers rather than less accessible. Archivists follow the motto of conservators and medical practitioners when considering treatment: "First do no harm." No action an archivist or conservator takes to preserve, repair, or stabilize archival material should be responsible for harm to the material over the long term, and ideally any preservation steps taken should be reversible. For this reason, only specific types of adhesives and other conservation supplies are used when treating archival materials. The idea is not just to repair a torn page but also to ensure that the materials used in that repair do not cause future damage such as staining or embrittlement of the page over time.

Some of the preservation steps taken with the James Berlin Papers will illustrate the application of these principles. The removal of metal paper clips and staples was a high-priority task because, after ten years, they had already begun to leave rust deposits on the papers. Removing staples and paper clips introduces some risk of separating materials that were originally together, but that can be ameliorated by replacing metal fasteners with plastic paper clips or folding acid-free, lignin-free paper around packets of papers that must remain together. Berlin's teaching materials included a number of newspaper clippings of articles related to the economy and education; because the high acidic content of newsprint causes it to deteriorate quickly—and to damage other paper it touches—photocopies of these clippings were made, and the originals were discarded. Though photocopying and then discarding the original clippings might seem to undermine the integrity of the original materials, it was justified for three reasons: the newsprint would damage the other materials, newspapers are mass produced and thus clippings have informational value but not artifactual value, and the clippings themselves were not created by Berlin. The *collection* of the clippings—that is, their selection and organization—was created by Berlin, and the integrity of that collection could be maintained with photocopies of the clippings.

Following standard practices and using standard materials, Shirley also replaced original folders and cardboard file boxes with acid-free, lignin-free folders and boxes, which slow the natural aging process of paper. These steps also make the materials much more accessible to researchers, because the standard folder sizes and uniform folder-tab length minimize the likelihood of overlooking a file, and the archival manuscript boxes are a convenient size for transporting and reviewing.

The steps described above were all consistent with standard practices and fairly common. Frequent users of archival materials will recognize them in the materials they consult. Two other preservation steps taken with the collection are less common and, because they are both more obvious and irreversible, seem more aggressive or proactive and therefore likely to raise more questions from users of the materials. The Berlin Papers included two wire spiral-bound notebooks containing notes from Berlin's participation in the 1978 National Endowment for the Humanities Seminar led by Richard Young at Carnegie Mellon University and a dozen or so legal-size yellow pads of notes. In consultation with Sammie, Shirley decided to cut and remove the rusting wire spiral from one of the notebooks that had already damaged several of the notebook pages. Removing the wire spiral risked undermining the order of the notebook pages and the papers inserted between the pages, so Shirley lightly penciled sequential page numbers on each notebook page and insertion. Also in consultation with Sammie, Shirley removed the cardboard backings from the yellow notepads to minimize the damage the highly acidic cardboard would do to the notepad pages. This step left the notepad binding still intact so that original page order could be maintained. Though these steps were appropriate and justified, they may seem more aggressive than other preservation steps because they alter the form of the materials and cannot be reversed. Furthermore, these are actions obviously not taken by the creator himself. For these steps, the archivist's hands became visible. However, a distinction must be made between altering the backing of a standard yellow legal pad and altering the form of, for example, a page on which Berlin wrote. The yellow pad itself was not created by Berlin, nor did removing its backing alter the appearance of the actual pages on which Berlin wrote.

Researchers need to be able to distinguish preservation steps taken by archivists from those taken by the records creator in order to avoid jumping to erroneous conclusions about the format or condition of materials. For example, in most cases, creators do not use or have access to professional archival preservation supplies such as acid-free, lignin-free folders, so their presence in a collection suggests a certain level of processing work by an archivist. As with many of the other steps of processing, some account of the preservation measures is likely to be provided in the collection file maintained by the archivist. Even if this is not the case, an archivist who does not know firsthand what preservation steps were taken during processing will very likely still be able to distinguish professional preservation work from steps taken by the records creator and will be able to advise a researcher who inquires about the preservation steps that have been taken. Researchers who become aware of preservation risks within an archival collection, such as torn pages, staples or metal paper clips, rubber bands, highly acidic newspaper or other damaging materials, should bring these to the attention of the archivist.

Archival Arrangement

As we explained earlier, the arrangement of archival materials is determined to a great extent by their creator and his or her context. This section describes how original order governed specific arrangement decisions for the Berlin Papers. Because James Berlin was a college professor, his professional work throughout his career had been assigned to the three general categories of research, teaching, and service. Regardless of how Berlin himself intellectually integrated his work across these categories or found them problematic, these categories organized his professional life insofar as he was assigned to specific classes each semester, served on specific committees, and worked on specific research projects. Each of these activities generated its own discrete materials; thus, the traditional triad for college faculty work also informed Shirley's decisions and choices for the archival arrangement of these materials.

A second example of how the creator's original order determined arrangement is in Shirley's decision to arrange the teaching materials by course number after dividing them into groups based on the institution where Berlin taught the courses. This division by institution could have easily been placed in chronological order. But because Berlin often reused teaching materials when he taught a course numerous times, grouping materials by course was more in keeping with how Berlin would have arranged the files and thus determined Shirley's final decision about arrangement. Yet, because chronology is also relevant, Shirley drew from various sources in the collection materials to create a chronological list of courses taught by Berlin from 1981 through 1993. That list became part of the collection file and can be consulted by any user of the collection in the future, if he or she knows to ask for it. That list is not filed with the collection itself because it was not created by Berlin, and a researcher is unlikely to learn of its existence if he or she doesn't ask about the contents of the repository's own files on the collection—another reason a researcher should not skip the reference interview with the archives staff or forgo an onsite visit to the archives if possible.

Archival Description

Description is the general term archivists use to describe the activities involved in creating a narrative account of the contents of a collection. Archivists prefer the term *description* to the library term, *cataloguing*, because describing archival materials involves more than creating catalog records, a complexity that rhetoric and composition researchers can appreciate. Archival description can include creating finding aids, collection guides, machine-readable cataloging records (MARC), encoded archival description (EAD), and other files and/or documents describing the collections themselves. Description is not simply a matter of listing the contents of boxes and folders; its purpose is to record the information necessary to composing a narrative account of the collection. In other words, description documents—which provide information about the creator of the documents and the context of their creation—provide information from which a story about the collection and its contents could be constructed.

Usually, this work of description begins at the point of accessioning materials into the archival repository's holdings, with a brief and general statement noting the number and size of the containers and their contents and continues through the creation of a finding aid prepared with the audience of potential users or researchers in mind. Several factors govern an archivist's decisions about the extent of description, and an awareness of these factors can help a researcher to accurately interpret the finding aids and other descriptive documents. Some factors relate to available resources such as staff expertise and time for doing description, which often translates into financial resources. Here again, the more communication between researcher and archivist, the better the choices made. Other factors relate to the archivist's assessment of potential users' interests in the collection materials. Effectively, the archivist must make cost-benefit analyses in order to determine where to direct limited resources.

The purpose of description is to let researchers know the general content of the collection, not the content of individual documents within the collection, although it is sometimes difficult to distinguish between the two. For example, Shirley had to decide whether or not to mention the existence of copies of William Blundell's *Wall*

Street Journal article "The Days of the Cowboy Are Marked by Danger, Drudgery, and Low Pay" in various files in the Berlin papers, because she knew that a researcher familiar with Berlin's work would be likely to immediately recognize this title as a text used in the writing courses in which Berlin was developing a cultural-studies pedagogy for composition studies.[4]

The location of multiple copies of the "Days of the Cowboy" essay in the Berlin papers also serves to illustrate that while some materials in a collection have intrinsic value, other materials are important only because of their relationship to the collection's creator. Although the essay copies are self-evidently not one-of-a-kind materials, their presence among the teaching materials for one of Berlin's courses has evidentiary value because they could be interpreted as evidence that the course was one in which Berlin used a cultural-studies pedagogy.

The "Days of the Cowboy" essay also illustrates how the archivist's familiarity with the creator's work can influence decisions about processing a collection from appraisal through arrangement to description. As a specialist in contemporary rhetoric and composition studies, Shirley was familiar with Berlin's published scholarship, and as a Purdue faculty member, she was familiar with the curriculum of the graduate rhetoric and composition program, the mentoring program for first-year composition instructors in which Berlin taught, and the daily practices of life in the English Department. This meant that her context for identifying, interpreting, and evaluating collection contents was especially rich. Often, the archivist who processes a collection does not have the advantage of working from so rich a context, and when that is the case, researchers using a collection may discover that they can provide valuable information that can be used to revise or supplement finding aids.

Decisions about describing items found in archival collections must be made throughout the processing phase, so archivists must be trained to recognize items in collections that are either confidential by law or may infringe on the privacy rights of individuals. For example, while processing materials, archivists often must make decisions about how extensively to describe materials that are confidential. This is particularly important for materials that can legally be made accessible after the passage of sufficient time. The public finding aid should not include any information that would effectively undermine the confidentiality of the materials, yet enough information must be included to help ensure that potential users know of the materials' existence if appropriate. For example, the James Berlin Papers included confidential materials of several different kinds, each requiring a different means of arrangement and description. Information about students' course enrollment and grades is protected by law, so Shirley removed course rosters from folders of teaching materials in order to make the remainder of the folder contents accessible to researchers. Separation sheets noting the removal of the rosters were placed in each folder, and the rosters were then collected in a separate folder and filed with other confidential materials from the Berlin papers.[5] Other confidential materials found in the Berlin Papers included tenure and promotion reviews Berlin wrote for colleagues around the country. Such letters are typically considered confidential by their writers and readers. Though individual institutions' actual practices in this regard vary, and, typically, a review writer would be informed about whether his or her letter would be treated confidentially, the Berlin papers included no information about which of these reviews Berlin had written with the expectation that they would be kept confidential. Therefore, Shirley decided that all of them should be filed with the confidential materials and remain inaccessible for seventy years, a standard length of time used by archivists for restricting information that may infringe on privacy rights, as well as a sufficient amount of time to ensure the letters had no potential to affect the professional careers of their subjects. For these materials, however, no separation sheet was filled out and left with remaining materials because to do so would be a clear sign that a letter had been written, undermining an important element of the confidentiality of the process of tenure and promotion review. Instead, Shirley prepared a list of the folders of tenure and promotion reviews and related materials that were placed with confidential materials and included this list in the collection file. This provides an example of an instance in which consultation with the archivist, who will have access to the contents of the collection folder, could be particularly helpful to a researcher.

The collection folder often contains additional details about the collection that will be of interest to researchers and especially likely to be significant to scholars of rhetoric and composition. Information about the history of the collection, such as the details of its acquisition, and rationales for processing decisions, such as arrangement choices, are often included in the collection file and can provide explanations for aspects of a collection that might otherwise be puzzling or mysterious. For example, the collection file for the James Berlin Papers includes an account of Shirley's work with the collection over several years, explaining that when she first received Berlin's papers from Sandy Berlin in 1998, she worked with several graduate students in a "Documentation Strategies in Writing Programs" seminar to develop an initial general inventory of the materials, place them in sturdy standard-sized cardboard file-storage boxes, and remove rusting paper clips. That account clarifies that, although the seminar members' work focused primarily on developing recommendations for processing and included minimal hands-on work with the materials, Shirley did have a general idea of the overall contents of the collection.

When Shirley's fellowship project began in 2006, her first step in developing a description of the collection was to create a complete list of the file folders (using folder names already assigned by James Berlin or others) in each box. The second step was to develop more detailed notes on the folder contents that would be used later in the scope and content notes for the collection. It is important to note that listing each item in the collection was not part of the project; instead, notes were taken on types of materials found in the collection, inclusive dates, overall subjects included, and so forth. Once that was done, Shirley had the basis for identifying suitable series titles for describing the arrangement and content of the papers. Though some of the materials had clearly been displaced, most of Berlin's original organization seemed to be still evident and suggested the following six series titles as the major components of the collection:

Series 1. NEH Seminar Materials, 1978–1979. Documents Berlin's participation in the seminar. Included are meeting handouts, notes, and readings.

Series 2. Teaching Materials, 1981–1994. Documents Berlin's teaching career, with most materials related to his tenure at Purdue University (1987–93). Included are materials related to his development of a cultural-studies composition pedagogy for graduate teaching assistants.

Series 3. Research Materials, 1984–1994. Includes handwritten research notes from composition-related journals, annotated copies of articles, unpublished drafts, and notes for conference papers.

Series 4. Collegial correspondence, 1979–1994. Includes letters and notes from colleagues and copies of works in progress sent to Berlin for review.

Series 5. Faculty Governance and Community Activism, 1987–1994. Includes faculty meeting minutes, proposals, and materials related to governance and activism.

Series 6. Confidential Student Records, Correspondence, and Committee Work, 1981–1994. Contains student records (course rosters and grade sheets, dissertation prospectuses, exams), letters of recommendation, tenure and promotion reviews, and confidential notes from faculty searches. (Rose 5–6)

Shirley ordered the series according to best archival practice by ranking the series according to importance to the creator: she placed materials that represented the creator's overall achievement and contributions first. In addition, materials created by Berlin such as his teaching materials ranked higher in the hierarchy of the finding aid than materials not created by him such as the faculty-governance materials. Due to the importance of Berlin's attendance at the NEH seminar to rhetoric and composition, this series was placed first.

Familiarity with standard archival description practices benefits researchers by helping them more efficiently locate information in typical archival finding aids. A researcher needs to know the various documents of description and their purpose to determine what kinds of information can be gleaned from them. First of all, it's important to understand that even a descriptive document so apparently straightforward as a list of folder titles is a report on the archivist's examination of the materials and has been shaped by the sense the archivist is making of the apparent order and organization of the folders. A finding aid is a text that is not transparent but must be interpreted by a researcher. At the same time, standard practices of description have evolved, and a set of conventions is developing—in part as a result of technology's effects on the profession's descriptive practices— and the capabilities for developing searchable electronic databases radically alter researchers' virtual access to finding aids and, in some cases, digital versions of documents themselves.

A finding aid may be viewed as a map of a collection, designed to help the user find his or her way. The main purpose of the finding aid is to let researchers know that a collection exists, where it can be found, and how to access it; ideally, the finding aid will also provide a general idea of the collection's contents so users can judge the material's relevance to their research projects. However, it must be kept in mind that archivists are trained to describe collections at different levels: *fonds* (collection or record-group level), *series* (major categories within the collection), *box* (general summary of each container's contents), and *folder* (general summary of each folder's contents). Although researchers are usually interested in specific items in a collection, archivists are strongly discouraged from describing collections at the item level.[6] Researchers may wonder why archivists do not describe in detail each letter, photograph, artifact, diary, or other item in a collection. After all, it is undoubtedly easier for the researcher to know if the exact item he or she seeks is contained in the collection. Archivists do not describe to this level because of lack of resources. There are too few staff members to document every piece of paper in a typical archival collection, usually thousands of individual documents, photos, and related materials. This can be likened to the cataloging of books: When books are described in library catalogs, they are described in an overall summary—each page of the book is not described because it would be time and cost prohibitive. The same is true for archival collections—they are most often described as an overarching unit, with some detail added but usually not to the individual page level. Ultimately, the researcher must be willing to invest time into finding details that may not be included in a summary catalog record.

Most archival repositories are understaffed and face an enormous backlog of unprocessed collections that are practically inaccessible to researchers due to their lack of description. The archivist must choose between devoting limited staff resources to creating a small number of detailed, item-level finding aids for select collections and leaving the bulk of the collections undescribed and therefore inaccessible or using staff time to create quicker, more summarized descriptions or finding aids of the bulk of the collections but relying on researchers to delve into the collections themselves to discover particular documents. Neither choice is ideal, but archivists usually decide to spread out their staff resources over many collections rather than spending all of their staff time describing in great detail a select grouping of collections in their repository. Researchers should be aware of the benefits of this—after all, if the archives devoted the bulk of its staff resources to describing only a select few collections, what collections might remain invisible to researchers because they are not described or cataloged yet? Additionally, archivists must prioritize which collections to process first and to what level. In prioritizing processing, the archivist considers the mission, goals, and objectives of his or her institution; the collection development policy that provides guidance and outlines collection strengths; and the current and potential future use of the collections themselves. In addition, some collections are more problematic for processing due to their size, the nature of their content, their lack of arrangement, or the condition of the collection. For example, if a collection was in complete disarray and would require considerable time and effort to put in useable order, it might be lower priority due to time and staff constraints. Often, the collections with the highest potential for research use are processed earlier out of a commitment to accessibility. The level of processing will also differ among collections. For example, collections that contain unusually valuable documents, such as autographs by celebrities or historic figures, may be described at a more detailed level for security purposes so that if an item is missing, the archivist will have a record that it at one time was part of the collection. And collections that are digitized, as more and more are each year, are often described in more detail.

Researchers also need to understand that more than thirty years ago, typical finding aids appeared to be created as much for the archivists themselves as they were for researchers. For example, many older finding aids included numerous abbreviations that only archivists could decipher. This is because in the past serious researchers tended to visit the archival repository and speak directly to the archivist about the collections. The archivist would often keep notes and supporting documents about a collection that would help him or her assist the researcher in using the collection. Over time, archivists began to compare differences in finding aids created by different repositories, and they started focusing on making the finding aids easier for researchers to use. Attempts were made to use less archival jargon, improve the format and layout of finding aids, and to include more-helpful information for researchers so they could work more independently of the archivist. Now that finding aids are often posted on the Internet, their level of descriptive content, visual design, and layout are more important than ever, because many researchers are likely to refer to them without first consulting the archivist. It is especially interesting for rhetoric and composition scholars to see the changes that have taken place in finding aids since the creation of the Internet and to acknowledge the dramatic increase in researcher queries for particular collections that may have not been used heavily in the past before the finding aids for those collections were made available online. Even with these changes, however, a researcher should not forego direct consultations with the archivists in whose custody the research materials are held.

Researchers should be aware that various finding aids/descriptive documents created at the time of original accessioning of materials for current audiences or research situations may not address all subjects of interest to researchers of today and tomorrow. Archivists must base their decisions about what aspects of a collection need to be mentioned on their assumptions about who is likely to be using the collection and for what purpose. As research topics grow and change over time, finding aids created decades ago may or may not address current research topics such as women's studies, ethnic studies, and so forth.

Making Effective Use of Archival Finding Aids

By becoming familiar with the typical components and layout of finding aids, researchers can more effectively utilize finding aids to locate the information they are seeking. Although finding aids differ greatly across archival repositories in form, style, layout, and language, good finding aids all contain certain basic elements: introductory and administrative information; biographical or historical sketch of the author or creator of the collection; scope and content note providing a brief overall summary of the collection; and a container list or inventory of the contents of the collection. (See the appendix to this chapter for an annotated version of part of the finding aid for the James Berlin Papers.)

The introductory and administrative section includes information on how the collection is to be used: for example, if there are any restrictions on access to the collection. Often, archival collections are stored outside the main repository in offsite storage, due to space restrictions. A good finding aid will let researchers know if they need to contact the archives in advance of their visit to allow time to retrieve offsite materials. The administrative section of a finding aid may also include information on how the collection was acquired—in other words, its provenance.

The biographical or historical sketch is usually a brief biography or history of the person or organization that created or brought the materials together as a collection. Researchers already familiar with this information often skip over this general introduction to the creator, but it can contain important information. Sometimes, archivists will include a timeline relating to the person or organization, and this may be helpful to researchers.

The purpose of the scope and content note is to provide a quick summary to the overall collection. It includes information on how the collection is arranged, a description of the series or major parts within the collection, any major subject areas or important people or events covered, a range of inclusive dates for the collection, and types of materials included, such as documents, photographs, artifacts, and so forth.

The heart of the finding aid is the container list or inventory. Here, contents of the boxes, series, and/or folders are listed out in greater detail. Although it is rare to include listings of actual items in the collection, some repositories do provide this information. The container list or inventory is often the first place a researcher looks for the information, and it is helpful to know that in most archival finding aids, this information is located toward the end of the finding aid. A researcher seeking something very specific in the collection—such as a letter with a particular date from a particular correspondent—will find it most helpful to scan the series descriptions first, to see if "correspondence" is a series in the collection and if so, where it will be located in the more detailed container list.

Finally, although rare, some finding aids include indices that list personal and corporate names and topical subjects. These are often found at the end of the finding aid after the container list. Often, different archives describe or catalog their holdings differently.

The project of processing the James Berlin Papers presented a unique opportunity for a researcher and an archivist to work together to understand each other's perspectives when approaching archival collections. Reflecting on the experience, the most important insight Shirley gained was recognizing how her decisions about processing had to be informed by knowledge and understanding of the materials themselves. Because archival materials are one-of-a-kind, there is no one right way to arrange or describe them, and the archivist will always have to make his or her own decisions about how to proceed, informed by an understanding of the materials, their creator, and the context of their creation. Though professional archivists have, over time, developed a set of agreed-upon best practices that continue to evolve as technologies evolve and be refined as historical understanding is refined, those best practices are more like guidelines and principles than like a rulebook.

Shirley also learned how time- and labor-intensive the work of archival processing is. Not including the time spent rereading some of Berlin's publications or reading about archival theory and practice in the professional literature, Shirley devoted about a hundred hours to work on physically arranging and describing the James Berlin Papers. She acknowledges that as a novice, she worked less efficiently than a seasoned professional archivist would because she hadn't determined the most streamlined procedures for handling materials. To be fair, she felt that she lost some time because she would occasionally revert out of her novice archivist's role and back into her more familiar role as researcher. She would often find that she was reviewing materials more for the researcher's purpose of answering specific questions or analyzing documents for evidence to support arguments than for the archivist's purpose of identification and description.

Shirley also found that it took time to learn how to do the appropriate level or degree of description. She learned that appropriate description of folder contents was not a matter of listing every item in the folder but of characterizing the folder contents in a way that would help a researcher locate the materials if they were of interest. To do this, of course, she had to construct this figure of the "researcher" from her own experience of research, from her knowledge of the significance of Berlin's work in contemporary composition and rhetoric, and from her knowledge of the contents of the James Berlin Papers themselves.

Shirley is now much better able to understand that the professional archivist's intellectual work comprises a series of judgment calls from accessioning materials to providing access to those materials. Of course, archivists must make judgments about their priorities for expending their always limited funds, time, and staff. Yet, even in an ideal world of limitless resources, archivists would still have to make choices about how to arrange and describe those materials to best reflect their original state. And, ideally, the outcome of those choices would be finding aids that were so extensive (yet easy to read) and so precisely attuned to multiple users' interests as to seem transparently composed, so that readers would need no further help finding materials. Thus, ironically, under ideal circumstances, the archivist's best work might well be invisible to most researchers.

For her part on the project, Sammie learned how rhetoric and composition researchers differ from most researchers in the amount of context and detail they require about steps taken during processing archival collections. While the average researcher may not care how a collection was acquired by the archival repository, or why the collection is organized a particular way, or what preservation steps have been taken by the archivist, it has become clear to Sammie that rhetoricians need such information for drawing conclusions from their research. In addition, as she discussed archives work in more detail with Shirley, Sammie began to think about how exposing the details of the archivist's often "invisible" work might benefit the archives profession itself. For example, by explaining what decisions have been made when processing a collection and what theories and principles guided those decisions, the archivist is not only better able to justify her actions but also to illustrate to researchers the amount of time, resources, and expertise needed to make collections accessible. In addition, when archivists include more information in finding aids about the steps that have been taken in processing collections, it increases the accountability of the archivist's work by presenting it for critique and discussion. It also helps prevent researchers from drawing false conclusions and assuming that steps taken by the archivist were taken by the creator or author of the papers.

Many researchers may not understand that, unlike file clerks, archivists base their actions on not only their practical training for processing collections and describing them but also the theoretical foundation of the archives profession. Archivists must themselves be good researchers to be effective archivists; after all, how can an archivist adequately write a biographical sketch of the record's creator without researching the creator's life? How can the archivist reconstruct the original order of the creator's papers without understanding the different facets of the creator's activities? Archivists often feel undervalued, but perhaps by documenting more of the work they do in publicly accessible finding aids, they will achieve more recognition for their efforts.

In addition, the profession as a whole should open itself up for study by being more forthright about steps taken in processing collections. Just as the archives profession was an outgrowth of the need to make the government accountable to its people, offering evidence of its activities through access to its official records can make the archives community more accountable for its actions. This can only happen when archivists are more forthcoming about the steps they take processing collections. This is not to say that archivists as a rule purposefully seek to hide their actions from those outside the profession; instead, it has been a result of archivists' assumptions that researchers do not have the time or inclination to be interested in that level of detail.

We hope this brief explanation of professional archivists' work will help our readers to see the extent and significance of the often invisible work archivists do every day to preserve and make collections accessible for research and to better understand why so many archival collections remain "hidden" to researchers. If nothing else, we hope that our essay will prompt a dialogue between researchers and archivists that will ultimately result in increased accessibility and use of archival collections—bringing the work of archivists' invisible hands within reach of many more researchers' hands.

Appendix

INVENTORY TO
THE JAMES BERLIN PAPERS, 1978-1994

Comment [s1]: Title of the collection appearing on the cover sheet to the finding aid. This finding aid adheres to template developed by Purdue University Archives and Special Collections.

PURDUE UNIVERSITY LIBRARIES
ARCHIVES AND SPECIAL COLLECTIONS

http://www.lib.purdue.edu/spcol/

Revised: December 8, 2006
Compiled By: Shirley K. Rose

Comment [s2]: Name of the person who wrote the finding aid; often this is the same person who processed the collection, although not always.

Descriptive Summary

Creator	Berlin, James, 1942-1994
Title	James Berlin Papers
Date Span	1978-1994
Abstract	Papers relating to the academic career of James Berlin, Professor of English at Purdue University and major figure in the development of cultural studies pedagogy in rhetoric and composition.
Quantity	7 cubic feet
Language	English
Repository	Archives and Special Collections, Purdue University Libraries

Administrative Information

Access	Collection is open for research. The collection is stored offsite; 24 hours notice is required to access the collection. One box of confidential student records and peer evaluations is restricted from access until 2064.
Preferred Citation	James Berlin Papers, Archives and Special Collections, Purdue University Libraries
Copyright Notice	Rights transferred to Purdue University by Sandy Berlin, June 2006
Acquisition	Donated by Sandy Berlin, wife of James Berlin, June 2006. Papers were transferred from Berlin's office at Purdue University and from his home in West Lafayette, Indiana to Archives and Special Collections in June 2006.
Accession Number	20060619
Location	HKRP 340
Processed By	Shirley K. Rose, 2006

Comment [s3]: These are the dates of the materials in the collection.

Comment [s4]: Significance of Berlin's work might be characterized differently by others

Comment [s5]: The size of archival collections can be expressed in various ways, but normally the designation is by cubic foot, linear foot, number of containers, or number of individual items in the collection. Typically one cubic foot is equal to one linear foot when collections are shelved in boxes, with one foot equaling a standard records size storage box, or two manuscript boxes. The Berlin papers are in 14 manuscript boxes, so this gives researchers a general idea of the size of the collection before consulting it.

Comment [s6]: These notes indicate that although the collection is accessible, it requires 24 hours notice to use it because it must be retrieved from offsite storage. It also tells researchers that portions of the collection are restricted due to confidentiality and privacy laws. It is common, due to space limitations, for archives to use offsite storage so calling ahead before visiting the repository is strongly recommended.

Comment [s7]: This information lets researchers know how to cite the use of the collection in papers or other publications.

Comment [s8]: Although the materials had been in Shirley's custody since summer of 1998 the formal deed of gift legally transferring the collection to Purdue University Libraries was not signed until June 2006, when Berlin's wife agreed to donate the materials permanently to Purdue.

Comment [s9]: Accession numbers are often assigned to archival collections or objects in order to identify them and track them to their physical location in the library. At Purdue Libraries, the accession number reflects the date the collection was acquired: 2006, June 19. If more than one collection or object is acquired on the same day, the number is followed by a dash and then a number indicating which order the collection came in (for example, the first collection acquired on this date would be 20060619-1 and the second collection acquired the same day would be 20060619-2).

Subject Headings -

Comment [s10]: These subject terms will be used by cataloging staff in creating the MARC record for inclusion in the online catalog at Purdue and subsequently in OCLC's WorldCat, a database including the holdings from libraries and archives around the country. For example, an author search on "James Berlin" will generate a record describing his collection, as will a subject or keyword search on "cultural studies theory" or "composition studies."

Persons
Berlin, James

Organizations
Purdue University- Department of English

Topics
Cultural studies theory
Cultural studies pedagogy
Composition studies
Writing instruction
Rhetoric- history of
Rhetorical theory
Composition theory

Biographical Sketch of James Berlin -

Comment [s11]: The biographical sketch, or, in the case of the records of an organization, the historical sketch, is meant to provide a brief summary of the highlights in a person or organization's history. It is not meant to be comprehensive, but it serves to introduce the author or creator of the collection to researchers who may not be familiar with this information.

James Berlin was a faculty member in the Department of English at Purdue University from 1987 to 1994. He was a nationally renowned educator and scholar in rhetoric and composition, valued for his leadership in the development of a cultural studies approach to teaching writing. He was also known for his scholarship on the history of rhetoric and composition theory.

Berlin was born in 1942 in Hamtramck, Michigan. He attended St. Florian High School, where he played football and basketball. He entered Central Michigan University on a football scholarship, receiving his Bachelor of Arts degree and graduating summa cum laude in 1964. Berlin began teaching in elementary schools in Flint and Detroit, Michigan. In 1969 he entered graduate school at The University of Michigan, working towards a degree in English. He received his Master of Arts degree from Michigan in 1970, and his Ph.D. in Victorian literature from there in 1975. His doctoral dissertation was on the relation of German Idealism to Tennyson, Browning, and Arnold.

After he received his Ph.D. he accepted a position as Assistant Professor of Composition at Wichita State University (1975 until 1981). While at Wichita State, Berlin served as the first director of the Kansas Writing Project. Berlin later worked as Associate Professor of English at University of Cincinnati (1981-1985), where he was also Director of Freshman English. In 1985 he joined the faculty of the University of Texas at Austin as a Visiting Associate Professor of English; at the same time he was serving as a visiting professor at Penn State University. Berlin joined the Purdue University faculty as Professor of English in 1987.

Berlin was a member of the National Council of Teachers of English, the Modern Language Association, the Ohio Council of Teachers of English and Language Arts, the College English Association of Ohio, and the Rhetoric Society of America. He published numerous journal articles on rhetoric and teaching composition, and was the author of *Writing Instruction in Nineteenth-Century American Colleges* (1984) and *Rhetoric and Reality: Writing Instruction in American Colleges, 1900-1985* (1987). Berlin died suddenly of a heart attack on February 2, 1994. He was survived by his wife, Sandy, and his sons Chris and Dan.

Scope and Contents of the Collection

The James Berlin Papers (1978-1994; 7 cubic feet) contain papers and other materials created or collected by James Berlin during his academic career, with an especially extensive representation of his work during his years as a Professor of English at Purdue University (1987-1994). The Berlin Papers include research and writing notes, instructor's class notes and other teaching records, as well as correspondence with a large and varied group of scholarly colleagues. The collection generally reflects the state of Berlin's academic files at the time of his death in 1994.

The papers document Berlin's participation in the 1978-1979 National Endowment for the Humanities seminar on rhetoric invention led by Richard Young at Carnegie-Mellon University. This seminar has been recognized as among the most significant events in the early development of the contemporary field of rhetoric and composition studies. The bulk of the papers relate to Berlin's work in developing a cultural studies composition pedagogy, particularly materials from seminars in Purdue's graduate program in rhetoric and composition and from mentoring graduate teaching assistants in Purdue's first-year composition program.

The papers also include copies of articles and book chapters Berlin used for his research; the majority of these contain Berlin's marginalia. The papers also include extensive correspondence with Berlin's academic colleagues, who often sent Berlin drafts of their scholarly works in progress. Materials related to Berlin's work on faculty committees at Purdue University include minutes and notes from committee meetings and activities. Berlin was a member of the School of Liberal Arts Senate when it was reviewing the proposal for its major curriculum revision "Curriculum 2000," a member of the English Department Policy Committee, and a member of departmental committees related to the development of composition and professional writing curricula.

Confidential materials such as student records, letters of recommendation, and tenure and promotion reviews have been separated into one restricted box. Restrictions on access to these materials will be lifted in the year 2064.

Comment [s12]: The Scope and Contents note is meant to provide researchers with a quick summary of the collection; rather than including the entire finding aid in a library catalog record, the Scope and Content is often used to briefly describe the overall collection. This is because library catalog records based on the MARC format cannot accommodate entire finding aids.

Comment [s13]: In the first sentence of the scope and content note, researchers are given a wealth of information: the title of the collection, the inclusive dates of the collection, the collection's size, the author of the collection, and a general idea of what the bulk of the collection relates to—this is meant to save the researcher time by preventing the researcher from having to read through the entire finding aid if all he or she needs is something from a date not represented in the collection, or items relating to Berlin's personal life, for example, which are not represented in this collection. By knowing immediately that what is needed cannot be found in the collection, the researcher saves valuable time reading through sometimes extensive finding aids.

Comment [s14]: This description of contents reflects Shirley's judgment about why materials not created by Berlin should be included in the collection and in the description.

Comment [s15]: This division is an example of when original order could not be used, as confidential material had to be physically separated from the nonconfidential material it was grouped with in order to allow access to the nonconfidential material without risk of allowing access to the restricted material.

The arrangement of the papers reflects Berlin's original order, with a few exceptions. Teaching related materials from Berlin's papers were used and subsequently returned by faculty members who taught Berlin's classes after his unexpected and sudden death; thus, the original order of these materials cannot be certain. Berlin's handwritten research notes have been organized chronologically. Readings included in Berlin's research materials are organized alphabetically by subject or author, reflecting Berlin's own folder titles and order.

The papers are divided into six series:

Comment [s16]: This division imposes a conceptual arrangement on the physical order.

1. NEH Seminar Materials, 1978-1979 (0.5 cubic feet)

The series documents Berlin's participation in the National Endowment for the Humanities year-long seminar in twentieth century rhetorical theory led by Richard Young at Carnegie Mellon University. Types of materials include Berlin's reading and discussion notes from the seminar, copies of assigned readings, and other materials developed by seminar participants.

Comment [s17]: By providing information on the size of each series, the finding aid shows researchers that the bulk of the materials in the collection are related to Berlin's teaching, whereas only small parts of the collection relate to Berlin's participation in the NEH Seminar and his faculty governance activities.

2. Teaching Materials, 1981-1994 (2.5 cubic feet)

The teaching materials document Berlin's teaching career from 1981 to 1994, which the bulk of the materials relating to his graduate teaching at Purdue University from 1987 to 1993. Included are materials related to his development of a cultural studies pedagogy for graduate teaching assistants whom he mentored in the first-year composition program at Purdue and materials related to graduate seminars in rhetoric and composition. Types of materials include syllabi, exams, lecture and discussion notes, and copies of course readings.

3. Research Materials, 1984-1994 (1.5 cubic feet)

The series includes handwritten research notes from an extensive historical review of composition-related journals, annotated copies of printed scholarly articles and book chapters, and unpublished drafts and conference papers. Included in the papers are numerous note pads filled with Berlin's research for his publications *Writing Instruction in Nineteenth-Century American Colleges* and *Rhetoric and Reality: Writing Instruction in American Colleges, 1900-1985.*

4. Collegial Correspondence, 1979-1994 (1 cubic foot)

Items in the series include letters and notes from national and international academic colleagues as well as copies of works in progress Berlin's colleagues sent to him for review.

5. Faculty Governance and Community Activism, 1987-1994 (0.5 cubic feet)

Faculty committee meeting minutes, proposals developed by faculty committees, and other materials related to university community governance and activism in which Berlin participated are included in the series.

6. Confidential Materials, 1981-1994 (1 cubic foot)
Confidential materials include student records such as grade sheets and examinations, confidential collegial correspondence such as letters of recommendation, tenure and promotion reviews, and confidential committee materials such as notes on candidates applying for faculty positions.

Preservation Note
All materials have been housed in acid-free, lignin-free folders and boxes. All newsprint has been photocopied and original newspaper clippings have been discarded.

Separations or Transfers of Materials
Confidential student records, letters of recommendation, peer reviews and candidate evaluations have been separated and placed together in a restricted box.

Comment [s18]: This note lets researchers know some of the ways the collection has been altered through preservation activities.

Comment [s19]: This note explains that original order was not retained when processing restricted material, by clarifying that this material was physically separated from its original location in the collection.

INVENTORY OF THE COLLECTION

Box 1
Series 1: NEH Seminar Materials, 1977-1979 -

NEH Seminar Notes, 1977 [notebook]
NEH Seminar Notes, 1978 [notebook]
NEH Seminar Readings and Assignments, 1978-1979 [four folders]

Box 2
Series 2: Teaching Materials, 1980-1994

Subseries 1: Prior to Purdue University, 1981-1987

English 825, Wichita State University, undated
English 826, Theories of Rhetoric, Wichita State University, 1981
Director of Freshman English, University of Cincinnati, 1981-1987
E 360M, University of Cincinnati, 1985-1986
Theory and Practice of Composition, University of Cincinnati, Fall 1986
English 730, Teaching College English, University of Cincinnati, 1981-1986
English 325M, University of Texas at Austin, Fall 1985 [materials appear to have
   been used again in PU English 304]
ENGL 597B and E 387M, Twentieth Century Rhetoric, 1986
ENGL 382, History of Literary Criticism, University of Cincinnati, 1987
English 103, University of Cincinnati, Summer 1987
English 489, Advanced Composition, University of Cincinnati, Spring 1987

Box 3
Series 2: Teaching Materials, 1980-1994

Subseries 2: Purdue University, 1987-1993

Mentoring materials, 1987-1993
   Orientation, 1987- 1990 -
   Mentoring, 1987-1990
   English 102, 1988
   English 102CS, 1992-1993
   English 304, Advanced Composition, 1990-1991
   English 502, Fall 1989
   English 502, Spring 1993
   Orientation, 1991-1992
   Orientation, Fall 1992
   English 596, Cultural Studies and Rhetorical Studies course proposal, undated

Comment [s20]: Text in bold illustrates the box number where the items can be located along with the particular series or subseries the materials belong to. A range of inclusive dates for each series is also provided.

Comment [s21]: Rather than listing the same title and date information four times, archivists typically indicate instead the number of folders that share this title. This decreases duplication and the overall length of the finding aid, while making it easier for researchers to browse through it.

Comment [s22]: The hierarchical nature of archival finding aids is illustrated here. Items in box 3 are part of the Teaching Materials series, which is further subdivided into two subseries: classes taught prior to Berlin's tenure at Purdue University and classes taught after that period. Even within subseries there may be additional layers or groupings, as shown here. All items that are tabbed under the heading "Mentoring materials" relate to mentoring. Archival finding aids often reflect the use of tabs to show when information is going from general to more specific within the finding aid.

Comment [s23]: Archival finding aids sometimes differ in how they indicate when items are undated. Some finding aids write out the term "undated," while others use the initials "n.d." to stand for "not dated."

Notes

1. A pdf of the finding aid for the James Berlin Papers is available at <http://www.lib.
purdue.edu/spcol/fa/pdf/berlin.pdf>.

2. A *finding aid* is "a tool that facilitates discovery of information within a collection of
records." The *finding aid* is "a description of records that gives the repository physical and
intellectual control over the materials and assists users to gain access to and understand
the materials" (Pearce-Moses 168).

3. *Creator* is the term archivists use for "author" or "artist."

4. Berlin discusses his use of this article in his *Rhetoric Review* essay "Poststructuralism, Cultural Studies, and the Composition Classroom."

5. *Separation sheets* are forms that let the researcher know that an item or items were
originally part of the folder's contents but were removed during processing. Ideally, separation sheets should identify the reason for the removal and the new location for the items
that were separated.

6. Museum professionals differ from archivists in this manner, instead relying on their
training for describing each item in their collections.

Works Cited

Berlin, James. "Poststructuralism, Cultural Studies, and the Composition Classroom."
    Rhetoric Review 11.1 (1992): 16–33.

Blundell, William E. "The Days of the Cowboy Are Marked by Danger, Drudgery, and
    Low Pay." *Wall Street Journal* 10 June 1981, sec. A: 1+.

Burke, Frank G. *Research and the Manuscript Tradition.* Lanham, MD: Scarecrow, 1997.

Pearce-Moses, Richard. *A Glossary of Archival and Records Terminology.* Chicago: Society
    of American Archivists, 2005.

Posner, Ernst. *Archives in the Ancient World.* Chicago: Society of American Archivists,
    2003.

Rose, Shirley K. "Inventory to the James Berlin Papers, 1978–1994." James Berlin Papers,
    Archives and Special Collections. Purdue University Libraries. 2006. <http://www.lib.
    purdue.edu/spcol/fa/pdf/berlin.pdf>.

VIEWING THE ARCHIVES:
THE HIDDEN AND THE DIGITAL

Alexis E. Ramsey

A common assumption about archives is that, once inside, the researcher can access all their holdings or that all their holdings are available for public use. Yet, in reality, most archives have more unprocessed or partially processed collections than they do fully processed collections, creating, in effect, three distinct archives—the hidden, the partially hidden or partially processed, and the visible archive, which itself encompasses both traditional archives and, increasingly, digital archives. In order to effectively research on a given topic, a researcher must be aware of these three types of archives, as well as learn how to (potentially) access hidden and partially processed collections. Because of the huge quantities of hidden collections, the Association of Research Libraries is considering new initiatives to help make hidden collections more visible and thus accessible, even as archivists continue to work processing and preserving these collections. Further, researchers must learn how to navigate digital archives, especially in relation to or alongside more traditional archival research practices. Thus, novice and seasoned researchers alike need to be aware of how much information is held within a given archive (which often means turning to the archivist), how to access that information, and how the processing and digitizing protocols used by archives help turn hidden collections visible and visible collections digital.

Hidden Collections

Although collections are quickly and preliminarily processed when they arrive at the archives, the actual, in-depth processing is often delayed for months, if not years. Archivists, who are specifically trained in appraisal, begin by determining the research value of a collection. The research value influences the level of priority given to processing collections. Archivists also evaluate the collection based upon its size, the nature of its contents, and the resources available for processing. For example, a collection needing lots of preservation work or a collection of unusually large size might by necessity wait longer for processing until needed resources and personnel can be attained. There may be things of a confidential nature within the collection, such as Social Security numbers or credit-card numbers, that should not be made accessible to researchers because such things may cause harm to either the donor or the person to whom the papers belonged. Usually, however, it is the anticipated research value that determines when collections are processed. This value is often based on research patterns in the past and user demand as observed by the archivist. For example, at the Purdue University Archives and Special Collections, processing priority was given to the Herbert C. Brown Collection, donated to the university in spring 2006, even though it is quite large at over three hundred cubic feet. The papers are from Purdue's only Nobel Laureate, and Library Administration provided special funding for the processing of this collection because of its highly anticipated research demand.

Another example of how processing decisions are made stems from my own work with the Albert Viton papers. The collection comprises the business papers from his fifty-plus-year career as a representative with the United Nations Food and Agriculture Organization. Although Viton did not attend Purdue University and the collection makes no reference to the University, he does have some connection to Purdue. In 2004, the Purdue University Press published his book *International Sugar Agreements: Promise and Reality* (chapter drafts are included in the collection), and in 2005, Viton endowed a scholarship in his name to recognize the top undergraduate who worked in the Purdue library system. His collection was accepted conditionally, provided that he would financially support processing—essentially providing funds for materials and for someone to do the actual processing. As a result, the archive was able to hire an archival assistant, and Viton's collection was processed almost immediately. Such processing decisions only serve to highlight the created nature of both the accessible/viewable and the hidden/invisible archive. The created nature of archives demands that researchers ask why certain collections are readily available, when these collections were processed, what the archive gained from the processing of these collections, and the purpose of processing these collections. This is not to suggest a conspiracy on the part of the archivists to keep certain collections hidden, but it does suggest that researchers must understand that there are very limited resources for processing, and, therefore, priorities must be set based on anticipated research use, cost for processing due to the nature and size of the collection, and relevance to the archive's collecting mission. Such priorities should be known to the researcher.

According to Purdue University Archivist Sammie Morris, the majority of archives have only a portion of their holdings processed and available for researchers. Further confirmation of this statistic is found in a survey conducted by Morris with the Committee on Institutional Cooperation (CIC), University Archivists Group, in December 2005. Morris compares the archives of all CIC institutions (the Big Ten, plus the University of Chicago) and reports that, on average, member archives had about 46 percent of their collections unprocessed, with a high of 80 percent processed and a low of 6.4 percent processed. While Morris cannot speak to how the other CIC institutions responded to the survey results, she has been actively working to process Purdue's collections. As of summer 2009, there are minimal catalog records for 90 percent of the archives and manuscript holdings. This minimal catalog means that the majority of the holdings have at least a title-level record in Archon, the university's online finding-aid database. As other authors within the current volume have stressed, communication between researcher and archivist is key for information retrieval, and in this case, I suggest that researchers directly ask their archivists for the amount of processed versus unprocessed collections, as well as about any unprocessed collections that may be of interest to the researcher. As I note later, interest in unprocessed collections may help make them accessible, even if conditionally, to researchers.

The problem of these unprocessed and as it were hidden collections is so pressing that a special task force was created by the Association of Research Libraries (ARL) to study and report on these collections. The task force operated from 2001 to 2005 and examined special collections, looking specifically at how to lessen the number of hidden collections and how to further systematically and broadly digitize collections ("Special Collections"). In 2003, the ARL task force published a white paper,[1] assessing the problems associated with hidden collections and the scholarly barriers they create. Their bulleted list began with accessibility issues:

- Hidden or underprocessed collections are at a greater risk of being lost or stolen and are difficult or impossible to recover from legal authorities if they are underdocumeted. Unique and rare materials are particularly vulnerable.
- They are inaccessible to the scholarly community and thus hinder research and research results. Even when unprocessed collections are made available—which is a security risk—they are difficult, if not impossible, for researchers to locate unless they happen to suspect that the institution in question might have such a collection.
- Undergraduates, graduate students, and junior faculty, many of whom lack the financial wherewithal to travel to other institutions, are particularly affected by the lack of access to unprocessed collections in their own institutions. (Jones 3)

Another challenge associated with hidden collections is staffing priorities where access to these hidden collections is "staff dependent." This means that staff may be the only source of expertise on these collections or that staff resources may be diverted from processing collections to digitizing already processed collections. There is a strategic plan to this staff shift: the more items are digitized, the more effective public relations, and, therefore, the publicity of digitized collections begins to generate additional interest and financial support, which can then be used for processing the unprocessed collections. The problem remains, however, of "staff expertise," particularly when staff knowledgeable about certain collections retire before those collections can be processed.

An initiative proposed by the white paper and agreed upon by attendees at the 2003 Exposing Hidden Collections Conference at the Library of Congress is that "it is better to provide some level of access to all materials, than to provide comprehensive access to some materials and no access at all to others" (Jones 5). In other words, hidden collections should get acknowledgment in the catalog of holdings and at least be brought to the attention of researchers, even if they remain unusable. Some archives create minimal finding aids and/or catalog entries for unprocessed collections precisely so they can be found by researchers who arrive preprocessing. Extended availability is becoming more common every year, especially with the Greene-Meissner model of "more product, less processing" growing in popularity among archivists. The Greene-Meissner models suggest a set of processing guidelines that "expedites getting collection materials into the hands of users, that assures arrangement of materials *adequate* to user needs, that takes the minimal steps necessary to physically preserve collection materials, and that describes materials *sufficient* to promote use" (Greene and Meissner; italics in the original). The goal is to give researchers access to more or less the entire holdings of archives.

In July 2006, the ARL task force published its final status report, encouraging all member institutions to "address of all types of hidden collections: archival, rare books, audio, video, and other media" ("Special Collections") and to do so by following four recommendations: first, to test and use a "preliminary record" format; second, to encourage collection mapping to reveal both overlaps and hidden collections; third, to demonstrate how work processing hidden collections can provide learning opportunities and faculty-student collaboration; and fourth, to work with historically black colleges and universities (HBCUs), which often do not have archivists or special collections librarians, to train archivists and thereby expose their collections. Overall, however, the task force stressed the need to find funding to support these processing efforts. One newer source of funding available to institutions is a program created by the Council on Library and Information Resources and funded by the Andrew W. Mellon Foundation. The nationwide program, begun in June 2008, provides funding to institutions to help them identify and catalog collections of high scholarly value ("CLIR Issues").

On a more individual level, a way to alleviate the problem of hidden collections is for the researcher to take the initiative and inquire of the archivist about other collections that may be related to his or her research topic but are not yet publicly available. Some archivists are willing to allow a researcher to look through, under carefully guarded conditions, the unprocessed collection. Even if a researcher is unable to work directly with an unprocessed collection, at the very least the researcher can include a footnote in his or her project about the hidden collection, thereby aiding future researchers. The researcher's inquiry may also cause the collection to get a level of preferential treatment and a timelier processing schedule. Again, unprocessed collections are highly susceptible to theft and damage because no complete finding aid exists that catalogs each item within the collection as well as its condition, meaning that work with unprocessed collections requires a great deal of trust between researcher and archivist and, thus, access is not always a realistic expectation. These suggestions emphasize the importance of a researcher actively working with archivists and not being shy in asking for help with collections or suggestions on other potentially useful collections.

The (In)Visible Digital Archive

Another way archivists are actively working to make collections both more accessible and more widely available is through digitizing certain collections or key parts of collections. Currently, the National Archives and Record Administration Electronic Records Initiative is working to provide long-term access to electronic contents "free from dependence on any specific hardware or software" ("Electronic Records Archives (ERA)"). This initiative demonstrates how seriously archives are taking the digitizing of collections, and understanding that digitizing will exponentially aid users in research may help to further and more broadly publicize the archives. The Library of Congress is currently digitizing its special collections "hewing to a philosophy that it should be digitizing objects that cannot be seen elsewhere" (Hafner 4). Yet, as Donald J. Waters, program officer for scholarly communication at the Mellon Foundation, asserts, "As interesting and as important as standout collections in individual libraries and archives might be, the mere fact of digitizing them does not mean that once they are online they will attract and sustain an audience" (Hafner 5). In other words, digitizing does not equal automatic profitability. Yet, the necessity and value of digital archives stems from the possibility of access. Further, digitizing can be another means for preserving extremely fragile documents. For example, digitizing a document that is already torn or disintegrating may decrease the amount the document is handled, helping to stave off further damage.

The choice to digitize certain collections over others is indicative of which collections are prioritized for the university archives. Karin Becker of the Nordic Museum in Stockholm, Sweden, writes that in being "charged with documenting and preserving that which is considered valuable, the museum has also become the institutionalized arbiter of value" (3). For the Purdue University Archives and Special Collections, value is assigned to those collections that, in relating to Purdue history, also showcase the contributions of Purdue faculty members to a more national or international audience. The University Archives values those collections that emphasize the role of Purdue in the life of these otherwise-famous individuals. The first collection to get fully digitized is the George Palmer Putnam Collection of Amelia Earhart Papers. A quick inventory of the other digitized collections reveals that all have Purdue affiliations, but most have not been digitized to the level of the Earhart papers.

The drive to digitize collections is hampered by three main impediments: "money, technology and copyright complications" (Hafner 2). Indeed, even the Library of Congress forecasts that "only 10 percent of the 132 million objects held will be digitized in the foreseeable future" (Hafner 2) because of the cost prohibitions. "Scanning alone on smaller items ranges from $6 to $9 for a 35-millimeter slide, to $7 to $11 a page for presidential papers, to $12 to $25 for poster-size pieces. (The cost of scanning an object can be a relatively minor part of the entire expense of digitizing and making an item accessible online.)" (Hafner 2). For smaller archives, such as county or business archives, the cost of digitizing may preclude any objects whatsoever from getting scanned or put online. Yet, to not digitize collections is to leave these items behind where they might "disappear from the collective cultural memory, potentially leaving our historical fabric riddled with holes" (Hafner 2). The problem with the latter statement is that it assumes archive holdings form any type of complete history, when, in reality, they themselves are just as "riddled with holes" and incomplete as any digitizing effort; however, the popularity of online research does suggest that nondigitized collections may become invisible for the average researcher.

Another difficulty with the digital archive—and by this I mean digital renderings of traditional archives—is that only certain items may be fully digitized. Items such as textiles, coins or medals, or other three-dimensional objects, lose detail when scanned—if scanning is possible at all. Indeed, one can argue that all texts, when digitized, lose something when confined to a screen. And the goal of digitizing is often to entice the researcher into the archive to see, touch, and smell the real thing. Being able to touch and smell documents are important aspects of archival work because a researcher should be able to take account of the collection for him- or herself and not only through digital renderings. For example, in "Historians Who Love Too Much: Reflections on Microhistory and Biography," historian Jill Lepore opens the piece with the confession of how holding a piece of Noah Webster's hair made her feel "an eerie intimacy with Noah himself. And, against all logic, it made me feel as though I knew him—and, even less logically, *liked* him—just a bit better" (129; italics in the original). Being physically with archived objects allows for a level of intimacy with the collection. The importance of the senses in archival work also suggests that being inside or in physical contact with a collection is paramount for a researcher to write with any level of authority on the collection. For instance, as beautiful as a dress looks on screen, something of its research value, its uniqueness, is lost when I cannot hear how the fabric sounds as it moves, or smell the fabric, or cannot observe the rips, stains, or stitching up close and in person because imagining how the dress functioned as a wearable object becomes too difficult. The same is true for scanned documents and other more traditional archival holdings. I may note that a document looks fragile from its digital image, but I cannot see how truly fragile and thin the paper is. Nor, for instance, can I feel how hard a pen might have pressed into the paper. And while some scanning may be highly detailed and have the option of zooming into a document, not all scanning is so advanced. A researcher using digitized collections must take into account how using a digital collection affects research outcomes in both positive and negative ways.

Considerations about the link between traditional and digital collections, and how research is completed with digital collections, are evidenced in the digital processing decisions made in regards to the Putnam Collection of Earhart Papers at Purdue. The digital collection has its own Web site linked off the Archives and Special Collections homepage (http://www.lib.purdue.edu/spcol/aearhart/). The Earhart page features digital images of all the photographs and documents in the collection, access to the collection's finding aid, biographical information, news about the search for Earhart, and directions for physically accessing the collection. Each document or photograph has its own page, on which details of the digitizing process are noted: date scanned, capture device, capture details, resolution, color depth, color management, as well as information about the physical document: title and description of the object, extent of original, language, type. The page also allows viewers to magnify sections of the document/photograph.

The digitizing is part of the Digital Initiatives @ Purdue University Libraries Project, and its mission is "committed to the production and maintenance of archival quality digital reproductions from the unique collections in the Purdue University Libraries Archives and Special Collections to be delivered via state-of-the-art networking technology to the University scholarly community and to the world." The focus of the Digital Initiatives is to make the collections accessible, though a long-term purpose of the digitizing team is to utilize "Encoded Archival Description (EAD) to make the contents for finding aids for archival and special collections available in major bibliographic databases, as well as [. . . for] a future digital (institutional) repository" ("Digital Initiatives"). E-Archives developed from the Digital Initiatives to house scanned archival content. The site debuted in 2006 and by summer 2009 included about 107,000 digital objects from many of the university's major collections. Thus, there are two Web sites for Purdue's collections: Archon for finding aids and e-Archives for collections. The immediate result of digitizing is that the collection has been saved twice within the archives, both as documents in boxes and as documents on hard drives, and then again whenever images-of-documents are downloaded or printed by a researcher.

The collection demonstrates how the process of transforming traditional archives into digital archives reinterprets the singular topology of the archival space. The digital archive does not exist in one, centralized location but in the nonlocation of cyberspace. The "dismissal" of the physical archive space also lends to the collections a sense of informality as some of the strictures of researching within the archive are voided (namely, where and when a person can use the collections). The result is a sense of pliability, or perhaps even *playfulness*, in and with the collections because the actual collections themselves are not affected. Closing the browser replaces the collection as it was when the researcher first opened the page. Researchers can therefore continually "play" with the documents, examining how the importance of the materials varies when positioned in different ways (one is no longer limited to going folder by folder because the folders themselves are gone). Thus, the act of preserving documents on hard drives and showcasing documents online affects how we access and research "in archives."

If digitizing is causing a renegotiation of the archival space, digitizing is also reinterpreting the relationship between archivists and researchers. For instance, when examining collections online, researchers may assume that the archivist has been eliminated and no longer stands between the researcher and total access to the collection. Such an idea is misguided because it is the archivists who decide which collections warrant digitization and how that process will occur and be rendered on the computer screen. The archivist, though invisible, still controls access to collections. At the same time, because the archivist is not necessarily present when the researcher logs into the collections, the ability of the researcher to manipulate and realign collections is all the greater. Digital collections do not render one party obsolete, but they do force an altered understanding of how researcher and archivist "work" together, sometimes blurring the line between researcher and archivist. Some archives are making their finding aids and digitized collections available for comment and keywords by researchers. A researcher looking at a digital item could tag onto the item a comment that there is a similar item of importance available at another archives. Or a researcher could provide caption information for an unidentified photo or provide cross-references or additional details in a finding aid.

The Putnam collection also showcases how digitizing artifacts can allow an object to stand alone, rather than as yet another piece in a large collection. Digitizing can reassign the (potential) meaning(s) of objects, perhaps distancing them from their intended or original meaning, or give prominence to a hitherto ignored object. Such reinterpretation is not necessarily negative because it privileges the documents, but it also has the potential to deny the objects a context. Archivists are concerned about this problem; some archives are providing the links to the digital objects from within the finding aid itself, allowing the researcher to see the digital item in context and original order. (Provenance, the theory that the contents of one collection must not get mingled with another collection's materials, is still intact. The only way to affect provenance is if digitized collections cannot be separated and searched on their own. With the Earhart collection, searching is limited to that collection, so provenance is always apparent. Also, the chain of custody and ownership information vital to provenance is available in the finding aid. Ideally, all digitized collections would be available for viewing within or alongside their finding aids.) The digital images of the Earhart documents remain grouped together on a single Web page, and the collection as a whole is given its own Web site, but the original order of the collection is lost. The Web site does not tell, other than through the finding aid, how the objects are situated against/next to each other in the file folders and boxes. The documents and photographs are linked to one another through keywords, but they are also highlighted individually. For instance, one photograph is titled "Amelia with unidentified person after arrival in Oakland" ("Amelia"), and each of the words in the title, except for the prepositions, are all links to other elements within the collection. One can also use a subject search to categorize the Earhart photographs or an advanced keyword search of the Earhart documents to pull up specific groupings of documents.

Although the digitizing of documents might make visiting the hard copies obsolete and although the crash of a computer threatens the digital archives in much the same way that fire and floods threaten "real" archives, digitizing cannot threaten the objects themselves because they have intrinsic value beyond their intellectual content. Similarly, good digitization projects such as Purdue's include off-site backup tapes and on-site backups on gold archival CDs so that if a computer crashed, the digital archives could be easily restored. Yet, Purdue University Archivist Morris is emphatic that "digitization is not the same as preservation" (Morris, interview), nor does digital equal forever, and, thus, the digital archive can never be anything but a supplement to the traditional archive. Further, "recourse to the virtual archive does not mean that their posterity is any more secure. . . . The archives which cyberspace houses are no less fragile or vulnerable to disappearance, for a variety of technological, economic, and political reasons" (Burton 3). Indeed, part of the reason for the level of detail on the digital document pages regarding scanning procedures is for preservation reasons, or what Morris refers to as "preservation metadata." The information is intended to be helpful for both the researcher and later archivists or IT staff who may need to update the technology that input the collections. Digitizing for that reason remains an ongoing process for archives because "digital material is ephemeral, and digital files must be maintained, backed up, refreshed, and migrated on a regular, ongoing basis to remain accessible with current hardware and software" (Morris, "Preservation" 2). In order for the collections to remain digitally accessible, archivists must have both the resources and the knowledge to continually update their digital collections. In "Preservation Considerations for Digitization of Archival Materials," Morris suggests that archivists create both a "digital surrogate" (4) and a print copy of the original document to benefit researchers and the archives alike. Yet, the question remains, what happens with nontraditional collections? How does one digitize a three-dimensional object? Such questions are a reminder of why digitization cannot threaten the archive—because digitization is not tangible. As realistic as a document looks on-screen, the image remains an image, a representation. Thus, Morris point outs, most scholars will still come to the archive for the experience of being in the archive and for the experience of being near the original collection.

Awareness of the relationship between the digital and traditional archives, as well as how collections are catalogued and processed in each setting, should encourage researchers to ask questions, explore both types of archives, and consider how each venue shapes research. Digital archives call attention to the created nature of all archives. The digital archive is just as, *if not more*, created than traditional archives because digitizing is expensive and time-consuming work. What is digitized is specially selected. Thus, in addition to negotiating new archival spaces, researchers must understand that the application of the terms *hidden*, *digital*, and *archive* are continually shifting: a collection may be hidden one visit and viewable at the next visit, and vice versa. A collection may be removed from active circulation for restoration or digitizing reasons, or a collection may be undergoing processing during one visit and completed the next. Furthermore, more and more collections are creating at least some type of online presence. At the same time, researchers must be aware of the difficulties faced by archivists who not only have to process hidden collections but also, nearly simultaneously, digitize their holdings. As archives evolve into the twenty-first century, researchers and archivists alike are confronted with new research questions, procedures, and decisions that necessitate both parties working together to preserve, yet make accessible, the fragile and fascinating items held by archives.

Note

1. *White papers* are short treatises written to educate industry customers.

Works Cited

Albert Viton Papers. Archives and Special Collections. Purdue University Libraries, West Lafayette, Indiana.

"Amelia with Unidentified Person after Arrival in Oakland." Photograph. New ID number b10f5i51, Putnam Collection of Earhart Papers. <http://earchives.lib.purdue.edu/cdm4/item_viewer.php?CISOROOT=/earhart&CISOPTR=164&CISOBOX=1&REC=10>.

"Archon." Archives and Special Collections, Purdue University Libraries. 16 June 2009 <http://www4.lib.purdue.edu/archon/>.

Becker, Karin. "Picturing our Past: An Archive Constructs a National Culture." *Journal of American Folklore* 105.415 (1992): 3–18.

Burton, Antoinette, ed. *Archive Stories: Facts, Fictions, and the Writing of History*. Durham, NC: Duke UP, 2005.

———. "Introduction: Archive Fever, Archive Stories." *Archive Stories: Facts, Fictions, and the Writing of History*. Durham, NC: Duke UP, 2005.

"CLIR Issues." Purdue University Libraries. 16 June 2009 <http://www.clir.org/pubs/issues/issues62.html>.

"Digital Initiatives @ Purdue University Libraries." 31 Aug. 2005. *Purdue University Libraries*. 10 July 2007. <http://www.lib.purdue.edu/spcol/digit/index.html>.

"E-Archives." Purdue University Libraries. 16 June 2009 <http://earchives.lib.purdue.edu>.

"Electronic Records Archives (ERA)." National Archives. 6 July 2007 <http://www.archives.gov/era/>.

George Palmer Putnam Collection of Amelia Earhart Papers. Archives and Special Collections. Purdue University Libraries, West Lafayette, Indiana. <http://www.lib.purdue.edu/spcol/aearhart/>.

Greene, Mark A., and Dennis Meissner. "More Product, Less Process: Pragmatically Revamping Traditional Processing Approaches to Deal with Late 20th-Century Collections." 18 July 2007. <http://ahc.uwyo.edu/documents/faculty/greene/papers/Greene-Meissner.pdf>.

Hafner, Katie. "History, Digitized (and Abridged)." *New York Times* 10 Mar. 2007. June 30 2007. <http://www.nytimes.com/2007/03/10/business/yourmoney/11archive.html?_r=1&scp=1&sq=%22History,%20digitized%20(and%20Abridged)%22&st=cse>.

Jones, Barbara M. "Hidden Collections, Scholarly Barriers: Creating Access to Unprocessed Special Collections Materials in North America's Research Libraries." 6 June 2003. Association of Research Libraries Special Collections Task Force. 30 June 2007. <http://www.arl.org/bm~doc/hiddencollswhitepaperjun6.pdf>.

Lepore, Jill. "Historians Who Love Too Much: Reflections on Microhistory and Biography." *Journal of American History* 88.1 (2001): 129–44.

Morris, Sammie. Personal interview. 3 Nov. 2006.

———. "Preservation Considerations for Digitization of Archival Materials." *Archival Outlook* 2005: 26–33. *Purdue E-Pubs.* 10 Nov. 2006. <http://docs.lib.purdue.edu/lib_research/14/>.

———. "Status of the CIC University Archives: A Survey." 27 Jan. 2006. Committee on Institutional Cooperation, University Archivists Group. 10 Nov. 2006. <http://www.cic.uiuc.edu/groups/UniversityArchivistsGroup/>.

"Special Collections Task Force Final Status Report 2006." 5 June 2007. Association of Research Libraries. 7 July 2007 <http://www.arl.org/rtl/speccoll/hidden/status0706.shtml>.

Viton, Albert. *International Sugar Agreements: Promise and Reality.* West Lafayette, IN: Purdue UP, 2004.

LOCATING THE ARCHIVES: FINDING AIDS AND ARCHIVAL SCHOLARSHIP IN COMPOSITION AND RHETORIC

Chris Warnick

Revisionist historians in composition and rhetoric have written extensively about the materiality of the archive and the ideological questions researchers face when confronted with the necessary knowledge that archives, whether they are official documents housed in climate-controlled libraries or student papers gathering dust in an attic, are highly mediated constructions of the past. Jean Carr, Stephen Carr, and Lucille Schultz, in their expansive archival inquiry into nineteenth-century rhetorics, readers, and composition textbooks, make a similar claim when they observe, "Any particular archive is at once a *fragmentary* and an *interested* record of textual production, the consequence of innumerable local decisions and unforeseen contingencies about the production and preservation of a large array of texts" (19; italics in the original). Wendy Sharer goes one step further to discuss the impact this materiality of the archive has for our ideological understanding of writing. Drawing on James Berlin, she writes, "[H]istorical versions of 'what is good' depend on 'what exists,' or specifically what *materially* exists as sources for histories, and on 'what is possible' for revisionist historians of rhetoric to do with what exists" (120; italics in the original). Yet, while recent inquiries into the past material traces of composition and rhetoric scrutinize the composition of the archives, remarkably little is said in these studies about the methods used to locate these archives in the first place.[1] In other words, recent historical scholarship into the archives of composition and rhetoric, despite its increased attention to the materiality of these archives, obscures an important material consideration of archival work—specifically, the sources and interpretive processes researchers draw on to locate archival materials.

This essay looks into this issue by examining several types of finding aids available to scholars interested in recovering material traces of writing, rhetoric, curricula, and pedagogy. Drawing on my experience working with these resources as part of my ongoing research into personal writings composed by 1960s-era college students, I discuss some problems these finding aids pose, especially for historians of composition and rhetoric, and offer practical suggestions for using print bibliographies, online databases, archive catalogs, and other finding aids. One objective of this essay is to share with other interested researchers resources that can potentially expand our historical understanding of writing and writing instruction; that being said, it should go without saying that the listing of resources offered here is by no means exhaustive. Additional finding aids relevant to the historical study of composition and rhetoric undoubtedly exist, and interested scholars might take the opportunity provided by a range of disciplinary forums—including those on a local level, such as undergraduate and graduate seminars, as well as those on a national level, such as the Wiki site CompPile or the National Archives of Composition and Rhetoric Special Interest Group at the Conference on College Composition and Communication (CCCC)—to collect and disseminate resources for further inquiry.[2]

This essay is aimed at scholars already experienced in archival research, as well as graduate students and other intellectuals less versed in the arts of the archive. Thus, I have at times written this piece more like a review essay on finding aids rarely discussed, at least directly, in the research literature; at other moments, this is a narrative of my own individual research process in the hopes that the insights I have learned, as well as the mistakes I have made, will encourage researchers new to archival work to seek out primary materials and provoke all of us interested in material histories of writing and pedagogy to think critically about the processes we draw on to construct the archives we create through our research.

Electronic, Print, and Local Finding Aids

Within the professional archivist community, the term *finding aid* refers specifically to a guide or index listing the materials held in a particular archival collection; however, for the purposes of this essay, I want to broaden this term to include general archival directories, or electronic and print databases that assist researchers in locating relevant archival sources. This section describes some of the different types of finding aids available to locate archives of student writing, syllabi, departmental records, and other documents important to historical inquiry in composition and rhetoric. In addition, it details several examples of different finding aids and offers information about the kinds of materials and collections they privilege—as well as those materials not included as part of the archive. These finding aids may be broken down into at least three broad categories: online databases, print bibliographies and directories, and catalogs specific to particular archival collections.

Online Databases

The National Union Catalog of Manuscript Collections (or NUCMC) and ArchiveGrid are two electronic resources useful for locating unpublished materials housed in publicly accessible U.S. libraries, museums, historical societies, and other repositories. Essentially, the NUCMC and ArchiveGrid provide libraries and researchers access to the RLG Union Catalog, a database maintained by a nonprofit consortium known as the Research Libraries Group, which includes Harvard, Yale, Columbia, the New York Public Library, and more than 150 other research institutions ("About RLG"). Both the NUCMC and ArchiveGrid only retrieve data on manuscript collections, which means that archives comprising published materials, such as the John A. Nietz Old Schoolbook Collection, discussed in Carr, Carr, and Schultz's history, are not indexed. Thus, the NUCMC and ArchiveGrid are more useful resources for locating syllabi, student papers, lecture notes, textbook manuscripts, correspondences, and other manuscript materials. They are of little use to those researchers who focus on textbooks and other published traces of writing pedagogy. For a more thorough discussion of these and other online databases, see Elizabeth Yakel's essay "Searching and Seeking in the Deep Web: Primary Sources on the Internet" in the current collection.

Print Bibliographies and Directories

Because the NUCMC and ArchiveGrid only search for relevant collections indexed through the RLG Union Catalog, they are not, by any means, exhaustive. Thus, print bibliographies and directories specializing in manuscript collections are an additional resource that may be consulted alongside electronic search aids. One bibliography that is geared more toward newcomers to archival research than veterans is *Archival Information: How to Find It, How to Use It*, edited by Steven Fisher. (Fisher states in the introduction, "This book is aimed at the general researcher who finds the need to conduct archival research" (ix).) Besides containing a brief introduction that covers the basics of archival research—including tips on how to efficiently contact library staff, how to conduct oneself in the archive, and how to follow copyright law relevant to archival materials—Fisher's collection consists of eleven essays, each written by different authorities in library science and records management, that gloss archival collections specializing in government, science, fine and performing arts, genealogy, film, business, and other broad research areas.[3]

Unfortunately, none of the chapters focus on issues such as education, universities, students, or writing—an absence that plays itself out in other bibliographies, as I discuss in a moment. However, the collection contains one chapter entitled "Women's History Archives," written by Wendy Chmielewski, a valuable resource for scholars working on women's histories in composition and rhetoric. This chapter contains extensive information on well-known archives on women's history at the Schlesinger Library and Smith College; noteworthy microform collections; published bibliographies that catalog the records of various women's organizations; and digital archives, such as the African American Women Online Archival Collections, sponsored by Duke University. Chmielewski's chapter would make a useful starting point for scholars interested in locating diaries, collected papers of well-known activists, documents charting the development of women's clubs, or other archival materials on women's literacies and history.

A slightly different type of printed archival finding aid is *Articles Describing Archives and Manuscript Collections in the United States: An Annotated Bibliography*, compiled by Donald L. DeWitt. Rather than putting together a directory of archival locations, DeWitt cites over two thousand secondary sources that evaluate the holdings of archival collections. Thus, Dewitt's bibliography represents an even more highly mediated construction of the archive, as it reports on journal articles and other sources that describe specific archives—including collections of literary manuscripts, government records, political and legal documents, sound recordings, film, musical scores, and a range of other materials. DeWitt describes the contribution of the bibliography:

> For decades, the bibliographical article has been a traditional way to publicize and improve access to unique collections of unpublished resources that are potentially valuable to researchers. . . . The authors of these articles sought to inform readers about the existence of specific collections and to analyze collections of papers or records in a way that might help researchers formulate reference questions or make a decision to personally visit an archive. The purpose of this bibliography is to further assist researchers in locating and evaluating primary sources pertinent to their research by bringing together articles describing unpublished resources into a single volume. (ix)

In other words, DeWitt devises this bibliography as a preliminary step in the research process where scholars assess the value of a given archive with little to no risk. DeWitt cites articles published as recently as ten years ago and as far back as the late nineteenth century, although he says remarkably little about the value these more historical examinations of the archive might have for contemporary researchers.

Another type of published search tool to consider at the beginning stages of a project is a bibliography that indexes catalogs, guides, inventories, and other finding aids. In *Guides to Archives and Manuscript Collections in the United States*, DeWitt attempts "to bring together in one volume finding aids to unpublished materials" (ix). DeWitt further suggests that his book is the first of its kind when he remarks that "it was surprising to discover that no comprehensive bibliography exclusively of guides to unpublished materials existed" (xi). DeWitt's claim to novelty notwithstanding, the text proves valuable to composition historians because it identifies a number of finding aids that catalog the holdings of archival collections that could potentially fuel numerous archival studies of writing and pedagogy. The bibliography annotates finding aids relevant to collections focusing on education specifically, but most of the particularly exciting archives are those indexed under general, ethnic, and women's history. They include state archives documenting the Federal Writers' Project instituted as part of the Works Progress Administration; records of the American Missionary Association and its efforts to educate African Americans; teaching materials and other documents composed by Horace Mann Bond, father of civil-rights activist Julian Bond; and records from midwestern Catholic mission schools designed to educate American Indians.

Distinct from bibliographies that list secondary sources and finding aids are books that catalog diary and journal manuscript holdings. William Matthews's *American Diaries in Manuscript, 1580–1954: A Descriptive Bibliography* represents an important example of this genre. According to Laura Arksey, Nancy Pries, and Marcia Reed, Matthews was a linguist who "began the study of diaries as a means of analyzing linguistic change but quickly discovered in them such antiquarian, historical, and human interest values as to claim his attention for the remainder of his life" (ix). Matthews's earlier work, titled *American Diaries: An Annotated Bibliography of American Diaries Written Prior to the Year 1861*, which lists diaries published up until the start of the Civil War, influenced several later bibliographies focusing on diaries and journals that found their way into print.[4] In his later book, *American Diaries in Manuscript*, Matthews identifies unpublished personal writings held in over 350 libraries, historical societies, and other research institutions. He indicates archives where researchers can find diaries and journals written by travelers, housewives, farmers, infantrymen, military officers, clergy, adventurers, politicians, diplomats, business leaders, academics, and a host of other occupations and identities. Most relevant to composition research, though, Matthews references several holdings that include the personal writing of students, including nineteenth-century diaries kept by students at Harvard and the University of Minnesota, as well as at boarding schools and military academies in the American south.[5]

The last kind of source I want to mention here are print directories that contain basic information about individual archives (i.e., contact information, inclusive dates, and volume) and gloss what they deem to be some of the most-noteworthy holdings. Two directories frequently consulted in bibliographic scholarship are *A Guide to Archives and Manuscripts in the United States*, edited by Philip M. Hamer, and *Directory of Archives and Manuscript Repositories in the United States* of the National Historical Publications and Records Commission (NHPRC). Both texts were underwritten by the NHPRC, an arm of the National Archives and Records Administration. The information found in these directories is not as up-to-date as that found online in ArchiveGrid or the NUCMC, but it nonetheless illustrates a similarly colossal investment of time, labor, and money as these online databases. The compilers of the second edition of the *Directory of Archives and Manuscript Repositories*, which sought to expand on the work done in Hamer, speak to the difficulties of putting such a directory together: "From . . . completed questionnaires, from additional information solicited by telephone, and from comprehensive field surveys conducted . . . in Kentucky, New York State, and Washington State, the *Directory* staff prepared approximately 1,400 new entries and revised the majority of first-edition entries" (xi). This work wasn't always valued, though, as the compilers also mention the setbacks they faced in the wake of federal budget cuts and layoffs (xi). The second edition of the *Directory of Archives and Manuscript Repositories*, published in 1988, is the most recently published directory that I have been able to locate, with the bulk of archival indexing now understandably being done online because of decreased, although still substantial, costs in terms of maintenance and publication.

Given that directories like those compiled by the NHPRC print information that is in some cases no longer accurate, it would appear as if they have little relevance to scholars currently conducting archival research in composition and rhetoric. However, this would overstate the case as these texts, and indeed all of the bibliographies discussed here thus far, can teach those of us in the field doing archival research how to better disseminate information among one another and to others about how to locate archives of composition. Although archival research has grown tremendously over the last two decades, bibliographic scholarship that would assist further historical inquiry is generally absent from the field. Prominent journals such as *College Composition and Communication* and *College English* no longer publish bibliographic articles as they did earlier in their history, and graduate programs in composition and rhetoric, too, place less of an emphasis on bibliographic knowledge. (Speaking anecdotally, I attended a graduate program that offered courses in historical and archival scholarship; however, these courses stressed archival theory over methodology.)

The greatest limitation of print bibliographies and directories is that they do not mark composition and rhetoric as specific archival interests. Education appears as a category in most bibliographies and directories, and one can page through a back index and occasionally find entries under *writing, students,* or *colleges and universities.* But these do not always prove to be useful search categories. In essence, bibliographies and directories reproduce the problem scholars in the field face every time they enter the archive: These texts, like archives in general, do not recognize composition and rhetoric as valid research fields. But this limitation also points to their greatest potential strength because this absence underscores the important need, evidenced by the current collection of essays, for those of us in composition and rhetoric to further educate ourselves concerning the practices of archival scholarship.

Catalogs Specific to Particular Archival Collections

These finding aids typically represent the last step of preliminary research before one examines the holdings that make up a specific archive. In other words, it is only after processing and evaluating the information found in search engines and published directories or bibliographies that one usually consults a finding aid that inventories a particular record collection—and this depends on whether or not the collection is indeed catalogued. These finding aids are often produced by archive staff or by graduate students completing projects as part of their coursework. They come in a variety of forms: They may consist simply of a list of documents alphabetized by the authors' last names, or they may be detailed inventory sheets that organize the collection into generic categories and indicate what documents are held in which file folder.

Using Finding Aids Critically

Given most finding aids' inability to recognize composition and rhetoric as productive areas of inquiry, how does one use these imperfect resources to identify relevant primary sources? Furthermore, when thinking about archival inquiry beyond the local level, how can researchers use finding aids to gather materials across different archives that, when taken together, allow them to make critical claims about writing, students, and pedagogy that have regional or even national implications? The scope of this essay prevents me from addressing these questions as fully as I would like, so I conclude with two practical observations that I hope may point to some tentative conclusions to these questions and offer other researchers, especially those new to archival work, effective strategies for initiating long-term research projects. These observations are drawn from my archival work with student writing in the 1960s and 1970s, and they presume that the issues one faces when working with these materials are representative of the problems encountered in archival research in composition and rhetoric more generally.

First is the issue of how best to conduct a search using tools such as the NU-CMC and ArchiveGrid. When searching online directories such as these, it is important to key in search terms that prompt whichever search engine used to retrieve relevant listings. Terms such as *composition* and *rhetoric* are too broad to retrieve a manageable number of results. This is a common piece of advice, so let me be more specific. If one searches ArchiveGrid for archival collections related simply to *composition*, it pulls up almost three thousand entries, ranging from archives documenting the process of noteworthy composers to those containing the sketchbooks of famous artists. Using the phrase *composition book* narrows the field to almost two hundred results, which enables one to identify a number of different collections that contain the composition or commonplace notebooks of selected individuals, although these notebooks are typically among the holdings documenting the lives of prominent local community members. For instance, one of the entries that comes up under the search for *composition book* in ArchiveGrid is a composition book held in the special collections department at Brigham Young University, dated 1876–1917, belonging to Clarissa Young Spencer, the daughter of Brigham Young.

Conducting a search using the phrase *composition book* therefore proves less fruitful if one's objective is to examine everyday instances of student writing, which was the aim of my dissertation research. However, this example also suggests that archivists at times understand artifacts like school writing in ways similar to how they understand correspondences; that is, student essays are oftentimes collected as if they are personal papers that help shed light onto the historical actions of noteworthy individuals. Thus, one place to find student writing is among collected personal papers. Most of us in the field do not normally approach student essays in similar ideological terms—as if what is said in them gives us insight into the writer's personal development—but if our aim is to locate student writing to work with in the first place, we must be conscious of our ideological assumptions, as well as archival-processing theory, and be willing to think differently.

The other observation I have is more practical. Perhaps the most effective and time-saving step in assessing an archive's value is to verify its holdings by contacting archive staff, describing to them your interest in the archive, and asking them to confirm the integrity of the archive or, better yet, send a collection catalog. The accuracy of the RLG Union Catalog, whether it is searched through NUCMC or ArchiveGrid, is dependent upon the information provided by archivists, and in some cases, the description of the collection on the RLG Union Catalog may bear little resemblance to the actual condition of the archive. For instance, when I was in the process of determining the archives I wanted to visit to conduct my dissertation research, I became interested in a collection housed at the State University of New York College at Oneonta, *Student Essays, Orations, and Notebooks*. The entry for the collection on the RLG Union Catalog, which I searched through the NUCMC, described it as "Miscellaneous student essays and orations. Also students' class notes, notebooks, and papers, including a complete set of one student's course notes and papers, 1965–1969." In my dissertation, I was interested in exploring whether and to what degree students' personal writings in the 1960s and 1970s could accurately be characterized as "expressive," and I remember feeling as if I had found my dream archive since the collection at SUNY Oneonta seemed to afford me the rare opportunity to see the development of one student's work over four years, which I felt might give me some insight into how pivotal a role personal-writing assignments may have played in Vietnam-era pedagogy. I eagerly phoned the head archivist only to learn that no such papers actually exist in the archive. Whether they were destroyed due to a lack of use, she could not say; however, she was kind enough to send me an inventory sheet that indicated the collection had a number of student essays written between 1900 and 1950. The only materials from the 1960s that she could point me to were student newspapers and periodicals. In telling this anecdote, I do not mean in any way to criticize the special collections department at SUNY Oneonta—quite the contrary, for the archivist saved me from making an unnecessary trip. The point I wish to make is that the descriptions of an archive on the RLG Union Catalog cannot always be taken as an accurate depiction of the actual state of the archive.

These examples illustrate an important lesson of using finding aids: namely, that in order to efficiently locate archives one must think like an archivist. More often than not, materials important to the study of composition and rhetoric are not gathered in official archives. These documents may, of course, be found as part of larger official archives, but of the thousands of archives that exist, relatively few are nominally devoted to students, pedagogy, writing, and rhetoric, which makes it difficult to quickly and efficiently locate materials. Archival finding aids can point researchers to those types of manuscript materials that are often the hardest to find—syllabi, student papers, assignments, program documents, and other supposed ephemera—but only if one is willing to think of these materials in different ideological terms. Thinking like an archivist also means, however, that we as a field need to learn more about the process of archival work and create disciplinary space for bibliographic scholarship and other aspects of archival research that can, in turn, expand the field's historical knowledge.

Notes

1. One exception to this is the almost commonplace narrative archival enthusiasts tell one another about the chance or random acquisition of materials. This narrative most

often surfaces in offhand comments made during the delivery of conference papers or in informal conversations; such accounts, because of the methodological questions they raise, rarely occur in published research.

2. It should be emphasized that the databases, bibliographies, and other finding aids I discuss here do not offer information on all known archives. Thus, it is necessary to consult additional resources, such as local library catalogs. In my own research, I identified one important archival collection—the Alternative Curriculum records collection at the University of Pittsburgh, which documents the activities of a 1970s experimental-learning program—by searching the university's library database. To my knowledge, this collection is not indexed in any of the finding aids discussed in the current essay.

3. Another resource useful for scholars new to archival research is the *Researcher's Guide to Archives and Regional History Sources*, edited by John C. Larsen. Although it is published almost twenty years prior to Fisher's collection, Larsen's *Researcher's Guide* presents a more thorough introduction into how archives are organized and accessed.

4. See Patricia Pate Havlice as well as Arksey, Pries, and Reed. I have chosen to put aside these bibliographies for the purpose of this essay because they deal with published texts rather than unpublished manuscripts. However, they are valuable resources to use alongside archival finding aids, for they can point to published materials that may potentially corroborate, contextualize, or complicate findings derived from archival manuscripts.

5. See entries 4323, 4333, 4349, 4544, and 4617.

Works Cited

"About RLG Programs." *Research Library Group*. OCLC. 2006. 14 Dec. 2006. <http://www.rlg.org/en/page.php?Page_ID=2>.

Arksey, Laura, Nancy Pries, and Marcia Reed. Introduction. *American Diaries: An Annotated Bibliography of Published American Diaries and Journals*. 2 vols. Detroit: Gale, 1983. ix–xiv.

Carr, Jean Ferguson, Stephen L. Carr, and Lucille M. Schultz. *Archives of Instruction: Nineteenth-Century Rhetorics, Readers, and Composition Books in the United States*. Carbondale: Southern Illinois UP, 2005.

DeWitt, Donald L., comp. *Articles Describing Archives and Manuscript Collections in the United States: An Annotated Bibliography*. Westport, CT: Greenwood, 1997.

———. *Guides to Archives and Manuscript Collections in the United States*. Westport, CT: Greenwood, 1994.

Fisher, Steven, ed. *Archival Information: How to Find It, How to Use It*. Westport, CT: Greenwood, 2004.

Hamer, Philip M., ed. *A Guide to Archives and Manuscripts in the United States*. New Haven, CT: Yale UP, 1961.

Havlice, Patricia Pate. *And So to Bed: A Bibliography of Diaries Published in English*. Metuchen, NJ: Scarecrow, 1987.

Larsen, John C. ed. *Researcher's Guide to Archives and Regional History Sources*. Hamden, CT: Library Professional, 1988.

Matthews, William. *American Diaries: An Annotated Bibliography of American Diaries Written Prior to the Year 1861*. Berkeley: U of California P, 1945.

———. *American Diaries in Manuscript, 1580–1954: A Descriptive Bibliography*. Athens: U of Georgia P, 1974.

National Historical Publications and Records Commission. *Directory of Archives and Manuscript Repositories in the United States*. 2nd ed. New York: Oryx, 1988.

Sharer, Wendy B. "Disintegrating Bodies of Knowledge: Historical Material and Revisionary Histories of Rhetoric." *Rhetorical Bodies*. Ed. Jack Selzer and Sharon Crowley. Madison: U of Wisconsin P, 1999. 120–42.

SEARCHING AND SEEKING IN THE DEEP WEB: PRIMARY SOURCES ON THE INTERNET

Elizabeth Yakel

Access to primary sources has never been easier; however, the proliferation of information about archives and manuscript collections on the Web also raises issues for scholars. First, archival materials are often considered to be part of the "deep Web," that portion of the Internet not easily indexed by search engines and therefore difficult to retrieve. As a result, comprehensive searching requires scholars to master different search strategies than they have previously employed. Second, after data on collections is retrieved, examination of the information (e.g., surrogates or representations) or actual digital documents necessitates a new but complementary type of textual analysis than scholars have utilized in the past. The first issue relates to access, or the online publication of information about archives and special collections. The second issue concerns accessibility, which refers not just to the availability of descriptions or digital materials but also to the intellectual and cognitive accessibility and the ability of researchers to make sense of and use primary sources appropriately. This chapter addresses the issues of searching online for and then selecting archival materials based on their virtual descriptions. It begins with an overview of Web-based information about archives, continues with an introduction to search strategies for primary sources on the Web, and then addresses the selection process. This piece concludes with some observations about the future of archival finding aids and online access tools in the Web 2.0 environment and the potential effects on scholarship and teaching.

Online Sources of Archival Materials

When using primary sources, a sound research methodology includes a systematic search for archival and manuscript materials on a given subject. Planning a search strategy is key for a successful project. The "deep Web" offers a great deal of archival information, but navigating Web sites or online databases that yield different levels of detail can be very confusing. In increasing order of detail, the sources with information about archives and manuscripts are:

1. Directories of archival repositories
2. Web sites for archival organizations
3. Online bibliography networks and catalogs with brief descriptions of collections
4. Inventories (also referred to as finding aids) to collections in various online formats
5. Digitized reproductions of primary sources

Knowing how to locate and use these online tools enables more comprehensive identification of sources and is the first step in researching for primary sources online.

Directories

Directories of archival repositories used to be large, clunky books only available in library reference rooms. Now, researchers can locate general information online. The most comprehensive and up-to-date directory is the "Repositories of Primary Sources" site (http://www.uidaho.edu/special-collections/Other.Repositories.html) compiled by Terry Abraham at the University of Idaho Special Collections Department. This site provides links to archival collections around the world. It is organized geographically, so if you know the repository, you can go directly to it. If you do not know the repository but suspect that manuscripts may be in a certain geographic area, you can identify repositories in that area. The "Repositories of Primary Sources" site also links to more specialized lists, such as the Society for the History of Authorship, Reading, and Publishing (SHARP). Recently, the Online Computer Library Center (OCLC) launched the WorldCat Registry (http://www.worldcat.org/registry/institutions) a directory of libraries and archives with such information as repository Web sites, e-mail addresses, and telephone numbers.

Web Sites

Most archives and special collections have a Web presence. The completeness and navigability of these sites vary considerably. Some just list contact information, rules for use, and hours of operation; others provide detailed, comprehensive lists of all holdings. There are several key details to note about archival Web sites. First, is the database or listing of collections complete? In most cases, these are not comprehensive. Second, is there information about searching for collections in their systems? Because archival systems are idiosyncratic, reading this will help to optimize your search. Third, whom do you contact for more information? It is always helpful to talk with reference archivists to ascertain the appropriateness of collections for specific projects, to verify special arrangements for collections because many archives have off-site storage requiring twenty-four hours' notice for retrieval, and to help you judge how much time to allocate for research at a repository.

Online Bibliographic Catalogs

Archives and special collections, particularly in colleges and universities, have taken advantage of their institutions' online catalogs by including information about archives and manuscripts. This provides members of a learning community with an overview of the local sources. A benefit of this approach is that primary and secondary sources are integrated. A downside is that the number of manuscripts is usually small, and they can get lost in these catalogs. In some newer catalogs, there is a standard icon (📖) to denote archival manuscript materials.

Typically, catalog records contain brief descriptions of collections including the creator/author, title, date range of the materials, access or use restrictions, a brief biography of the person or administrative history of the organization, and a paragraph describing the topical contents of the collection. This description of the topical coverage should not be considered comprehensive; rather, it is highly selective. If you suspect that a collection may hold relevant materials, locating more detailed information or contacting the reference archivist is necessary. The current generation of these online catalogs, referred to as integrated library systems or ILS, links to more specific information about archives and manuscripts, such as inventories or finding aids or actual digital documents.

In addition to appearing in local online catalogs, archival and special collections also are listed in what is referred to as a union catalog, a large database that searches the holding of libraries and archives in the United States and, to a lesser extent, around the world. The major bibliographic database is the OCLC's WorldCat. As of June 2009, the OCLC WorldCat database contains 136,924,136 bibliographic records. Of these, almost 1.9 million entries are archives and manuscripts.

There are three ways to search the WorldCat database. First, there is a free version available on the Web at http://www.worldcat.org/. Second, most colleges and universities also subscribe to the WorldCat database, and it is available with other licensed online reference sources. Third, the Library of Congress also offers free WorldCat access at http://www.loc.gov/coll/nucmc/ under "Searching Manuscripts" and then "Searching on OCLC WorldCat." Each of these methods of accessing the WorldCat catalog leads to a different interface, but the underlying information is the same.

What follows is an example of a search for Kenneth Burke manuscripts. This search utilizes WorldCat, local online catalogs, online finding aids, and Web pages; please note that catalogues change frequently and rapidly, and as a result, you may not be able to replicate this search—it is an example only. In figure 1, I used WorldCat's "Advanced Search" option, which enabled me to select "Archival Material" as the desired format. I also indicated I wanted Kenneth Burke as an "Author" so I would find items he wrote in the manuscript collections of other people. Figure 2 shows the initial four (out of thirty) collections retrieved in my search. I then selected the second record retrieved, "Kenneth Burke letters to William H. Rueckert, 1959–1987," to see whether this might be a fruitful collection for research. Figure 3 is the "Item Details" view, which provides a descriptive summary of this collection at the Special Collections of Pennsylvania State University. In figure 3, I follow the link to Penn State's online catalog, The CAT,

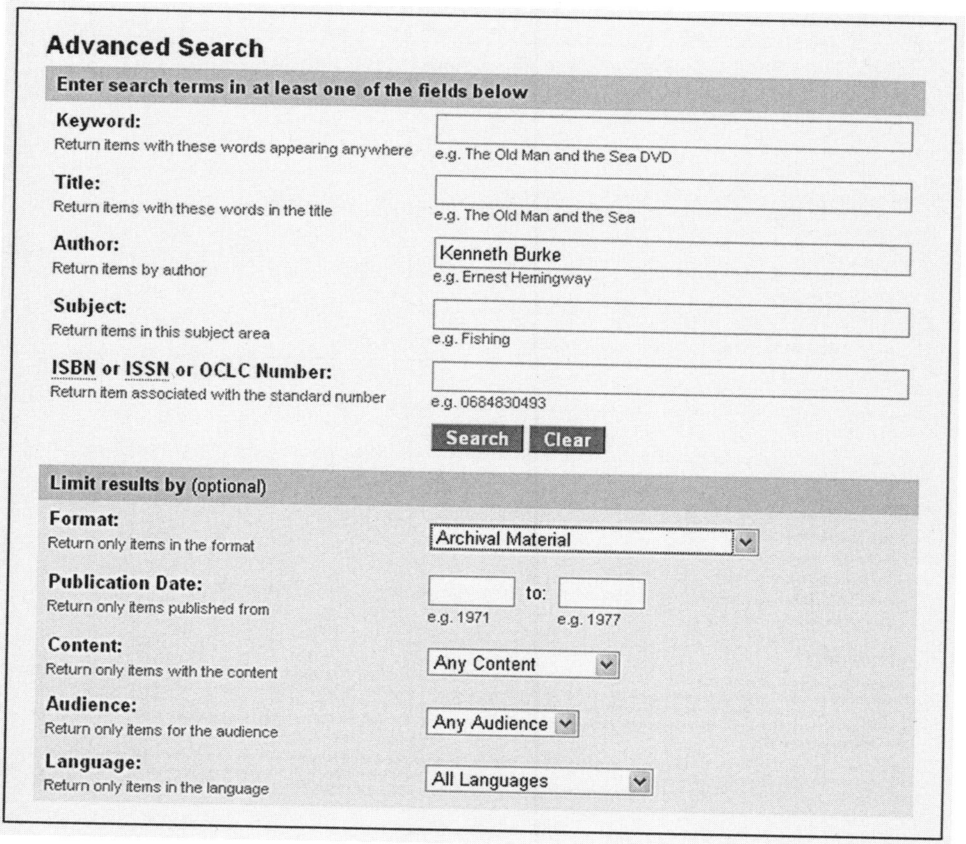

Figure 1. WorldCat advanced search for "Kenneth Burke." Used with the permission of OCLC. WorldCat is a registered trademark of OCLC Online Computer Library Center, Inc.

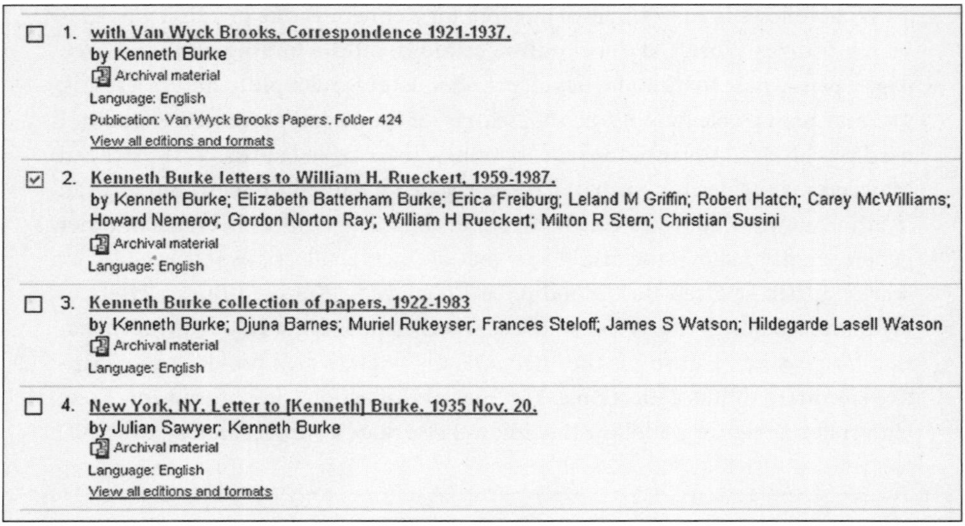

☐ 1. with Van Wyck Brooks. Correspondence 1921-1937.
by Kenneth Burke
Archival material
Language: English
Publication: Van Wyck Brooks Papers. Folder 424
View all editions and formats

☑ 2. Kenneth Burke letters to William H. Rueckert, 1959-1987.
by Kenneth Burke; Elizabeth Batterham Burke; Erica Freiburg; Leland M Griffin; Robert Hatch; Carey McWilliams; Howard Nemerov; Gordon Norton Ray; William H Rueckert; Milton R Stern; Christian Susini
Archival material
Language: English

☐ 3. Kenneth Burke collection of papers, 1922-1983
by Kenneth Burke; Djuna Barnes; Muriel Rukeyser; Frances Steloff; James S Watson; Hildegarde Lasell Watson
Archival material
Language: English

☐ 4. New York, NY. Letter to [Kenneth] Burke. 1935 Nov. 20.
by Julian Sawyer; Kenneth Burke
Archival material
Language: English
View all editions and formats

Figure 2. WorldCat search results for "Kenneth Burke." Used with the permission of OCLC. WorldCat is a registered trademark of OCLC Online Computer Library Center, Inc.

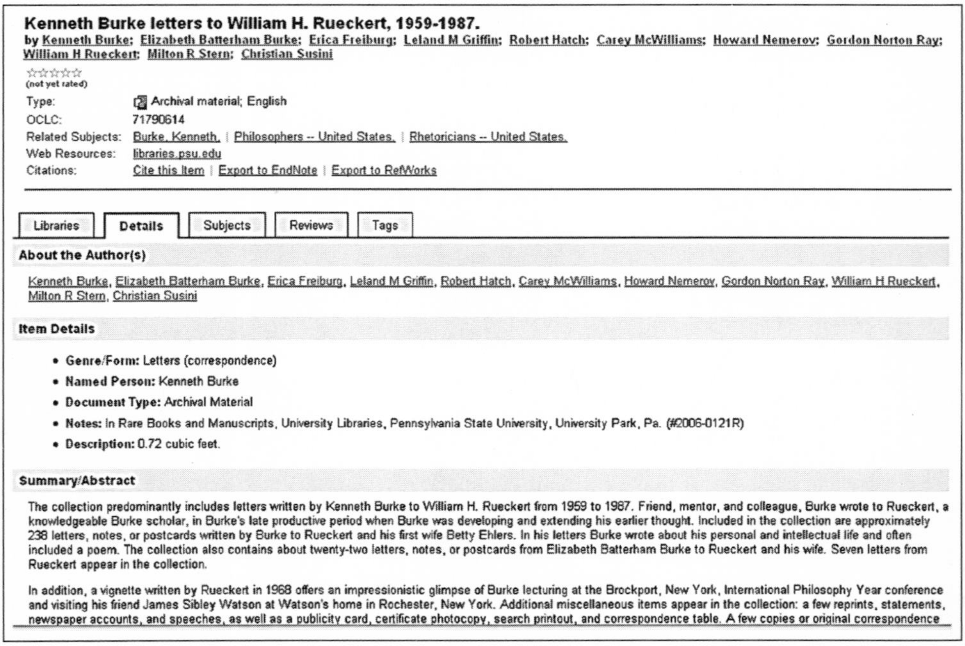

Kenneth Burke letters to William H. Rueckert, 1959-1987.
by Kenneth Burke; Elizabeth Batterham Burke; Erica Freiburg; Leland M Griffin; Robert Hatch; Carey McWilliams; Howard Nemerov; Gordon Norton Ray; William H Rueckert; Milton R Stern; Christian Susini
(not yet rated)

Type:	Archival material; English
OCLC:	71790614
Related Subjects:	Burke, Kenneth. | Philosophers -- United States. | Rhetoricians -- United States.
Web Resources:	libraries.psu.edu
Citations:	Cite this Item | Export to EndNote | Export to RefWorks

Libraries | Details | Subjects | Reviews | Tags

About the Author(s)

Kenneth Burke, Elizabeth Batterham Burke, Erica Freiburg, Leland M Griffin, Robert Hatch, Carey McWilliams, Howard Nemerov, Gordon Norton Ray, William H Rueckert, Milton R Stern, Christian Susini

Item Details

- **Genre/Form:** Letters (correspondence)
- **Named Person:** Kenneth Burke
- **Document Type:** Archival Material
- **Notes:** In Rare Books and Manuscripts, University Libraries, Pennsylvania State University, University Park, Pa. (#2006-0121R)
- **Description:** 0.72 cubic feet.

Summary/Abstract

The collection predominantly includes letters written by Kenneth Burke to William H. Rueckert from 1959 to 1987. Friend, mentor, and colleague, Burke wrote to Rueckert, a knowledgeable Burke scholar, in Burke's late productive period when Burke was developing and extending his earlier thought. Included in the collection are approximately 238 letters, notes, or postcards written by Burke to Rueckert and his first wife Betty Ehlers. In his letters Burke wrote about his personal and intellectual life and often included a poem. The collection also contains about twenty-two letters, notes, or postcards from Elizabeth Batterham Burke to Rueckert and his wife. Seven letters from Rueckert appear in the collection.

In addition, a vignette written by Rueckert in 1968 offers an impressionistic glimpse of Burke lecturing at the Brockport, New York, International Philosophy Year conference and visiting his friend James Sibley Watson at Watson's home in Rochester, New York. Additional miscellaneous items appear in the collection: a few reprints, statements, newspaper accounts, and speeches, as well as a publicity card, certificate photocopy, search printout, and correspondence table. A few copies or original correspondence

Figure 3. WorldCat "item details" on the Kenneth Burke Papers. Used with the permission of OCLC. WorldCat is a registered trademark of OCLC Online Computer Library Center, Inc.

Search Results

Author "kenneth burke" search found 7 titles.

#1 Details Mark	RGN 41.29 box01 **The Year of the Pennsylvania writer collection. [archival material]. 1984-1986** Pennsylvania State University. Copy available at Special Collections Library (UP) in P.S. Univ. Archives, 1st Floor Paterno, Univ. Archives & Mss	1984
#2 Details Mark	2006-0121R Box2 **Kenneth Burke letters to William H. Rueckert, 1959-1987** Burke, Kenneth, 1897-1993. Copies available at Special Collections Library (UP)	1959
#3 Details Mark	1976-0164R VF Lit **Hugh Dalziel Duncan papers, 1954-1969** Duncan, Hugh Dalziel. Copy available at Special Collections Library (UP) in Rare Books & Mss, 1st Floor Paterno, Vault	1954
#4 Details Mark	1997-0074R VF Lit **Marianne Moore letters and other material, 1952-1972** Moore, Marianne, 1887-1972. Copy available at Special Collections Library (UP) in Rare Books & Mss, 1st Floor Paterno, Vault	1952
#5 Details Mark	XXXX-1094R VF Lit **Erskine Caldwell letter to Kenneth Burke, 1935 April 7** Caldwell, Erskine, 1903-1987. Copy available at Special Collections Library (UP) in Rare Books & Mss, 1st Floor Paterno, Vault	1935
#6 Details Mark	MGN 197 box01 **Joseph Leonard Grucci papers. [manuscript]. 1932-1983. (bulk 1949- 1982)** Grucci, Joseph Leonard, 1908- Copies available at Special Collections Library (UP)	1932
#7 Details	1974-0202R VF 2-1 **Kenneth Burke papers. 1906-1960** Burke, Kenneth, 1897-1993	1906

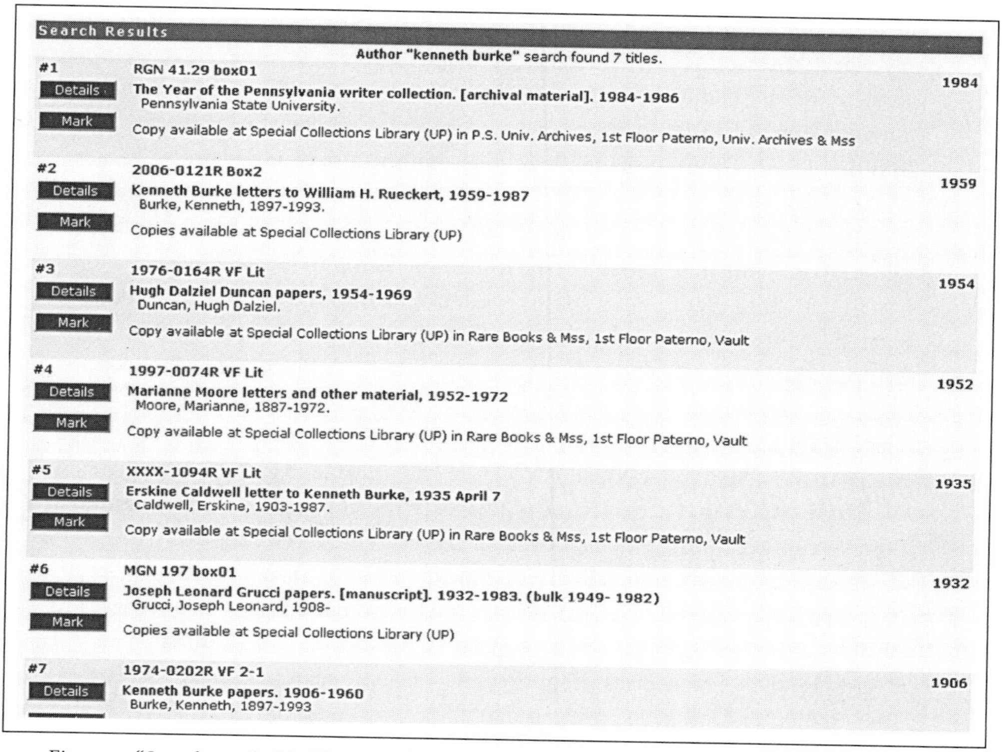

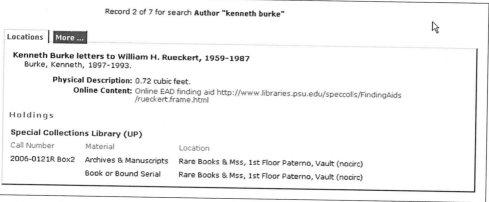

Figure 4. "Search results" in The CAT for the Kenneth Burke papers in the Pennsylvania State University online catalog.

Record 2 of 7 for search **Author "kenneth burke"**

Locations | More ...

Kenneth Burke letters to William H. Rueckert, 1959-1987
Burke, Kenneth, 1897-1993.

Physical Description: 0.72 cubic feet.
Online Content: Online EAD finding aid http://www.libraries.psu.edu/speccolls/FindingAids/rueckert.frame.html

Holdings

Special Collections Library (UP)

Call Number	Material	Location
2006-0121R Box2	Archives & Manuscripts	Rare Books & Mss, 1st Floor Paterno, Vault (nocirc)
	Book or Bound Serial	Rare Books & Mss, 1st Floor Paterno, Vault (nocirc)

Figure 5. "Details" view in The CAT of the Kenneth Burke letters to William H. Rueckert, 1959–87.

to search locally for "Kenneth Burke." Again I use "Advanced Search" and limit my search to "Archives & Manuscripts." This search retrieves seven collections, some of which did not appear in the original WorldCat search (see fig. 4). Since I am following the Burke-Rueckert papers, I select the second choice (see fig. 5) and find that I can now link to a more detailed finding aid, termed here as "Guide" to this collection (see fig. 6).

After making notes on this collection, I return to my list of Kenneth Burke materials at Penn State and select the link to the Kenneth Burke Papers (number 7 in fig. 4). I find that there is no link to an online finding aid for this somewhat extensive collection (twelve linear feet) but that it is in Special Collections. Examining the "More" view (see fig. 7), I see that the Rare Books and Manuscripts, Special Collections Library has a "card index available in repository."

In order to find out more about the Kenneth Burke papers, I go directly to the Penn State Special Collections Web site and am able to locate a Web page on the Burke papers that provides me with access and copyright information and a fifty-seven-page online guide naming all correspondents (see fig. 8).

This search demonstrates the interlocking nature of information about primary sources and how searches jump institutional boundaries. In summary, there are several actions to highlight and search heuristics to note in this process. First, I always use the advanced search option and limit my search to primary sources. These materials are variously referred to as "archival material" and "archives and manuscripts" in the systems highlighted here, but other systems employ yet more terms. Second, different views in the online catalogs, such as "Details" in WorldCat and "More" in The CAT, provide additional scope and contents information. These screens should be read to determine whether a collection is worth pursuing. Third, had the initial search when I requested information about Kenneth Burke as an author been unsuccessful, I would have searched his name as a title, subject, or keyword. For example, in a search for the Gertrude Buck papers, a subject search

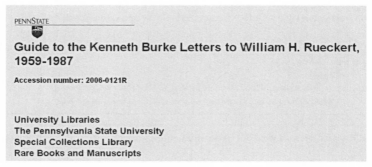

Figure 6. Online finding aid in The CAT for the Kenneth Burke letters to William H. Rueckert, 1959–87.

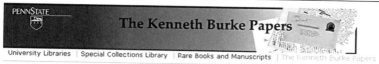

```
Locations | More... |                                              ⌖

Kenneth Burke papers. 1906-1960
  Burke, Kenneth, 1897-1993
      Personal Author: Burke, Kenneth, 1897-1993
              Title: Kenneth Burke papers. 1906-1960.
Physical Description: 12 linear ft.
Organization/arrang.: Chronological organization. Arranged alphabetically by surname.
  Access restriction: Unrestricted access.
            Summary: Contains personal and professional correspondence. Correspondents include Malcolm Cowley,
                      Stanley Hyman, Theodore Roethke, Allen Tate, Robert Penn Warren, Hugh Dalziel Duncan, John
                      Crowe Ransom, Robert M. Coates, Hart Crane, Jean Toomer, Waldo David Frank, R. P. Blackmur,
                      James T. Farrell, Francis Fergusson, Charles Henri Ford, Lincoln Kirstein, Sidney Hook, Marianne
                      Moore, Gorham Bert Munson, Howard Nemerov, Gilbert Vivian Seldes, and William Carlos Williams.
   Reproduction note: Correspondence with Malcolm Cowley, 1916-1959: Microfilm. University Park, Pa.: Pennsylvania
                      State University Libraries, Photographics Department, 1969. 1 microfilm reel ; 16 mm ; master
                      negative.
   Reproduction note: Card index: Microfilm. University Park, Pa.: Pennsylvania State University Libraries, Photographics
                      Department, 1969. 13 microfiche ; 16 mm ; negative.
   Reproduction note: Card index: Microfilm. University Park, Pa.: Pennsylvania State University Libraries, Photographics
                      Department, 1969. 1 microfilm ; 16 mm ; master negative.
  Acquisitions source: Purchase. Kenneth Burke. 1974.
          Finding aids: Card index available in repository.
              Subject: Burke, Kenneth, 1897-1993--Correspondence.
              Subject: Cowley, Malcolm, 1898-1989--Correspondence.
              Subject: Hyman, Stanley Edgar, 1919-1970--Correspondence.
              Subject: Roethke, Theodore, 1908-1963--Correspondence.
              Subject: Tate, Allen, 1899-1979--Correspondence.
              Subject: Warren, Robert Penn, 1905-1989--Correspondence.
              Subject: Duncan, Hugh Dalziel--Correspondence.
              Subject: Ransom, John Crowe, 1888-1974--Correspondence.
              Subject: Coates, Robert M. (Robert Myron), 1897-1973--Correspondence.
              Subject: Crane, Hart, 1899-1932. Correspondence.
              Subject: Toomer, Jean, 1894-1967--Correspondence.
              Subject: Frank, Waldo David, 1889-1967--Correspondence.
              Subject: Blackmur, R. P. (Richard P.), 1904-1965--Correspondence.
              Subject: Farrell, James T. (James Thomas), 1904-1979--Correspondence.
              Subject: Fergusson, Francis--Correspondence.
```

Figure 7. "More" view in The CAT of the Kenneth Burke papers, 1906–60.

PENNSTATE

The Kenneth Burke Papers

University Libraries | Special Collections Library | Rare Books and Manuscripts | The Kenneth Burke Papers

Introduction | Background Note | Burke-1 | Burke-2 | Burke Exhibition 2005 | The Bust of Burke

Introduction

The Kenneth Burke Papers contain the personal and professional papers of the philosopher of language Kenneth Duva Burke (1897-1993). Spanning over eight decades, from 1906 to 1993, the multifaceted papers illuminate not only the personal and intellectual life of Burke, but also the lives of many twentieth-century figures. The papers are housed in the Rare Books and Manuscripts division of the Special Collection Library at The Pennsylvania State University Libraries.

Respecting their different provenance, the Kenneth Burke Papers consist of two collections. The first Burke collection, Burke-1, dating from 1906 to 1961, was purchased by The Pennsylvania State University Libraries from Kenneth Burke in 1974. Although it includes a few manuscripts, it is primarily a correspondence file of letters written to Burke. It measures twelve linear feet.

The Pennsylvania State University Libraries purchased the second Burke collection, Burke-2, from the Kenneth Burke Literary Estate in 2005. This collection dates from 1950 until Burke's death in 1993, with the bulk of its correspondence written between 1960 and 1987. Burke-2 contains Burke's later correspondence (including many carbon copies of Burke's own letters), news clippings, article reprints, a few typescripts, many poems, and several photographs. Burke-2, more than double the size of Burke-1, measures twenty-five linear feet.

Both Burke-1 and Burke-2 follow Burke's original order: chronologically, and then alphabetically by the correspondents' last names, year by year. This arrangement allows researchers to investigate a select time in Burke's life or Burke's interchanges with particular correspondents.

Figure 8. Web page on Kenneth Burke from the Pennsylvania State University Special Collections.

works best because a major group of her papers are within the Collection of Laura Wylie at the Vassar College Archives. Researchers need to be flexible and creative to accommodate the vagaries of cataloging practices. Fourth, the Burke-Rueckert letters gave me an "information scent" and led to another catalog (The CAT) where I was able to find additional manuscripts. From there, I was able to link to an online finding aid but still had to go to the Special Collections' Web site to find further information about other Kenneth Burke collections. Finally, this search demonstrates the variety of indexes available that are connected, or not, to one another. These include the WorldCat and The CAT records, an online finding aid, a Web page, and a reference to a card index that I would have to go to Penn State to use. At the end of this search, if I decided that I remained interested in these materials, I would still contact the archivist to confirm that a trip to Penn State would be productive and to learn of any further details that would expedite my research in these and other collections at Penn State.

Online Inventories and Finding Aids

Online inventories and finding aids provide the most in-depth information about collections. In addition to the data found in online catalogs, finding aids also contain more detailed information on the contents of the collection including box, folder, and occasionally item-level descriptions. Finding aids appear on many archival Web sites. In some cases, these are searchable. In others, researchers must browse through the collections. It should also be noted that access to archival collections is idiosyncratic. Some collections have online catalog records, others only have finding aids; some have both; and some neither. Furthermore, since finding aids can be decades old and may have been originally typed on a manual typewriter, many are not available on the Web. As a consequence, many archives have some percentage of finding aids that are not online and still only available in paper format. Unfortunately, few archival Web sites specifically give the percentage of their collections that are represented by online finding aids. Researchers should approach archival Web sites and finding aids online with the assumption that not all finding aids are online.

Searching through individual archival Web sites for collection information is not time efficient. Luckily, consortia and union databases of archival finding aids have emerged. These are not nearly as comprehensive as the union catalogs previously described, but they are growing daily. The most comprehensive of these databases is the OCLC's ArchiveGrid (http://www.oclc.org/archivegrid/default. htm). ArchiveGrid contains almost one million descriptions of archival collections and links to over seventy thousand finding aids. ArchiveGrid is a subscription service, and libraries must license ArchiveGrid for access. Currently, over twenty-five hundred libraries, museums, and archives worldwide provide descriptions of archival and manuscript collection to ArchiveGrid. Institutions do not have to be OCLC members to contribute information; any archives or special collections can take advantage of ArchiveGrid to improve the discoverability and usage of their collections.

Figure 9 shows the results for a general search on "rhetoric teaching" in ArchiveGrid. Note the varied types of collections retrieved through this search. If we were to select any of these collections, more detailed information about each collection would appear as well as contact information for the repository. It is worth searching both ArchiveGrid and WorldCat for the same collections because ArchiveGrid can provides more detailed information than WorldCat.

In addition to ArchiveGrid, several geographically based finding-aid databases have emerged. These include the Online Archive of California (http://www.oac.cdlib.org/), the Rocky Mountain Online Archive (http://rmoa.unm.edu), and the Northwest Digital Archives (http://nwda.wsulibs.wsu.edu/). Each of these is freely available on the Web. It is important to realize that geographically based means that the contributing archival or manuscript repositories are located in

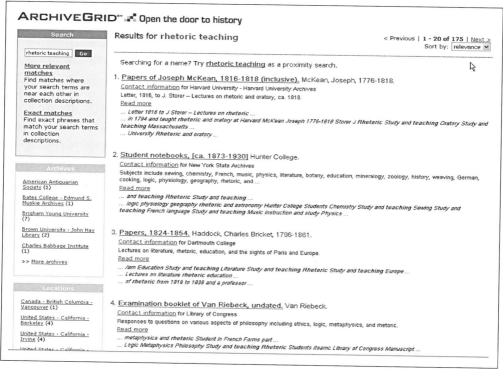

Figure 9. ArchiveGrid search and results screen. Used with the permission of OCLC. ArchiveGrid is a registered trademark of OCLC Online Computer Library Center, Inc.

a geographic region. The primary sources listed in these databases can be from anywhere. For example, the New Jersey Infantry (Fourth Regiment, Company B) Morning Reports from the Civil War are found in the Online Archive of California because they were donated to the Department of Special Collections, Santa Barbara Library, University of California.

Researchers will find many different interfaces for online finding aids. The illustrations in this chapter demonstrate this diversity. Some consistency in the types of information provided about archival and manuscript collections, system functionality, and navigational elements is emerging. For example, an initial screen provides general information about the collection. Navigation is usually on the left side; researchers can select the section of the inventory that best suits their needs. Headings in the navigation bar are also becoming more similar. For example, "Access and Use" is an important piece of information because it provides copyright information or other important notes about access and restrictions. The "Collection Scope and Content Note" gives a detailed narrative view of the contents. Finally, the "Contents List" gets at the heart of the collection and provides series- and/or a folder-level listing of the materials in the collection.

Digitized Primary Sources

There are two types of digital primary sources on the Web—*digitized documents* that were originally in analog format but have been scanned and published on the Web and *born-digital materials* whose original format was digital. Most archives now have digitized documents online, and many of their Web sites feature digital materials and exhibits. The most well-known site with digital materials is the Library of Congress's American Memory site (http://memory.loc.gov/ammem/index.html), which features digital primary sources from across the country. The strength of the Library of Congress site is its critical mass. Searching is possible within collections from individual repositories or across related collections from many repositories. Keep in mind that few of the digital collections on the American Memory site or on any archival Web site are complete. Usually, materials are selected out of a larger collection. Therefore, although these are excellent for use in classroom demonstrations on reading and analyzing individual sources, the collections themselves are usually not complete and therefore pose evidentiary problems if used alone and out of context in the research process.

Few entire collections of primary sources have been digitized at this point. Notable fully digital collections include the several collections at Carnegie Mellon University, including the Senator H. John Heinz III Archives, Allen Newell Collection, and Herbert A. Simon Collection (see http://diva.library.cmu.edu/) and the Polar Bear Expedition Digital Collections (http://polarbears.si.umich.edu) at the University of Michigan.

Although the digitization of entire collections is becoming more common, researchers should assume that most of the digitized collections are incomplete. When viewing and utilizing digital primary sources, it is always important to read the project descriptions to understand the selection criteria and whether additional documents or other materials are available elsewhere. Communicating with an archivist to understand the nature and comprehensiveness of digital collections is essential. If any research is solely based on a digital collection, this should be stated as part of the overall discussion of the methodology as the context of archival and manuscript collections is important for their interpretation. Researchers should be aware that one's sense of context varies between physical and digital collections and that this can impact interpretation (for better or worse). Even if all the textual materials in a collection have been digitized, items difficult to digitize, such as oversize maps, may not have been. Also, since many collections are split between several repositories, one archive digitizing its entire collection does not mean that all of a person's extant papers are available electronically.

Searching and Seeking
Why Not Just Google It?

Using Internet search engines (Google, Yahoo, and the like) to locate primary sources is a good first step in the research process, but it should not be the only step. As previously noted, archival and manuscript materials are part of the "deep Web." The "deep Web" often cannot be retrieved by these search engines. The *deep Web* refers to items in databases, nontextual files, and content requiring passwords or subject to other access restrictions. Much of the archival information previously discussed is contained in databases that contain information stored in tables, making discovery by these search engines problematic. In essence, what you see on the screen is only created "on the fly" when a search is conducted. This is unlike static, fixed Web pages, which are accessed directly.

Search Strategies

Searching is both an art and a science. It requires planning, patience, and persistence to achieve the desired results and to ensure that a comprehensive search has been done to locate primary sources or to fully discount their existence. The two factors in the search process are the search strategy itself and the delimiters within the search systems. Each of these is discussed separately.

Search strategies include: synonym generation, chaining, name collection, pearl growing, and successive segmentation (Drabenstott). Each of these can be used alone or in tandem in searching for primary sources. Synonym generation is a key element in most searches. This comes into play in a number of ways. First, archival collections are rarely described in the ways in which researchers think about them, and, thus, generating synonyms is always a valuable strategy. For example, if a researcher is interested in basic writing, potential search terms might include *remedial writing* and *basic English*. When thinking of synonyms, it is important to consider the language and time period in which the manuscripts originated as word meanings and phrases change over time. Thus, a researcher interested in free writing might also use terms such as *invention* and *brainstorming*. If at all possible, archivists tend to use the language of the collection in the contents listing.

In online catalogs and archival finding aids, archivists add controlled-vocabulary subject terms to enable information discovery. These terms come from authorized lists and enable disparate collections covering the same topics to be linked together in spite of the varied terminology in the collections themselves. Searching controlled terminology or subject searching, as opposed to keywords, means that disparate collections can be linked together. These subject terms can then be used in chaining and in name collection to search for additional collections.

Pearl growing occurs when you begin your search with a series of smaller, narrow searches and eventually are able to identify additional terms with which to build searches. Constant refinement of search terms, identification of promising sources, and citation chaining in the results all lead to pearl growing. Successive segmentation is the opposite strategy: a researcher starts with an overarching concept and then slowly whittles the results away to identify a few select collections.

Whatever search strategy is used, it should be documented. Happily, many systems now allow you to save your searches. This not only assists researchers by enabling them to repeat successful searches but also helps them to remember previous searches and not go over unsuccessful ground twice. Because archives are constantly putting more information on the Web, repeating successful searches periodically for ongoing projects is essential in a comprehensive search strategy. Finally, a search strategy should not only be seen as a direct path to getting information. Colleagues, friends, and competitors of an individual being researched can emerge through the search process; major events and activities can come to the fore. All of these create opportunities for chaining and offer new terminologies for searching.

Search Systems

Search systems allow different types of searching. Most offer a basic search where researchers type in a term or string of terms and an advanced search where researchers have many options such as preferred language or format of the material as well as the ability to use the Boolean operators (*and, or, not*). In basic search mode, entering multiple terms should be done carefully. Simply adding search terms alone does not increase search accuracy. Often, systems insert the Boolean operator "and" into the basic search so the system will search for records containing the terms anywhere. To avoid this, many systems allow the use of quotation marks in order to keep phrases, such as "horseless carriage," together.

In online catalogs, the most effective searches for archival materials are done using the advanced search mode, as demonstrated in figure 1. By using the advanced search option, researchers can restrict a search to only archival and manuscript materials. Online catalogs may also include the option to restrict the search to one library or one collection (e.g., special collections or university archives) within the system. This also narrows the search results considerably and helps researchers to hone in on the desired set of materials more quickly.

Use of the Boolean operators can reinforce synonym generation and is preferred over utilizing search strings in the basic search. By using the Boolean operator *or*, a researcher can try multiple terms and see the search results for each term. This enables researchers to more quickly identify the language used in the system.

Finding-aid systems also offer different search options. These include searching across many finding aids and/or using Boolean operators. Many of the finding-aid systems also provide researchers with the ability to search within a single finding aid or its subsections, such as names, subjects, collection description, or collection inventory. These options result in very different types of searches, and the results need to be carefully analyzed. For example, searching an entire finding aid for the term *rhetoric* will show matches in all parts of the finding aid including the biography. This does not necessarily mean that there is actual archival or manuscript content on that subject in the collection. Additionally, searches can yield results in the Scope and Content note and not in the Contents List, as materials are described differently in various sections of the finding aid. Researchers need to be attentive to these variations to interpret search results.

Accessibility: Analysis

Reading archival online catalog records and finding aids is an art. Yet, this is an essential part of the research process because it is key for making decisions about the appropriateness of collections for one's research and in prioritizing which leads to follow first. Often, there are too many potential collections for the researcher to write to all the archives and ask for information. As one historian notes, "Deciding which are relevant sources is rarely straightforward.... Making judgments about the value of sources cannot be done in a vacuum. Sources need to be compared to one another" (Jordanova 128).

Catalog records are necessarily brief and often contain only a very general overview of the types of materials in the collection and the major topics. These can be tantalizingly vague and often require contacting reference archivists to fill in the gaps.

Finding aids, particularly older finding aids, can be suspect. In general, archives are not publishing older finding aids online. One of the main reasons for this is that archivists realize their drawbacks and want to redo the finding aid before it is published on the Web to be used without any mediation by the reference archivist. Still, finding aids can be difficult to understand, particularly if they are describing a large collection and there is only a box listing.

Reference archivists prefer to be asked about collections prior to a visit rather than to greet a researcher, who has usually traveled a long way to read manuscripts, with the news that the materials do not actually pertain to his or her topic. Subjects to discuss with the archivist include the topical coverage and the depth of the coverage, information about the organization of the collection that is not apparent from the finding aid, and the existence of related collections on the research topic. Researchers can also begin to get a sense of the context of the collection from the reference archivist. There may only be one item in a collection that directly addresses a research topic, but there can be hundreds that help to contextualize that issue and show its importance for the individual or organization in question.

Researchers should also get an idea from the reference archivist about working with the collection. Questions to ask might be: How long will retrieval take? Is the handwriting in the collection difficult to read? Is the collection fragile, and will it require more time in handling? Ultimately, analysis of online information about the archival and manuscript materials along with a frank exchange with the reference archivist should provide a sound basis for decision making about whether to visit a repository and how to prepare for that visit.

The Next Generation

The tools scholars are using to mine the Internet are increasing, and search engines are getting stronger and more precise. Yet, searching for archives and manuscripts remains an inexact art or science. Movements are afoot to create greater intellectual access to primary sources. Social software tools could enable researchers to exchange ideas about manuscripts among themselves and comment or annotate collection descriptions along with archivists. OCLC is already experimenting in their WorldCat catalog by encouraging users to comment on items and to download citation information. The Everglades Digital Library (http://everglades.fiu.edu/), a composite collection of primary and secondary sources about the history and ecology of the Everglades, encourages visitors to rate finding aids and other digital objects in its collection. The Polar Bear Expedition Digital Collections Web site. (http://polarbears.si.umich.edu), allows researchers to comment on the collections and has instituted a process for changing erroneous information (such as death dates, military rank, and the like) in the official archival descriptions in response to evidence provided. This type of shared authority for archival collections is just now emerging but will most likely become more prevalent in the future.

Another social software application with potential for assisting researchers in identifying collections is collaborative filtering, which can link seemingly disparate collections together. (Think Amazon.com's "Customers who bought this item also bought . . . ") The Polar Bear Expedition Digital Collections Web site uses collaborative filtering by noting "Researchers who viewed this collection also examined these manuscripts . . . " Current systems that display finding aids, such as the Digital Library eXtensionService (DLXS) system, also contain bookmarking functionality and the ability to save previous searches. The Zotero application allows Web searchers to grab citations for a variety of digital objects. Imagine a system that allowed tagging and the addition of folksonomy terms alongside controlled vocabulary headings. In the sciences, the trend is for greater information and functionality to be placed on the researcher's desktop. This could also work well in the humanities and social sciences where searching for primary sources is laborious. Keeping track of basic search strategies is often difficult, let alone efficiently capturing and tracking citations to potentially relevant collections. This vision of the future for primary sources research is just emerging. For now, searching and seeking primary sources may be easier today than it was before the Internet, but researchers must still hone a variety of techniques for discovery and analysis to locate and use archival and manuscript materials.

Works Cited

Drabenstott, Karen. "Web Search Strategy Development." *Online* 25.4 (2001): 18–27.
Jordanova, Ludmilla. *History in Practice.* Oxford, Eng.: Oxford UP, 2000.

Web Sites Mentioned

"American Memory." Library of Congress. <http://memory.loc.gov/ammem/index.html>. Features digital primary sources from across the United States.
ArchiveGrid. OCLC. <http://www.oclc.org/archivegrid/default.htm>. The most comprehensive site for consortia and union databases of archival finding aids.
Everglades Digital Library. A composite collection of primary and secondary sources about the history and ecology of the Everglades that encourages visitors to rate finding aids and other digital objects in its collection. <http://everglades.fiu.edu>.
Northwest Digital Archives. <http://nwda.wsulibs.wsu.edu/>. A geographically based database of finding aids.
Online Archive of California. <http://www.oac.cdlib.org/>. A geographically based database of finding aids.
Polar Bear Expedition Digital Collections. University of Michigan. <http://polarbears.si.umich.edu>. A fully digital collection.
Repositories of Primary Sources. <http://www.uidaho.edu/special-collections/Other.Repositories.html>. The most comprehensive and up-to-date directory of links to

archival collections around the world. Compiled by Terry Abraham, University of Idaho Special Collections Department.

Rocky Mountain Online Archive. <http://rmoa.unm.edu>. A geographically based database of finding aids.

Herbert A. Simon Collection. <http://diva.library.cmu.edu/>. A fully digital collection.

WorldCat Registry. A directory of libraries and archives that includes repository Web sites, e-mail addresses, and telephone numbers. Available through <http://www.worldcat. org/registry/institutions>.

WorldCat. <http://www.worldcat.org/>. Free database through the Library of Congress <http://www.loc.gov/coll/nucmc/> under "Searching Manuscripts" and then "Searching on OCLC WorldCat."

FINDING AND RESEARCHING PHOTOGRAPHS

Helena Zinkham

Photographs provide a vivid connection between the present and the past that can inspire new interest in old subjects and also improve understanding of diverse peoples, places, and subjects. The special power of this visual language to aid explorations of history was recognized not long after photography was invented. The New-York Historical Society, for example, published a report in 1862 to urge the acquisition of photographs to benefit future scholarship:

> Within a few years there has been given to the world one of the most curious & useful inventions of human genius. Sufficient time has not elapsed to enable us to ascertain its exact influence upon historical inquiries, but we doubt not it will furnish most valuable materials to future Prescotts, Irvings & Bancrofts. . . . If Art had been able to preserve for them the actual reflections, as in a looking glass, of the scenes they describe, what life would animate, what truth would dignify their pages! . . . how many questions it would solve in architecture & costume & history about which hundreds of dull & unsatisfactory books have been written.

Photographs not only illustrate history but also they themselves can be rich primary source materials. In addition to studying the content of images, considering why photographs were created and for whom can shed new light on research topics. In a biography of Sojourner Truth (1797?–1883), historian Nell Irvin Painter devotes an entire chapter to the photographic portraits that Truth commissioned (see fig. 10.) Truth, a well-known public speaker on women's rights and abolition, tapped into the popular craze for *carte de visite* photographs of celebrities. As early as 1863, she sold these calling-card-size portraits by mail and at public appearances. Her signature phrase "I sell the shadow to support the substance" appears below many of the images.

Today, seeing a portrait of Truth while reading about her speeches reinforces the sense of her strong personal presence. Delving deeper into the original context of the images, Painter points out Truth's astute use of a new technology as a source of income. Painter comments on Truth's choice to present "the image of a respectable, middle-class matron" by posing in the well-fashioned clothing she wore for public speaking (187). According to Painter, Truth's portraits did not invite donations based on charity for an ex-slave. Instead, the images insist on Truth's womanhood and refute the idea that anyone deserves slavery. Painter based her analyses on fourteen portraits from seven sittings that she found at libraries and museums as dispersed as the Detroit Public Library, the University of Michigan in Ann Arbor, and the National Portrait Gallery in Washington, D.C.

Overall, photographs are a very new means of communication compared to written words. But so many public and private repositories have accumulated so many photographs that finding images for a specific research project can be a challenge. And, as approachable as photographs might seem at first glance, visual literacy is essential to the researcher's ability to understand and use images effectively.[1] This chapter is organized like a tutorial, and the sections follow the typical sequence of steps for undertaking research with photographs. The first two sections focus on preparation steps by describing strategies for finding sources of photographs and, then, by presenting ways to learn about general picture research techniques. The last two sections introduce techniques for working with whatever photographs have been found and offer exercises for reading photographs and caption images and tips for researching subject matter, creators, dates, archival context, and material culture.

Finding Photograph Sources

Research with photographs is often as complex as it is rewarding: a wide variety of organizations hold photographic collections, including archives, libraries, historical societies, museums, and commercial stock image services. Although growing numbers of historical photographs are available online as digitized images, photographs are still more likely than books and manuscripts to be uncataloged, undercataloged, or represented only in card catalogs and browsing files. In-depth research with photographs requires visiting repositories in person to examine original images and explore the numerous "off-line" collections. Researchers use a variety of tools to track down likely sources of photographs, including printed reference works, general Web searches, subscription databases for visual resources and finding aids, lists of online visual catalogs, and guides to collections. Access tools differ among repositories, ranging from collection-level summary

I Sell the Shadow to Support the Substance.

SOJOURNER TRUTH.

Figure 10. Sojourner Truth. Albumen photo on *carte-de-visite* mount by unidentified photographer, 1864. Courtesy Library of Congress, Prints and Photographs Division, Gladstone Collection of African American Photographs, LC-DIG-ppmsca-08978.

descriptions supported by general finding aids to detailed, item-level databases with online images. Thus, in-depth research requires casting a wider net to locate sources of enough photographs to constitute a sufficient body of evidence for the subject being explored.

Although interesting pictures can be found through the Web and most contemporary researchers turn there first, any comprehensive search for pictures should also include printed books and magazines. Among the traditional picture reference works that remain valuable are the *A.L.A. Portrait Index*, which contains an estimated 120,000 citations of portraits published in books and periodicals before 1905. Books such as the heavily illustrated *Chronicle of America* offer visual time lines of history and indicate the kinds of pictures available for different eras and their sources. Already published histories of specific research topics are a way to find potential sources of images or to learn about a subject through a visual overview. Checking image credit lines and citations in bibliographies and footnotes can lead to the names of repositories that might have additional images on the same subject. To locate printed visual histories, search in library catalogs or at bookseller sites for the desired topic combined with such phrases as "illustrated history," "views of," "pictorial," "photographs," and "portraits."

General Web searches are a useful strategy for a rapid introduction to archival and published resources that often include photographs of popular subjects. Researchers should use more than one search service, such as Google and Yahoo, and compare the top few pages of results. Researchers should also be wary of depending solely on "image search" tools because many pictures are presented in online exhibits, essays, and blogs without being separately indexed as images. Among the search-result lists, Web sites that tend to cite the sources for the historical images, including Wikipedia, PBS stations, and specialized subject sites, are especially helpful. Searching eBay for pictures of research topics can lead to interesting images, but researchers should be aware that many of the photos that look old are actually uncredited modern reproductions. Such images are risky to use as primary resources because they may have been significantly altered in appearance from the original and may lack crucial caption information such as the original creator names and image dates. Researchers should rely instead on sources that can provide authenticity and context for their images.

Subscription databases available through many research libraries are also worth consulting because they increasingly incorporate photographs and other pictures. Examples include the American National Biography Online (illustrated with many portraits) and HarpWeek (illustrations published in *Harper's Weekly* from 1857 to 1912). At least one new nonprofit subscription service has begun to focus on visual materials. ARTstor "is a digital library of nearly one million images in the areas of art, architecture, the humanities, and social sciences with a set of tools to view, present, and manage images for research and pedagogical purposes" (ARTstor). The AccuNet/AP Multimedia Archive includes more than two million images from the 1800s to the present. The ArchiveGrid from the Online Computer Library Center (OCLC) offers access to collection descriptions from thousands of repositories.

Photographs are among the most heavily used resources in archival repositories. As a result, separate access tools often exist to assist researchers who need images. These special databases and checklists for visual materials can be difficult to locate through general Internet searches because their names vary so widely. Phrases such as *digital images, historical photographs*, and *visual resources* are used in numerous combinations with the words *archives, catalog, collection, gallery, library,* and *online*. To help researchers get started in finding the specialized catalogs for documentary and historical images, the Library of Congress's Prints and Photographs Division offers a list of about fifty representative online picture catalogs at http://www.loc.gov/rr/print/resource/223_piccat.html.

Collection guides, both online and printed, also provide valuable access routes to pictorial holdings in libraries, archives, and museums. In addition to summarizing each collection at a repository, guides can highlight relationships among collections and provide in-depth indexes. The introductions to these guides also convey valuable information that helps researchers comprehend the collections' strengths and weaknesses. The old directories such as *Picture Sources* and *Picture Researcher's Handbook* that summarize public and commercial sources of pictures can still be useful to build awareness of the kinds of organizations that offer photographs. Researchers new to working with photographic collections can benefit from selecting a guide to review for an archive in their geographic vicinity and then asking the archives for an orientation session with the collections. The dual activities of reading about an archives and visiting in person can help researchers learn how written descriptions of photographs translate into the different types of images available at archives. For ready reference, the Library of Congress's Prints and Photographs Division has compiled an online list of more than sixty guides to visual collections at http://www.loc.gov/rr/print/resource/227_picguides.html.

A search for photographs of the United States Indian School in Carlisle, Pennsylvania, illustrates how picture research benefits from pursuing images through a variety of general Web and deep-Web sources and also printed reference works (see fig. 11). The school's now controversial assimilation program operated from 1879 to 1918. The founder, Richard Henry Pratt, used photographs from the school's earliest years to promote his program. The images could be useful for comparative studies of educational facilities and teaching methods as well as for investigations of cultural interactions. Starting with Google and Yahoo searches for the phrase *Carlisle Indian School*, several common sources surface: a Wikipedia article, photo collections at the Cumberland Historical Society in Carlisle, the Carlisle Indian Industrial School Research Pages site, and *Visualizing a Mission*, the latter of which is an exhibit catalog from an art historical-methods seminar at Dickinson College and includes essays on the major Carlisle photographer John Choate and visual propaganda. The references at these sites to photos at the National Archives and Records Administration, the Smithsonian National Anthropological Archives, and the Library of Congress lead to exploring the deep-Web catalogs at each institution where hundreds more photos are described.

The Cumberland Historical Society offers the most comprehensive array of photographs by a variety of photographers, with extensive indexing of individual student names online and helpful summaries of relevant holdings at the National Archives and Records Administration. The National Anthropological Archives collections can help a researcher compare Carlisle photographer John Choate's

Figure 11. "Conversation Lesson—Subject, the Chair," Carlisle Indian School, Carlisle, Pennsylvania. Cyanotype photo by Frances Benjamin Johnston, 1901. Courtesy Library of Congress Prints and Photographs Division, F. B. Johnston Collection, LC-DIG-ppmsca-18486.

student portraits with images of Indians at other boarding schools. The general visual resources at the Library of Congress can facilitate exploration of photographic studies of diverse schools from the same time period because the Frances Benjamin Johnston collection includes about one hundred views of the Carlisle Indian School from 1901 to 1903. In addition, Johnston's many views of Hampton Institute, Tuskegee Institute, and the Washington, D.C., public schools are available for comparison. Her extensive correspondence and personal papers are also available to check for information on when, how, why, and for whom she photographed schools (see fig. 12). Printed resources should be consulted, too. The Cumberland Historical Society offers relatively few photos online but has published an illustrated history of the Carlisle Indian School with about two hundred images (Witmer). The American Heritage Web site provides the text of articles about the Carlisle school and students, but the printed volumes must still be consulted to view the illustrations for the articles.

Figure 12. Washington, D.C., public schools—Sixth Division children in geology class. Cyanotype photo by Frances Benjamin Johnston, 1899. Courtesy Library of Congress Prints and Photographs Division, F. B. Johnston Collection, LC-DIG-ppmsca-18487.

Learning General Picture Research Techniques

Time-tested techniques for locating images remain worth learning. The book *Picture Research: A Practical Guide* describes in detail what it is like to do research with both public repositories and commercial stock image agencies and also covers the special considerations involved in buying photographs for publication, including reproduction permissions and fees. The manual *Photographs: Archival Care and Management* provides a behind-the-scenes view of how repositories select, preserve, and access images. Knowing how archives acquire and arrange visual records can simplify use and improve understanding of collections.[2] Tip sheets or pathfinders compiled by libraries to orient researchers are helpful for getting acquainted with visual-research strategies. For example, "Women's History Resources in the Library of Congress Prints and Photographs Division" describes in detail how to use collections relevant for many subjects at http://www.loc.gov/rr/print/coll/237_path.html.

Pictorial research can be simplified by answering several questions before beginning a project. A handheld camera for visual note taking is also helpful, when allowed.

- How will the photographs be used? As illustrations (a few selected pictures can suffice) or as historical evidence of information not available through other sources (all relevant pictures are needed)?
- How exhaustive a search is planned, and how much time is available?
- Will original materials need to be seen, or will reproductions suffice?
- What kinds of copies will be wanted? Digital, xerographic, or photographic; color or black-and-white? Ready reference or publication quality?
- What types of pictorial material need to be seen? Is the medium or format important? Should the images be contemporary to the historical era, or can they be an artist's interpretation?
- Has enough background information been gathered about the topic to be able to evaluate and interpret the images that are found?
- What words will be searched for to locate pictures, including subjects, dates, and names of associated individuals, organizations, places, and events?
- Which repositories will be consulted to do the research?

Seeking illustrations for teaching or for publishing projects is one of the most frequent situations for picture research. The following scenario indicates how the project-preparation questions influence a search for photographs. The scenario also underscores the importance of trying many different words when seeking pictures. Assume that a researcher has one week to find ten images to illustrate a lecture about the impact of diverse learning environments on children's education in the early 1900s. To limit the time invested, the researcher turns to a single, general picture source such as the Library of Congress's Prints & Photographs Online Catalog at http://www.loc.gov/rr/print/catalog.html. This resource describes more than eight million items, and more than one million are viewable online as digital reproductions with most available for downloading. The catalog has many features that facilitate visual research such as display of images and records together. Researchers should try combinations of many different words to facilitate retrieving relevant photographs.

Starting with the phrase *children's education* yields more than five hundred records for posters and cartoons as well as individual photos and groups of photos spanning the 1860s to 1970s. While browsing the digitized images and descriptions, the researcher observes that the photos of most interest have titles or subjects with the words *classroom* and *student*. Searching for those two words together narrows the display to about 250 images. Searching for *students* alone broadens the results again and brings up more than four thousand photos, including views of adult students. The catalog's online *Thesaurus for Graphic Materials* (http://lcweb2.loc.gov/pp/tgmiquery.html) has an entry for *students* that suggests additional words to try, including the more specific *school children* that leads to many highly relevant images. Searching for names of specific educators and educational institutions could also be useful.

An investment of about one hour leads to more than ten photos of the desired topic, including an open-air classroom in Chicago (see fig. 13). Reading the catalog records for these photographs helps confirm the time period of the images and the subject matter as well as the collection names. The Chicago school photo, for example, is one of hundreds of photos and periodical illustrations gathered by Louise Goldsberry in the early 1910s to document the benefits of open-air education in schools throughout the world. Using the collection name "Goldsberry Collection of Open-Air School Photographs" in a search reveals related images described with words not yet tried, such as *toothbrush drill, kindergarten,* and *manual training.* The catalog records also clarify the status of publication rights: public domain or permissions required. Rights concerns can be a major consideration for reproducing photographs, even for educational purposes, but a tip sheet is available to guide the risk analysis at http://www.loc.gov/rr/print/195_copr.html.

Reading Photographs

Once photographs are found, they need to be looked at carefully—analyzed and deciphered. "The ability to understand (read) and use (write) images and to think and learn in terms of images" is often called *visual literacy* (Hortin 25). The researcher can gain a basic skill level through simple exercises that involve looking at photos systematically and by becoming aware of common visual-presentation conventions. Archival research also emphasizes the importance of exploring

Figure 13. "Graham School, Chicago, Interior: Children Seated at Desks." Photographic print by F. P. Burke, ca. 1910. Courtesy Library of Congress Prints and Photographs Division, Goldsberry Collection of Open Air School Photographs. LC-DIG-ppmsca-18484.

the context of image creation by looking at textual and visual resources related through a common source or provenance. Knowing who made the photographs, for which clients and audiences, and under what circumstances is critical for understanding the meaning of images.[3]

An instructive case study for learning to read large archival series of photographs is available in *Image Worlds*, which describes the massive photographic archive at General Electric from which author David E. Nye develops new insights into "the nature of ideology in a capitalist society" (9). Nye explains well the intentions of the corporation and its photographers and the technical constraints on capturing images that influences the results. He also deciphers the original order of the archival photographs to reveal their evolving functions. Advanced visual literacy involves iconography, semiotics, and other formal-analysis methods that are beyond the scope of this chapter. Several recent books describe the field well and increasingly incorporate material culture considerations.[4]

In order to learn methods for reading photographs, the researcher can start by looking for a full two minutes at one photograph and listing all the things seen in an image such as the English class by Lewis Hine (see fig. 14) or the Lopez family by John Collier (see fig. 15). Awareness of the researcher's own, possibly false, assumptions is important to recognize, along with checking for discrepancies between what a picture shows and what its caption says. Expanding the looking activity into writing one's own caption and verifying the information further develops visual literacy. Steps for scrutinizing photographs are these:

- Capture a first impression in a few words about what the image shows.
  - Name everything seen in the image.
  - Look at each part of the picture again.
- Write a narrative caption about what the picture might mean.
  - Read any existing information that accompanies the image.
  - Draft a short paragraph to describe not only what the photo shows but also to account for who made the picture, why, when, where, and how.
  - Identify any assumptions with question marks.
- Finalize the caption.
  - Verify the caption information by fact checking with reference sources and related textual and visual records.
  - Show the picture and caption to colleagues, and ask what they think.
  - Discuss how and why initial assumptions changed through research.

Hands-on experience with original photographs is invaluable. The researcher can develop appreciation for typical sizes, styles, functions, and subject matter by asking to use collections at a local archives or library, by going to see exhibits of old photographs, or by window-shopping at photo sales that feature historical images. Nothing beats the experience gained from time spent looking at original images, especially in a world where the usual fare is digital reproductions that mask some aspects of original visual artifacts.

Researching Photographs

Many photographs lack key pieces of the basic "who, what, when, and where" identifying information that is necessary for their use as historical evidence. The names, dates, and places provided in old captions may also need to be verified to confirm their accuracy. As with any research project, assumptions must be tested. What researchers think they see through the filter of modern perspectives may not be at all what is going on in photographs. For example, smiling prisoners might represent fear of reprisal rather than a happy situation. Empty streets might signify a camera's inability to capture moving traffic rather than a deserted town.

Figure 14. "Class in English for employees. Pocasset Mill. After day's work." Location: Fall River, Massachusetts. Photographic print by Lewis Hine, 1916. Courtesy Library of Congress Prints and Photographs Division, National Child Labor Committee Collection, LC-DIG-nclc-05025.

Figure 15. "Trampas, New Mexico. Mrs. Maclovia Lopez can read and write English well; she also keeps the family books in the evening and helps the children with their homework." Safety film negative by John Collier, January 1943. Courtesy Library of Congress Prints and Photographs Division, Farm Security Administration/Office of War Information Collection, LC-DIG-fsa-8d12762.

The following four research techniques can help with understanding the subject content of photographs and also the purposes for which they were made.[5]

Gather the Internal, Physical, and Contextual Evidence

The first step is to look at the photographs. Really look at them! Check the fronts and the backs of the pictures for both visual and textual clues.

- Study the photographs and their housings closely (e.g., envelopes and albums). Use a magnifying glass and adequate light to read the details. Note carefully any written information—from cryptic abbreviations or signatures to formal studio imprints and full titles.
- Describe all the things that could be checked in reference sources to help identify a place. Look for clues to help estimate time periods, including styles of buildings, clothing, equipment, furniture, and/or transportation systems.
- Ask what events or activities might have caused the creation of the photographs for insight into the images' original function and viewers. Family albums, for example, may represent only special events rather than daily life.
- Determine the images' style, form, and/or genre for clues to the creator and to unmask any hidden provenance information.
- Identify physical characteristics to check in histories of photography for clues to time periods. Are the image processes, formats, or sizes unusual? Is there color? What types of image mounts were used? What are the image bases—film, glass, metal, paper? Film negatives, for example, are unusual before 1900.
- Consider each image's placement within its collection. Is there an original order preserved from the photographer's own use of the image? Does that order offer clues to approximate dates of the image? Does a numeric arrangement indicate the availability of a photographer's logbook or a coded scheme to decipher and reveal client, date, or place name information? If an archive rearranged the photographs, does it have acquisition or processing records that document the original order that might reveal the original purpose of the picture?

Look for Similar Photographs and Text Sources

After developing a general idea of the subjects, creators, time periods, and functional roles, seek out identification and context information in related textual or visual records. Comparing images of the same general topic can either verify an educated guess about a subject or disprove a false identification. Consult other holdings at the archive. For example, are there dated photographs on similar mounts or identified images with the same backdrops and props?

- Check for related textual records and finding aids that might describe the source for the images, why the photographs were taken, and additional caption notes.
- Use online picture catalogs and Internet search tools to track down related material at other repositories.

Consult Reference Sources

Online as well as printed reference works can help verify a subject and time period or determine photographers' names and dates. When possible, verify the information in more than one source. The types of reference sources most frequently used to research photographs include the following printed and online sources:

- Pictorial histories provide clues for dating subjects and identifying buildings.
- Histories of photography help establish a general date span, media type, and/or functional role for images.
- Photography dictionaries and professional directories help determine photographers' full names, addresses, and dates.
- Biographical dictionaries and genealogical sources help verify names for people shown in portraits as well as photographers.
- City directories, business directories, telephone books, and yellow pages help identify street locations, match photographers' addresses to particular ranges of years, or obtain the full names of businesses that appear in the photographs.
- Maps help confirm addresses and positions for places and structures shown in photographs. Fire-insurance maps and atlases provide valuable information about individual structures in many cities and towns.
- Specialized registries provide dates and names for such things as aircraft, hotels, railroads, schools, ships, and sports events and athletes.

For a representative list of free Web sites useful for picture research, see "Online Reference Sources for Cataloging Visual Materials" at the Library of Congress, Prints and Photographs Division, http://www.loc.gov/rr/print/resource/vmrefcat.html.

Ask for Help

Don't be shy about asking for assistance. Show the photographs to people familiar with the suspected subject matter or with photographic history in general. Requesting advice is a good way to learn more about a specific photo and to gain clues to new sources for finding images related to the topic. Many people enjoy sharing their knowledge or solving mystery-identification puzzles. For example, when a researcher has trouble finding a photo of a particular individual or event, checking personal papers and corporate records that seem to contain only textual information can yield treasures. Unidentified photos tucked inside of a letter might turn out to be the only known portraits of the researcher's subject.

Photographs not only enliven historical presentations, they can provide primary resource evidence of past lives, events, places, and ideas. Images already available online are likely to suffice when only a few illustrations are needed for a lecture or article. When undertaking in-depth or exhaustive research, however, it is benefi-cial to contact and visit archives to look at a comprehensive array of images and to gather all available contextual and textual clues to the meaning of the images from the perspective of the image creators and the intended audience as well as the subject content and cultural material characteristics.

Finding and researching photographs can be a complex endeavor. But more and more descriptions of archival images are available online each day, numerous tip sheets are available, and friendly archivists, librarians, and curators are ready to help. Learning to look at photographs and taking the time to look closely are the key ingredients to successful visual research.

Notes

1. For additional information on photographs as primary research sources, see Edward Linenthal, ed., with the assistance of Donna Drucker, "American Faces: Twentieth-Century Photographs"; John E. Carter, "The Trained Eye: Photographs and Historical Context"; Walter Rundell, "Photographs as Historical Evidence: Early Texas Oil"; Thomas J. Schlereth, "Mirrors of the Past: Historical Photography and American History," and Joan M. Schwartz and James R. Ryan, eds., *Picturing Place: Photography and the Geographical Imagination*.

2. For more information, see John Schultz and Barbara Schultz, *Picture Research: A Practical Guide*, and Mary Lynn Ritzenthaler and Diane Vogt-O'Connor, *Photographs: Archival Care and Management*.

3. For articles that explore the role of visual literacy in archives, see Elisabeth Kaplan and Jeffrey Mifflin, "'Mind and Sight': Visual Literacy and the Archivist." Additional sources are cited in the "Visual Materials: Processing & Cataloging Bibliography" at the Web site of the Library of Congress, Prints and Photographs Division: http://www.loc.gov/rr/print/resource/vmbib.html#research.

4. For thorough descriptions of formal visual-analysis techniques, see Peter Burke, *Eyewitnessing: The Uses of Images as Historical Evidence*; Gillian Rose, *Visual Methodolo-gies: An Introduction to the Interpretation of Visual Materials*; and Elizabeth Edwards and Janice Hart, eds., *Photographs Objects Histories: On the Materiality of Images*.

5. Most of these tips are from Helena Zinkham, "Reading and Researching Photo-graphs."

Works Cited

A.L.A. Portrait Index. Washington, DC: U.S. GPO, 1906.
"American Faces: Twentieth-Century Photographs." *Journal of American History* 94 (June 2007): 97–202.
ARTstor. "Overview: What Is ARTstor?" <http://www.artstor.org/what-is-artstor/w-html/artstor-overview.shtml>.

Burke, Peter. *Eyewitnessing: The Uses of Images as Historical Evidence.* Ithaca, NY: Cornell UP, 2001.

Carter, John E. "The Trained Eye: Photographs and Historical Context," *Public Historian* 15 (Winter 1993): 55–66.

DK Publishing. *Chronicle of America.* Rev. ed. New York: DK, 1997.

Edwards, Elizabeth, and Janice Hart, eds. *Photographs Objects Histories: On the Materiality of Images.* London: Routledge, 2004.

Evans, Hilary, and Mary Evans. *Picture Researcher's Handbook: An International Guide to Picture Sources and How to Use Them.* 6th ed. London: Routledge, 1996.

Hortin, John A. "Theoretical Foundations of Visual Learning." *Visual Literacy,* ed. David M. Moore and Francis M. Dwyer. Englewood Cliffs, NJ: Educational Technology, 1994. 5–29.

Kaplan, Elisabeth, and Jeffrey Mifflin. "'Mind and Sight': Visual Literacy and the Archivist." *Archival Issues* 21 (1996): 107–27.

New-York Historical Society. *Annual Report of the Committee on the Fine Arts.* New York: New-York Historical Society, 1862.

Nye, David E. *Image Worlds: Corporate Identities at General Electric.* Cambridge, MA: MIT P, 1985.

Painter, Nell Irvin. *Sojourner Truth: A Life, a Symbol.* New York: Norton, 1996.

Ritzenthaler, Mary Lynn, and Diane Vogt-O'Connor. *Photographs: Archival Care and Management.* Chicago: Society of American Archivists, 2006.

Robl, Ernest. ed. *Picture Sources.* 4th ed. New York: Special Libraries, 1983.

Rose, Gillian. *Visual Methodologies: An Introduction to the Interpretation of Visual Materials.* London: Sage, 2001.

Rundell, Walter."Photographs as Historical Evidence: Early Texas Oil," *American Archivist* 41 (Oct. 1978): 373–98.

Schlereth, Thomas J. "Mirrors of the Past: Historical Photography and American History." *Artifacts and the American Past,* ed. Schlereth. Nashville, TN: Amer. Assoc. for State and Local History, 1980. 11–47.

Schultz, John, and Barbara Schultz. *Picture Research: A Practical Guide.* New York: Van Nostrand Reinhold, 1991.

Schwartz, Joan M., and James R. Ryan, eds. *Picturing Place: Photography and the Geographical Imagination.* London: Tauris, 2003.

"Visual Materials: Processing & Cataloging Bibliography." Library of Congress, Prints and Photographs Division. <http://www.loc.gov/rr/print/resource/vmbib.html#research>.

Witmer, Linda F. *The Indian Industrial School, Carlisle, Pennsylvania, 1879–1918.* Carlisle, PA: Cumberland County Historical Society, 1993.

Zinkham, Helena. "Reading and Researching Photographs." *Archival Outlook* (Jan./Feb. 2007): 6–7, 28. <http://www.archivists.org/periodicals/ao_backissues/AO-Jan07.pdf>. Reprinted courtesy of the Society of American Archivists.

LOOKING FOR LETTERS

Margaret J. Marshall

On and off for the last fifteen years, I've hunted for the correspondence regarding an essay written by the U.S. Commissioner of Education William Torrey Harris published in the June 1892 edition of the *Atlantic Monthly*. If this were the usual magazine article, such correspondence would be confined to the editor and the author, and so the search, one would think, would be rather simple and straightforward. If this were the usual magazine article, a rhetorical scholar would probably be interested in the correspondence only as an aside—the text itself would give plenty of material to analyze and interpret. But, as you can probably already tell, this is not the usual magazine article, and so my troubled search taught me lessons about archival work that might well be useful to others working with late-nineteenth-century materials.

What makes Commissioner Harris's essay, "The Education of the Negro," especially intriguing is its unusual rhetorical deployment of footnotes; the editor, Horace E. Scudder, solicited comments from others prior to publication and inserted those comments as footnotes. Though the commentators are identified in the piece and introduced as "four Southern Gentlemen," there is very little information in the piece itself to answer such questions as the following: Did Harris know that his essay would be treated in this way? Did he agree to the insertion of comments? Did he participate in selecting the commentators? Were these four the only people invited to comment? What criteria were used to select them for this unusual public forum? Did the editor modify the notes he received? Why was this piece chosen for such treatment, and why was the form not repeated? Such questions simply cannot be answered without contemporaneous documents of the kind usually located in manuscript and archival holdings.

As it turns out, Scudder's letters to these gentlemen did survive, are housed at Harvard's Houghton Library, and do help explain his intentions for the piece. Scudder's diary, also preserved at the Houghton Library, provides little insight into his thinking about the article, however. Copies of the original manuscript are available in Harris's papers at the Library of Congress and help to clarify which elements of the essay were shaped by Scudder's suggestions for revision, though Harris left no diary to corroborate our guesses about his revisions. Though I have looked for correspondence or draft copies from the commentators, none have yet been located. I hesitate to say that these documents do not exist because, as my experience makes clear, our search for remnants of the past is complicated by a whole host of practices—both past and present—that make it very difficult to be certain that what hasn't yet been found was not preserved. Though I will tell the story of the search for these particular documents, the case has broad implications for scholars working in archives.

Caution 1: Business Practices and Technology

Archival and manuscript collections of correspondence are almost always collections of incoming mail, but the value of keeping outgoing correspondence was recognized early in the nineteenth century, and many corporations began to keep copies of letters they sent in bound ledgers. According to JoAnne Yates, a historian of early corporations and business technologies, pressed letter books emerged when the volume of correspondence and the expectation of speed fostered by the pony express and the telegraph made it impossible for clerks to keep up. Pressing letters instead of copying them by hand required that the original be written in special copying ink. The original letter was then placed between a moistened sheet of tissue paper in the ledger and oil cloth, which protected the other pages. A screw device brought enough pressure to produce a dim copy on the back side of the tissue paper (see fig. 16). By 1856, the invention of aniline dye improved the quality of the reproduction enough that the technology became widespread, especially in offices with a large volume of outgoing mail. Not only was pressing faster than hand copying, but the task did not require the advanced skills of an

Figure 16. The letter press in action. Illustration from Yawman and Erbe Office Supply Catalogue, 1905. Courtesy of Hagley Museum and Library.

office clerk, so duplication became cheaper as well. Apparently, several letters could be copied at once, but if the proper amount of compression was not used, the letters would be either too faint to read, or both the copy and the originals would be blurred (Wigent, Housel, and Gilman 53–54). Another disadvantage of the pressing process was that the procedure had to be done soon after the letter was produced, for once the ink set, copies could not be made (Yates 26–28).

Letter book ledgers typically consist of three hundred to five hundred sheets of tissue paper bound together with each page given a prestamped number. These ledgers are larger than the paper typically used at the time for correspondence, so a page of a ledger typically includes two pages of correspondence. If the letter is very short, two different letters appear on the same page of the ledger. In the

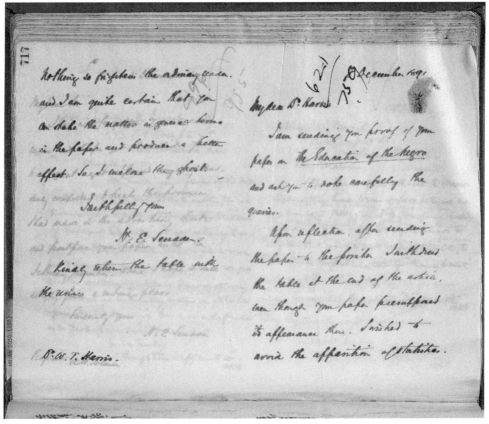

Figure 17. Example of pressed letter page from the ledger of the editorial department for the *Atlantic Monthly* with the letter from editor Horace Scudder to William T. Harris, 8 December 1891, on the right. Handwritten numbers and checkmarks refer to earlier and later correspondence to the same party, notations apparently made as the letters were indexed. Used with permission of Houghton Mifflin Company and Houghton Library, Harvard University.

example shown in figure 17, first pages are entered on the right and subsequent pages on the left, contrary to our expectations for texts to read from left to right. If the letter is longer than two pages, the text continues on subsequent sheets though occasionally the different pages got reproduced out of sequence. The tissue-paper pages of the ledger are fragile, so text from surrounding pages bled through either in the pressing process or over time, and wrinkles and tears often obscure the print. Scudder's pressed letter ledger, for example, includes some pages where the ink is flaking off the page, erasing individual words or whole lines in the process. Such irregularities in quality mean that when these materials were copied onto microfilm, as is the case with the Bureau of Education letters, whole volumes or individual letters were lost.

Occasionally, individual letters—perhaps those written at home rather than at the office—would be copied and filed individually, but this would have been the exception rather than the norm during the time that ledgers were in use. Even before the introduction of pressing letters, larger businesses and government agencies employed clerks to hand copy individual letters into ledgers, creating a chronological record of correspondence. An alphabetical index of names, often, though not always, included at the front or back of the ledger, directed the user to the appropriately numbered page. Some ledgers included letter tabs that made the creation of the index somewhat easier, but the care and completeness of the ledger are entirely dependent upon the skill of the clerk who generated the index originally. Figure 18 shows the index for the *Atlantic Monthly*'s editorial department for 1892. The numbers after each name refer to the numbered sheets in the ledger, so it is easy to see that Harris received four different letters during this time period. Note how some names are squeezed in because the indexer did not leave adequate room to keep the names in alphabetical order.

Because the technology and prominence of pressed letter books endured for only the fifty years or so when the volume of correspondence outpaced technology, they are easy to overlook. Letter books or copybooks were used earlier, however, so in a business or government office where the correspondence would have been considerable, it is very possible that important documents are waiting to be discovered in these bound collections. Historians I consulted often had used such volumes but had learned to do so in the process of a specific study rather than as a routine part of their training in archival research. Working with ledgers can be time consuming; locating them can take even longer.

Caution 2: Finding the Archival Repository

Finding letter books is not straightforward for two reasons: the difficulty of finding the archive where the collection might be held and the cryptic nature of the indexing of these bound collections. Following the usual routine of searching for

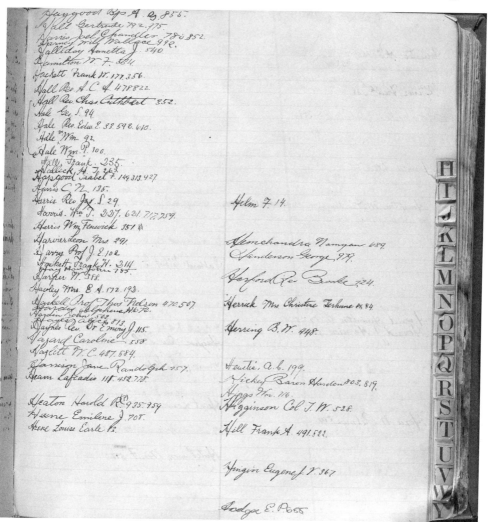

Figure 18. Example of pressed letter index from the ledger of the editorial department for the *Atlantic Monthly* showing letters written to correspondents whose last names began with *H*. Used with permission of Houghton Mifflin Company and Houghton Library, Harvard University.

archival records, I began by consulting the National Union Catalogue of Manuscript Collections (NUCMC). My original search found collections listing letters by Scudder in twenty-four repositories, but most of these were individual letters sent to authors, and none had any obvious connection to the men involved in the Harris essay. The collections at Washington University Library and Harvard's Houghton Library seemed more promising, and both NUCMC descriptions include a notation of an "unpublished finding aid" but more on that in a moment.

I also found collections for William T. Harris and two of the four commentators. Current researchers would find NUCMC now has a searchable database linked to WorldCat, but because holdings from the print version of NUCMC are not transferred to the online system except under special circumstances,[1] only twelve repositories appear for "Horace Scudder" in the WorldCat system. The material housed at Harvard's Houghton Library does not appear in that system and was not listed in the print version of NUCMC until the 1983 volume. Thus, a researcher must check both online and print copies, including the multiple print indexes created between 1959 and 1993. Not all libraries, even at research universities, have been able to keep up with the cost of subscribing to multiple indexing services, and if a print copy of NUCMC has gone missing or was never purchased, it is virtually impossible to replace it. Because the WorldCat system is only the latest database to attempt to index archival and manuscript collections and probably won't be the last, researchers have to consult with librarians who specialize in archival searches to be certain they are consulting the full range of databases and indexes. Moreover, a failed search needs to be regularly repeated to catch newly catalogued materials that might contain the "missing" documents.

Though both researchers and librarians can get the impression that NUCMC is complete, the print editions cover only 1,406 of the estimated 9,000 to 10,000 repositories in the United States (Burke 45, 50); the online version represents only 462 repositories for 1996 to 2006. As a result, the indexing of the past is incomplete, and the turn to electronic databases has not replaced earlier print editions nor begun to fill in the glaring omissions. In addition to the possibility that the material a researcher seeks has not been catalogued, the structure of the indexes means that even if materials have been catalogued, they may be missed. NUCMC's cumulative indexes for some years are separated by subject, name, and corporate listings; in other years, these three categories are combined. Searching for the letters by an editor of a magazine requires checking both the personal names and corporate indexes in those years when they are separated. But, what corporate name to search for may not be immediately obvious. My initial search included looking for archival collections for any of the six men involved in the essay as well as for records of the *Atlantic Monthly*, but a more experienced researcher would have to know, as I did not when I began my search, that because the *Atlantic* was owned by the Houghton Mifflin Company until 1907, the editors' letters have been archived with those corporate records rather than with their personal papers or as a separate collection identified by the name of the magazine. Holdings for other major nineteenth-century periodicals appear to work the same way, so a search for an editor's letters must include the parent publishing company as well as the individual and the magazine. In a quick test of this idea using the WorldCat system, I found corporate records for Charles Scribner's Sons and Henry Holt and Company as well as several manufacturing companies that list pressed letter books in the description. Because WorldCat allows searching by subject terms like "publishers and publishing—19th century" or "business records—19th century," researchers might be able to locate corporate correspondence more easily, but the gaps in these indexes are still problematic.

Another example of the less-than-obvious location of letters is that William Harris's outgoing correspondence is not part of his personal papers housed at the Library of Congress and cannot be found by looking for the Commissioner of Education or even the Bureau of Education. Rather, Harris's letters are filed with the Bureau of the Interior records at the National Archives because in the nineteenth century, the commissioner of education reported to the secretary of the interior. Editors and government officials are, of course, not the only individuals who wrote letters in the official capacity of their positions, so it is very likely that all sorts of documents might be hiding in corporate or government records rather than being housed with the manuscript collections of prominent individuals.

Unfortunately, the corporate structure of nineteenth-century publications is not always easily visible. If, for example, a researcher looks at the "Making of America" project that has digitalized many of the most prominent nineteenth-century magazines,[2] the publisher of the *Atlantic* is listed as "Atlantic Monthly Co." However, according to Frank Mott's *History of American Magazines, 1850–1865*,[3] the Atlantic Monthly Publishing Company did not exist until Ellery Sedgwick joined with MacGregor Jenkins to buy the magazine in 1908 and severed the relationship to the book publishers, who had previously owned it (513). The title page of each *Atlantic* volume lists the publishing company, but it is easy to assume that the publisher and the operation of the magazine would be separated. However, in the nineteenth century, the publisher was most often also the owner, and despite an appearance of independence, the magazines were frequently run as an appendage of the publishing house. The editors themselves were sometimes drafted from the publishing company and had a longer tenure with the publisher than with the individual magazine they edited. Scudder, for example, worked for Houghton from 1863 until his death in 1902, first to produce the *Riverside Magazine for Young People* and then as editor-in-chief of the trade division (Sedgwick 201) but served as direct editor of the *Atlantic* for only six years.

The reason why publishing companies owned or created magazines in the nineteenth century involves both the economics of printing and distribution and the legalities of copyright for literature that so often appeared as both books and serialized installments in periodicals. Many magazines, even the most well-regarded and successful, operated at least in part to review and promote the publisher's book list and shape a reading public that would buy more books. When Houghton appointed Scudder as editor in 1890, he reasoned that because the *Atlantic* should serve to develop new authors and manuscripts for the publishing house, coordination would be easier if the editor had dual responsibilities (Sedgwick 206). Of course, many of these magazines were named for their publishing houses. *Scribner's Monthly* was published by Charles Scribner's Sons. *Harper's Monthly* and *Harper's Weekly* were both produced by Harper and Brothers. Most magazines' ownership and publishers cannot be derived simply from the title, however, and almost all were taken over by different publishers during their lifetimes. *The North American Review*, to name but one prominent publication of the time, was owned and published by at least twenty different companies between its founding in 1815 and the end of that century. From its inception in 1857, the *Atlantic* was owned and published by three different companies before becoming a part of the Houghton Publishing House in 1874. Such information is rarely self-evident in historical publications any more than it is obvious today that the Washington Post also publishes *Newsweek*, that CBS owns Simon and Schuster, or that Time Warner produces not only *Time Magazine* but also *Fortune, Money, People*, and *Sports Illustrated*.[4] How businesses other than publishing houses and magazines were organized is probably equally important for locating archival records, so researchers would be wise to read secondary histories for the business relationships and corporate structures that may well determine how the materials they seek were preserved and catalogued.

Caution 3: (Mis)understanding Descriptions of Holdings

An additional challenge for researchers arises from the ways these correspondence books are indexed. Because letter books, whether produced by hand copying or by pressing, are chronological records, they are typically listed in finding aids as simply "pressed letter book" or "bound letter book" followed by the date. The general description of the Houghton Mifflin Corporate Records, for example, has the notation that the collection "Includes cost books, sales books, invoice books, sheet stock books and ledgers; letterbooks, containing copies of outgoing letters; scrapbooks; clippings" (1) and the more detailed listing at 182–235 F reads, "Pressed letter books, including letters from Henry Oscar Houghton (1879–1885), George H. Mifflin (1894–1909), the editorial department (1890–1909), the treasurer (1908–1916)" (6). Even these descriptions don't mention the specific editors or the *Atlantic Monthly*, so a researcher hopes for the best and travels to the archive or begins corresponding with librarians on site to seek further details (a better, potentially cheaper option).

The finding aid for the Office of the Commissioner of Education[5] is even more cryptic with no correspondence or pressed letter books immediately visible. Only by accessing the more detailed description for Record 12.2.1: "General Records" does the researcher find the notation "Press copies of letters sent, 1870–1908, with gaps."[6] Note that this time span includes the first five Commissioners and reflects the phasing out of bound letters once the technology of typewriters and carbon paper allowed multiple individual copies of correspondence to be produced, and vertical filing allowed documents to be sorted by subject or correspondent rather than simple chronology. Note also the phrase "with gaps," an indication of the documents that were unreadable by the time the ledgers were transferred to microfilm in the 1960s. A pamphlet listing the contents of the seventy-one individual reels of microfilm was produced when this transfer occurred, but that document also lists only the ledger dates rather than reproducing the individual indexes of each ledger. Despite this pamphlet's introductory statement that "Filmed on the 71 rolls are 130 unnumbered *but indexed* volumes of letters sent from 1870–1909 by the Office of the Commissioner of Education," (National Archives and Records 1; emphasis added), the notation is easy enough to miss that a National Archives' librarian assumed that no index existed based on the document description.

An alternative explanation for the "with gaps" notation arises from the unusual way in which I found this collection. While searching for the original manuscripts and drafts of the *Atlantic* article in Harris's papers at the Library of Congress, I happened upon a file of correspondence with Harvard President Charles Eliot. I looked at that file only for idle curiosity, since Eliot had nothing to do with my project. In that file, however, I found a letter from Harris that seemed to be torn from a pressed letter book; the letter had a printed number at the top and was printed on tissue paper, and the ink seemed similar to those of Scudder's pressed letters. Apparently, someone, at some time, decided that this letter was worth removing from the bound volumes and incorporating into a file with other materials by subject. It is quite possible that other historical records have been removed from bound ledgers and incorporated into vertical files, and while such disassembling might increase the chance that individual letters will be indexed, it is also very possible that the dispersion of materials will make them ultimately harder to locate. It would take careful study of the microfilms of the commissioners' letters in comparison with their internal indexes for a researcher to determine who the letter was written to, and that name would be essential in searching for the *possibility* that the individual letter was removed yet preserved separately. If a separated letter were classified by its subject matter, the chance that a researcher would locate it in a systematic search is even slimmer.

Even when the researcher is lucky enough to find a likely collection appropriately catalogued, searching for individual documents, especially letters, within corporate records is fraught with difficulties. Key elements of the collection will very likely be missed even with a searchable database unless the researcher employs multiple strategies for locating specific documents. William Torrey Harris's letters are a good example of the difficulties of such a search. Remember that

Harris's letters as commissioner of education are housed in the National Archives with the Records of the Bureau of the Interior. Though the "Guide to Federal Documents" has been digitalized,[7] entering Harris's name, even with variations, will not locate his letters. Entering "Commissioner of Education" with quotation marks will call up the appropriate record, but forgetting the quotations will produce more than four hundred hits, and limiting by dates or names does not match the system's coding well enough to yield the relevant record. Sometimes, searchable databases are case sensitive, and if material has been indexed under a misspelling or a variant of some kind, the relevant item will not be identified. Searching by general terms like "letters" or "correspondence" is rarely helpful.

The descriptions of the archival holdings in the print versions of NUCMC, like most of the online descriptions, are likewise abbreviated and depend upon the information supplied by the institution or library. The Houghton Mifflin collection at Harvard in the NUCMC print edition for 1982 (MS 82–628) is longer than most—nearly two full columns—and includes an alphabetical list of correspondence. It is easy to miss that this is the "unbound" correspondence, especially because there is no mention of "bound" correspondence or "letter books" in the NUCMC description. A current researcher would simply turn to Harvard's online archival database,[8] which includes the complete finding aids. Of course, in the early 1990s, when I first began this project, online systems were not available. Instead, I wrote to individual archivists at each of the repositories where I had identified possible connections to my project, a practice that is still necessary for the many libraries and repositories that do not have online databases or for when the researcher needs more details than the finding aid can reveal. I also wrote the *Atlantic Monthly* directly because I could find no listing of where the magazine might have placed historical documents and, as discussed earlier, did not recognize at that time that the Houghton Mifflin Company entry included all of the *Atlantic* business records.

I received many helpful responses, including a letter from the editor of the *Atlantic,* who informed me that all their historical papers had been turned over to the Massachusetts Historical Society. The letter from a reference librarian at the society, however, noted that only the papers of Ellery Sedgwick were in their collection but also that she had called the archivist at the *Atlantic* and had been assured that business records for the period of my search did not exist. The letter from Harvard's Houghton Library was equally insistent that they had no correspondence related to the Harris article. A few years later, I sent a second letter to Houghton's librarians asking more specifically about Scudder's papers, the unpublished finding aid, or the possibility of an uncatalogued collection. This time, the librarian assured me that she had searched the Scudder papers and found no correspondence listed for any of the gentlemen involved in the essay. I received similar discouraging news from every collection I contacted, and many of these librarians included photocopies of finding aids so I could see for myself that there was no indication of relevant documents. The archivists were not, I am certain, intentionally misleading me. Indeed, the extra effort to contact another library on my behalf and read unpublished finding aids or make photocopies of indexes is indicative of just how helpful librarians can be to researchers. But the business structures and practices of the past are not necessarily known by archivists either. Indeed, one of the problems I hope my experience makes clear is that even when possible collections are listed—and, as noted above, many collections remain invisible because they are not included in NUCMC or any other archival database—the in-library finding aids are rarely complete enough to list outgoing letters in a way that would enable librarians or researchers to search for individual correspondents.

What finally gave me the hint that correspondence did exist was first reading histories of the *Atlantic Monthly* and then of the Houghton Mifflin Publishing Company. Such background reading may be routine and necessary, but it is hardly the first avenue researchers follow in looking for archival materials. Although luck is always a part of the process of historical work, had I known more about historical literacy practices, especially those practices related to business correspondence, I might have saved myself a good deal of time or at least asked the librarians better questions. In looking for Scudder's letters, I was looking not only for the originals that would have been sent (and so more likely to be housed in the manuscript collections of the recipient) but also for copies that Scudder would have kept. And, what I did not recognize initially was that in the nineteenth century, copies of outgoing correspondence would not have been filed individually and subsequently indexed later as "unbound" correspondence but would have been in a bound letter book, copybook, or pressed letter book. So, even where the finding aid listed "letter books," neither the librarians nor I recognized that these might contain the correspondence I was trying to locate.

In short, the researcher hunting for letters from the nineteenth century needs to recognize the additional obstacles to finding correspondence. First, because individual outgoing letters are not included in the finding aids, researchers must be on the look-out for bound letter books and be prepared to visit the archive in order to examine these letter books directly. What I should have asked the librarians is not whether the finding aids recorded the individual letters I was trying to locate, but whether their collections contained letter books of outgoing correspondence, especially letter books that would have reflected the position these men occupied rather than them as individuals. Though librarians in most archives are willing to help researchers from afar, few libraries have the resources to allow individual records to be examined, so researchers using bound letter books have to either pay for a surrogate researcher on-site or locate travel funds to visit the archives. Asking specifically if the letter book includes an internal index might speed the process, for those few pages might be easily photocopied and save the researcher considerable extra expense. Finding aids that list pressed letters or copybooks are a clue that additional correspondence has not been indexed, but as librarians of special collections have explained to me, there is a growing consensus within that field that librarians ought to spend their time cataloguing materials that have not been previously indexed rather than producing more-detailed finding aids. In other words, relying on finding aids, even when they exist, will become only more problematic.

Second, researchers seeking information about particular individuals, publications, agencies, businesses, or other small entities must consider whether their papers might be housed within the records of the larger firms or agencies that controlled or sponsored them. Because letter books are so often a part of a larger organizational structure, the researcher must know what that structure was and look for archival holdings for the parent company or agency rather than concentrating only on individuals or even smaller subsidiary enterprises. In the case of nineteenth-century magazines, for example, it is the publishing house that controlled them, and so historical records of individual publications are very likely subsumed in the records of the publisher. Likewise, records of government agencies are more likely to be housed under the division to which they reported, and these reporting structures frequently have changed from their original incarnation. Understanding corporate and bureaucratic structures of the past means researchers have to turn to secondary histories that may seem tangential to their immediate interests to learn about the structure and evolution of the larger enterprise within which their interests operated. Such secondary sources are thus more than a way of contextualizing one's project; they may well offer essential clues to the location of manuscript collections and surviving archival records or at least provide researchers with alternative search strategies.

Third, because the technology of pressing so often produced unreadable copy and some letters might have been removed, the researcher can expect the records to be incomplete even if they can be located. More important, however, the example of pressed letter books suggests other technologies of the past may have impacted literacy practices and opens up an entire area of additional research we might pursue as a field interested in writing and literacy. I had never considered, for example, when filing cabinets were invented or how people stored written documents prior to their creation. There are very few histories of these earlier technologies and their uses, but Joanna Yates's book on corporate communication is suggestive of the many interesting possibilities for further research into literacy practices that are waiting for us; from in-house corporate magazines, instruction manuals, or corporate policy statements to the creation of business forms, stenography, telephones, typewriters, or duplicating equipment, it is clear that past technologies played an important if little understood role in literate practices. Further, these technologies influence how documents of the past were preserved and thus how they might be found by those interested in working in the archives.

Notes

I would like to thank my historian colleagues who made suggestions that helped me figure out where to look and how to understand pressed letter books, particularly Robin Bachin of the University of Miami, Richard John of the University of Chicago, and Ken Lipartito of Florida International University. I would also like to thank the Hagley Museum and Library, particularly Ben Blake and Max Moeller and the staff at the Houghton Library at Harvard for their help in obtaining the illustrations used in this essay. Funding to travel to the archives at Harvard was supplied by the Department of English at the University of Miami. A University of Miami General Research Support Grant enabled my research at the Library of Congress.

1. See question 11, "Frequently Asked Questions," NUCMC site http://www.loc.gov/coll/nucmc/index.html.

2. See, for example, the "Making of America" project at Cornell University Library, http://cdl.library.cornell.edu/moa/.

3. Mott's five-volume history of American magazines is the most comprehensive source for magazine publishing, but recent scholarship has begun to fill in the finer details of this history especially in regard to African American publications and the role of women in early magazine history. See, for example, Sharon M. Harris with Ellen Gruber Garvey, eds., *Blue Pencils & Hidden Hand: Women Editing Periodicals, 1830–1910,* or Armistead S. Pride and Clint C. Wilson II, *A History of the Black Press.*

4. *Columbia Journalism Review* provides an updated list of "who owns what media" that can be searched at its page "Resources," http://www.cjr.org/resources/.

5. See Record Group 12, 1870–1983, Records of the Office of Education, "Guide to Federal Records," National Archives, http://www.archives.gov/research/guide-fed-records/groups/012.html.

6. 12.2.1 General Records, Record Group 12, 1870–1983, Records of the Office of Education, "Guide to Federal Records," National Archives, http://www.archives.gov/research/guide-fed-records/groups/012.html#12.2.1.

7. The digitalized guide is available at "Guide to Federal Records," National Archives of the United States, http://www.archives.gov/research/guide-fed-records/.

8. The searchable database is at "OASIS: Online Archival Search Information System," Harvard University Library, http://oasis.harvard.edu:10080/oasis/deliver/home?_collection=oasis.

Works Cited

Ballou, Ellen B. *The Building of the House: Houghton Mifflin's Formative Years.* Boston: Houghton Mifflin, 1970.

Burke, Frank G. "Personal Communication in the Electronic Age." *Research and the Manuscript Tradition.* Chicago: Scarecrow and Society of American Archivists, 1997. 269–85.

Harris, Sharon, with Ellen Gruber Garvey, eds. *Blue Pencils & Hidden Hand: Women Editing Periodicals, 1830–1910.* N.p.: Northeastern UP, 2004.

Harris, William T. "Education of the Negro" *Atlantic Monthly* 69. 416, June 1892: 721–36.

———. Letter to C. W. Eliot, Chairman, Committee of Ten. 22 November 1893. Library of Congress. MSS 25056. Container 15, Folder 310.

———. *Letters Sent by the Commissioner of Education, 1870–1909.* United States Department of Education. National Archives and Records 12.2.1 (microcopy No. 635 reels 27–35).

———. Manuscript of "Education of the Negro." Library of Congress. MSS 25056. Container 13, Folder 256.

Houghton Library On-Line Guide. *Houghton Mifflin Company. Records: Guide MS AM 2030–2030.4.* Cambridge, MA: Harvard University, 1997.

Mott, Frank Luther. *A History of American Magazines, 1850–1865.* Cambridge: Harvard UP, 1957.

National Archives and Record Service. *Pamphlet Accompanying Microcopy No. 635: Letters Sent By the Commissioner of Education, 1870–1909.* Washington, DC: General Services Administration, 1966.

Pride, Armistead S., and Clint C. Wilson II. *History of the Black Press.* Washington, DC: Howard UP, 1997.

Rathbun, Jennie. Reference librarian. Houghton Library, Harvard University personal correspondence. 6 July 1990 and 16 August 1993.

Scudder, Horace E. Diaries. 58 M-231. Boxes 1, 2, 3, and 6. Houghton Library, Harvard University, Cambridge, MA.

———. Letters written as editor of *Atlantic Monthly.* MS Am 2030. 192–94. Pressed Letter Books. Editorial Department. Records. Houghton Mifflin Company.

———. MS AM 2030. 252–59H. Records. Houghton Mifflin Company.

Sedgwick, Ellery. *The Atlantic Monthly, 1857–1909.* Amherst: U of Massachusetts P, 1994.

Smith, Virginia H. Reference librarian, Massachusetts Historical Society. Personal correspondence. 1 April 1993.

Whitworth, William, ed., *Atlantic Monthly.* Personal correspondence. 1990.

Wigent, William David, Burton David William Housel, and Edward Harry Gilman. *Modern Filing and How to File: A Textbook on Office System.* Rochester, NY: Yawman and Erbe, 1916.

Yates, JoAnne. *Control through Communication: The Rise of System in American Management.* Baltimore: Johns Hopkins UP, 1989. 25–28.

Yawman and Erbe Manufacturing Company. *Rapid Roller Letter Copier: Catalogue 901.* Rochester, NY: 1905.

INTERVIEW: LYNÉE LEWIS GAILLET—
THE UNEXPECTED FIND

Lynée Lewis Gaillet's historical scholarship includes articles in *Rhetoric Review* and *Rhetoric Society Quarterly*, as well as an edited collection on *Scottish Rhetoric and Its Influences*. Gaillet admits that for her, "the best part of archival research is the unexpected find." And as her narrative below illustrates, her research into the history of rhetoric has been complemented by a number of serendipitous and unanticipated discoveries.

My primary area of research falls within the history of rhetoric and composition pedagogy. In researching the work of our forebearers (especially teachers), I examine student notes, early textbooks, university and national reports, wills, letters, newspaper clippings, personal journals, published accounts of pedagogical practice, university calendars and catalogs, student writings, commencement speeches, and inauguration addresses. In my research of Scottish teaching practices, I've visited national libraries, university libraries and collections, government offices, portrait galleries, church repositories and headquarters, religious publications' offices, and the like.

As I was researching the rhetorical theory and practice of Scottish rhetorician George Jardine (1742–1827), I happenstanced upon a reference to Jardine's letters. After some digging, I found a University of Glasgow library notation of 136 letters that Jardine had written. In these letters, written throughout his lifetime to a college friend, Jardine discussed personal events but also worked out some of his early teaching ideas. The librarians took forever to find the letters, and when they brought them to me (in a crushed-in, flimsy cardboard box), it was with a sense of reverence. For you see, I don't think anyone had taken a look at these letters since they were initially archived in the nineteenth century. The stack was tied with a red (faded to pink) satin ribbon, and I carefully opened the folded pages with a due sense of awe and respect. Five years later when I returned to the library, I requested the letters out of a sense of nostalgia more than a need for research. They were brought to me bound in a large notebook, each one catalogued and secured in a plastic slipcover—not exactly a repeat of my earlier experience.

The value of Jardine's letters to my research was a no-brainer. Notes taken by his students (in their own handwriting) proved "golden" as well. But prior to my first visit to Scotland, I found a reference to a copy of a synopsis of Jardine's notes, bound and housed in the Yale library (not in rare books but on the shelves). I requested the book through interlibrary loan. A couple of weeks later, I received a call from the librarian at my institution, Texas Christian University. She told me that my book was in, and I should come right over to retrieve it. Bound in a very groovy, yellow-and-orange-flowered covering was the copy of Jardine's lecture synopsis—including marginalia and the name of the student who apparently took Jardine's class. In those notes, I found many references that helped me plan my research trip to Glasgow. When I first held that volume, I knew I had struck gold.

On another occasion, I was researching Jardine's influence upon American educator Alexander Campbell of Bethany College. I kept coming upon references to Jardine and Princeton and so began following that lead—to little avail. I *knew* there was something out there but couldn't find it. In the middle of the night, I awoke and (on a hunch) decided to try "F"ardine instead of Jardine as a search term—both because of (1) the opposite placement of the "f" and "j" key on the typewriter and (2) eighteenth-century orthographic symbols that don't translate when scanned into online documents. This hunch led me to a fabulous online source (citing "Fardine") that effectively changed (and expanded) the trajectory of my research project. At the time, I had a National Endowment for the Humanities summer grant to research Jardine's influence in America. Although I didn't go too far afield the scope of that project, this find greatly expanded the "reach" of Jardine's influence.

Certainly, researchers should approach archival research with a list of research questions in hand. That said, the best part of archival research is the unexpected find—and sometimes what one finds necessitates rethinking the research questions and the scope of the project. My advice to researchers is as follows: Leave yourself room to expand your topic and add several (perhaps unexpected) subheadings to your write-up or include information in an appendix—and later embrace other projects that perhaps build on the "extra" finds. But by all means, don't ignore information when you unearth it. Take careful notes, and photocopy materials when possible. You never know what ideas may emerge once you've left the archives and have time to mull over your finds. Often, you can't easily go back to the site, so plan ahead and gather carefully to make room for "chance."

My poor husband and my students are exposed to my archival "tales" regularly. I get extremely excited when researching archives. Certainly, I tell the Jardine/

Fardine anecdote and the "decrepit box of Jardine's letters" story to anyone who will listen. The archival research that excites me the most (and reaps the greatest scholarly rewards in the form of grants and publications) are instances of seren- dipity . . . just being in the right place at the right time.

INTERVIEW: JESSICA ENOCH—STRIKING METAPHORS

In addition to her chapter in this collection and her recent book *Refiguring Rhetorical Education: Women Teaching African American, Native American, and Chicano/a Students, 1865–1911* (2008), Jessica Enoch's work has appeared in *College Composition and Communication*, *College English*, and *Rhetoric Society Quarterly*. In her response to interview questions, Enoch questioned the use of metaphors when asked to describe a time when she had "struck gold" in the archives: "I'm actually uncomfortable with the 'striking gold' metaphor. I think it has some pretty problematic implications especially when researchers work in smaller, community archives or cultural centers." In a presentation at the Modern Language Association in 2005, Enoch argued that scholars working in community archives should not view their work as a kind of "treasure hunt or an exploration into new frontiers (two metaphors often used to describe archival research)." Instead, she suggests that smaller archives are anything but passive repositories of information; instead they serve as "*productive* site[s] for civic participation," in the present tense [emphasis hers]. In the work that follows, Enoch details some of her experiences visiting a number of smaller, community archives around the country.

My book [*Refiguring Rhetorical Education*] examines female teachers and rhetorical education from 1865 to 1911. In particular, I look at five turn-of-the-century women and their work with African American, Native American, and Chicano/a students. I've worked at archives for all three of the main chapters. I've gone to the American Antiquarian Society, the Library of Congress, the Cumberland County Historical Society in Carlisle, Pennsylvania, the Webb County Heritage Foundation in Laredo, Texas, and the University of Texas libraries in Austin. For other smaller projects, I've also researched the Kenneth Burke Papers at Penn State's library as well as the Chicano Studies archives at UCLA and the National Archives for Criminal and Civil Cases in Laguna, California.

Finding the smaller archive that holds materials for figures who might not be widely recognized is an important moment for archivists. When I was working on Jovita Idar, Marta Peña, and Leonor Villegas de Magnón, I couldn't find any archives that held materials for these women. In fact, these women are rarely referenced in secondary materials at all. But when I called the Laredo city information center and asked them about possible archives, the person there referred me to the Webb County Heritage Foundation. I would have never found that archive on my own—that is for sure—but once I got there, I was able to find a lot of really good information.

When I was at the Webb County Heritage Foundation, I asked the archivist if she had materials about these women and she said, "No." I then started talking with her about the holdings she had on turn-of-the-century teachers and education more generally, and she said she did have a few documents I might want to look at. When she brought them out, I was shocked to see that she had found pictures of Villegas's students. Villegas's great-niece had submitted them to the archive.

When I visited the archives in Carlisle and the archive in Laredo, I had the opportunity to see where the women in my chapters lived and worked. I was able to visit the former grounds of the Carlisle Indian School, and I was able to see the town in which Idar, Peña, and Villegas taught and published their work. Being at both of these places helped me to see how and why these women made the arguments that they did. For instance, Laredo is situated directly on the border of Texas and Mexico—the Rio Grande certainly separates the two, but the bridge across it is about two hundred yards. It made sense, then, that these women would argue for bilingual education for their students living on the Texas side of the border.

For another project examining Burke's pedagogical work in "Linguistic Approaches to Problems in Education," I found that Burke taught something like a teacher-training course when he was at the University of Chicago during the 1950s. While I was in the archive reading letters about his time there, I became interested in what he might have done in that class. I proceeded to work on the article and forgot about the Chicago lead, though. Later that summer, Jack Selzer took a group of us to Burke's home in Andover, New Jersey, where there remains a good bit of Burke's writing, letters, and the like. In his study, I saw an envelope that said "Chicago 1950s," and when we looked at it, we saw that it contained some really interesting material on his time there and the course itself. We also found that a mouse had made his way through about an eighth of the documents. I haven't pursued that project, but I know where to go when I do—unless the mouse has gotten to it first!

I try to keep really good notes of what I find and where it is, so that if one accidental discovery becomes something that I want to continue working on later, I can find the material. The worst experiences I've had are when I can't locate something I know I saw because I didn't make a note as to where it was.

PART THREE

Working with/through Archival Material

READING THE ARCHIVE OF FRESHMAN ENGLISH

Thomas Masters

When I began doing research, I had twenty years of experience in the classroom, as well as extensive study in literature, composition, rhetoric, and empirical research methods. My exploration of the teaching and learning of writing led me, however, to switch strategy from empirical design to archival research, a move I made with only informal training in historiography and library science. What I discovered through instinct and trial and error might be useful to someone contemplating working in the archives.

Archival research, I would emphasize, is not the passive recording of objective data but a reader's constructive, subjective ordering and making meaning out of what he or she chooses to examine. Archival research is a form of reading. But what does it mean to "read" an archive? Certainly, it requires locating repositories, finding materials, and examining them. But this kind of reading—perhaps all reading—is essentially constructive. Alberto Manguel's anecdotal description suggests what I mean:

> [S]itting in front of my book, I . . . do not merely perceive the letters and blank spaces of the words that make up the text. In order to extract a message from that system of black and white signs, I first apprehend the system in an apparently erratic manner, through fickle eyes, and then reconstruct the code of signs through a connecting chain of processing neurons in my brain—a chain that varies according to the nature of the text I'm reading—and imbue that text with something—emotion, physical sentience, intuition, knowledge, soul—that depends on who I am and how I became who I am. (38)

Manguel's description highlights the importance of having a clear notion of yourself as a reader, as a researcher. What you dismiss and what you deem meaningful depends upon who you are and your prior experience. In turn, thoughtful, reflective, constructive reading reconstructs the reader. A researcher's investigation gradually assembles the archive, while in turn the archive shapes the research and the researcher.

Using this definition of *archive*, I would like to offer my experience of researching and writing *Practicing Writing: The Postwar Discourse of Freshman English* as an illustration of how to do archival work. *Practicing Writing* examines the first-year writing course, generally known at the time as "freshman English," during a pivotal era: the mid-twentieth century, beginning with the waves of World War II veterans who attended college on the GI Bill. Using evidence from the archives at three Midwestern schools—Northwestern, Wheaton (Illinois), and Illinois—it analyzes the reforms during the late 1950s following the launch of Sputnik and, in 1963, the establishment of composition as a separate discipline. Through voices often taken for granted or forgotten—those of students and their instructors—*Practicing Writing* reveals the tacit rules that constituted the discursive practice of teaching and learning writing then and perhaps now.

The book began as a response to a pedagogical imperative: my desire to "make sense of what I perceived as nearly random patterns of success and failure in my classroom" (22). I began by taking what Stephen M. North calls an "experimental" or "clinical" approach, but the more I studied the problem, the more I intuited that my teaching and my students' learning were not complex acts that cognitive science could explain but the manifestation of a historically constituted discursive practice. I could best examine the problematic events in my classroom today by visiting classrooms of the past, and I could do so by reading the archive of such experiences.

James Berlin locates the roots of contemporary writing instruction in the nineteenth century and its stages of development up to the 1990s. Others, such as Sharon Crowley and Robert Connors, have explored its problematic aspects ("current-traditional" pedagogy, textbooks). They explore the bankruptcy of the most common pedagogy—the current-traditional model—and using the critical lexicon provide a theoretical basis for more vibrant or intellectually consistent ways of teaching writing. Even as I tried to enact more liberating approaches, such as the epistemic rhetoric that Berlin discusses in *Rhetoric and Reality* (165–79), a powerful centrifugal force seemed to pull me and my students back into the current-traditional. What made it so difficult to enact a more constructive pedagogy, one more coherent with critical theory and cognitive psychology? Certainly not a lack of energy and goodwill. I and my colleagues struggled to make a difference by trying enlightened approaches consistent with the findings of empirical research and critical examination, but our "scene of teaching" never improved.

It seemed that resistance came from the very shape of the scene of teaching—the students who enrolled, the relationship between writing instruction and the rest of the curriculum, the structure of the school itself that compartmentalized writing as a subject. What might explain that resistance? North, as well as Susan Miller and Richard E. Miller, were calling for critical historical work that began with "concrete instances drawn from everyday reality that lie outside or just beyond the interpretive area necessarily designated in advance and thereafter inscribed by every theory" (R. E. Miller 174). It seemed that a careful examination of such materials might reveal the tacit rules of formation for the practices my students and I enacted every day, even when we tried to resist them.

Archival research allows exploration of such "concrete instances drawn from everyday reality." To focus my research, it seemed that I—as had many other researchers—might begin at the most common site for writing instruction in North American schools, the first-year composition class. To focus on a particular time period, I relied on Berlin's observation that "economic, political, and social developments between 1940 and 1960 had placed in motion a current of ideas that would profoundly affect the teaching of writing" (*Rhetoric and Reality* 119). Given those two parameters, I contacted the English departments and libraries of colleges and universities mentioned prominently by other researchers, asked prominent figures in the history of the discipline for advice, and posted an author's query in the *Chronicle of Higher Education*. I explained that I was interested in the relation between composition and literary theory in the context of the larger intellectual and social environment and listed the materials that I was seeking. Contacting likely repositories of information as well as knowledgeable figures who could provide relevant information, give me interviews, or suggest further or alternate avenues to explore served two important functions. This method of research identified as many sources as possible, something vital to archival research. Just as important, however, it produced unexpected and useful feedback from a number of expert sources. Guidance early in the process helped me allocate my resources most efficiently.

While waiting for replies—this was in 1988, when *inbox* denoted an actual metal compartment that I visited expectantly every day on my way into the office—I explored library sources. For current information, I consulted printed yearly indexes, each searchable by author, title, and/or subject. Using a computer required an appointment with a research librarian; in the one precious hour allotted to each graduate student, we ran as many of my carefully selected search terms as possible past the Dissertation Abstracts and the ERIC databases. I had to wait a day for printouts of matching studies and other sources. Even though the process today is much more efficient, the point from which research begins—finding search terms that lead to desired information—is just as important for using Google as it was for using *The Readers' Guide to Periodical Literature*. By June, I began sending inquiries and evaluating library resources; by October, I began exploring particular collections and contacting individuals for interviews.

Once begun, the process, like all authentic research and writing, became self-generating. Sources begot other sources; within a month, I needed to evaluate my leads and narrow my efforts to those most suitable among sources all over the United States. Fortunately, I found useful repositories at four nearby sites that represented a cross-section of the era that I was investigating: Northwestern University, a large private institution; Wheaton College, Illinois, a small liberal-arts school; and the two campuses (Chicago and Urbana) of the University of Illinois, a large public institution. Each of their libraries had extensive special collections and archives administered by helpful, knowledgeable staff. Given my research objective, to examine the actual practices of composition teaching during the post–World War II era, I hypothesized that taken as a whole, these places represented the gamut of experience I sought to investigate. Given my time and finances, it was attractive that all lay within a day's drive or less.

I began to explore these repositories by learning how to use their finding aids. In 1988, Wheaton's Buswell Memorial Library and the libraries of both campuses of the University of Illinois had searchable databases, which now can be accessed online; the Northwestern University Library had printed finding aids, now available on its Web site as PDF images. There is no equivalent of the Library of Congress index that archivists use. As with any indexing tool, discovering the nomenclature used at a particular site is the key to finding useful material, and doing so comes through trial and error. Through telephone calls, correspondence, and initial visits, I assembled a list of search terms and possible files. Then, I made an appointment at each school to review the nature of my search and my preliminary findings. The archivists suggested other terms, different collections within the archive, and material not yet cataloged that I might investigate.

At that point, I laid out a research calendar and began to handle actual documents, photos, books, and other materials. Looking back now, I realize that I had only begun to assemble my archive. I learned by experience to take careful notes concerning materials that seemed useful and to keep my own annotated list of promising indexing codes. Photocopying was cheap enough that I could make copies of materials as I found them, then take them to my office for review. Wheaton, Northwestern, and Illinois–Urbana let me make my own copies; Illinois–Chicago required a written request for each item, and the special collections staff made the copies. I took pains to label each document with its indexing code, which I sometimes needed to locate the item again, as well as to assemble the list of sources to be included with my dissertation, "Freshman English as a Discursive Practice, 1947–1960." I followed the *MLA Style Manual*, the style sheet that the guidelines requested. Once I had found a publisher, I had to modify some documentation according to *The Chicago Manual of Style*, which the University of Pittsburgh Press uses. Content remained the same, but certain formatting had to be changed, such as using endnotes instead of footnotes. Keeping a careful file of sources with complete information arranged according to a uniform system prevented errors and wasted time and effort.

As I surveyed my initial materials, I began to sketch out the shape of the concepts that they were communicating. Periodic notes to myself reveal how I was reading the archive as I was assembling it. As Manguel describes the process, "I first apprehend . . . and then reconstruct the code of signs through a connecting chain of processing neurons . . . that varies according to the nature of the text I'm reading—and imbue that text with something" (38). I did that reconstructing through a research diary, a set of almost daily notes in which I reflected on the work to that point. For example, a note dated 21 April 1988 reads, "What I hope to do: Given a few years of historical perspective, I propose to describe the 'shape' English had taken in the 1950s. What were the forces, and how did they coordinate with one another?" By August 17, a structure began to emerge from the data. I wrote this, which resembles an extended marginal reading note:

General statements about comp so far

1. Accidental nature . . . almost an *arbitrary* nature.
2. Search for a sound basis for the course: Semantics. Literature. Structural Linguistics, but a tremendous inertia here; a continual questioning of the "current-traditional" model; but the model always seems to survive.
3. Powerlessness of the comp staff . . . tied to English department . . . some attempts to spin off into sub-departments; but my three models [I was considering the two Illinois programs as one] all kept comp within the English department. . . . [C]omp is . . . not *really* wanted, but once obtained it really takes over the department
4. Content/no content of course . . . but in fact, the content inevitably seems to become the students *themselves.*
5. Connection between New Critical reading & writing as taught. . . .
6. Outside compulsion to offer the course. . . . "service" . . . universal literacy . . . economic/mercantile needs . . . *Status*: somehow (how?) what the current-traditional notion of writing espouses is what people (businessmen, gov't administrators, etc.) claim to desire: correctness, logic & organization, clarity.
7. Larger contexts—The notions of *literacy* operative at that time: "general semantics," "liberal arts education" (prevailing notions of what constitutes education)

8. What are the reasons for "English"—esp. English comp.—being taught?—Is it something that gets relabeled in each age to account for the prevailing notion of education. . . . like Derrida says—looking for a center . . .

9. The impossibility of *any* pedagogical scheme to break out of the restrictions which make English what it is (. . . can the course be other than what it, historically [and what the schools have been historically] has been?)

10. From W. Douglas[1] referring to a student, but we can substitute the entire course: f[reshman]. e[nglish]. "is the nexus in which the various forces do meet and interact."

11. Q: *Who* is the student here? According to what model is the student constructed? And is that construction part of a larger picture?

Over time, the underlying relationships among the particulars in my sources were beginning to come into focus. I cite these notes at length because they show how, through interacting with the material (and with advisors and peers[2]), I was beginning to give shape to what I had found.

I allowed plenty of time just to look, to gather, to write notes, and to ponder. In this part of the process, the archive, the text I intended to read and interpret, was assuming a distinct form. I let the sources speak to me and take me to further information. It turned out that the libraries' collections led in interesting directions.

At Northwestern, for example, the head archivist knew many of those who had figured prominently in the English A-10 program in the 1950s. Although some had already passed away or were too ill to be interviewed, others welcomed conversation about the early years of their careers, what had changed, and what had remained the same. At Wheaton, one archivist recalled a history-department project from the early 1970s in which students interviewed alumni about events from different eras of the school's history. The students' essays led me to contacts who supplied personal materials they had prepared while taking Wheaton's Writing 111 and 112. The alumni office provided the addresses of certain persons from whom I wanted further details or whose materials I needed permission to cite. At Illinois–Chicago, I found names of retired faculty who had figured prominently in Rhetoric 101 and 102; I interviewed them face-to-face, over the telephone, or through correspondence. Several gave me additional materials such as personal files or annotated textbooks. They also steered me to documents (literally, closets full of them) that had been stashed in the English department. At Illinois–Urbana, the archivists put me in touch with the English chair, who in turn let me examine files kept in the departmental office. He told me how to contact retired faculty members who could share personal experiences or documents. The Illinois archivists also suggested a community resource, the Urbana Free Public Library, where I found useful articles in its collection of newspapers from the 1950s.

I discovered many, many such coincidental links as I explored freshman English during the post–World War II era. These anecdotes illustrate the nature of the process. The archive, tremendously rich and variegated, requires time for the shape of the concepts that it can yield to emerge. In my case, I worked full time—about forty hours per week—for four full months before I'd seen enough to begin answering the question I'd posed in my author's query: "What is the relation between composition and literary theory in the context of the larger intellectual and social environment?"

Once I was relatively sure of the thesis that the information could support and the specific evidence that was available, I outlined a research plan. I sketched the principal categories for which there seemed to be useful evidence. A note from October 19 reveals how that evidence seemed to fall into six binary oppositions:

Organicity		its opposite would be randomness/mutation. . . . *spontaneity*
Individuality	vs.	identification, predictability, sameness, *corporateness*
Transferability	vs.	immutability; *specific*, rather than general value
Compositeness	vs.	essential unity; impermeability
Instrumentality	vs.	self-value
Progress	vs.	stasis—*circumstance*. Change but *quality* remains the same

> Writing not about the *course*, so much as I am about the conditions within which it operates . . . *Is* there continuity? What stays the same, and why does it remain so?

These headings provided an itinerary for return visits to examine in detail the sources I had identified as being possibly useful. In a note to myself on 23 November 1988, I sketched a tentative thesis:

> I would like to contrast the stated purposes of the course with the sub-textual assumptions which were deemed necessary to the course, to show the tension within the course. Those involved in the course made certain moves in order to "improve" the course, to make it serve the needs of the institution, the students, the faculty better . . . but these moves often have created unintended crisis, because they were based on an understanding of the course as a simple instrument, a straightforward procedure, rather than a complex discursive practice.

At this point, echoes from my own Rhetoric 101 teacher, Jeff Stiker,[3] came back to me: Paraphrase documents as you read them. Copy precisely what you intend to repeat word-for-word. Label each note with a heading from your research outline and with its source code. For each document or source, prepare a card with complete and accurate information required by the style sheet you are using. The time and effort I put into bibliography and note taking paid dividends (and came back to haunt me when I cut corners). Today, I use a laptop to generate databases of notes and sources but maintain the same basic principles of research.

My archive included almost forty interviews, some with the widows of men whose papers I had investigated, some with retired professors or office staff. I took pains to explain to them the nature of my research and to secure a release to use their words in my study. I was not scrupulous enough in doing this during the first round of my research, and when it became clear that my dissertation would be published as a book, I needed to revisit several people to obtain these releases, a painstaking but necessary part of publishing.[4] When subjects consented to be recorded, I kept an outline of our conversation, which proved valuable in transcribing the tapes, as not every section of an interview proved relevant. I kept both the audiotapes and the typed transcripts. Interviews as well as private papers, letters, or students' work require permission to be published, and I labeled everything and kept a file of contact information for the authors.[5] Although tedious, I found it easier to document the sources as I used them rather than to revisit the repositories or recontact my live sources for information that I could have—and should have—obtained the first time through.

I ran across some fascinating material that didn't fit my research plan. "The Pier Glass," a journal of exemplary student work that the rhetoric department at Illinois–Chicago published each semester, contains freshman essays by contemporary scholars Gerald Graff and Mihaly Csikszentmihalyi. The Northwestern archives include Wallace Douglas's correspondence with a woman from rural Indiana regarding the relationship between evangelical Christianity and the academy. At Wheaton, Clyde Kilby's papers contain a trove of information about his role in establishing the archive at Buswell Library of C. S. Lewis's work. I took careful note of these and many more tantalizing nuggets of information, then set them aside in a separate folder. Some of these orphans proved useful as I expanded the introduction to include more information about each of the four schools I profiled. Most of them, however, await future research projects.

Like reading and writing, archival research is recursive. Some material that at first seemed promising proved not useful. Documents or files listed on an index did not exist or had been stolen or were in use by someone else. Some, particularly personnel files, could not be viewed without special permission or were sealed for a certain number of years. I was wary of coming across an unexpected document that might have required modifying my thesis, outline, or both, but my initial intuitions proved reliable; the more I researched, the more sure I was that I had found something true about the discipline.

I came across sources that might have proved interesting, such as a large archive of student writing at the University of Minnesota, but I had reached a point at which the additional information would not have had a significant impact on the fundamental purpose of the project. On the other hand, such unexpected finds sometimes helped to deepen my insights. One day at Wheaton, the archivist turned up a file with the original typescripts of a pair of speeches delivered at oratorical contests by Ed McCully, a notable Wheaton graduate who gave up a career in law to work as a missionary in Ecuador, where he was martyred by Auca natives.[6] At first, the typescripts seemed an interesting curiosity, but later I found McCully's words and ideas useful in developing one aspect of my argument—how New Humanism was construed in an overtly Christian atmosphere like Wheaton's.

The digging, culling, thinking, and writing that constitute the physical reality of doing research take time. The research that led to a 225-page dissertation took six months of steady work. Getting it published later as a 250-page book required another fourteen years' work (albeit intermittent) in the archive. Had circumstances been different, I would have needed much less; but I had only six uninterrupted weeks each year because I was teaching high-school English, which left me little time or energy for other pursuits. Maintaining our marriage, raising three children, and a chronic back problem that led to a couple of surgeries kept me from completing the work more quickly. I was fortunate to have appreciative and patient family members and editors.

By January 1989, I had visited each of the four repositories and had interviewed fifteen or so of the people who had been associated with programs at Wheaton, Northwestern, and Illinois. I had gathered a thick file of notes on each of the six categories that had been emerging. I also had accumulated anecdotal information that did not fit in any one category but suggested a more global picture of the functions of teachers, students, and the course itself. Reviewing these notes, which represented four months of reading and research, gave me the sense that things had reached a critical mass and that I was ready to begin writing. I refined the thesis that I had used to guide my research and reconsidered my research outline. The directions I had developed for finding and organizing materials in the archive suggested another set for shaping my argument. I transformed my preliminary thesis and notes into a working thesis and outline, using the following statement as a guide for shaping an argument from the archival evidence:

> My study suggests that we look elsewhere besides the psychology of the individual learner (or groups of learners) or even the "needs" of specific disciplines for a rationale for courses such as Freshman English. When we enter this field of discourse, we are joining in a play of forces which has its own history and life; if we wish to change it, we must consider the complexity of our task.

The notes to myself included earlier in this article gave rise to a tentative outline. One section, "The Discourse of Freshman English," included the six "features": organicity, individuality, transferability, compositeness, instrumentality, and progress; another section, "The Practice of Freshman English," discussed students, faculty, and the course itself.

As I wrote, I needed to revisit the four libraries as well as other places where I had found documents and to interview subjects whose names came to light only after my first round of research. I needed to confirm intuitions that emerged as I was writing, to rectify inconsistencies that appeared as I began to assemble my material, to flesh out part of my argument that lacked sufficient support, and to satisfy my trusted readers who offered feedback on my work in progress.

As I continued to write and revisit my sources, my thesis emerged into a statement about the value of archival research for people in their classrooms: "[P]ractitioner-based history can enable teachers to bring about far more important and subtle changes than adopting a more self-reflexive theory or choosing and deploying more effective means of delivering education" (25). The outline, however, still resembled the one I used as I began to write: Part 1, "The Discourse of Freshman English," retained six chapters but with refined nomenclature—no longer features but "presumptions": "Instrumentality," "Priority," "Efficiency," "Individuality," "Transmission," and "Correspondence." Part 2, "The Practice of Freshman English," kept its three chapters: "The Course," "The Student," and "The Teacher."

After completing the dissertation draft, I found myself with a large collection of documents useful in developing my thesis as well as many more that seemed repetitious or perhaps unnecessary. I labeled everything and organized it for ready reference. Working toward publication, I did not know what my colleagues, advisors, reviewers, or editors might want me to revisit or refine or expand. My initial research turned up hundreds of samples of student writing. I had selected one or two for each of the six presumptions that emerged as the tacit structure of what it meant to "do" freshman English in the post-war era. The anonymous readers from the University of Pittsburgh Press who critiqued my manuscript found those samples the most powerful and interesting part of my argument and suggested including more of them. These initial responses (some of which were frank, even harsh) demonstrated also that they had understood only part of the thesis that I thought the evidence supported. I had not explained sufficiently my rationale for choosing the four schools as representative examples, nor had I put enough of a human face on their policies and practices. I needed to select more samples of student writing, to document the differences among the four schools, and to find a representative who embodied what it meant to be a teacher at each school during that era. Before revising, I revisited my collection of notes and documents as well as the libraries at Northwestern, Wheaton, and the two Illinois campuses. I knew where to look, but even with that knowledge, I found useful things that I had dismissed or overlooked during my earlier research—collections of papers, biographical files of administrators and teachers in the rhetoric and composition programs, and institutional histories.

Although no piece of writing is ever truly finished, this phase of my involvement with the archive of freshman English in the post–World War II era had concluded. I satisfied myself and my critics that I had produced a cogent argument with sufficient evidence to demonstrate my thesis. In May of 1989, my dissertation was accepted, and fifteen years later, the reviewers and editors at University of Pittsburgh Press agreed that the book was ready to be published. This project is finished, but the experience has produced more possibilities than conclusions—for an academic, a fortunate problem.

Notes

1. Wallace Douglas of Northwestern University is one of the figures I profile in *Practicing Writing*.

2. Three other graduate students and I formed a dissertation support group, which became a forum of trusted yet frank peers against whom we could test our ideas. At weekly meetings, one of us would present some aspect of his or her work in progress. At milestones (a completed chapter, a job interview, a successful oral exam), we would celebrate. The stick of honest feedback coupled with the carrot of another dinner at Florence Restaurant motivated all of us.

3. I profile him and his class on pages 6 and 7 of *Practicing Writing*. The habits of mind he and a succession of rhetoric and English professors taught me proved invaluable in this research.

4. The University of Pittsburgh Press Web site offers useful resources for authors at http://www.upress.pitt.edu/htmlSourceFiles/pdfs/manuscriptpreparation.pdf. It contains a sample release form and guidelines for what an author must obtain permission to publish.

5. Federal law in the United States has made uncovering and using such personal information more difficult. The 1974 Family Education Rights and Privacy Act (FERPA) states, "The parent or eligible student [that is, one over eighteen] shall provide a signed and dated written consent before an educational agency or institution discloses personally identifiable information from the student's educational records." Some of the archivists with whom I worked think that this regulation may make it illegal for student papers to be made available unless the author has provided written permission to do so.

6. The manuscripts of these two speeches, "Alexander Hamilton" and "Patrick Henry," can be found in the special collection archives of the Buswell Memorial Library at Wheaton College, Wheaton, Illinois. "Alexander Hamilton" is discussed in Masters, *Practicing Writing* 153–54.

Works Cited

Berlin, James A. *Rhetoric and Reality: Writing Instruction in American Colleges, 1900–1985.* Carbondale: Southern Illinois UP, 1987.

———. *Writing Instruction in Nineteenth-Century American Colleges*. Carbondale: Southern Illinois UP, 1984.

Connors, Robert J. *Composition-Rhetoric: Backgrounds, Theory, and Pedagogy*. Pittsburgh, PA: U of Pittsburgh P, 1997.

Crowley, Sharon. *The Methodical Memory: Invention in Current-Traditional Rhetoric*. Carbondale: Southern Illinois UP, 1990.

Manguel, Alberto. *A History of Reading*. New York: Penguin, 1997.

Masters, Thomas. *Practicing Writing: The Postwar Discourse of Freshman English*. Pittsburgh, PA: U of Pittsburgh P, 2004.

Miller, Richard E. "Composing English Studies: Toward a Social History of the Discipline." *College Composition and Communication* 45 (1994): 164–79.

North, Stephen M. *The Making of Knowledge in Composition: Portrait of an Emerging Field*. Upper Montclair, NJ: Boynton-Cook, 1987.

JOURNEYING INTO THE ARCHIVES: EXPLORING THE PRAGMATICS OF ARCHIVAL RESEARCH

Katherine E. Tirabassi

I deposit my jacket and bag in the entryway of the University of New Hampshire Archives, stopping at the front desk to sign in and taking only my laptop, a notebook, and a pencil with me to one of the long, wooden tables. Because I visit the archives almost daily, the staff has assembled several boxes for me on a cart; I select the box I ended with yesterday, carry the box to a table, looking for one of two cushioned chairs because I plan to remain here for several hours. Opening the box, I pull out a folder and turn each page slowly, reading through the miscellaneous brochures, letters, and conference registration records for serendipitous finds—answers to my evolving research questions. Occasionally, I find an artifact that I want copied, and I place the long, thin, white paper bookmarks supplied by the archives to indicate which document I need. As I look through the folders, I take notes—possible leads to other boxes and folders, quotes that I will want to refer to, new questions that arise as I read, and connections that I want to remember later. Sometimes, I type out whole sections of an archival text, looking for patterns or information that I might not see otherwise.

The process I describe above presents a snapshot of my many days in the University of New Hampshire Archives as I conducted research for my dissertation. This scene is likely quite familiar to researchers who have worked on long-term archival projects. In some ways, my research process was random, as I sifted through folders that might or might not yield information useful to my study. In other ways, this research process was ordered; I developed a list of materials to look through, adding to that list as I learned of new resources and searching through these documents sequentially, folder by folder, box by box. The method itself was organic, shaped by the research process itself and shaped by other key theoretical and pragmatic factors that I discuss in this chapter. In developing this method, I read what I could about archival methodology, but after finding few pragmatic suggestions for conducting archival research, I ultimately found it was my entry into the archives itself that shaped my approach most significantly. Drawing on my work in the UNH Archives, as both a researcher myself and as a cocreator of a writing program archive, I present four principles of archival research that grew out of these experiences and that speak to some of the pragmatic concerns of archival research. This experiential model of archival research will, I hope, prove useful to researchers developing their own personal approaches to archival research.

How Archival Definitions Shape Research Approaches

In her article "X-Files in the Archive," Susan Miller argues that understanding what one means by archival research is an important consideration in taking up this work because "queries about how one does archival research rarely specify what it is that one learns how to do. That is, when we make prior assumptions about what 'archival research' is, we may erase many options and experiences that composition scholars haven't yet taken up" (1). Though the brief narrative at the beginning of this chapter presents my apparent familiarity with the UNH Archives, this familiarity developed over a series of encounters. With each visit to the archives, my understanding of the nature of archival research continued to shift as I encountered new surprises and struggled with seemingly irresolvable gaps within the archives. Each encounter also influenced every aspect of my research process—from designing my research project to negotiating the archives to deciding when to stop gathering data and begin data analysis.

Before spending time in an archive, I viewed an archive in terms of its apparent and obvious function: as a storage facility or repository preserving historical materials that might otherwise be lost in closets, attics, barns, and local landfills. But my first direct encounter with the UNH Archives, as part of a collaborative team designing a local writing program archive, reshaped my definitional views of archival research in significant ways. In the summer of 2003, Cinthia Gannett, then director of the UNH Writing Center and Writing Across the Curriculum (WAC) Program, created a research team that included herself, me, fellow graduate student Amy Zenger, and composition historian John C. Brereton to create an archive for ten years' worth of writing center and WAC records (1993 to 2003) at UNH.[1] The generative work of creating this archive reshaped my view of an archive as an inert repository of artifacts to a layered, historical record of dynamic stories. I saw firsthand how artifacts already housed within a university archive could be reimagined with a fresh perspective by a researcher asking a different set of questions than those implied by the archive's established categories. I also saw that artifacts could be added to the archive to extend the historical picture of a given collection or collections. This new conception of the archive aided me as I began my dissertation project on the history of writing instruction in the 1940s, a study I refer to throughout the rest of this chapter as I outline some practical approaches and challenges of archival research.[2]

Key Principles Shaping Archival Spaces

As I worked with materials to be submitted to the university archives, I developed not only a deeper theoretical understanding of an archive but also a better sense of the kinds of organizing principles governing the construction, maintenance, and investigation of an archival collection. In conducting research for my dissertation project, I recorded my personal observations of how the archives was constructed—where I found artifacts, how particular artifacts were labeled or linked in ways that I did not expect, and how this archival construction impacted me as a researcher. Through these observations, I came to see that there were four main research principles driving my work in the archives. These four principles helped me to negotiate the array of archival artifacts I encountered daily, formed my essential conceptual framework, and guided my day-to-day work in the archives, thus influencing my evolving understanding of the archives. I want to note here that the archival field has its own complex, defined, and clearly articulated series of organizing principles for archival construction requiring a great deal of study and expertise. In contrast, the principles that I outline here originated from my experiences researching in the UNH Archives and, as I show, served as a means of understanding and navigating *this* particular archival space. Because I realize that not all researchers will have the opportunity or resources to develop a writing program archive or to spend the amount of time that I did in an archive due to constraints of time, location, or deadlines, I offer these principles to those embarking on archival research projects, particularly projects in an unfamiliar archive. The four principles I have named and their descriptions are as follows:

> *Principle of selectivity*: the researcher's understanding of how archivists select and omit artifacts for a given collection.
> *Principle of cross-referencing*: the practice of searching across documents for contextual traces that clarify an archival document's rhetorical situation or that confirm, corroborate, clarify, or contradict a fact or point cited in a given document.
> *Principle of categorization*: the development of keywords and finding aids that help researchers access information in the archive.
> *Principle of closure*: the researcher's understanding that there are inherent gaps in archival records and that while the archive is complex and rich, it

cannot be searched exhaustively. Finding the ending point or knowing when to make an exit is an essential part of archival research.

The remainder of this chapter focuses on defining and discussing these principles in greater detail, presenting my personal observations based on my work in the UNH Archives and explaining the applicability and importance of understanding each principle for researchers preparing to enter an archive. Although earlier I pointed out that each archive is different in methods and policies, I submit that some version of these principles is applicable in most, if not all, archival settings.

Principle of Selectivity

First, I observed that archivists need to be selective in developing a usable archive. For researchers, this means developing an understanding of how archivists select and omit materials for an archival collection; this is the application of the *principle of selectivity*. Including all of the materials from a donor into a given collection has the potential to create an archive that is too cumbersome for researchers and that could overwhelm the physical space of the archive. Some artifacts have to be omitted, while others are selected; applying a principle of selectivity allows the archivist to sift materials that are appropriate for a particular archival category and to negotiate with the donor(s) about what materials are most interesting or historically significant for the archive.[3] Keeping this principle in mind is important to the archival researcher because it emphasizes the need to interrogate the archival record and to enter the archive with questions about what kinds of stories aren't being told, can't be told, and won't be told given the data available. Because the archival record is inevitably incomplete, an awareness of such silences and gaps leads the researcher to look past established categories, established in the finding aids, in the archive in an attempt to fill in gaps, to ask new questions of the current archival record, to conceive of new labels for materials in the archive, and to look for materials that are not yet in the archive but that corroborate the researcher's developing thesis or fill in certain gaps in understanding. These materials might be found in a department's filing cabinets, in a community member's attic or basement, or on the shelves of a local historical society.

Principle of Cross-Referencing

Ironically, one of the places where archival researchers locate gaps is in the artifacts themselves, in artifacts that are acontextual—with no clear author and, at times, just a vague temporal marker. In order to look for contextual traces for these documents, if they can be found, we look, as we do in other cases of missing information, in new places and are, at times, willing to do more with less, or, as Ruth M. Mirtz puts it "to conduct research when we must fill in many blanks with what we know from events outside the documentary materials" (121). Because most archival materials reach the archivist, and consequently the researcher, in the form of boxes and folders that provide a marginal context at best and more often than not no context at all, the researcher needs to look for *contextual traces* that situate the document in time and place. Without these traces, the researcher has to infer the document's context and should, ethically, make it clear in the resultant historical narrative when intuitive leaps have been made. Carol Steedman notes that the historian is, after all, "the reader of what is never intended for his or her eyes" (30); the historian, then, needs to locate contextual traces to help him or her make interpretive connections about and between artifacts.

Understanding that such acontextual gaps are inherent in the archive, the researcher must apply a *principle of cross-referencing* in attempting to read across the documents to fill in some of these gaps. In reviewing documents to be submitted to the writing program archive and documents for my dissertation research, I learned how important a document's contextual traces can be. Whenever possible during my research process, I tried to develop notes that described a document's rhetorical situation—the author (when knowable), the intended audience, and the purpose of the document.[4] Finding these contextual traces helped me to determine whether certain documents were vital, useful, or tangential to my study, to confirm what I thought were emergent trends or developing traditions, and to reassess my understanding of the types of documents that could or should be relevant to my study. For example, when I first began my dissertation study, I looked at a series of letters focusing on the annual University of New Hampshire Writers' Conference, started by Carroll S. Towle and held from 1938 to 1961. Some of these letters were written on stationery that told me far more about the author than simply the signature—previously unknown information such as a home address or institutional affiliation. However, the letters also contained language that was understandable only to the members of that particular community. By searching the official brochures of the conference, I located some contextual traces within the letters; for example, in a letter signed by "John," I determined from the letter's content, from the writer's mention of a collaborative lecture that he was designing with the American poet Rolfe Humphries, and from the conference schedule and brochure of that year (1945) that this signature referred to John Holmes, American poet and teacher at Tufts University, who lectured and led writing groups at Towle's writers' conference for several years.

But in my experience, finding these contextual traces was not always so easy, apparent, or possible. Some documents were in folders assembled by faculty or staff members who could no longer be contacted, and the rhetorical situation of other documents was hard to decipher because quite simply too much time had passed or too much information was missing in the documents themselves. As I examined whole folders, I could sometimes find contextual traces in what archivists call the "original order"[5] within the folder; for example, if a document's temporal context was in question, as in an undated letter, the surrounding documents sometimes provided insights into the chronological order of the documents. And, as noted above, the concept of original order was helpful as I worked to piece together the story behind incomplete documents in a file, such as an incomplete series of letters between two writers.

Another means of finding contextual traces is by cross-referencing archival documents with other related documents, as I did with the Holmes letter, or with artifacts found in unofficial archives—student newspapers, college and university publications, departmental filing cabinets, historical societies' records, and public library special collections; researchers could also, as I did, interview faculty, staff, students, or local specialists who might shed some light, directly or indirectly, on gaps within certain documents. As I conducted my research, I developed particular questions to ask of the archival materials that I encountered in my study to extend my understanding of their context and of their appearance in the archive itself:

- Who included this document in the archival record, and why?
- Why is this document included in this location?
- Who created this document originally and for what purpose/audience?
- What gaps do I see in the archival record that might be filled in other places in the archive or in other unofficial archival sites? And, what gaps can't be filled?

The answers to these questions may be found in unexpected places. For example, after discovering a box of letters and poetry by Robert P. T. Coffin, American poet and long-standing "leader" (as they were called) at the summer UNH Writers' Conference, I found a few letters indicating Coffin's assessment of the writers' conference and a few letters describing the political climate of the Bowdoin College English Department during the 1940s. These discoveries were crucial to my study because I wanted to know how the writers' conference staff felt about its practices and emergent traditions and because I wanted to know more about the structures and debates in English departments at colleges and universities geographically close to UNH. Had I not searched a folder that seemed to be unrelated to my study, beyond Coffin's connection with the writers' conference, I might not have made this discovery, and I would have missed out on this piece of the contextual puzzle.

Principle of Categorization

As I conducted research in the archives, I also learned that, as they organize the documents found in an archive, archivists use what I call a *principle of catego-*

rization to develop finding aids that make an archive accessible and navigable for researchers. When a researcher begins an archival research project, he or she should develop as many classification terms and key questions as possible in order to make the search more fruitful. However, because the archival record is incomplete, historical research is often messy, unwieldy, unexpected, and ultimately is always constructed by the historian's selections, omissions, and biases. Despite the laudable efforts of archivists who develop categories and multiple finding aids for archival materials, there will always be a researcher coming to the archive with a question that is not best served by these finding aids, though material in the archive might exist to respond to the question itself[6] (see Elizabeth Yakel, "Searching and Seeking in the Deep Web," and Sammie L. Morris and Shirley K Rose, "Invisible Hands," in the current collection). In short, finding aids and keywords cannot account for every research question. As Robert J. Connors notes, "archival papers and notes tend to be cataloged separately," and "usually researchers have no way to know what college archives contain without hands-on examination, and that can be expensive and difficult for many scholars" (20). For the researcher, then, it is important to take note of where a document is found and to consider why it is catalogued in this manner, considerations that provide insight into the archive's categorizing structures and allow the researcher to imagine additional potential locations in the archive that could yield relevant data.

In exploring the UNH Archives, for example, I determined that documents were organized based on four primary criteria:

- As a collection of artifacts donated by a certain person, as in Coffin's papers
- As a collection of artifacts created by university staff members, as in presidents' papers
- As a collection of artifacts created in connection with a given event or institutional tradition such as the UNH Writers' Conference (1938–61)
- As a collection of artifacts created in connection with a specific course, such as Freshman English, an academic department, or a university committee

I found that as I learned more about the archives' layout, I could cross-reference materials more easily because I could look for material about a specific person or course in two, three, or even all four categories.[7] Understanding the principle of categorization also provides the researcher with information about the ways that certain artifacts have been valued or viewed by archivists and, potentially, by the institution and can allow the researcher to consider how he or she might recategorize or resee the document in the context of his or her study. For example, in my dissertation study, I looked at a box containing the papers of Edward Eddy, assistant to the president during the early 1950s. This box was categorized by one of the roles that Eddy held at UNH, but the reason I was interested in the box was that it contained pedagogical information on the Freshman English course and documents created by the English Department regarding this course. Although Eddy's papers and his lesson plans for Freshman English were important, the more useful information for my purposes was the insight into the policies and practices of the English Department that this resource provided.

Principle of Closure

For the archival researcher, the time comes when following new leads and the search for cross-references must end. This principle of closure is inherent in the archival structure itself because collections—even while containing gaps—must eventually be opened to the public. In a similar vein, the archival researcher, too, must plan an exit from the archive in order to present his or her discoveries to a larger audience. As I spent hour after hour in the archives, observing the comings and goings of researchers, I began to recognize the importance of knowing when to make an exit from the archive or what I've called the principle of closure in archival research. Even when there may be more materials to investigate or cross-reference, there comes a time when the researcher needs to find closure for a given research project. The archival staff is available to help researchers locate and contextualize artifacts, but they obviously leave it up to the researchers to organize their time and to develop an exit strategy. This exit strategy can be shaped by external factors such as travel arrangements, financial resources, or project deadlines (or, in my case, the need to begin writing my dissertation). A key factor in finding closure can also arise from the researcher's need to make sense of the data already collected and/or to find out what more, if anything, needs to be gathered.

Archival research takes a researcher on a journey of surprises and serendipities and, at times, fruitful tangents. But the tangents can also become dead ends, consuming time and energy that he or she cannot afford to expend for too long. Although the researcher wants to be thorough, there needs to be an ending point, a clear deadline to archival research. Sometimes, that deadline comes in the form of a publication due date or a need to get to the writing. Or, the deadline comes as one's planned visit to an archive comes to an end, and there is a need to return home. As a researcher living close to the archive I was searching, I constantly struggled with the question of closure, wondering if and when had I cross-referenced enough or gathered enough data. But Carol Steedman points out that the researcher must accept that she "will not finish, that there will be something left unread, unnoted, untranscribed" (18). It is possible, of course, that a study need be long-term, stretching across months or years, and located in multiple archives; that all depends on the scope of the project and what the researcher's writing goals are. And, it is possible that a researcher might return to an archive while writing about the research to confirm certain hypotheses or fill in gaps. But one danger in archival research is that the research can go on endlessly and can become consuming without a deadline. Returning to primary research questions can help a researcher evaluate whether he or she's gone too far off track or whether the search, while tangential, is still productive. There will always be one more box or folder that might bring a new discovery. But the researcher must, at some point, accept the need to stop researching, realize that some discoveries are best left for another time or another researcher, and engage in the process of writing—to share his or her research with the world.

Applications of Archival Research Principles in Local Contexts

This final section considers why the principles I've outlined in this chapter can help the researcher use his or her time in an archive productively. Understanding these principles of archival research allows the researcher to become acquainted with the richness and limitations of the local archive and to design a research study that takes these issues into account. As I have shown, they also provide strategies for the researcher to begin negotiating the archive. Connors argues that early in the research process, as questions are forming, researchers need to "know their archives," to know what materials are available and how to access them (25). I agree; researchers need to comb archival finding aids for terms that might yield partial answers to their research questions and to familiarize themselves with the policies, procedures, and terms of access of a given archive. For example, at the UNH Archives, the policies and procedures are outlined in a document that the researcher signs prior to working in the archives; the document focuses especially on how researchers should handle, obtain copies, and secure the "right to publish" archival materials. Understanding these policies early in the research process helps researchers prepare for the workday itself—to bring the proper note-taking materials, to gain access to materials stored in alternate facilities, and to plan for expenses related to archival research such as travel, length of research time, and photocopying documents.[8]

Part of knowing the archive is locating and accessing materials in the archive itself. Though I had some prior experience exploring the established archive before I started my dissertation research and had accessed online lists of finding aids telling me what materials I could expect to see, I found that I still needed to learn more about the archive itself, its structure, policies, and procedures, and the staff working daily in the archive to help me negotiate the distance between my research questions—what I wanted to know—and the artifacts that would give me answers or lead to more, nuanced questions. Another important part of knowing the archive is researching the archive in its local context, not only its specific policies and procedures but also its theoretical underpinnings and priorities. These factors affect the type and scope of archival collections and whether the researcher needs to pursue local resources beyond the archive. I developed the four principles described above by spending a significant amount of time in the local site of the UNH Archives.[9] Given that many researchers do not live in proximity to the archives they explore, I present these principles to provide researchers with initial points of consideration as they enter new archival spaces.

Approaches to archival research must be built, in part, in response to the local archive itself. Each archive has its own distinctive structures, strictures, procedures, and policies, and exploring materials as well as taking note of organizing features specific to a given archive are vital activities for archival researchers. As Gesa Kirsch comments, "being there physically, both in the archives and actual location where the historical subject lived, is invaluable. There are many things I would not have been able to explore virtually or online" (20). I have endeavored to provide specific suggestions for approaching archival research, shaped by my experiences working in the UNH Archives, but these suggestions are generalizable only to a point because the pragmatics of archival research are inextricably linked to the local archival context, and a researcher must negotiate strategies that fit within these local contexts as well.

When we choose to conduct archival research, it is because we have a passion for the work and the questions that are pushing us to find answers. Archival research can be exhilarating in the wake of a new discovery, but the overall research experience can be a slow, even painstaking, search for insight amid folders and boxes. A challenge in archival research is learning to negotiate the seeming idiosyncratic nature of an unfamiliar (or even a familiar) archive in pursuit of answers to our questions while remaining open to new directions that the artifacts might take us. Such pursuits take a great deal of time. Understanding—and adding to—the principles of archival research that I have outlined can help researchers navigate local archives more efficiently and lead the field of rhetoric/composition to serendipitous insights we might not otherwise have.

Notes

1. As we developed the materials, this work expanded to include other UNH writing programs as well. For a fuller account of this partnership, see Cinthia Gannett, Elizabeth Slomba, Katherine E. Tirabassi, Amy Zenger, and John C. Brereton, "'It Might Come in Handy': Composing a Writing Archive at the University of New Hampshire: A Collaboration between the Dimond Library and the Writing Across the Curriculum/Connors Writing Center, 2001–2003." *Centers for Learning: Libraries and Writing Centers in Collaboration* (Chicago: Association of College and Research Libraries Publications in Librarianship, 2005), 115–34.

2. See Katherine E. Tirabassi, "Revisiting the 'Current-Traditional Era': Innovations in Writing Instruction at the University of New Hampshire, 1940–1949," Diss. University of New Hampshire, 2007.

3. There are moments, of course, when these principles of selectivity change, due to theoretical shifts in a field; in her work with the writing program archive, UNH Archivist Elizabeth Slomba notes that her field is just beginning to recognize student writing as valuable artifacts to be preserved. Her work with the team to develop a writing program archive helped her to see the importance of student writing to the field of composition:

> In some archival literature, archivists are encouraged to collect student papers to document student life on campus. But in practice, there is a tacit bias against collecting papers because they are difficult to collect, do not have inherent research value as secondary sources, and do not immediately reflect in themselves the student experience. But what Cinthia, John, Kate and Amy were advocating was the collection of papers for documenting both the process of writing as well as the textual products and along with evidence of writing pedagogies. This triangulation of materials made a difference in my understanding of the desirability of collecting all levels and stages of student work along with other program materials. And it also emphasized the advantages of studying writing in a university or college archive because the whole process could be studied from course development, to the kinds of specific genres assigned, to the resulting papers and teacher's responses and evaluations. (Gannett, Slomba, Tirabassi, Zenger, and Brereton 123)

4. Through her example of researching the origin of the entrance exam for first-year composition, Mirtz provides a useful methodology for reading archival documents: considering authorship of the document when available, looking for the existence of documents in different departments or locations, and then analyzing the trails of history that researchers can find in the lines of each document (124). For further information on reading archival materials, see the series of articles by John C. Brereton, Linda Ferreira-Buckley, and Stephen Mailloux, "Archivists with an Attitude," *College English* 61.5 (1999): 574–90.

5. According to archivist Richard Pearce-Moses, original order is defined by the field as "the organization and sequence of records established by the creator of the records." Pearce-Moses explains that original order "is a fundamental principal of archives" because "it preserves existing relationships and evidential significance that can be inferred from the context of the records," and "it exploits the record creator's mechanisms to access the records, saving the archives the work of creating new access tools." In describing the development of the UNH writing program archive, Amy Zenger and Katherine E. Tirabassi note that as the group prepared materials to be sent to the UNH Archives, its members learned more about the program they were part of as a result of original order "because the way documents are ordered can reveal a great deal about how the creators and users envisioned their own work" (127–28).

6. Susan Miller, in her discussion of the challenges of negotiating the "spotty texts" in an archive, points out that "unless a relevant archive . . . is well-catalogued to guide a researcher to examples of assignments and student writing that are proofs for *one* perspective on this hypothesis, an archive is a difficult place to be" (2).

7. Categories other than the ones outlined here do not fit within this listing; however, these general categories were the main organizing features that I identified while researching in the archives and that proved useful as I cross-referenced materials.

8. See Lynée Lewis Gaillet, "Archival Survival," in the current collection for a discussion of policies and procedures in the archive. In my experience, the policies and procedures of the archives helped to shape my research methodology, due to specific rules regarding how documents could be accessed, handled, reproduced, and the like.

9. Because I did not have to travel far to the archives, I was limited only by the hours of operation and by the time constraints of my project.

Works Cited

Brereton, John C. "Rethinking Our Archive: A Beginning." *College English* 61.5 (May 1999): 574–76.

Coffin, Robert P. Robert P. Tristram Coffin, 1892–1955, Papers 1910–55. MC 46, Box 1. University of New Hampshire, Special Collections, Durham, NH.

Connors, Robert J. "Dreams and Play: Historical Method and Methodology." *Methods and Methodology in Composition Research.* Ed. Gesa Kirsch, and Patricia A. Sullivan. Carbondale: Southern Illinois UP, 1992. 15–36.

Eddy, Edward. Letter to Mrs. Arthur S. Adams. 5 October 1951. Edward Eddy Papers. UA 2-2-3. University of New Hampshire University Archives, Durham, NH.

Ferreira-Buckley, Linda. "Linda Ferreira-Buckley Responds." *College English* 62.4 (March 2000): 528–30.

———. "Rescuing the Archives from Foucault." *College English* 61.5 (May 1999): 577–83.

Gannett, Cinthia, Elizabeth Slomba, Katherine E. Tirabassi, Amy Zenger, and John C. Brereton. "'It Might Come in Handy': Composing A Writing Archive at the University of New Hampshire: A Collaboration between the Dimond Library and the Writing Across the Curriculum/Connors Writing Center, 2001–2003." *Centers for Learning: Libraries and Writing Centers in Collaboration.* Chicago: Association of College and Research Libraries Publications in Librarianship, 2005. 115–34.

Kirsch, Gesa. "The Importance of Location: Place, Serendipity, and Archival Research." *Beyond the Archives.* Ed. Kirsch and Liz Rohan. Carbondale: Southern Illinois UP, 2008. 20–27.

Mailloux, Steven. "Reading Typos, Reading Archives." *College English* 61.5 (May 1999): 584–90.

Miller, Susan. "X-Files in the Archive." *Peitho* 8.1 (Fall 2003): 1–4.

Mirtz, Ruth M. "WPAs as Historians: Discovering a First-Year Writing Program by Researching its Past." *The Writing Program Administrator as Researcher.* Ed. Shirley Rose and Irwin H. Weiser. Portsmouth, NH: Heinemann, 119–30.

Pearce-Moses, Richard. "Original Order." *A Glossary of Archival and Records Terminology.* Archival Fundamentals Series II. Chicago: Society of American Archivists, 2005. *Society of American Archivists.* 15 July 2007 <http://www.archivists.org/glossary/term_details.asp?DefinitionKey=69>.

Steedman, Carol. *Dust: The Archive and Cultural History.* Piscataway, NJ: Rutgers UP, 2002.

Tirabassi, Katherine E. "Revisiting the 'Current-Traditional Era': Innovations in Writing Instruction at the University of New Hampshire, 1940–1949." Diss. U of New Hampshire, 2007.

Writers' Conference. F.15, brochures 1938–45, series 4: brochures, box 1, Writers' Conference Files, 1935–1962 (UA 17/6), Miscellaneous Units (UA 17) Subgroups, University of New Hampshire Archives, Durham, NH.

———. F.16, brochures 1946–61, series 4: brochures, box 1, Writers' Conference Files, 1935–1962 (UA 17/6), Miscellaneous Units (UA 17) Subgroups, University of New Hampshire Archives, Durham, NH.

(EN)GENDERING THE ARCHIVES FOR BASIC WRITING RESEARCH

Kelly Ritter

> I analyze a frankly male tradition. Sometimes the people quoted here
> wrote as though they considered women to be part of humanity, and
> sometimes they wrote as if they did not. My decision to write about a male
> tradition does not mean that I am not forwarding a feminist agenda.
> —*Sharon Crowley,* Composition in the University

> Rhetoric and composition scholars have been making use of an
> archive assembled by others, with other purposes in mind.
> —*John C. Brereton, "Rethinking Our Archive: A Beginning"*

I am new to the work of the archives. I became interested in researching the
past—specifically the early twentieth century—while re-reading James Berlin's
Rhetoric and Reality when I happened upon Berlin's quick note mentioning the
"Awkward Squad" at Yale in the 1920s. The Awkward Squad was the label given
(by Yale faculty) to the students who placed into basic (remedial) writing there—
students who took drill courses in grammar and style "off the books" until they
could meet the institutional expectations for writing and be allowed back into
"regular" first-year English literature courses. I was fascinated by this stratified
notion of writing instruction—especially at Yale. As a teacher of basic writing at
primarily urban, public institutions, I wanted to understand this decidedly elite,
male tradition of basic writing and put that instruction in the context of what
basic writing pedagogy means today. So I headed to the Yale University archives,
just a few miles down the road, to find out more.

As a woman researcher into this somewhat alien world of men's-only writing, I tried in the summer of 2006 to create a cohesive story out of a great number of dirty, ragged, yet pristinely indexed and catalogued documents related to first-year writing in Yale's manuscripts and archives collection. I sat quietly among other scholars, all of whom were set upon the same general detective work as myself—piecing together clues about the past from the displaced locale of the present—but none of whom were *composition* scholars, I thought, as I peered casually over their shoulders. Some were sprawled over maps of antiquity; some were holding magnifying glasses to yellowed manuscripts written in other languages. Others were furiously typing notes on their laptops while balancing three or four books in their laps, fiercely protecting their findings. But no one was talking; no one was noticing me, either, as I wandered, a little aimlessly, back to a seat in the far reaches of the reading room, near the oscillating fan. My nervousness—(*Am I the only one who sweats in the summer?* Apparently.)—led me to other questions, ones that very much resemble the questions we often ask ourselves when we first begin to teach. Am I the only one here who is a visitor, who doesn't have some "legitimate" affiliation with this institution? Does anyone know that *I* don't know what I am doing? Or, to put it more boldly, am I the only *imposter* in the room?

My feelings of loneliness in that elongated, musty room—and my growing paranoia that my archival research was not nearly as legitimate as these other scholars' work—may have been a symptom of something larger—akin to John C. Brereton's comment about the relationship of the archives to rhetoric and writing. As a writing teacher, I felt not only a little lonely, missing the lively exchanges of my classrooms of writers, but also in uncharted research territory—to be at work on such an investigative project without the lively input of other composition and rhetoric scholars nearby, physically or virtually. The archives are a place of hallowed silence, often with no phones, Internet, or other connections to the modern world (yes, they allow laptops, in an odd way privileging the clean, streak-free shine of computer notetaking to the buzz of pens and paper, which may pollute or even ruin the archival materials altogether). And no personal effects—kind of like how prison must be, I thought, or high school gym class. All my belongings had to stay in a neat, little space just outside the reading room. In a gesture that harkened to nicer, simpler times, the surprisingly friendly staff attendant kept a stash of quarters for scholars who lacked the necessary money for the coin-operated lockers. If you borrowed the quarter, you gave it back after the locker spat it out and released your belongings. I wondered how many times that same quarter had been used and for what research. Did Jerome Karabel, for example, use that quarter to research into the anti-Semitic practices of Yale's admissions for his book *The Chosen*? Did George Pierson use that quarter to complete his two-volume, seminal history of Yale? How long had that quarter been jangling around, exactly? How long do the archives hold their accidental artifacts before letting them return to the open world?

I asked myself this last question, and ask it still today, because as a composition scholar, I found the archives a mysterious, secretive place—a club to which I had been granted temporary, if not full, membership. In addition to feeling alone in my historical query, I also had a difficult time tracing a clear, linear path to any information about basic writing at Yale, given the documents I culled from the archives for review. As Susan Wells notes, the archive often "resists knowledge in a number of ways. It refuses closure; often, it simply refuses any answer at all" (58). I, too, deduced that there was a clear resistance to closure in the scattering of documents that I found, none of which spoke directly to what I wanted to know about first-year writing, let alone basic writing. Importantly, there was *no* archive for the English department or for first-year writing itself. Nearly every other department had a box of archives (or multiple boxes) but not English.

My past perceptions of the openness of composition's history—and its collegial, shared present—was swiftly contradicted by this glaring absence of documentation regarding Yale's own first-year writing histories and larger English department. This was quite unlike the copious documents in Harvard's archives—as detailed by David Joliffe in his own archival reconstruction of student writing in the nineteenth century at Harvard. Joliffe's study was, in many ways, a more difficult undertaking: to analyze the themes (compositions) written by Harvard students in order to ascertain their social and political attitudes toward what Joliffe terms a "morality of instruction." But he had primary materials to work with; his search allowed for textual analysis to take place. Comparatively, I was hoping to find departmental curricular committee notes (or something equivalent), records of the construction of the Awkward Squad course, group, or classification, or, ideally, student accounts of participation in the course or discussions of its value (or lack thereof). No such luck.

Instead, I had to reconstruct a history of basic writing at Yale by thinking "outside the box," to use that corporate cliché. And what a box it was—with solid sides and hidden trap doors. Begin a search with "composition" and "Yale" in the online archival records—nothing. Try searching for "basic writing" and "Yale"—still nothing. Realizing that I was using modern terms to do distinctly unmodern work (a lesson of the archives for a scholar of the present like myself), I tried "remedial" and "Yale." Found some things—in related databases—but none of them archival, and none of them housed at or written by Yale divisions or officials. Finally, I *eliminated* composition-related search terms altogether and used "admissions" and "Yale," or "first year" and "Yale," or "undergraduate education" and "Yale." *Now* I got somewhere. Hence, the first lesson learned: Composition scholars, don't call it what it *is*; while scholars in other fields—literature, history, philosophy—may have their own clearly labeled archives, especially at elite institutions where our work is not a "subject," we do not have such luxuries of documentation. Instead, compositionists traversing the archives at such institutions must walk in a large circle *around* where key documents might be hidden, then move in smaller, concentric circles, closing in on the small scrap that might bear some archival fruit. Particularly for scholars working with early-twentieth-century or late-nineteenth-century archival materials, remember to consider past parlance for first-year writing. It's not "basic," it's "remedial" (or "hospital," or "dummy," or "zero" English, as Andrea Lunsford and Mike Rose have shown in their own historical work). Writing teachers who think not only in that perpetual present but forward to the future, the outcomes of today's writing projects, must in the archives reconstruct themselves as detectives of the past, which includes the pejorative past and all its labels. In doing this detective work, I thought immediately of that old comedy sketch "Think like a Phonebook." It's not "clothing," it's "apparel." Makes perfect sense.

Second lesson: Composition scholars cannot do archival work alone, just as in our larger professional lives. We need help from the inside. In writing program administration, for example, this help may be most readily found not in one's historical department but in the admissions office, the dean's office, the registrar, other departments—roundabout but valuable sources and locations. In archival work, the most obvious source—the archives themselves—similarly may not yield results. One needs an interpreter, an interloper who lives intimately on the inside of the institution but away from its academically driven biases and political locations (*Remedial Composition? Eek! We don't DO that here . . .*). My insider came in the form of Diane Kaplan, the director of Yale's archives, who rushed to my rescue just as I was about to throw in the towel and leave with the two pages of notes about the curricular offerings in first-year writing between 1920 and 1955 that I had gleaned from studying Yale undergraduate course catalogues (which cannot lie; they are contractual, as well as historical, fixed records of presence and absence).

Diane encouraged me to look at archival documents constructed elsewhere in the university to reconstruct what *may* have been the conditions for basic writers and basic writing at Yale from the perspectives of those other stakeholders in the process (dean, provost, president, scheduling officers). Diane helped me form those predatory-like circles around broad swaths of information in hopes of finding a few good traces of history in Yale's composition and rhetoric experiences. In doing so, Diane allowed me to conclude that the trajectory of first-year writing, especially basic writing, has *always* been intensely political; when no direct or primary documents would tell me about its institutional history at Yale, surely its ancillary documents, those which spoke of its budgeting, its faculty involvement, its curricular import schoolwide, would tell the tale.

Some of the types of documents are detailed below. These documents were housed in nonobvious places, such as the files of the dean and the president, the undergraduate admissions files, and, in one case, a private collection of student papers.

- *Memos* between the English department chair(s) and the dean, and/or the dean and the president. These memos were frequently cordial exchanges about staffing, budgets, or other faculty accomplishments (such as "congratulations to Professor X on the publication of his fine volume on DeFoe"). Other times, the memos were barely polite back-and-forth conversations about a troublesome faculty member or another departmental problem. Given that many of these problems concerned staffing the courses "nobody wants" (first-year writing), I was able to glean quite a bit of context and history from reading these memos and letters, as they discussed first-year writing as part of a larger problem or the end product of another, that is, student literacy concerns. Composition scholars must be willing to slog through these often lengthy exchanges and pull out the useful slivers of evidence. For example, a long letter about Professor Henry Canby, who in 1932 apparently wanted to reduce his teaching load, involved a discussion of how relieving him of his duties would compromise the overall staffing picture, including having to "omit provision for the Awkward Squad."
- *Annual reports* to and from the president. These invariably include the dollar amounts allocated for staffing courses, including first-year writing, as well as important figures such as enrollment numbers, number of students who failed a particular course, and sometimes grade distribution. Any composition scholar seeking an overall view of the state of a writing program at a particular historical marker can use these numbers to paint a larger picture of things.
- *Administrative documents* from university curriculum committees and other similar bodies. Sometimes, these committees have special names depending upon the subject—for example, the Committee on the Use of English by Students at Harvard. At Yale, more general curriculum committee files at the university level yield results, such as sample syllabi from the Basic Skills courses for the Army Specialized Training program, which included an early basic writing syllabus from the mid-1940s.
- *Sample student papers*, not from any English department archival collections but from the private collected papers of alumni. These were few and far between—and time-consuming to locate. I found few samples that I could use, one being a very nonfascinating paper on the poem "Low Barometer" written for English 15 (the literature-composition course at Yale) in 1953. This

student's collected papers also included his informal writing from preparatory school (in England) and some other exams. In sum, they did not help me significantly, but scholars in the archives should know that many alumni may keep their early papers in the archives.

- *Sample placement examinations* as well as sample entrance exams from the United States Armed Forces Institute and the University of Chicago Scholarship Exam, designed to determine higher-level placements in English literature as well as other subjects. Again, these documents were not archived by the English department but by the Records and Reports of the Office of Institutional Research. Current scholars may believe that "Institutional Research" only became an office in the university's current assessment craze. Not so. Yale's OIR had volumes of records, many pertaining to placement and admission, such as the examinations above and many cross-indexed with organizations such as ETS.

- *Articles* about Yale and first-year students, such as "The Brightest Ever," written by Katherine Kinkead in 1960 and archived under Yale's Office of Public Affairs. Scholars working in the archives and seeking materials about mass-required subjects such as first-year composition should consider what delving into these publicity files might garner. As we know, many a university reputation is built on the success or failure of its general education curriculum. Kinkead's article gave me a valuable context for the curricular developments happening at Yale during this time; in addition, I was able to access memos regarding the article, correspondence with Kinkead, and other related documents by searching through the public-affairs archival records.

As I read through these widely categorized, inner-sanctum documents and memos, I not only observed the lack of *direct* attention to first-year writing as a subject, let alone a scholarly endeavor on campus (a finding that did not surprise me, but I was eternally hopeful that my expectations would be overturned), but I also observed the total lack of women's involvement in this reconstructed history. Third lesson learned: The archives make a female scholar, especially a composition scholar—one who spends her life making meaning of writing as a path to identity—look at herself more closely and find that self objectified through history. In other words, I have always assumed that writing teachers are doing some agreed-upon, universal "good" in their work. Regardless of our gender or our "social standing," writing instruction is *good* work, not tempered by who we are socially or demographically. But I remembered myself in this work—remembered that I have "grown up" in composition studies benefiting from a highly liberal, democratized field since the 1970s. This position of particular subjectivity caused me to initially be limited in my archival research—unable to understand, for example, why there were no files for the writing program at Yale, let alone the English department. I had not understood, or had not been able to understand, what earlier *versions* of composition instruction looked like or for whom they were created. I expected volumes of information from an English studies/composition studies perspective, which in my experience, was also significantly created and maintained by women.

Instead, I found myself staring for inordinate periods of time at the handwritten correspondence that had been dictated to women to type for formal distribution to other male faculty and administrators, who were doing the "real" work in the field at this particular institution during this time period. I found myself wondering, therefore, was I the only Woman besides the secretary who had ever looked at these documents? And if so, why was that—especially because composition studies has, in my lifetime, been a field of women scholars, researchers, as well as teachers. Had no woman ever sought to interpret these documents before?

I tried to put this potential discovery in the context of how I had been trained to view composition studies—as someone who came to the field from creative writing, where gender ascriptions are less pronounced in favor of other political demarcations associated with the cultivation of "talent" (read: breeding, training, external and internal patronage of one's work). I knew that a traditional cultural label for the teaching of first-year composition—"tradition" encompassing notions of the pejorative, in its effort to maintain a practice that does not disrupt the status quo—has been "women's work." This label, however, as publicized and politicized by Sue Ellen Holbrook, has come to stand for renewed power and agency for women in composition studies—scholars, teachers, researchers—who are acutely aware of their positioned history in this heavily gender-coded field. The root of this label is academia's view of the teaching of first-year composition as a labor-intensive but critical duty of irritatingly enormous proportions, much like the mothering of numerous small children. Such a duty is best relegated to women whereas the "serious" work of teaching literature (and other subjects that are truly "about" something), the site of ideology, free-thinking, and philosophy, is best suited to men.

As Alice Gillam argues in "Feminism and Composition Research: Researching as a Woman," such a dichotomy can be attributed to "the equivocal term feminization, a term that can be read as meaning either a female takeover of composition or a composition takeover of the feminine" (48). I felt, in the archives, as if I were embarking on that "female takeover" in a particularly hostile—if inanimate—environment. Citing Elizabeth Flynn, Gillam notes further that Flynn's notion of "feminization" is "not equivalent to a feminist presence in composition discourse" (48). In other words, deconstructing and claiming the field of composition studies, for women, are Catch-22s: If we overtly claim the field for research and scholarship, it becomes highly feminized and thus marginalized by definition, but if we reject ownership of the field and equally overtly attribute masculine attributes to its methodologies, it becomes less gender coded but also less powerful as an arena of significantly women's work, in the positivist sense. Susan Miller argues that this is why "composition professionals have found it entirely reasonable, if not entirely successful, to redefine their hitherto blurred identity in more crisply masculine, scientific, terms" (123).

Perhaps because higher education in general and composition and rhetoric specifically have made these rather enormous strides in the last forty years, we often don't stop to consider what was happening, politically speaking, to the ultramarginalized world of basic writing before even *women* were allowed into its negatively constructed confines—that is, before composition itself was a discipline. More to the point, we rarely consider how it is for women to now reconstruct that all-male history in a field where the research, writing, and publishing of seminal documents that will characterize the field for the next generation of researchers and scholars are frequently done *by* these very women. This realization is part of the third lesson for new composition studies archival historians like myself: in order to understand the history that you seek to uncover, you must denounce your complicit ignorance *of* that history and recreate what has been lost, even if what results is in direct conflict with how and why the field is operating today.

As a woman researcher—one who never attended an Ivy League institution and one who works at an institution of more than 60 percent women students and faculty—I was also struck by my own emotions that arose when I encountered archival documents from this historical phenomenon, the pre–"women's work." Like Crowley, I encountered a set of documents that, in their rhetorical aggregate, sometimes did not seem to consider women "part of humanity." Also like Crowley, by investigating these documents and reflecting on their effect on me as a scholar, I believe I am now considering a more "feminist agenda" than I had previously envisioned when first undertaking this research. Now, I want to approach these archives that, in Susan Wells's words, are "full of echoes" where I must "suture together the relation between one text and another" (55) as the primary (historical) and secondary (political) meanings of these materials are often at odds with one another.

In particular, I have come to a secondary—though by no means less important—argument in my archival research. Though historical research such as mine has its cause rooted in the discussion and dissemination of essentially "men's work" during one portion of composition studies history (i.e., roughly 1920 to 1960) and its impact on the modern history of basic writing at selective institutions, *the reflection* on that research process can also be of value to other scholars—women scholars in particular. Every time we bring research to our composition studies community, diverse in its needs and interests as it is, we need to think about *audience*. What kind of rhetors would we be otherwise? Investigating my own investigation of these archives—a kind of meta-analysis of the archival work—is a means by which I can reconsider these particular historical documents and their various audiences from a gendered, ergo inherently political perspective. And perhaps such a perspective can raise new questions about how and why we choose our historical research subjects and the ways in which we need to prepare ourselves for historical research in which our "selves" may be absent altogether.

Thus, I believe my research was affected by my identity as a reader—a woman, for whom these documents, memos, curricular plans, were *not* written and by whom they were never supposed to be seen. Perhaps giving readers a sense of a few key documents that I encountered in the Yale archives will provide some perspective on what is like to spy—and I use that word deliberately, to invoke the violation of boundaries and transcending of intended communications and confidences—into one setting for the all-male world of basic writing.

Here are some examples of the specific archival documents that caught my attention as I was doing my research in the Yale archives:

1. A faculty member who, after being denied tenure in Yale's English department in the mid-1930s, lamented that this meant he would have to teach at a "girl's school" for "much lower pay," thereby not only jeopardizing the financial welfare of his family but also his own career path—that is, that the girl's school was less career-worthy than his current position at Yale. He cites these as primary reasons for why he should be renewed/reinstated in Yale's English department. This memo I found among the records of the chairman, in otherwise pedestrian files detailing reappointments and awards of tenure. This faculty member was characterized as somewhat disgruntled for his complaint—but not a word was said to contradict his perception that a "girl's school" would, indeed, be a step down on the food chain. Such a research finding echoes another memo I later found when working in the Harvard archives, wherein a professor requests an assignment to English A (first-year writing) at Radcliffe, so that he might "try his hand at teaching girls," as if it were a new and amusing hobby, like stamp collecting.[1]

2. A bulletin from the late 1950s, published by the College Board (now ETS) but included in the Yale newspaper and archived in the files of the English department, that forwarded a proposal that the reading and grading of "freshman themes" should be done by "housewives" with college degrees, as a way to parse out the arduous labor associated with the teaching of writing (i.e., the *reading* of student writing). This document surprised me because I did not immediately see its connection to Yale, other than its publication in the Yale newspaper. But after some further thought, I realized that this news release fit into the archival

materials perfectly, as it reflected (if accidentally) the beginning of the end of "gentleman's" instruction in first-year writing. This news release served as the icing on the cake, the cake being represented by lament after lament in the archives—from the chair to the dean, the dean to the president—about the taxing, backbreaking work of grading "freshman themes." Such work took time away from the valuable work of literary instruction for these *scholarly men*. Such work was relegated to the faculty of the freshmen year, a male faculty of mostly junior professors and lecturers (or the pre-1950s equivalent). Around the time of this news release, the climate for research versus teaching was shifting to allow for the 2/2 (or less) teaching load now present in the Ivy League. I believe that the call to shift such menial tasks to "housewives" signaled the beginning of the end of overworked men teaching writing.

3. The visual representation of the Yale English department in 1924—a solemn photograph of about thirty men between the ages of twenty-five and seventy—published in the Yale English Department newsletter of that year. The men look intently at the camera, stately and formal in their appearance, collective in their presence. This is less a group of *faculty* than a group of *distinguished men*. Long before scholars were thinking or writing about visual rhetoric, the photographer for this newsletter was surely thinking about the photographic presence of these men *as* the English Department itself. I was thinking about what these scholars would think of *me*, jeans-clad, dusty, girly me, looking at their pristine, posed photograph. Would I have even been *good* enough to teach their young men how to write?

4. The same newsletter's standing column, entitled "Father to Son," which included a letter of sendoff from a father *and mother* to their son, entering Yale, about his upcoming college experiences:

> When you receive this you will have attained your majority—the time when boys are conventionally supposed to take on the responsibilities of manhood. In other words, you have technically at least, ceased to be *our* boy and have become *your own man*. There is something inexpressibly sad to us in the thought; and if we did not realize that *our boy* is passing into good hands as he becomes *your man*, we should find it difficult to be reconciled to the change. . . . We love you not alone because you are our son, but because you have by every consideration of filial devotion and regard provided yourself worthy of it. (italics in original)

And so on . . . signed "your father and mother" (in the year 1899). Women and their concomitant social roles did not fit into this paradigm; the mother of this boy even appears as only a silent partner in the letter-writing enterprise. As a mother myself, I would feel slighted if I had to sign on to such a column and be such a silent agent in the creation of my child's intellectual identity. Again, such a heavily patriarchal tone echoes historian Samuel Eliot Morison's explanation of how those students relegated to remedial writing at Harvard in the 1920s were regarded by their tutor/instructor, who "takes in hand the pupils reported to him by various departments, gives them *fatherly advice,* and sees to it that they receive the steering that should be theirs" (70).

Of course, none of these documents themselves explicitly say "women excluded," but they do, in varying ways, create a world for men, by men, about men—or *gentlemen,* more acutely—with no future intention of being open or available to women readers. In addition, they allocate women very little space in these men's educational process, except to be approving mothers, at best, or silent workhorses, at worst, assigned to grade college writing from the secluded (and perhaps quite isolated) space of their own domestic spaces. These documents are the product of an age, to be certain, and are endemic of the culture much more than the discipline. But as archival documents that led me to other intellectual conclusions about basic writing, they redirected my research.

They caused me to consider what basic writing meant not only to Ivy League students of the time but also to *men* in general—especially the teaching of writing, the division of labor practices in writing, and the moral associations made between good writing and "good order" throughout the documents. Whether it was to account for returning servicemen in the 1940s who needed particular kinds of social and intellectual training based on their veteran and (implicitly) lower-intelligence status or whether it was to account for the increasing number of "less-prepared" men that Yale was forced to admit to stay financially afloat in the 1920s, first-year writing, archivally speaking, had as its central aim the intellectual *and* social growth of these young men in order that they be cleanly prepared for the higher-order task of literary analysis, the true province of men.

David Joliffe observes that Harvard composition students in the late nineteenth century were "urged to choose as their subject matter some aspect of contemporary manners or morals, to try to construct some ideological system to account for the phenomenon, and often to urge upon their readers a sense of what they see as their moral obligation for dealing with the issue at hand" (163). This is an interesting way to connect to the tone and register of the memos going between deans and chairs and deans and provosts in the early part of the twentieth century at Yale. I was struck by the rigorous formality of these exchanges—not because I expected the correspondence to start, "Hey Jim! What's up?" or be overloaded with modern slang or mannerisms. No, I was struck because the memos each had a significant amount of ethical appeals to them—that is, for the good and decency of the college, please allow Mr. X to remain on faculty, or please allow us $500.00 more for Project Y. Rarely did I see the politics of the larger university at play; instead, I primarily found men making appeals to other learned men, for the benefit of the young men taking the English courses and the only slightly older men teaching those courses.

For example, take this snippet of an annual report from 1929–30 that, rather than beginning with departmental needs or appeals, refers first to the retirement of an elderly dean:

> ... his manifold services to every important aspect of teaching, scholarship, and administration will find appropriate recognition throughout the whole University. Here, his closest colleagues within his own Department unite with one accord in voicing Loyal admiration of his distinguished accomplishment and deepest gratitude for their Privilege of intimate fellowship with him. (Nettleton, "Report")

The notion of "intimate fellowship" in particular is pervasive in the archival materials that I uncovered—a kind of unspoken gentlemen's bond that unites these chairs and administrators. I further find this sort of discourse jarring to read as a woman—as I believe my presence in this "intimate fellowship" was never intended nor particularly foreseen. Unlike the kind of mixed-sex bonds that might be formed at a public, coed university, Yale's male faculty were heralded in these documents as the sheer *embodiment* of the quality and value of the English department. As Nettleton puts it in the 1924 English department newsletter, "the Yale English Department is no more and no less than the men who make it" ("English" 1061). While I concede that every department is proud of its faculty, Nettleton emphasizes not these men's scholarship or teaching acumen but their simple *presence* (collectively, as represented in the group photograph on the page of this newsletter) as evidence of its "substance" ("English" 1061).

Ultimately, the ways in which this gendered reading of the archives affected my research were many. First, I began to think of the homogeneous population at Yale in the early twentieth century as not just of primarily one social class, or one race, but very much of one gender. I had deliberately wanted to research this population for its homogeneous properties, but I had not fully considered how an environment of writing that in no way included women could color the tenor and scope of that writing instruction, at least in interuniversity documents and policies. Second, stemming from this, I began to see myself in a unique position as a researcher—as a teacher of basic writing who had always taught in diverse, mixed-gender classrooms and who considered single-gender settings from the perspective of *women's* education but never men's. Finally, my experiences in the archives allowed me to translate the notion of "access" quite differently. No longer was my research primarily about class distinctions or issues of economic access or educational status. Now I was more fully considering how gender—and the aims of gendered instruction—indeed played a large role in the construction of these basic writing courses and—though this is speculative—may have contributed to their usually "secret" position in the curriculum, a curriculum of honor and good standing.

My archival experience has caused me to think carefully about Brereton's call to "begin asking what is missing from the archive and how it can get there" (574). But I mean to translate this call quite specifically as a call for missing perspectives *on* our archival material. We cannot change the facts when confronted with very specifically gender-coded materials such as the Yale archives; we cannot make women live and work where they were once excluded. But we *can* think about how that restricted history might open doors for us, as scholars, to reinterpret the histories of our field and ask, "What can we gain by confronting the discomfort we feel when these historical assumptions are overturned, if unexpectedly, by archival research?" As I continue to engender these archives for our basic writing historians, I hope to continue to be aware of how my position as a woman scholar in the present is a critical component in the search for and translation of our composing pasts.

Note

1. For more information on writing instruction at Radcliffe, see Sue Carter Simmons, "Radcliffe Responses to Harvard Rhetoric: 'An Absurdly Stiff Way of Thinking,'" and JoAnn Campbell, "Controlling Voices: The Legacy of English A at Radcliffe College 1883–1917."

Works Cited

Berlin, James. *Rhetoric and Reality: Writing Instruction in American Colleges, 1900–1985.* Carbondale: Southern Illinois UP, 1987.

Brereton, John C. "Rethinking Our Archive: A Beginning." *College English* 61.5 (May 1999): 574–76.

Campbell, JoAnn. "Controlling Voices: The Legacy of English A at Radcliffe College 1883–1917." *College Composition and Communication* 43.4 (1992): 472–85.

Crowley, Sharon. *Composition in the University: Historical and Polemical Essays.* Pittsburgh, PA: U of Pittsburgh P, 1998.

Gillam, Alice. "Feminism and Composition Research: Researching as a Woman." *Composition Studies/Freshman English News* 20.1 (1992): 47–54.

Harvard University. Robert Hillyer to Professor James B. Munn. June 4, 1935. UAV 363.123.6. Harvard University Archives, Cambridge, Massachusetts.

Holbrook, Sue Ellen. "Women's Work: The Feminizing of Composition." *Rhetoric Review* 9.2 (1991): 201–29.

Joliffe, David. "The Moral Subject in College Composition: A Conceptual Framework and the Case of Harvard, 1865–1900." *College English* 51.2 (February 1989): 163–73.

Karabel, Jerome. *The Chosen: The Hidden History of Admission and Exclusion at Harvard, Yale, and Princeton.* New York: Mariner, 2006.

Kinkead, Katherine. "The Brightest Ever." *New Yorker* 10 Sept. 1960: 132–81.

Lunsford, Andrea. "An Historical, Descriptive, and Evaluative Study of Remedial English in American Colleges and Universities." Diss. Ohio State U, 1977.

Miller, Susan. *Textual Carnivals: The Politics of Composition.* Carbondale: Southern Illinois UP, 1991.

Morison, Samuel Eliot. *The Development of Harvard University since the Inauguration of President Eliot 1869–1929.* Cambridge, MA: Harvard UP, 1930.

Nettleton, George H. "English at Yale." *Yale Alumni Weekly* 1924, 1061–63, Yale University Archives, New Haven, CT.

———. "Report of the English Department, Yale University, 1929–30." June 18, 1930. Yale University Archives, New Haven, CT.

Pierson, George Wilson. *Yale College: An Educational History 1871–1921.* New Haven, CT: Yale UP, 1952.

———. *Yale: The University College 1921–1937.* New Haven, CT: Yale UP, 1955.

Rose, Mike. "The Language of Exclusion: Writing Instruction at the University." *College English* 47.4 (1985): 341–59.

———. "Remedial Writing Courses: A Critique and a Proposal." *College English* 45.2 (1983): 109–28.

Simmons, Sue Carter. "Radcliffe Responses to Harvard Rhetoric: 'An Absurdly Stiff Way of Thinking.'" *Nineteenth-Century Women Learn to Write.* Ed. Catherine Hobbs. Charlottesville: UP of Virginia, 1995. 264–92.

Wells, Susan. "Claiming the Archive for Rhetoric and Composition." *Rhetoric and Composition as Intellectual Work.* Ed. Gary Olson. Carbondale: Southern Illinois UP, 2002. 55–64.

Yale University. "The Departmental Staff." Photo. "English at Yale." *Yale Alumni Weekly* 1924, 1061. Yale University Archives, New Haven, CT.

———. "Father to Son." *Yale Alumni Weekly* 1924, 1063. Yale University Archives, New Haven, CT.

———. "Fifth Annual Conference of Teachers of English." Press release. 5 April 1959. RU 22, box 84, folder 755, Yale University News Bureau. Yale University Archives, New Haven, CT.

———. Letter from Frederick Pottle to Henry Canby, November 15, 1932. YRG 3-A, series 1, box 21. Yale University Archives, New Haven, CT.

———. Phillips, Ivan. "Low Barometer: Robert Bridges." 1953. RU 916, box 1, folder 6. Yale University Archives, New Haven, CT.

ARCHIVAL RESEARCH AS A SOCIAL PROCESS

Neal Lerner

Many of my experiences conducting archival research have been intensely isolating. Deep in university libraries, opening dusty boxes and leafing through yellowed papers that haven't felt a human touch in decades, I experience the stark contrast with the qualitative research projects I've conducted in which social interactions— interviews, participant observation, talk—*are* the research methods. In archives, I feel alone as I strive to grasp the worlds of Robert Moore, a graduate student at the University of Illinois in the late 1940s, or Francis "Mike" Appel, the director of the University of Minnesota General College Writing Laboratory in the 1930s. These efforts have offered me only glimpses of what the authors might have been thinking through the material that has somehow made its way into the archives. I emerge from these long sessions with only a partial knowledge of these previous worlds and disoriented to my present one, akin to coming back home after extended travel, the familiar made strange by my absence, to paraphrase Clifford Gertz.

The isolated nature of archival research conjures up notions of isolated writers producing texts that are the products of a benevolent muse. While such romantic ideals have long been countered by what we know about the essential social nature of composing, the social world created by archival research is due a similar treatment. In other words, my sense of isolation while conducting archival research is illusory, more of a statement about that particular moment (myself, alone, in a university archive) than about the larger enterprise. What I have come to realize is that the social forces that shape archival research are many, from a researcher's experiences and expectations, to contemporary events, to the choices made by those who have donated papers to an archive, leading to fragments of information that even the best archive will offer. In other words, archival research is not merely about the artifacts to be found but is ultimately about the people who have played a role in creating and using those artifacts, whether their authors, their subjects, their collectors, their donators, their readers, or a host of other players in the social worlds represented.

For those new to archival research, understanding these many influences is essential, lest they imagine some *pure* narrative that an archive will offer. One danger is that archives themselves hold great evidentiary power to researchers and readers. As described by Paul Ricoeur,

> the document sleeping in the archives is not just silent, it is an orphan. The testimonies it contains are detached from the authors who "gave birth" to them. They are handed over to the care of those who are competent to question them and hence to defend them, by giving them aid and assistance. In our historical culture, the archive has assumed authority over those who consult it. (169)

Ricoeur warns that such power might lead researchers to conflate archives as "facts" with the varied stories archival materials might tell researchers. In Ricoeur's words, "A vigilant epistemology will guard . . . against the illusion of believing that what we call a fact coincides with what really happened, or with the living memory of eyewitnesses, as if the facts lay sleeping in the documents until the historians extracted them" (178).

In this chapter, my intent is to disrupt the sleep of the archives and describe the social process of archival research, drawing on my experiences at the University of Illinois and the University of Minnesota. In each of those settings, I was attempting to re-create social worlds as I traced the histories of particular writing clinics or laboratories and the people who were represented in those histories. And in each setting, I was faced with at-times-conflicting forces: the partial documentary history as represented in the archives, the motivations and purposes for those who collected those particular documents, and the narrative that I constructed as a reader of those materials. As archival research becomes a wider practice in composition studies, an understanding of the social process of researching is essential for a variety of reasons: for readers to judge the veracity of archival accounts, for future researchers to be best prepared for the task ahead, and for our research to reflect our values of collaboration and our belief in social-epistemic knowing.

Searching for Robert Moore

In "Dreams and Play: Historical Method and Methodology," Robert J. Connors writes, "Seldom does anyone plunge cold into the Archive without something to look for, something they're hoping to find, hoping to see proof of" (22). One key player, then, is the researcher him- or herself, given the power of the intents that one brings to bear on the act of archival research. For some researchers, these intents are a product of the contemporary world's particular narratives of the past. My research into writing center history, specifically of the Writing Clinic at the University of Illinois, was informed by this present and my desire to disrupt it. But my archival research at Illinois was also influenced by additional social players: the person I was trying to trace, the archivist himself and what he granted me access to, the university personnel who long ago made decisions about what papers to donate to the archives, and, ultimately, the president of the University of Illinois, who needed to rule on my Freedom of Information Act request to view those papers.

My search for this history started with Robert Moore, director of the Writing Clinic at the University of Illinois in the late 1940s. I first became aware of Moore through his widely republished 1950 *College English* article, "The Writing Clinic and the Writing Laboratory," in which Moore described the one-to-one teaching of writing as "remedial agencies for removing students' deficiencies in composition" (388). For many contemporary writing center scholars, Moore's account represents an era of reductive notions of the teaching of writing, a dark time of grammar drill assigned by authoritative teachers to submissive students (for more on Moore and the history of the University of Illinois Writing Clinic, see Lerner, "Searching"). My reading of educational history, however, leads me to believe in a cyclic notion of reform, particularly in the teaching of writing where pedagogical ideas published a hundred years ago sound remarkably contemporary. Full implementation of such innovative ideas has been tempered by structural realities, including a reliance on part-time, contingent labor and the dominance of classroom solutions to educational *problems*. I suspected there was a rich writing center history out there, in a sense, an historical narrative that would run counter to prevailing notions of what Robert Moore represented.

With my motivation set, I figured it was now merely a task of digging in the University of Illinois Archives to find the narrative I imagined. This narrative, however, proved to be fragmentary. My first inkling of this partiality came before my visit to Illinois. After some investigating, I was excited to find references to Moore in multiple editions of the *Directory of American Scholars*. There he was, starting with the 1978 edition, an emeritus professor of English at George Washington University and resident of 314 Van Buren Street in Falls Church, Virginia. I scrambled around to local libraries, tracking down more recent versions of the *Directory*, all the way to the 1999 edition. Yes, there was Moore again, still residing in Falls Church. I calculated that he must be eighty-eight years old, and I had a vision of a quiet tea with him, surrounded by his books and personal papers, to which, of course, he'd grant me full access, his soft voice still holding strong traces of his Kentucky roots, telling me of the early days of the Illinois Writing

Clinic. Shortly thereafter, I found another reference, this one to an obituary in the *Washington Post*. Moore died of cardiac arrest on New Year's Eve, 1984, four days shy of his seventy-second birthday.

Without direct access to Moore, I turned to the Illinois archives and its holdings on the Committee on Student English and the Writing Clinic that Moore directed. Over two intense days in the archives and library stacks, I found a great deal about the Writing Clinic at Illinois, pages and pages of meeting minutes and early summary reports on its creation and sustenance. But what about Moore himself? The records in the archives told me very little about Moore, a PhD student in English while he was directing the Writing Clinic. This bogeyman, whose writing about "student deficiencies" seemed to define an era for many, was proving elusive to me. The best I could do, it seemed, was to retrace some of the steps of Robert Moore and the Writing Clinic, to try and relive in an oddly vicarious way, Moore's own social world. So on a cool and rainy June day, I toured the Illinois campus, looking for Moore's addresses as listed in the university directory of his time. For 1938, Moore's listed address was 803 Indiana, which is now a two-story brick house on a tree-lined, brick-paved street a block from campus. Perhaps Moore rented a room here, perhaps the third-floor room with the dormer window that I could see from the street. He was only here one year. Then, he married his wife, Marjorie. They needed a bigger place or perhaps there was a rule against couples renting a room in this house.

In 1939, Moore and his wife moved to 806 South Third. What was likely 806 South Third is an empty lot now, between a building facing John Street and a seven-story newish-looking apartment building that faces Daniel Street. From 1940 until 1948, he was listed at 907½ West California. For the 1948–49 academic year, Moore and his wife moved to 909 West California. The 900 block of California is mostly taken up by two parking lots now, Lot D22 on the south side and Lot D11 on the north. Bob and Marjorie would have lived on the south side.

My other excursion to find Robert Moore was to visit the listed sites of the Writing Clinic. During Moore's year and a half as director, it was in 202 Lincoln Hall and then moved to 135 Lincoln Hall before it found a more permanent home at 311 English. In 202 Lincoln Hall, I found a computer lab, about a dozen PCs humming away and generating more heat than an old building can handle. It was a fairly large room, at least nine hundred square feet, so it was difficult to imagine that it was all devoted to the Writing Clinic, assuming it had not been reconfigured. More fitting was 135 Lincoln Hall, now a women's bathroom amid the faculty offices and classrooms of the Speech Communications Department. Professors' names are painted on to the frosted glass of the heavy walnut doors here, and it was not hard to see "Writing Clinic" stenciled on to 135 Lincoln Hall instead of "Women."

Thus, my tour revealed more gaps in my research: parking lots and empty spaces where apartment buildings had been, computer labs and empty desks where the Writing Clinic had first set up shop. I was again finding only traces of Robert Moore, and it was time to return home.

My last gasp attempt to search for Moore came from my efforts to get copies of his Illinois personnel file. The archivist at Illinois was extremely helpful; however, he was bound by an additional social force: state law that protected the privacy of state employees' personnel records (a law that evidently has no statute of limitations). Thus, to see Moore's records, I had to file a Freedom of Information Act request, and my initial attempt was turned down. Two months later, however, after an appeal directly to University of Illinois President James Stukel, I was granted access to "information that bears on the public duties of public employees." The assistant to the associate chancellor sent me seventeen pages of Moore's personnel file, running from his initial application for an instructor position in 1938 and a copy of his grade transcripts from his MA courses at Indiana University, to the "acceptance of [his] resignation" in 1949. I learned a little about Moore from these materials, including that he had worked as a police reporter for the *Louisville Times* in 1936 and that he could read French and had studied Latin. But there was little else I didn't already know from the material in the archives and the information I had pieced together previously. Everything that was potentially interesting—the "remarks" sections in the forms used to reappoint Moore as instructor—were blackened out in heavy marker.

Moore's Illinois Writing Clinic did tell me a great deal about one early writing center, far earlier than many would guess such places existed, about the persistence of such places (the Illinois Writing Clinic was in operation from the late 1940s until the early 1980s), and about the work conducted in that clinic, which was not particularly different than the tutoring in writing that goes on in contemporary writing centers. I did have some evidence to counter those who might position writing centers as relatively recent or with an unfortunate past. However, rather than what they told me about Moore, those blackened-out comments on his personnel forms were more revealing of what I did not know—and still do not know—about Robert Moore and writing center history. Thus, my attempt to set the record straight only resulted in an even more complex record, and my search for Robert Moore offers a cautionary tale about the influence of what researchers bring to their attempts to understand composition history through archival research and the social forces that produce those archives, particularly in regard to what records get archived and how access to those records is controlled.

Connors invokes Kenneth Burke's idea of "terministic screens" to describe the powerful filters through which we sift archival research (21). In Connors's words, "We may not always be able to see all of our own terministic screens, certainly, but then again we cannot claim to know all of current reality or to have found all the possible archival sources" (21). I think of Jim W. Corder's book *Lost in West Texas*, in which my favorite chapter heading is "History Is Fiction, except for the Parts That I Like, Which Are, of Course, True." Our filters as researchers work in parallel with additional filters, a veritable purification process of social forces: the choices made by those who donate institutional and personal records, the choices made by those who collect and grant access to those records, and the choices we make as researchers in terms of what to examine and what motivates us to do so. Connors writes, "[The] archive is where storage meets dreams, and the result is history" (17). Whose dreams, of course, Connors does not specify, but the multitude of dreamers when it comes to writing center and composition history create rich possibilities and need to be accounted for in archival studies.

Present and Past at the University of Minnesota

Dreamers, of course, are not limited to those who study history. Higher education's past is also filled with those who dream of reform to current realities to bring about an ideal of educational practice. My research into the origins of the University of Minnesota General College Writing Laboratory was sparked by the desire to study one such dreamer, Malcolm MacLean, the first director of the General College, and the Progressive-era ideals that he instituted at Minnesota. A contemporary reform, however, provided a counterpoint to this search: During the time of my research in 2005, the General College was in the process of being shut down, a seventy-four-year experiment in developmental education succumbing to those who dream of *excellence* and *standards* and *exclusivity*. The social force of the present did, indeed, have an effect on my search for the past in this instance, though it was not my initial motivating force. I was just trying to understand an early, interesting-sounding writing laboratory, one that would offer more evidence that early writing centers were far more than sick wards for students suffering from the disease of bad writing (see Lerner, "'Laboring'").

First, some background on the experiment at Minnesota. The General College was founded in 1932 by University President Lotus Coffman, who felt that "the road to intellectual opportunity should never be closed" to any student (qtd. in Gray 309). As a two-year college within the university system, the General College was designed to attract students who were not succeeding in the four-year system or had not previously have thought of themselves as college material. In the face of the Great Depression, faith in higher education to provide solutions to societal problems took on increasing fervor, and Progressive-era ideals informed a general education movement that worked to shed higher education's legacy as primarily the stomping grounds of the privileged elite. Coffman hired Malcolm MacLean, whose PhD in English was from Minnesota and who had participated in experimental programs at the University of Wisconsin. MacLean established a college that was "to awaken in its students a social and civic consciousness, a sense of community responsibility, and a willingness to participate actively in the solution of common problems for the common good" ("Organization of the General College" 30).

When it came to instruction in writing, MacLean knew from experience that traditional composition classrooms were not going to work for the nontraditional students at the General College. Instead, consistent with the hands-on, experiential teaching and learning in other courses, teaching first-year English would be done in a Writing Laboratory with voluntary attendance and no grammar-drill workbooks in sight. Francis A. "Mike" Appel, the faculty director of the Writing Laboratory, described its procedures in a 1935 letter to Ena Marston of Saint Helen's Hall Junior College in Portland, Oregon:

> The procedure, then, is simply that of having the students write for two consecutive hours each week in a room equipped with special chairs and desks. During the laboratory period the instructor tours the class and confers with each student in turn. He may answer questions concerning the papers returned corrected to the student, or he may read part or all of the paper which the student is writing at the moment. Errors are corrected as they arise. No drills in grammar are assigned. (1)

When I first read about this writing-workshop approach, roughly thirty-five years before the writing workshop was promoted in composition literature, I felt a powerful connection to a historical past. Just as I hoped to discover with my research into Robert Moore, Minnesota seemed to offer compelling evidence that early-twentieth-century teaching of writing was far more sophisticated than is often assumed. However, by the time I made the first of two visits to the university archives to look for more details of the General College Writing Laboratory, my connection was disrupted by the forces of the present. In 2005, the University of Minnesota's Board of Regents endorsed a report calling for the General College to be dissolved and most of its functions integrated into the College of Education and Human Development:

> Changing demographics and the changing needs of an increasingly diverse student population have pushed [the existing] structure [of the General College] beyond its capacity and require the transformation of organizational structures that will assure not only access, but educational success, to all. (Academic Task Force 41)

Thus, in the tension between access and success, the regents' embraced the idea that "maintaining and enhancing excellence at the University of Minnesota is necessary to ensure the state's long-term economic and cultural success" (Academic Task Force 5), and the General College did not fit this goal. It was with a great deal of irony, then, that I read the banner hanging outside of the General College building during my last visit to the campus: "Achieving Access & Excellence since 1932," it said. Unfortunately, excellence was ruling the day, and the days were numbered for the General College.

With this contemporary reality as a backdrop for my archival research, the cracks in the façade of the General College seemed to increasingly stand out. For instance, Lorraine Kranhold, Mike Appel's coinstructor in the Writing Laboratory from its start, took a dim view of the progress of the college by the time she wrote to Malcolm MacLean in 1945:

> Perhaps I need not tell you that I have long been fed up with the increasingly sterile and uninspired character of the General College program in recent years and that I have been dismayed and disheartened by the progressive neglect of those educational principles that flourished in the old days. Watching the slow death of general education at Minnesota has sometimes been very painful. . . . I have told Dr. Morse that I am resigning.

Appel himself was consistently frustrated by the lack of resources that he needed in order to carry out the work of the Writing Laboratory. In his 1935 report to MacLean, he described the limitations and their effects:

> With the enrollment in each section of the laboratory (except one) averaging fifty students or more, most of the students have a conference, or comment, at best only once every three weeks. Each of the instructors has commented upon the sad state of affairs and has tried every device that has occurred to him in the hope of alleviating the situation. The immediate result seems to be a rapid cancellation of students from the various sections, not because they did not like the course, but because they felt they were not receiving enough attention. (1)

Or, as described by MacLean, looking back at his years at the General College, "We battled for room space, for supplies, equipment, academic and clerical assistance . . . for visual education men and machines to illuminate our general education and for budget allowances to support them all. And we ran into a multitude of problems, whipped many of them, made passes at others and left others still unsolved" ("General College" 34).

The General College, then, like many educational innovations, was always a work in progress, always struggling against the status quo and scrambling for resources. The archival record resisted my own imposition of a hero narrative on those early pioneers, despite the contemporary fate of the General College and my growing sense of something vital being lost. Before my second trip to the archives, before the final vote on the closure of the General College, I wondered if my access would suddenly be denied, if a conspiracy would be afoot to cut off the historical record and deny that appeal to longevity. But, no, if anything, the General College archives were instead being recategorized to improve access as the university archivist's impetus to preserve the General College's past was heightened by its imminent demise.

Connors states that "the most important data for the historical researcher in composition studies are perceptions of the present day" (16). At the start of my research into the General College Writing Laboratory, I could not anticipate the powerful role that the present would play. But play a role it did, providing a sense of urgency to my research and an ironic ending to the narrative.

Social Forces and Archival Research

The multiple social worlds that come to bear on any researcher's attempts at archival research create a rich complexity to what might be construed as a relatively simple act—just open up a box and look! The histories that emerge from archival research are also never simple, never complete. This conclusion should not be surprising of course, for good historical narratives are about people and the programs and practices that they have shaped. It does not take an advanced degree in psychology to know that people are very complex, and the records to be found in archives only hint at that complexity. Whether it was Robert Moore, Malcolm MacLean, or Francis Appel, I know a little about these early shapers of writing center history and a little about their social worlds. And, as I have noted, additional social worlds, additional figures came to play, particularly my own in the questions I asked, the choices I made, and the accounts I have written (including this one).

For composition studies, partial histories are both an indication of gaps to be filled in and a caution to mistrust the certainty of those who claim to know. After all, our field is built on knowing and forgetting: writing classroom practices and research into their effectiveness have run in cycles for more than a hundred years, tossed around by social, political, and ideological currents, and always subject to the robust resistance to reform that has marked the American educational system (Tyack and Cuban).

For Connors, a belief in the limits—but necessity—of archival work is essential: "All historical work, then, is provisional, partial—fragments we shore against our ruin. We are trying to make sense of things. It is always a construction. It is always tottering" (21). For those new to the work of archival research, such cautions are essential, as is a kind of self-check about the intents and biases that one brings to the act of research, just as one would with qualitative research when the researcher is attempting to render as accurately as possible the social worlds of the research participants. Stephen J. Ball's description of the ethnographer's *social stance* seems particularly appropriate to archival research as well: "Ethnography not only implies engagement of the researcher in the world under study; it also implies a commitment to a search for meaning, a suspension of preconceptions, and an orientation to discovery. In other words, ethnography involves risk, uncertainty, and discomfort" (157). Archival research will also be marked by some measure of "risk, uncertainty and discomfort," as my experiences at Illinois and Minnesota have shown. For new researchers, an attempt to be aware of the many social forces that come to bear on their work in the archives—forces literally from the past, present, and future—is essential. Researchers need to ask: Who are the people who have played a potential role in the narrative that might be constructed from archival evidence? Do the persons being studied, those who contribute to the archives, or those in the present have some stake in the stories being told?

Archival research that follows such questions has great potential power, allowing us to construct histories—if only partial ones—that speak to the continuing challenges of current times. Perhaps rather than Robert Connor's tottering tower, a more apt metaphor would be a map. In the archives with this crudely drawn map, we are not alone, for the map is the product of those who have come before, who have determined what will be in the archive, who control access. And each of our maps is different, shaped by the sensibilities and motivations that we bring to this research. It is a dynamic map and not a particularly accurate one, but it is the only map that we have.

Works Cited

Academic Task Force on Strategic Positioning. *Academic Task Force Report and Recommendations: Academic Positioning.* University of Minnesota. 30 March 2005. <http://www1.umn.edu/systemwide/strategic_positioning/pdf/SP_Acad_Task_Force_Report.pdf>. 12 June 2009.

Appel, Francis A. To Ena Marston, Saint Helen's Hall Junior College, Portland, Oregon, 7 May 1935. Folder "Correspondence: courses & programs in G.C., 1933–1935," box 24, General College, University Archives, University of Minnesota.

———. Report to M. S. MacLean, 11 Nov. 1935. Folder "Report on English Studies, 11/11/35," unnumbered box, General College, University Archives, University of Minnesota.

Ball, Stephen J. "Self Doubt and Soft Data: Social and Technical Trajectories in Ethnographic Fieldwork." *Qualitative Studies in Education* 3 (1990): 157–71.

Connors, Robert J. "Dreams and Play: Historical Method and Methodology." *Methods and Methodology in Composition Research.* Ed. Gesa Kirsch and Patricia A. Sullivan. Carbondale: Southern Illinois UP, 1992. 15–36.

Corder, Jim W. *Lost in West Texas.* College Station: Texas A&M UP, 1988.

Gray, James. *The University of Minnesota, 1851 to 1951.* Minneapolis: U of Minnesota P, 1951.

Kranhold, Lorraine Livingston. To Malcolm S. MacLean, 21 Aug. 1945. Folder "General College: correspondence, articles, Belt Line, 1932–1943," box 10, General College, University Archives, University of Minnesota.

Lerner, Neal. "'Laboring Together the Common Good': The Writing Laboratory at the University of Minnesota General College, circa 1932." *Teaching English in the Two-Year College* 33.3 (2006): 249–59.

———. "Searching for Robert Moore." *Writing Center Journal* 22.1 (2001): 9–32.

MacLean, Malcolm S. "The General College: Its Origin and Influence." *General Education in Transition: A Look Ahead.* Ed. H. T. Morse. Minneapolis: U of Minn. P, 1951. 29–44.

———. "The Organization of the General College." *The Effective General College Curriculum as Revealed by Examinations.* Ed. Committee on Education Research of the University of Minnesota. Minneapolis: U of Minn. P, 1937. 12–30.

Moore, Robert H. "The Writing Clinic and the Writing Laboratory." *College English* 11.7 (1950): 388–93.

Ricoeur, Paul. *Memory, History, and Forgetting.* Chicago: U Chicago P, 2004.

Tyack, David, and Larry Cuban. *Tinkering Toward Utopia: A Century of Public School Reform.* Cambridge, MA: Harvard UP, 1995.

Velazquez, Rita C., ed. *Directory of American Scholars.* Vol. 2: English, Speech, & Drama. 9th ed. Detroit, MI: Gale, 1999.

EMERGENT TAXONOMIES: USING TENSION AND FORUM TO ORGANIZE PRIMARY TEXTS

Tarez Samra Graban

In early 2004, through a cooperative effort between the county archives and the university where I was a doctoral student, I was given access to eleven boxes of miscellaneous papers and artifacts surrounding the political, philanthropic, and legal activities of a nineteenth-century American suffragist, Helen Gougar (1843–1907). The cooperation began as a twenty-five-student seminar with a service-learning component and resulted in hundreds of cumulatively logged hours spent processing over twenty different collections on behalf of the archives. Initially, the seminar focused on the theoretical workings of "the archive" and soon became a praxis-driven exploration of the intellectual challenges that archives pose for researchers in different disciplines, made richer by the fact that many of the collections we worked on contained intertextual links from one to another.

I knew nothing of Gougar before discovering her there—nothing other than that she was a local legend who employed fairly biting rhetoric from time to time, including clubbing the newspaper editor with her umbrella and shrieking her displeasure in the courtroom during an unsubstantiated slander suit—and thus considered myself well positioned to be impartial and efficient in my work. However, because of my dual involvement as archivist and researcher (i.e., I approached the collection with the primary task of processing it and with the secondary task of making it a research subject), organizing the Gougar Collection at times felt more like disrupting it than giving it order.

Throughout this process, I had an obligation to remain true to its arrangement and sensitive to its silences, yet I was also aware of its possibilities for future research, particularly as I began to pinpoint textual evidences showing that Gougar played a more significant role in rhetorical history than we may think. I wanted not to personify Gougar but to uncover her vital participation with other public personae, yet I could not infer participation or discursive relationships that were not already evident in the order of existing materials. In short, I could not insinuate that a letter or speech or activity was significant *to the collection* just because it began to take on a historical significance in my own mind.

The Need: Resolving Conflicts of De/Reconstruction

Carolyn Steedman's broad discussion of archival "memory" bears witness to how dilemmas like mine can sometimes drive an archival researcher's work. While we consider them to be fairly value-neutral, the acts of *biography, research*, and *remembering* can be understood as a rigorous exhuming of the dead's stories—reconstructed, taken, and then left (57). These acts tend to reconstruct the archival researcher's own desires for a particular collection; furthermore, they allow memory to subsume truth, for example, assigning significance to a particular document that may not have had it before or remembering a particular artifact within a photo that never showed it. My principal question should have been, "What is the most intrinsic way to *arrange* this information?" But I was most driven by the question, "What is the best way for rhetorical researchers to *access* the information that is here?" As my knowledge of Gougar's activities increased, I found it harder to prevent that question from driving my work.

It is precisely this question that causes the archivist's and researcher's missions to sometimes conflict. Archivists process collections by maintaining obvious relationships, typically resulting in record groups and series numbers because this helps them to arrange documents into consistent patterns. Rhetorical researchers and discourse analysts working with archived texts may fail to understand how these organizational patterns make sense to the collection's creator and why that structure needs to be maintained—particularly when vital or dynamic relationships could be discovered in a reorganization of the texts. The conflict becomes a question of purpose and function: How should researchers proceed if they need more than the text to help them locate the discourse? Can the collection serve as an artifact of discourse or as a grouping of discursive contexts? Should the collection serve as more than a record of intrinsic relationships?

Aside from arrangement, another conflict between archivists and researchers is the importance of provenance—or originary source—to a collection's purpose and functionality, specifically for governing its arrangement and description and essentially for keeping the "chain of custody" of a series of documents intact (Brunton and Robinson 223). This chain of custody represents what was meaningful to the collection's creator and has more to do with the order in which items are found rather than an order in which the documents might serve a research topic or question. I have found that this order is not so easy for rhetoric and com-position researchers to discern, let alone accept. For those researchers especially interested in discourse analysis, not disrupting the chain of custody often means suppressing the urge to mix or combine the archives of one agency or person with those of another. And for rhetorical theorists who strive to understand how texts function and are purposed together, it means having to study them apart. In short, researchers and theorists need methods that are more clearly developed for expanding the boundaries of a collection without blocking the archivist's mission to preserve and protect.

Thus, this essay offers one method for organizing texts according to their en-during rhetorical value without disrupting their provenance. It does so by utilizing the taxonomical system that emerges from the collection itself. It is my hope that this method as I describe it will help researchers and theorists to recognize their archival work through the same lens as Carolyn Heald's *diplomatics*—that is, as a research methodology that privileges certain facts in the interpretation of a col-lection by organizing texts within contexts that are broader than the collection, yet without imposing limits on the collection being studied. *Diplomatics* is the practice of reading texts whose principal function is documentary, and Heald argues for it as postmodern activity in surmising that—contrary to how we may understand their role—archivists have already been involved more in cultural and social deconstruction than in mere arrangement and preservation of texts (95). Recognizing archival organization as a deconstructive act underscores the need for taxonomical systems that emerge from the productive tension between document sets and the social strata out of which they were created.

The Taxonomy: Theoretical Foundations in a Contextualist Paradigm

This method relies on three assumptions. First, the best way to understand how certain texts in a collection inform other texts is by letting a new framework for analysis emerge from the texts themselves. Second, rhetorical analysis is situ-ational as well as functional (Fahnestock and Secor 178), which implies that even a singly authored text is best understood via the audience and moment out of which it was constructed and further when we can discern these from features inherent in the text itself. Third, discourse analysis is the study of how language is orga-nized in texts and contexts (Barton, "Linguistic" 57), which in turn implies that our goals with archived texts are similar to Ellen Barton's goals with any text—we examine them in light of their authorial contexts, and we are interested in how linguistic and rhetorical "rich features"—features "from all levels and registers of language"—allow us to identify, name, and evaluate a writer's strategies on all levels of language ("Inductive" 24).

To better describe how this taxonomy emerged in the Gougar collection, I will outline several steps, beginning with my application of Cindy Johanek's contextualist research paradigm for rhetoric and composition studies. Johanek developed this paradigm from the productive tensions often experienced by compositionists who see themselves as teachers and researchers simultaneously (1). These tensions occur when dichotomous methods or beliefs threaten to take over the research or when the situation provokes the question, "What makes good research in the discipline?" By adopting more fluid understandings of discipline and context, Johanek proposes that compositionists can become less burdened by making their research fit a purely quantitative or qualitative framework and more focused on innovating the kinds of questions that are needed to sustain the field (9). For example, they can question lore without discounting its significance on their inquiry, they can employ stories and narratives as legitimate forms of data gathering, and they can let questions of audience and presentation help guide these forms of data gathering. Thus, rather than applying a static method to a question, Johanek proposes a method that arises from the question—and from the processes and definitions that continue to drive it (186).

Although Johanek developed her paradigm largely to allow compositionists to situate their research in changing social and political contexts, the archival researcher also often situates his or her research in fluctuating contexts and historical moments. That is, the archival researcher's project is also often defined by inquiry rather than by method, and that inquiry sometimes strains against available methods. I propose that the archival researcher can paradigmatically realize the strengths and limitations of the historical moments depicted in what he or she is sorting, instead reframing the subject in less stable social and political contexts, where context means more than just place and is, as Johanek might say, "defined by its own power and its own variability" (3). The archival researcher can benefit from enacting Johanek's art of questioning of rhetorical contexts rather than by relying on prescribed dichotomies or anticipated findings (113) and without rearranging what the collection's creator has done.

Reframing my research as contextualist helped me to formulate questions about Gougar's texts by letting their various audiences, motivations, and outcomes determine what questions I should ask. One particular challenge I faced was situating Gougar's performances in the suffrage history we already know, fragmented and complex as that history is. The evidence provided in those eleven boxes did not present a very consistent figure. Gougar seemed to exemplify rhetorical practices that were shaped by combinations of different discourses and styles. Acknowledging the ongoing complexity of Gougar's participation in suffrage rhetoric was the first step towards getting at the questions that would become critical in organizing her texts. Thus, the emergent taxonomy must first define *context* broadly, to include "interlocutors and their social roles, their purpose, the genres of their oral or written texts, their institutional relations and frameworks, the prior text or talk, the setting, and other relevant factors" (Barton, "Inductive" 24).

Because the context from which questions about a population arise also determines how the population should be analyzed, Johanek places "Rhetorical Issues" such as audience, researcher, and evidence at the top of a matrix, and situates "Research Issues" of publication, methods, purpose, and question to one side of the matrix (112). Any intersection of rhetorical/research issues on the matrix results in a metaepistemology of sorts, where the analytical framework goes beyond the scope of what an archivist *thinks* he or she should ask. Metaepistemology is concerned with questioning the basic concepts employed in epistemology, concepts of *knowledge, truth, belief, justification*, and *rationality*. For the archivist, these tend to be determined by the given order of a set of texts. For the rhetorician, discourse analyst, or researcher, these are determined more by a(n ideo)logical order. That difference is key.

In order to more systematically approach the Gougar Collection with broader discursive goals that didn't disrupt the internal management of the collection, I used Johanek's matrix to formulate a question based on the most practical intersection of issues between researcher/method:

- How can I best search and organize my findings on over a thousand pages of text in fewer than three months? (To avoid an unwieldy and indiscriminate process of note taking, I needed a method that would also serve my future data management.)

The quickest way for me to proceed was to create a hierarchy of materials from largest to smallest (i.e., container to unit to folder to document or item) noting the *original* physical order of materials before deciding how detailed a description I should apply to the collection as a whole. This hierarchical arrangement began with an initial "first-pass description," and it was in several of these first-pass descriptions that I began to see a problematic organization emerge—problematic not only from my perspective as a discourse analyst who wanted to organize the collection according to how the texts related but also because previous efforts to process the collection had obfuscated any clear chain of events. From accession records showing early and late donations, it became apparent that at least one other archivist and author had started the work twenty-five years earlier.

My first-pass description of each folder, file, and text tended towards the rhetorical—as if questions of authorship and relationship and not questions of physical order constituted the collection. More often than not, these questions strained against the physical and chronological arrangement of the materials at hand. For example, I was intrigued by the location of certain *cartes-de-visite*, by the loopy handwriting on the backs of photographs telling narratives about who was pictured, by brief identification statements in the margins of letters or on the flaps of envelopes, by faded notes on older accession records indicating who had been in searching the collection before (who was speaking to whom in these notes?). But from the questions in these first-pass descriptions, more concrete discursive tensions and social strata began to emerge:

- Why is there no reference to Gougar's lecture activity after [Elizabeth Cady] Stanton's and [Susan B.] Anthony's volume 4 of *History of Woman's Suffrage*?
- Kriebel notes a "rhetoric to Henry Ward Beecher" (p. 50) and a "rift with Susan B. Anthony" (p. 66)—in what documents did these occur?
- Exactly what role did Gougar play in the 1892 and 1900 presidential elections?
- Are the irony patterns in her letters to [Benjamin] Harrison, Reverend [B. Wilson] Smith, and other male politicians the same?
- Who were her other principal correspondents?

My task soon became finding out how Gougar's rhetoric did (or did not) impact the larger movements with which she was involved. The social, personal, and factual questions that ensued show Johanek-like intersections among my sensitivity to the collection as an object, my concern with utilizing an analytical method that is transparent, and my desire to uncover textual evidences that were substantial yet "new" (i.e., to more adequately substantiate what Gougar's place was in rhetorical history):

Researcher/Purpose

- What is the best place for me to begin given my trajectory for analysis?

Audience/Question

- What forms of textual evidence (via internal and external references) does my audience need to see to understand Gougar's role in the suffrage movement?
- How do I make Gougar's extratextual connections with major suffrage figures more visible?

Evidence/Method

Questioning the authorship of and activity within this burgeoning collection—including trying to discern three different sets of handwriting on the backs of some documents—confirmed an important reality of archival work, and that is that a collection's donor need not be the same as its creator and almost always is not the same as its subject. Applying Johanek's rubric to these questions in turn showed a valuable evidence/method interaction in the following:

- What information about the collection can I get from within the collection itself?
- What information should I locate from outside the collection (e.g., secondary sources, other linked collections)?
- Who has used these materials before and for what purpose?
- How am I being guided by what Gougar has published—what am I prioritizing as a first source of knowledge? What other sources might I be leaving out?
- What am I inferring about the holes in this collection—such as lack of personal letters and family correspondence?

I call this interaction valuable because it led me to devise an internally consistent method for organizing Gougar's work. In other words, it led me to draw conclusions about her rhetorical participation based on the relationships that were evident in this collection at this time. My organizational tool, then, would have to be contextual and flexible and could change as further archival evidences emerged.

The Tool: Tension and Forum in Taxonomical Grids

While the rhetorical and research interactions on Johanek's matrix helped me to initially sort and catalog Gougar's texts without changing the physical arrangement of the collection, I still required a taxonomical framework that would uncover traceable features of her discourse in order to determine broader classifications for those items beyond the categories an archivist sets. For little known or unknown suffrage texts, such a taxonomy would need to privilege how the social, personal, and factual dimensions of the researcher's inquiry contend with certain characteristics that may or may not align with what we know as the suffrage "standard." For example, I considered this subset of questions:

1. Where did she stand on marginalizing issues, such as abolition, labor, and immigration?
2. How did her writings simultaneously reflect and resist popular nineteenth-century reform rhetoric?
3. What moves, characteristics, or strategies could have positioned her as a major rhetorical figure? As a dissenter?

I tried to provide alternative ways of naming and evaluating Gougar's strategies. Two guiding ideas helped me to discern Gougar's audiences, and in demonstrating how they work on my own research project, I posit them as the next step in devising an emergent (rhetorical) taxonomy.

The first is Karlyn Kohrs Campbell's notion of *double bind*,[1] a term implying that the opportunities and occasions for women to speak were at odds with discourse defending their participation in the public sphere. In "Gender and Genre:

Loci of Invention and Contradiction in the Earliest Speeches by U.S. Women," Campbell offers a reading of two women's speeches, Priscilla Mason's salutatory oration (circa 1794) and Deborah Sampson Gannett's public lecture (circa 1802), to argue two claims: first, the double bind that women faced as speakers actually spurred their inventional creativity by providing an opportunity for transcendence, and, secondly, the ensuing conflict they experienced between justifying their violation of taboos and speaking appropriately limited their ability to be seen as rhetorical artists (480). According to Campbell and Jamieson ("Rhetorical Hybrids"), whose concept of generic hybrid Campbell employs for her analysis of Mason and Gannett, in order to address the issue they embodied (whether women should have the right to speak in public), their discourse had to be consistent with audience expectations while justifying a violation of their gendered roles. Mason and Gannett had to "violate norms" for particular ways of acting and speaking and to speak in "unfeminine" masculine voices (491), yet they did so by appearing to speak in ways appropriate to their occasion and sex. I needed an archival classification system that was sensitive to these tensions.

The second guiding idea is James Porter's notion of forum. Unlike the classical rhetorical notion of audience as a one-way recipient of any text, Porter's forum allows me to consider Gougar's audiences as actors in or targets of certain ironic exchanges. It further allows me to consider Gougar's methods as uniquely feminist because she appears to be writing and speaking what is acceptable while using the irony to violate expected discourse conventions. Finally, it allows me to consider a classification based on the many situations in which she wrote.

Acknowledging the double bind or dual purpose of most of Gougar's performances and applying Porter's notion of forum analysis to Gougar's texts, I identified six "tensions," or strategic responses to audience and situation according to factors such as background (organizational affiliation, philosophy or expression of belief, reputation, membership, readership); speaker/writer status and credentials; addressee/assumed audience status and credentials; topic; form; and style ("Intertextuality" 46–47). These strategic responses (SRs) include the following:

1. Provoking women of means out of ambivalence into action and reprimanding dominant movements for their faltering efforts towards suffrage (1876–88)[2]
2. Appealing to women pragmatists by demonstrating the domestic and economic benefits of women's legal participation (1879–1900)
3. Undermining arguments against suffrage by condescending to gendered stereotypes of regional women in order to overturn them (1879–1907)
4. Appealing to male intellectuals by de-moralizing suffrage and repositioning Midwestern suffrage efforts as politically progressive (1881–1907)

5. Appealing to political power holders through electoral lobbying and by mentoring male politicians in social reform (1882–1900)

6. Criticizing U.S. policy makers by showing disparaging effects of immigration laws on state suffrage and by highlighting the progress of woman suffrage abroad (1888–1907)

While it would still be valuable to study Gougar's performances according to the terms, styles, and tropes already identified in the performances of her contemporaries (e.g., Frances Willard, Elizabeth Cady Stanton, and Lucy Stone), it is significant that within her own collection a classification for rhetorical practice emerged on its own.

The six-part classification allowed me to privilege the following categories which in turn influenced the organization of a flexible grid (shown in the table) that would track future documents I discover and denote significant relationships between them in what genres Gougar wrote or spoke most prominently: the nature and characteristics of her audience(s); the number and nature of references she made to people, places, or the movement at large; dominant arguments (hers and/or the movement's) in her texts; and her use of register (in this case, irony and sarcasm) to convey those arguments. Each category on the grid offered a way to track evidence that would guide a multilayered analysis into specific features of Helen Gougar's discourse. Internal and external references also helped me to position Gougar's speeches and writings within and alongside the suffrage movement as a whole.

Organizational Grid

Classification	SR 2: Appealing to women pragmatists by demonstrating the domestic and economic benefits of women's legal participation (1879–1900)
Text	"Industrial Training for Women" Address given for the Tippecanoe County Homemakers' Association at Trinity M.E. chapel on 29 January 1900 (Kriebel 188).
Source	*Lafayette Evening Call*, 3 February 1900
Record	117:2004.01 Helen Gougar Collection Newspaper 75.17.26: Folder of assorted clippings of Helen Gougar's writings and speeches from 1890–1900. Cf. Gougar's introduction to sister Edna Jackson Houk's Book 75.17.3 Cf. the B. Wilson Smith Papers (14:82.05)
Genre(s)	Public Address Newspaper Reprint

Audience/Characteristics	Gougar delivered this lecture between a series of trips to Joplin, Missouri, where she held business and speaking engagements for the WCTU. It became one of her most requested lectures. Gougar would later write columns under the title "Weekly Chat with the Call Readers" for the *Lafayette Evening Call* from 11/30/1903 to 12/15/1903. The paper became the *Weekly Call* in December 1903 and suspended the "chats" until 2/24/1904, before finally discontinuing them (Kriebel 198).
References to Suffrage Figures and Events	Passage B, line 3 (reference to *Uncle Tom's Cabin*) Passage B, line 4 (critics of Harriet Beecher Stowe misunderstand her role as little more than an overpaid domestic)
Argument	*Commonplace*: Logical expansion of the "women's sphere" into public life for the public good, and the positive effects to be gained from women's participation in political and economic life (Lomicky 103). Domestic and individual health contribute to the health of a strong nation. "In short she would represent the typical 20th century woman and stand for the highest civilization attained, for the status of woman always marks the status of her nation." *Gougar*: Promotes women's participation in education but preaches a particular kind of woman: someone who has liberty (but not license), temperance in all things, working over street-loafing. Differs from the WCTU by saying women can/should be able to participate on the basis of natural endowments and intellect, not on the basis of moral superiority. She outlines the curriculum she thinks all free schools (state institutions) should put into place for female students. Although this curriculum involves domestic training towards practical and common sense, individual health, and bodily comfort, not every woman is naturally endowed to be a housekeeper. "Inasmuch as there is no sex indicated in the divine decree that by sweat of the brow we must eat, and as I find that necessity knows no sex, I ask that there shall be no sex in the social or written laws pertaining to the industrial training of the young or old."

Notable Ironic Strategies	Uses exaggeration and metaphor to challenge stereo-types of Midwestern women (redirects her audience's attention to common but absurd beliefs about women's place)
	Embeds a high-context coarseness and bluntness in an otherwise plain style (uses understatement alongside exaggeration)
	Employs derisive adjectival construction to describe criti-cal subjects (rather than using self-deprecation)
	Draws connection between women's rights and abolition-ist possibilities
	"Strik[ing] the shackles from the lives of 4,000,000 slaves" and "washing dishes and ordering the domestic affairs of a home" are used within the same sentence, creating incongruity between women's social potential and men's domestic aims

While these categories are contextually appropriate given my specific research inquiry, I suggest them more generally even for texts not authored by women or little-known figures because they offer the researcher different levels of explanatory power. Practically speaking, these were the kinds of information I could glean fairly quickly, and they would allow me to do extensive cross-referencing of Gougar's texts. Most significant, they don't assume fixed or concrete categories. As more texts emerge and become subsumed into the collection demonstrating Gougar's rhetorical venues, these categories—and the six-part classification they came from—can and should change. (As a case in point, between 2004 and 2006 the list of SRs grew from five to six when I discovered references to three critical essays Gougar had penned on immigration policy, written after 1900 and from abroad, and in 2007, I happened across a collection of nineteenth-century news-papers featuring fifty-three short articles dating as early as 1882 that Gougar had written on foreign policy).

The organizational grid is not the same as a detailed collection inventory or even a finding aid. Both of those essential processing documents can and do make transparent how a collection works, and a detailed inventory can be gridlike to emulate a database that makes cross-referencing the content of items possible, but Johanek's and Porter's theorizing equips archival researchers to create other genres, allowing us to interpret documents in more than just their original order and beyond the creator's or archivist's leanings.

What distinguishes the taxonomical grid from other processing documents is its equal attention to the research trajectory and the inherent rhetorical nature of the collection. It allows the researcher to bring to archival work the impor-tant question of who is/was the audience for this collection. I note the following other benefits of creating organizational grids based on the taxonomical tensions inherent in a collection:

- holding the researcher accountable to the parameters of a collection without being limited by them
- allowing the researcher to augment limited public records by cross-referencing relationships to other figures, collections, documents, or performances
- compelling the researcher to look within the collection for information on how and how much to classify rhetorical performances, rather than imposing an external set of criteria
- focusing the researcher's analysis on the subject's performances by contextualizing them in other found texts
- causing the researcher to note pursuant areas of questioning
- preventing the researcher from trying to write only one coherent narrative of the subject's life or of approaching the subject's performances with the desire to personify through the limited evidence available

The Outcome: Recursive and Flexible Analysis

To summarize, my whole method consists of four steps:

1. I apply Johanek's matrix of rhetorical and research issues to do a first-pass description of the collection's contents and to organize the questions that ensue—that is, questions pertaining to method, authorship, and activity. In so doing, I differentiate between the collection's provenance and arrangement and the kinds of evidences I will need to glean in order to satisfy my overarching query.

2. I initially examine these evidences as cotextually and contextually derived, where the cotext is provided by references to—but outside of—the collection, and context is provided by materials existing within the collection. In my case, acknowledging Campbell's double bind and Porter's forum as co/contextual factors in Gougar's work helped me to focus methodologically on the tensions she was negotiating with her writings. But in any case, the point is to acknowledge identifiable, flexible relationships that occur between the subject and the subject's context (e.g., tension, forum, situation) as the topmost classification in the taxonomy.

3. From these relationships (i.e., Gougar's strategic responses), I select organizational categories that bear on the question of audience, that can be marked discursively and linguistically, and that can be noted fairly quickly. These categories are also flexible and unstable inasmuch as they can change when and if more texts are added to the collection. For example, knowing that I am dealing with an archival subject who worked alongside but not always with the women we remember as "pioneering" figures in the suffrage movement, I chose to examine how Gougar's arguments did or did not conform with what was considered

commonplace and to note how she used irony when her contemporaries did not. However, had Gougar already been one of the "pioneering" figures and had I been interested in how she positioned herself as a member of the movement, I would instead focus on the number of references she made to other suffrage figures, her method of attributing or citing ideas, and the type of forum in which she performed most frequently.

4. I apply the grid to a representative sample of texts in the collection, in order to select a minicorpus that best demonstrates the organizational categories and, eventually, to rethink and revise those categories in light of new textual evidence.

Beginning researchers who are new to a collection often do not know where to start, and even veteran researchers are often unaware of places to seek out alternative texts or are not practiced in how to mine unprocessed collections for inventive, productive taxonomical systems. Thus, they are at risk of glossing the essential characteristics of a collection by attempting to apply a prescribed organization to it or by evaluating its contents according to extant constructs. So one outcome of an emergent taxonomical method is that it helps researchers to recover authentic rhetorical features of understudied texts. Accounting for the relationship among "style, register, and situation" provides for fuller descriptions of how our archival subjects did and could communicate, not merely how they *should* communicate (Clarke 18).

However, this method can and obviously should be applied beyond just those texts. If what results from this volume is the realization that rhetoric and composition scholars are gradually gaining more access to archival collections—either because their projects are revisionist, or their institutional duties require that they create an archive from scratch, or their discursive or linguistic interests lead them to obscure but unprocessed work, or even because they view archival work as a kind of classroom-to-community engagement—then we should be aware of the difficulties of doing both processing and research in tandem with each other.

But we should also be aware that proceeding taxonomically can help us to more richly map intertextual activity in a collection by understanding documents within their social networks, yet without disrupting the nature of that collection if it is processed, and without erasing important provenance clues if it is not. In short, it helps us to devise a systematic method for organizing texts (and, hence, for classifying rhetorical practices) according to the communicative constructs inherent in that collection. It is in relating the documents within a taxonomical grid and not in disrupting the documents from a particular order where significant discursive relationships can be established and explored.

Notes

I thankfully acknowledge Paul Schueler, former Director of Special Collections at the Tippecanoe County Historical Association in Lafayette, Indiana, for granting me access to Gougar's work and for guiding me in several important lessons about archival processing.

1. Because the collection I use was principally authored by an understudied figure in the American Suffrage Movement, I employ Campbell's "double bind" as a product of (feminist) revisionist historiography. However, broader and more general applications of this methodology can still utilize the notion of rhetorical tension in order to determine how the archival subject upholds or violates discursive norms.

2. These dates reflect Gougar's range of involvement in each strategic response based only on the archival records available to me. They are approximate rather than binding parameters and subject to revision whenever new documents surface.

Works Cited

Barton, Ellen. "Inductive Discourse Analysis: Discovering Rich Features." *Discourse Studies in Composition*. Ed. Ellen Barton and Gail Stygall. Cresskill, NJ: Hampton, 2002. 19–42.

———. "Linguistic Discourse Analysis." *What Writing Does and How It Does It: An Introduction to Analyzing Texts and Textual Practices*. Ed. Charles Bazerman and Paul Prior. Mahwah, NJ: Erlbaum, 2004. 57–82.

Brunton, Paul, and Tim Robinson. "Arrangement and Description." *Keeping Archives*. Ed. Judith Ellis and D. W. Thorpe. 2nd ed. Port Melbourne, Australia: Thorpe/Australian Society of Archivists, 1993. 222–47.

Campbell, Karlyn Kohrs. "Gender and Genre: Loci of Invention and Contradiction in the Earliest Speeches by U.S. Women." *Quarterly Journal of Speech* 81 (1995): 479–95.

Campbell, Karlyn Kohrs, and Kathleen Hall Jamieson. "Rhetorical Hybrids: Fusions of Generic Elements." *Quarterly Journal of Speech* 68 (1982): 146–57.

Clarke, Danielle. *The Politics of Early Modern Women's Writing*. Harlow, England: Pearson, 2001.

Fahnestock, Jeanne, and Marie Secor. "Rhetorical Analysis." *Discourse Studies in Composition*. Ed. Ellen Barton and Gail Stygall. Cresskill, NJ: Hampton, 2002. 177–200.

Heald, Carolyn. "Is There Room for Archives in the Postmodern World?" *American Archivist* 59 (1996): 101.

Johanek, Cindy. *Composing Research: A Contextualist Paradigm for Rhetoric and Composition*. Logan: Utah State UP, 2000.

Kriebel, Robert C. *Where the Saints Have Trod: The Life of Helen Gougar*. West Lafayette, IN: Purdue UP, 1985.

Lomicky, Carol S. "Frontier Feminism and the *Woman's Tribune*: The Journalism of Clara Bewick Colby." *Journalism History* 28.3 (2002): 102–11.

Porter, James E. "Intertextuality and the Discourse Community." *Rhetoric Review* 5.1 (Autumn 1986): 34–47.

Steedman, Carolyn. *Dust: The Archive and Cultural History*. New Brunswick, NJ: Rutgers UP, 2002.

THE GUILTY PLEASURES OF
WORKING WITH ARCHIVES

Linda S. Bergmann

My work with archival sources has involved two projects, started at the beginning of my career, to which I return periodically to explore new understandings of the archives from which they were derived and the lives those archives have preserved. These projects, which have intersected each other over the past twenty years, are connected by my continuing interest in the relationships between public and private discourse. Moreover, since I first began working with them in the 1980s, they have assisted and recorded my transition from the study of literature to the study of rhetoric and composition. One project involved the private, unpublished papers (1958–65) of a deceased literature scholar, Marcia Tillotson, letters written mostly during her years in college, her postcollege travel, and when in New York working while deciding on her future course of life. These letters had been collected and cherished by her mother, at whose request I sorted the collection, transcribed a sample, wrote a paper about the documents, and tried—without success—to find a publisher for them. The other project involved investigating the work of Elizabeth Agassiz, who wrote both an expedition narrative (*A Journey in Brazil*, published in 1868) and a biography of her husband, the prominent American scientist (*Louis Agassiz: His Life and Letters*, published in 1886). The Agassiz projects began with my reading the published texts, searching the Schlesinger and Houghton libraries at Harvard, finding the original letters that Elizabeth Agassiz had worked from, and comparing them with the published texts. Early in the project, I was alerted by Stephen Jay Gould's argument in "Flaws in a Victorian Veil" that Elizabeth Agassiz had selectively quoted from her husband's original letters in ways that subdued his racist views and made them more acceptable to an audience of New England intellectuals. I did not then fully comprehend the relationships between Gould's analysis and my own developing interests, which were (1) to examine how she shaped her own letters (for *Journey*) and her husband's (in *Life and Letters*) to create public narratives about events that were crucial aspects of her private experience, and (2) to demonstrate how she developed a public voice and presence by doing this. I published several articles based on this work.

Working in Two Archives: Letters and Love

In pursuing these archival research projects, I shared many of the experiences described by others in this book: the thrill of the hunt, the help of archivists, their interest in my projects, my despair at ever getting the complete corpus of documents or their context, and the growth of new projects out of initial explorations. I also felt the thrill (sensual as well as intellectual) of touching letters written by people like William James and Henry Wadsworth Longfellow. But I also gradually became aware of my *emotional* responses to the women I was studying, responses ranging from close identification to anger, scorn, and contempt. Leon Edel discusses such identification as part of the experience of the biographer, as a quasi-Freudian phenomenon similar to transference. Perhaps. Or perhaps it comes from reading private texts, not intended (at least in these archived materials) for public scrutiny and from gaining access to the raw materials of the life narratives (written or imagined, for themselves and for others) that writers re-create for public consumption. This identification may also be precipitated by the ways writers of private documents create their audience. Walter Ong observed that even in personal letters and diaries, the audience is created; this audience, too, is a fiction because it must be imagined and addressed by the writer, and those acts of imagination help shape the discourse. It may be that reading over the shoulders of this audience can draw the researcher beyond the rational by the very power of this transgression. The worlds in the unpublished documents I have worked with are truly private worlds, and as I read and returned to these letters and diaries, I was drawn into relationships that allowed me to excuse rather than criticize the writers—and myself, for that matter.

My responses are, I would suggest, an aspect of scholarship that we seldom admit in print and therefore that we seldom "officially" investigate, although we do tell stories about them to our friends and colleagues in private. These responses, I would further suggest, constitute a kind of "guilty pleasure," because we cannot control our emotions about our scholarship as well as we can shape our written discourse about it, and so we (or I, at least) have trouble understanding the not completely coherent feelings I address in this chapter.

Violating Confidence

Marcia Tillotson earned her PhD in English at the University of Chicago and then taught at the University of New Mexico until her death in 1981, about five years before her mother contacted me at the suggestion of the chair of the English department at the University of Chicago, where I had also received my PhD. Her mother believed that the letters constituted a fine narrative (they did, indeed) and hoped to interest a publisher in them. My first reading of them was an experience of pure story; I strongly identified with the letter writer and was eager to learn what had happened next in her life. As though reading a fiction, I became engaged in the worlds she described: first, student life at Radcliffe College in the late 1950s and early 1960s, then traveling in Europe, and later working for a publisher in New York. But I was occasionally jolted back to a perception of their *reality*, because these were neither fictions nor archives safely buried in the past along with the bodies of those involved with them. One night as I was re-reading the letters, Marcia's mother (who lived in my midrise building in Chicago) knocked on my door with some newly discovered letters. I was jarred by the recognition that the letters I was experiencing as *story* were for this woman important aspects of her own *life*; it became clear that my work with them involved the interpolation of life and text in ways I had not previously imagined. I sensed that working with this archive was much more complex than the more formal considerations of public and private discourse I had hitherto encountered; and thinking about the position of these letters, somewhere between artifice and life, left me perplexed.

Reading the letters as "story" invoked in me another sense of guilty pleasure, the kind of pleasure I got from rummaging through the drawers of the parents of children for whom I babysat in high school; with this archive, as with the drawers, the pleasure outweighed the guilt. These letters were not written for public consumption, and yet here I was, a stranger who was "consuming" them. Moreover, in a January 13, 1965, letter, Marcia upbraided her mother for suggesting that the letters should be published some day, stressing that she would regard such publication as an act of betrayal and exposure:

> There is a difference between a gift for self-expression and a gift for creative writing. Self-expression without form is slop, and it's not for anyone else's consumption. Now I understand precisely the limit, the farther limit, of whatever talent I have: you, Mama, cannot understand it. I have an absolutely literal mind, both in writing and painting. I can invent nothing: I can only reproduce what I see, feel, and know. Within that limit, can I write anything? I don't know. That's what I mean by form. If I can discover a form for what I can write, then I may be able to do it. But if invention turns out to be necessary, which is likely, I can do nothing. . . .

And this, by the way, is why I could make nothing of my letters. They could be used as notes for a novel, or some such thing, if I were a novelist. They could be the material of a detailed biography, if I were a person that anyone wanted to biographize. But for my own writing, it's ridiculous to imagine they can be used. They've been written. Not for anyone else but my immediate family. (in Bergmann, "Women of Letters" 95)

I remained, in spite of this vehement refusal of permission, committed to working toward their publication, which would have been a major solace to her mother, a woman whom I greatly admired for her general courage, for her refusal to bow to convention, and even for her rejection of her daughter's clear prohibition.

I wonder now whether continuing with the project after reading this letter was ethical. I still don't know. Randy Cohen, in the *New York Times Magazine*'s "Sunday Ethicist," made a judgment on obeying the expressed desires of the deceased:

There are extraordinary cases when ethics compels us to disregard the demands of the dead in order to serve the profoundly important interests of the living. Several literary executors, for example, famously ignored a writer's instructions to destroy his papers as Max Brod defied Kafka's command and posterity applauds these acts of disobedience. (28)

I suspect that I noticed and embraced this opinion as a way of exonerating my own ambivalence about what I did and am still doing. What does "posterity applauds" mean, and how much does such applause count? Looking back, I admit that I must have been semiconscious of committing an act of betrayal, sufficiently conscious that I did not include the paragraph attacking her mother's desire to publish the letters in my first publication about them. I still wonder where I should have stood on this issue. Did I owe more to Marcia, whom I had never met? To her mother, who had paid me for my early transcription of the letters and for whom the letters remained profoundly important throughout her life? To my own conviction of their value and worth for women's history, accounts of experiences that otherwise would be lost from sight? When and how can we be sure that the "interests of the living" are "profoundly important" enough to ignore the intention of the dead writer?

My ambivalence was and remains complicated. For Marcia's mother, the letters were part of her intense love for her dead daughter, whereas my reading removed them from the context of both the writer and her primary audience and let the personality they expressed so strongly become an occasion for more distanced responses than simple love. In particular, my ambivalence raged when I read passages like the following, which Marcia wrote June 6, 1962, after finishing her last exam in college, to thank her parents for supporting her, financially and emotionally, throughout her education. My anger was a personal response from a stranger, clearly not the response she anticipated at the time from her intended and very well-known audience. I was profoundly jealous; I had never dared to think of myself to be as valuable as she considered herself; I had always been expected to consider first what I owed other people—parents, husband, son, professors, students—not what was owed to me:

> More than I thank you for sending me here, I thank you for making me able to come. Both by giving me whatever attitude of mind it took to make me choose Radcliffe and Radcliffe take me, and by making me such that I demand the best for myself as a right. After you had done all this to me you owed it to me to send me here, to put the picture you had painted in the proper frame, to polish the silver you'd spent money and taste in buying. This pompous tone, or arrogant, or egotistic—I cannot tell, only the listener can—I take is then also your fault. It is to blame or thank whatever is in me that is making me take this next year or two to indulge my curiosities and desires. The same conceited brat who tells you she deserved to go to Radcliffe at the cost of some $12,000 is now telling you she is not unusual for demanding for herself many months of undirected wandering. But it takes some confidence and a different kind of direction to permit me to dare it. So you are to blame and I thank you for doing what you have done, and for making me what I am, so far for making me even what I think should be polished further and what both wants to be polished and wants to spend the energy in polishing. By polished I don't mean finished, sophisticated. I mean seeing more and living more, a breadth of experience that gives a sheen, not a veneer. (in Bergmann, "Women of Letters" 92–93)

I found it hard to believe that any real person, any woman outside of a Henry James novel, could think so seriously about herself or take her own value so seriously. At the same time, I resented the freedom she felt to represent herself as so precious to her parents without fear of being "put in her place"—as I would have been. Twenty years later, I question the extent to which my resentment at her experience of family inclined me to ignore her insistence that the letters not be published. Perhaps because of the intensity and complexity of my responses, I came to share Mrs. Tillotson's conviction that the letters constituted an important account of the time and places they described. Because they could arouse interest and engage complicated emotions in an outsider like me, I believed, and still believe, that they could hold a wider appeal than the personal responses of a mother's love for and memories of her daughter. But I cannot rest comfortably and guiltlessly in that belief.

My feelings about these documents, then, helped shape my project, interfacing with the more abstract knowledge about personal writing I brought to it. They pushed me to study private writing by other women and to study research and theory about personal writing. On my second, third, and subsequent readings of Marcia Tillotson's letters, armed with a critical distance earned by this broader research, I developed a more distanced and theoretical approach to the letters. My 1989 article, "The Contemporary Letter as Literature," downplayed my personal responses, proposing a set of "distinctive attributes of the letter" (137) and analyzing this collection to discern the generic features of the letter. I suggested

> the possibility that women may choose the form of the letter because it offers an intense but accessible means of importing some of the order of literature onto the chaos of life, not in the retrospective manner of the autobiography, which looks back to find ultimate meaning, but in a personal and contingent manner appropriate to a genre in which closure is always tentative and resolution is left for the future. (137–38)

In this article, the first I published after finishing my dissertation, I carefully excised my personal responses to the Tillotson archive. Instead, I theorized how the writer created a coherent self and invented an interested, appreciative audience as she wrote the letters (Ong), out of her actual, living audience. As Marcia adopted a persona that she conceived of as her best self, she also envisioned her family audience as their own best selves. However, occasionally glimpsing her living family outside my window as I sat at my desk, I wondered how I could distinguish the textual best selves she had created from these real people, who were still so clearly and immediately visible, but who had probably aged into different people than the audience she had imagined years before. No matter how I tried to turn the letters into grist for a theoretical mill, they would not stay safely in the realm of an impersonal, professional analysis; the people who had known her, whose lives kept going on just outside my window decades after the letters were written, simply would not go away. I felt the guilt of knowing that I had not, and could not have, gotten it right—even if I had not ignored the clear directive of the letter writer to her mother that the letters should not be published.

Excusing the Writer

Intertwined with this work with the Tillotson letters was my study of the archival papers of Elizabeth Agassiz, a series of projects that engendered different kinds of "guilty pleasure." Working in the Schlesinger Library, the Radcliffe Archives, and the Houghton Library, I grew fascinated by the private life of a conservative, conventional nineteenth-century woman, quite different from the trailblazers

I normally admire. Elizabeth Cary Agassiz was the wife of the scientist Louis Agassiz, and after his death, she became the founder and first president of Radcliffe College. In my first project using her archived documents, I compared her journal/letters—sent home from an expedition to Brazil from 1865 to 1866, an expedition she undertook with her husband, his students, and other associates—to the published *A Journey in Brazil* (1868). In particular, I compared the public voice she developed in the published version with her husband's professional (but I considered bombastic) voice in both public and private. In this project, I argued that through writing and publishing the *Journey* and later preparing her husband's *Life and Letters* for publication (1886), Elizabeth Agassiz created the public self she needed in order to be taken seriously in the male-dominated Harvard of the last quarter of the nineteenth century.

My experience with this project resembles the ways Nan Johnson and K. E. Tirabassi describe their archival work in other chapters in this collection: I enjoyed the thrill of the archive, of exploring the unpublished, private realm of a person for what it might reveal, without knowing quite where the exploration might lead. And again I experienced the deep feelings about my subject that Edel describes, complicated by my own attempts to find my voice and my place in academic life at that time. In charting the differences between Elizabeth Agassiz's personal and public narratives, I learned much about the different tones that could be established through careful editing. That she asked her family to pass her letters around and then save them because "They may be useful" (May 6, 1865) indicates that even when writing to her family, she was thinking of publishing them. In these letters to her personal audience (the Higginson, Shaw, Agassiz, Cary, Felton, and Curtis families), she is openly critical and opinionated. Clearly, she knew she was writing to a primary audience that shared her values about self-presentation, education, and appropriate behavior, and who would keep her criticisms of the Brazilian way of life carefully under the wraps of polite discourse. For example, she is explicitly critical in an August 14, 1866, letter about the personal habits of some of the Brazilian ladies with whom she stays:

> You cannot fancy anything so limited and dull as the life of a Brazilian lady according to our notions. They never seem to read, they have not a thought out of the circle of their household duties, they are not expected to go out, and they have not the first idea what society means. Once in awhile they have a party and then they put on their diamonds and fine gowns & are much pleased to show themselves, but at home they have a most slipshod costume and never seem to think that a tidy and tasteful toilet is of the least importance if they have not some chance to display it. (in Bergmann, "Women of Letters" 97)

Even to her family audience, however, in spite of occasional confusion, complaints, and longing for order, Elizabeth Agassiz was clearly enjoying being a Boston lady traveling on the Amazons; this was a great adventure, and she clearly expressed to the folks at home how much she enjoyed it. Both to her family and later to the public, she gives cheerful accounts of sleeping in hammocks and making contact with various classes of Brazilians. She makes polite jokes about encounters with the rats, fleas, and other wildlife she occasionally had to tolerate, but she avoids the air of superiority Americans so much resented in the accounts of British travelers (like Charles Dickens and Frances and Anthony Trollope) about the dismal social conditions in the United States. Moreover, even in her private, personal responses, she shows a cultural relativism I had not expected of a well-bred, well-educated lady of her time, acknowledging that while she was judging her Brazilian hosts, they may have been judging her in return:

> I dare say she [a Brazilian young lady who rinsed her mouth and spat the water out of her window] may have thought me quite wanting in the proprieties of life, for after all peoples' own standard of cleanliness & propriety is always that by which they judge others. (August 2, 1865; in Bergmann, "Women of Letters" 98)

Elizabeth Agassiz tried not to be a prig.

The published *A Journey in Brazil* positions Brazil as a nation on the brink of modernity—a land of picturesque beauty with a hospitable upper class—with schools, hospitals, and other institutions of modern life being developed. It leaves out the dirty floors and spitting ladies and mutes her private criticism of the sexual and physical exploitation of the indigenous people. Although she occasionally criticizes Brazilian society and culture, Elizabeth Agassiz's polite, diplomatic discourse stresses the pleasures of the journey, the hospitality of the Brazilians, and a decided movement toward "improvement" in the country. As a private member of a semiofficial expedition (Louis Agassiz traveled with the sanction of the U.S. government and helped establish cordial relations between the United States and the emperor of Brazil), Elizabeth Agassiz formulated a careful public narrative and public persona. I argued then that assuming the public roles of writer and expedition member helped prepare her for life after the death of her husband in 1873, a public life primarily as a quite visible founder of Radcliffe College.

However, in focusing on her growth as an individual, my argument left out how Elizabeth Agassiz helped maintain the systematic racism that permeated both Brazilian culture and her own social milieu in Cambridge, Massachusetts. For example, her "diplomatic framing" enabled her to soften some of the racist premises and conclusions her husband drew from the expedition; reconsidering my work with these texts, I see that I was complicit in cloaking this racism. There are places in the book where Elizabeth Agassiz discusses and denounces the sexual exploitation of slave and native women in Brazil and their quiet acquiescence to this humiliation:

> [W]hen the daughter [of the "housekeeper" of an army captain] showed me two children of her own,—little fair people, many shades lighter than herself,—and I asked whether their father was at the war, like all the rest of the men, she gave me the same answer, "They haven't any father." It is the way the Indian or half-breed women here always speak of their illegitimate children; and though they say it without an intonation of sadness or of blame, apparently as unconscious of any wrong or shame as if they said the father was absent or dead, it has the most melancholy significance; it seems to speak of such absolute desertion. So far as this from being an unusual case, that among the common people the opposite seems the exception. (*Journey* 266–67)

She describes at even greater length in her letters the multihued slave children in the larger households of plantation owners and their wives; having spent time in the American south, she certainly knew about master-slave relationships and where these children came from.

However, while Elizabeth Agassiz expressed sympathy and sorrow for those she saw as neglected and denied women and children, this sympathy was laced with her husband's conviction that the mingling of races was undermining Brazilian civilization. This discomfort with miscegenation (a newly coined term at the time) was even more dominant in the parts of the *Journey* written by Louis Agassiz, who considered most of the Brazilian population as anthropological *objects* at best. For example, the *Journey* includes sketches and photographs of nude or scantily dressed men and women, serving as examples of elaborate tattooing and, as Christophe Irmscher notes, often exaggerating the "physical types" of various races and racial mixtures (274–77), which were elaborately described and named by Louis Agassiz in the *Journey*. At one point in her letters, she constructs a mildly humorous account of the "science" she encountered in the expedition's photography studio. In the *Journey*, she writes an account that assumes the scientific impartiality and objectivity of the scientists and the superstition of the native Brazilians who were reluctant to sit for nude photographs (276–77). To the contemporary mind, the pictures published in the book suggest considerable voyeurism in the [male] photographers' gazes. Irmscher describes the effect of one of the photographs by Walter Hunnewell, Louis Agassiz's photographic assistant, as "clearly not meant to seduce the viewer; if it served to stimulate the imagination at all, it was supposed to *repel* as it titillated" (277). This is clearly not the objective, scientific photography Elizabeth Agassiz addresses.

Because in both her published and unpublished accounts, Elizabeth Agassiz describes so much photographing and sketching (of fish, of course, but also of people), I expected to find unpublished photographs in the three archives I examined: the Schlesinger, Houghton, and Museum of Comparative Zoology Libraries at Harvard. I searched for several years for the complete collection of those pictures but was not able to find them. Ultimately, Irmscher found the three volumes of photographs preserved from the expedition; they had been transferred from Agassiz's Museum of Comparative Zoology to the Peabody Museum by Louis Agassiz's son. The larger body of pictures confirms that even if Agassiz and his assistants did not sexually abuse these men and women, they treated them in ways they would never have treated their white spouses, colleagues, and friends. Although my immediate feeling about Irmscher's rediscovery of these albums was chagrin that he had found what I could not, my greater regret is that I came way too close to ignoring the clear racism of the pseudoscientific photographs printed in the *Journey*.

In her letters home, Elizabeth Agassiz felt free to complain, brag, and criticize, as well as to observe, but she eschewed these freedoms in the published book. Initially, I considered these revisions as meant to construct her public self, no longer "Your own Lizzie" but rather "Mrs. Louis Agassiz" as a public voice. After some years away from the archive (although I still have boxes full of photocopies, some envelopes never opened), I have become much more critical about how she deleted and diluted her initial observations of Brazil to make them what she considered "fit" for publication to the American public. Moreover, as my identification with her has faded, I have become much more uncomfortable with the racism that permeates the volume, not only with Louis Agassiz's harsh, pseudoscientific denunciation of the "mongrel races" he found in Brazil but even more with *her* acceptance of his ideas, even when they contradicted her own recorded observations. She defers to her husband, "the scientist," even to his pseudoscientific analyses of the racial inferiority of the Brazilians of Native, African, and Portuguese descent—and particularly those of mixed races. She depicts individuals who do not fit her husband's hierarchy of pure and debased races as interesting exceptions, not as counterevidence to his theories. In the years immediately following the American Civil War, these reflections could be expected to apply to American concerns about the nature and appropriate roles of the newly freed African American slaves, and her implicit agreement with Louis Agassiz's conclusions, even when they contradicted her own observations, may have helped perpetuate the dominance of racial prejudice in the United States.

It now seems clear to me that I was seduced by the charm of the narrator and her air of innocent pleasure, both in the book and even more so in the private letters. I allowed myself to join that sympathetic family audience Elizabeth Agassiz had created and so was induced to take her observations and conclusions less critically than I should have. When a scholar enters the world of the archive, it is tempting and often necessary to "read with" what we find, to use Peter Elbow's concept. But I now believe I found it all too easy to accept that "everyone was a racist then," when reading letters with such a strongly conceived audience as Elizabeth Agassiz created. I neglected to identify myself with an audience more critical than the one she had shaped for herself in her letters and in her book.

The potential to identify closely and uncritically with selves represented in an archive can be greater than the temptation to identify with authors of published sources, I have come to believe, because of the material reality of the archive. One touches the actual paper and reads the actual words directly as they were written, and it is hard not to feel drawn into becoming a part of the particular, personal audience for whom they are written. This all too strong human sympathy can color the reading of unpublished work and impact responses to it. In her chapter Alexis E. Ramsey observed something of this feeling of connection while studying the clothes worn by nineteenth-century women and preserved in the Tippecanoe County Historical Association. There is something very strongly appealing about handling things the person we study has worn, of seeing the perspiration stains on the dresses, and handling papers written or touched by the writers we study, the inkblots and cross-outs that went into their writing. And yet the pleasures of that seduction, guilty pleasures or not, keep me returning to archives. I continue to think of new projects that will pull me back into that sense of personal involvement next time but, I always hope, with a more critical stance.

Works Cited

Agassiz, Elisabeth Cary. *A Journey in Brazil*. Boston: Ticknor, 1868.
———. *Louis Agassiz: His Life and Correspondence*. 2 vols. Boston: Houghton, 1885.
Bergmann, Linda S. "The Contemporary Letter as Literature: Issues of Self-Reflexivity, Audience, and Closure." *Women's Studies Quarterly* 17 (Fall/Winter 1989): 128–39.
———. "A Troubled Marriage of Discourses: Science Writing and Travel Narrative in Louis and Elizabeth Agassiz's *A Journey in Brazil*." *Journal of American Culture* 18 (Summer 1995): 83–88.
———. "Widows, Hacks, and Biographers: The Voice of Professionalism in Elizabeth Agassiz's *Louis Agassiz: His Life and Correspondence*." *A/B: Auto/Biography Studies* 12.1 (1997): 1–21. Rpt. with new afterword in *Widening the Discourse: The Florence Howe Award for Outstanding Feminist Scholarship, 1990–2004*. Ed. Mihoko Suzuki and Roseanna Dufault. New York: Modern Language Association, 2006.

————. "Women of Letters: Personal Narrative in Public and Private Voices." *The Personal Narrative: Writing Ourselves as Teachers and Scholars.* Ed. Gil Haroian-Guerin. Portland, ME: Calendar Island, 1999. 88–101.

Cohen, Randy. "The Ethicist: Attack from Beyond." *New York Times Magazine,* 4 Nov. 2007: 28.

Edel, Leon. "Transference: The Biographer's Dilemma." *Biography* 7 (Fall 1984): 283–91.

Gould, Stephen J. "Flaws in a Victorian Veil." *The Panda's Thumb.* New York: Norton, 1989. 169–76.

Irmscher, Christophe. *The Poetics of Natural History: From John Bartram to William James.* New Brunswick, NJ: Rutgers UP, 1999.

Ong, Walter. "The Writer's Audience Is Always a Fiction." *Cross-Talk in Comp Theory.* Ed. Victor Villanueva Jr. Urbana, IL: NCTE, 1997. 55–76. Rpt. of "The Writer's Audience Is Always a Fiction." *PMLA* 90.1 (Jan. 1975): 9–21.

THE PERSONAL AS METHOD AND PLACE AS ARCHIVES: A SYNTHESIS

Liz Rohan

In her 2002 presentation at the Conference for College Communication and Composition about methodologies for feminist research, "Innovative Research in the Study of Women's Literacy," Gesa Kirsch raised the stakes for researchers of historical work by suggesting that they should consider ethics of representation even when their subjects are dead. A member of Kirsch's audience wondered what an ethical feminist historical method "might look like," adding, "This would be very difficult to do": integrating ethics with historical research. Like Kirsch, Patricia Bizzell has also raised the stakes for researchers of historical work by asking feminist historians of rhetoric in particular to confront and theorize the "role of emotion" in historical research design (10). Jacqueline Jones Royster has argued, furthermore, that we should analyze "passionate attachments" with deceased research subjects because these affinities might reveal persisting patterns of habit and thought over time between a researcher and his or her subject.

As Kirsch, Bizzell, and Royster collectively theorized about how we should, do, or might care for others even when they are dead, I—at the turn of *this* century—was embroiled in emotions as well as ethical dilemmas while writing about a female missionary, Janette Miller, who came of age at the turn of the last century in a different world indeed. Even though she is no longer living and obviously would never read my research about her, I was concerned with representing Janette's writing and life with empathy and respect, even though at times I neither understood nor respected her. My passion came naturally to me at first when reading Janette's diaries set in a generally familiar turn-of-the-twentieth-century urban America but was eventually strained later in my investigation when I set out to read and understand the texts she wrote in a changed and charged setting while working as a missionary for sixty years in colonial Africa. Alienated by her reported evangelical initiatives, I had to work through my own prejudices as well as the prejudices of the academy because, as Anne Ruggles Gere points out, we lack language in the academy to talk about religious faith (46).

When working through my prejudices about Janette's past, geographic spaces in Detroit that we shared, although a hundred years apart, became texts in conversation and in tension with the other texts Janette left behind in the archives. Detroit the place became an archive to study Janette and later by default a subject from which to gain insight and answers. Detroit taught me how to think about Janette. I show that sharing the physical context of a subject by visiting the places where a subject lived and worked allows researchers to strengthen a bond with this subject, which teaches researchers how to better think about this subject, what Christine Mason Sutherland calls "living the research" (115). "Living the research," as I describe next, fuses interrelated enterprises: using place as an extension of the archive to imagine the past and recording my felt impressions, particularly when acknowledging the ethical dilemmas I had while and when representing a subject whose views conflict with popular and contemporary values, particularly in the academy.

Janette Miller was born in Michigan's Upper Peninsula in 1879. While she was a schoolgirl and young teenager, her family lived in Evanston, Illinois, and Omaha, Nebraska. When she was in her late teens, in 1899, her family finally settled in Detroit, where Janette eventually became a librarian at the Detroit Public Library. For most of her twenties, she lived with and supported Frank, her younger brother and only living sibling, so he could gain a foothold on a college degree, which he did in 1908. In 1910, the year she turned thirty, Janette decided to become a Congregational missionary and left for Angola, then colonized by the Portuguese government. She worked as a missionary for the next sixty years, eventually running a school for orphans. She died in Angola at the age of eighty-nine. She was born into a society when Christian evangelism was an authoritative world view maintained by the institutions of her girlhood through a comingling of church and state many would now find distasteful or illegal. By the time that she died in 1969, she knew that her particular religious views were no longer mainstream in the middle-class American culture she left behind. Janette nevertheless maintained her passion for these views and, by the end of her life, was running a mission, the Ebenezer Orphanage, with the help of a biracial, transnational administration. One of her partners was a Portuguese woman, the other an African woman. She created a conscious record of her endeavors throughout her life via a multitude of genres: diaries, letters, drawings, photographs, newsletters, and poems.

I do not have access much of Janette's later writing from Angola, including more than 150 poems she reportedly wrote in the African language, Umbundu. However, the materials she left behind, particularly a scrapbook and a dozen or so diaries she kept from 1894 to 1910, have shaped my life as a writer and scholar for over fifteen years—ever since I discovered her papers at the University of Michigan's Bentley Historical Library when I was a senior at the university in 1990.

Like many researchers, I found my subject by chance. I was led to Janette's diary after discovering the holdings of diaries at the library because I had been looking at the diary of a man who owned a house in Ann Arbor that I had been studying for an architecture class. I was immediately intrigued by two of Janette's diaries that I perused during my initial discovery of them. Like me, Janette began her diary when she was a teenager. I had read other published diaries before, but this was the first time I had seen another woman's unpublished diaries, and it had a profound effect on me—so much so that I went back to visit these diaries over the course of seven years and wrote a scholarly article about these diaries when I wasn't even in a graduate program or a full-fledged academic. Then, as it came time to choose a dissertation project when I was a PhD student in Writing Studies at the University of Illinois, I knew I had to write about Janette's texts.

When first admitting and using my personal attachments to Janette Miller, I was inspired by Ruth Behar's method of the "vulnerable observer," when the researcher describes what happens to her when she is at work (9). I also extended Behar's method by using it for historical research. (Because Ruth Behar is an anthropologist, she naturally developed her vulnerable observer theory in conjunction with the demands of ethnography.) I was also inspired, as mentioned, by Royster's observations that a subject, in her case, historical African American women, might serve as "teachers," "mentors," or "guides" (278).

I haven't the space to fully outline every other scholar who inspired my work and my entire vision about how I came to mine my own subjectivity to shape the way I thought about and represented Janette Miller's writings and their contexts. However, a few transformative episodes foreground my vulnerability as a researcher, my ethical dilemmas, and how I used geographic spaces to process my emotions. These dilemmas surfaced especially when I tried to find the house where Janette lived in the early 1900s, on Avery Street, near Wayne State University in Detroit. Janette's former high school, Central High School on Cass Avenue, is now one of Wayne's landmark buildings. During my trips through Detroit to look for this house, I confronted my ambivalent relationship to the space where Janette once lived—a now socioeconomically depressed Detroit, arguably a postcolonial space. My obvious task overall, according to standard academic practice, necessitated an interrogation of Janette's subjectivity as a white, middle-class woman working in a politicized situation, in Africa "converting natives." However, my recursive trips to find Janette's former home resulted in revelations to my own self about my subjectivity as a white, middle-class woman myself who grew up in the racially polarized space of Metro Detroit. My trips to Detroit made me think about and value Janette's experience; my trips urged me not to simplify her situation. By recounting these transformative episodes when I was "living the research," I invite readers into my world as a researcher to see both my struggle to delay conclusions about my subject's evangelical projects and my intimidation when considering the setting of many of her texts—colonial Africa. First, however, I will describe how I got to this place of transformation—both figuratively and literally—as I struggled to be less "presentist" about my historical subject.

Thanksgiving Weekend 2000

Shortly after deciding to make the story of Janette's writing the topic of my dissertation, I planned to stop in and look at Janette's work in Ann Arbor, about an hour away from my parents' home in the Detroit suburb Grosse Pointe where I would spend the holiday. I came to the library armed with very focused questions. I had just spoken to Rick Layton, a religion professor at the University of Illinois, and he had explained how significant the split between the modernists and the fundamentalists/evangelists had been to religious discourse and missionary endeavor in the United States. Janette struggled with this schism during this period and in 1929 resigned from the more "modernist" Congregational mission to join a more evangelical mission, effectively choosing the "conservative" side. Modernist Christians rejected the use of the Bible for teaching indigenous people while the evangelists, some known as fundamentalists, continued to embrace the Bible as a sacred text for teaching. Layton suggested that I find out where Janette's family had come from to learn the history of her faith, to perhaps figure out why Janette had rejected modern views. At that point, I thought that there might be information in Hancock, Michigan, the first place that the Millers had lived and where Janette was born. The city's clerk kindly did some research: the Congregational Church that the Miller family attended in the late 1900s was now a parking lot; all of the other churches in Hancock that had once been Congregational were now nondenominational. A metaphorical thinker, I began brainstorming themes for organizing my data about Janette (a bit prematurely, as I will explain) and conceived of the idea of "sacred space" as an overarching theoretical frame and perhaps a catchy title for my project. "Sacred space" would refer to the religious views important to Janette, like Bible teaching, as symbolized by the loss of architectural spaces like the Hancock Congregational Church—space that became vulnerable or even destroyed. The idea being: these places and ideas were "sacred" and mostly gone, outdated, and forgotten. It was a sad theme. After all, Janette was dead.

On my way to Michigan, I visited friends in Chicago and also had stopped to investigate the First Congregational Church of Evanston, just outside Chicago's city limits, to which Janette and her family once belonged and where Janette had made her Confirmation. I had once worked at a Montessori school down the street from this church, but that blustery November Saturday was the first time I had ever taken a good look at it. I circled the grounds and then attempted to open its doors in search of some kind of historical pamphlet. Just then, a man opened the church door. He told me to get information at the church office but added that the original building had burned down. Remarkable, I thought, considering my sacred-space theme. It was all fitting together, the religion Janette found sacred paralleled the destruction of the space where this religion was once valued and taught. That the First Congregational Church of Evanston retained its title, even if fatally forsaking its structure, and that the Congregational churches in Hancock were now nondenominational, and perhaps evangelical, reflected what I had read in a book by James Davidson Hunter about evangelism. Contemporary evangelists typically live in rural areas like Hancock and are less dedicated to modern life styles; modernist Christians tend to live in more cosmopolitan areas (60). Hancock, located in Michigan's remote upper peninsula, is obviously far removed from the modern setting of suburban Chicago.

So when I arrived in Michigan and sat down at the library with Janette's materials, I was looking for some evidence that I recalled reading in her diary about the coming schism between the modernists and the evangelicals, something her preacher had spoken about and that she copied down in her diary. Also, having read many books on diaries the previous month, I realized impressions I had about Janette's diary writing when I had read them in a few previous visits to them had been unfair. I had looked at these diaries as record keepers (dull) that contained occasionally juicy tidbits (fascinating) when Janette wrote about her feelings. I had learned, however, that it has only been in the last one hundred years or so that diaries have been explicitly used to record a "secret inner life" (Culley 3). Although girls' diaries had confessional elements in the nineteenth century, middle-class female diaries like Janette could also be "semipublic family records" (Jane Hunter 43). Because Janette began writing in the nineteenth century, it made sense that she would be unfamiliar or uncomfortable with the concept of a diary reserved for confession; this type of diary was being conceived as she wrote. I decided to stop hunting for those confessions measuring a so-called deficit of information to figure out what kind of history she was actually making. How was she using these diaries if not for confessions?

Looking at Janette's scrapbook, I noticed for the first time how indebted she was to multimedia for meaning making, using pictures and drawings as a form of record keeping and description. In the last couple pages of this scrapbook,

Janette had written down all the births and deaths in her family up until about 1902, when her mother died. This record also told a story. Apparently two of Janette's siblings, Katie and Bertie, died during their births before Janette was born. I noticed that next to her mother's death date, February 18, 1902, Janette had scribbled, "221 Avery," the Miller's home in Detroit where Janette nursed her mother for more than a year before she died. As I had learned from Janette's diary texts, her mother's death precipitated a string of related losses for her. Shortly after her mother died, Janette's father moved the Miller family to a new home and insisted that the then-twenty-two-year-old Janette abandon her long struggle to get a high-school diploma, a goal that had been disrupted by the Millers' frequent moves. He also insisted that Janette work, which led her to a job at the Detroit Public library, a job she kept until leaving for Angola. Not too long after his wife's untimely death, after a hasty courtship, Mr. Miller married a woman named Alice. Janette was displaced as tensions ran high with Alice, whose presence threatened to erase her mother's memory.

Knowing the profound effect her mother's death had had on Janette's life, I thought I might visit this house in Detroit as a kind of pilgrimage. (Because of the house's location, Detroit, where much of the domestic architecture is dilapidated, I assumed that 221 Avery met the same fate as the Millers' two previous churches. The alleged state of 221 Avery would therefore fit nicely with the developing sacred-space theme, which provided a connection between the loss of support for vital ideals, like Bible teaching, with the loss of architectural structures.)

I could not find the remembered diary passage about evangelical and modernist tensions. But another passage I did come across was equally interesting because it featured Evanston. In 1909, Janette was in Chicago training for her upcoming missionary career, and this was the first time she had been to Evanston since the family moved away from this Chicago suburb in 1894. "It looks queer around here," she wrote, "the house where I used to live, 1362 Ridge Ave, is only a hole in the ground. Kate's house next door is also a hole in the ground. The lots are deserted and neglected and even the fences [are] down. Under one of the big trees (dying now) is, I suppose, a little tin box containing a penny, 'buried treasure' it was, in fairy story days." I chuckled to read Janette's description of a desolate Evanston, not only because I had just been in Evanston but also because I had just pictured the Millers' house on Avery Avenue in Detroit as similar to the desolate scene Janette found in Evanston in 1909. This irony was one hint that "221 Avery" would be both a clue *and* a teacher. That I was attracted to the stories told by material structures—and places—was not necessarily a step towards the organizing framework as I had hoped. At least not yet. Instead, historical texts were pulling me into the contemporary material world as I paradoxically set out to better imagine the past.

The addresses on Avery had changed over a hundred years, and the mapmaking software on the Internet, Mapquest, seemed to know all about it, directing me to the 3900 block of Avery when I typed "221 Avery" into its search engine. The following day I planned a trip to this street, about ten miles from my parents' home in Grosse Pointe. I began my journey, however, with something familiar, at the Detroit Library's Burton Collection, where I went to see if I could get copies of the photographs of the old main library, now torn down, where Janette had worked from 1903 to 1910. I had looked at these photographs already a year before. Unfortunately, the Burton Collection was closed due to a flood (which seemed strange), so I crossed the street to the Detroit Historical Museum (I had never noticed this museum before) and walked through its main exhibits, "Frontiers to Factories: Detroiters at work: 1701–1901," and then the "Motor City Exhibition," which naturally was about the car industry.

The tone of the museum exhibits was quite optimistic, hedging on absurdity, when the decayed landscape outside was considered, symbolizing to me what the museum didactics had censored: the wounds experienced by those who did not benefit from a capitalistic society. I felt sad instead of cynical about the tone of these exhibits as I traveled them with two giggling French women next to me. I was alone in the last exhibit in the basement, "The Streets of Old Detroit, 1895–1905," a life-size depiction of old storefronts complete with real cobblestone "streets." In one of these storefronts was a dummy dressed like turn-of-the-century Janette. I became suddenly motivated to find Avery then, to get there, to touch this historical Detroit.

Back at the library, a librarian helped me find an old map of Detroit. The closest we could get to 1902 was 1919. I copied the map and then got in my car to try to find Avery, off of a larger street I kind of knew, Grand River Avenue, not too far from the library. In the Detroit Historical Museum store, I had been able to actually look at several old photographs of the city's buildings, many which, like the old main library, have also been torn down. As I drove, I noted the Wayne County Court Building, built in 1902, was still up and functional. Janette lived in Detroit in 1902. She might have seen it go up. I squinted at this building, maybe to see it as it was a hundred years ago, rather than in its contemporary condition, across from an abandoned building literally crumbling from the roof down.

In truth, I didn't like going into Detroit alone very much. I didn't really know where I was going in the city. The architectural decay of the city's buildings, accelerated by years of poverty and white flight after the riots in 1967, had always made me feel depressed when I drove through it. That day, the irony that I was looking for the home of a white woman who lived in Africa, whom the world might consider a type of colonialist, in a city where the majority of the people are African American, was not lost on me as I pondered other politically loaded locations: Janette's house in Detroit, Janette's home in Angola. While driving, I thought about my conversation about Janette with another University of Illinois professor, a history professor. In a meeting the previous summer and before I had read about the "vulnerable observer" concept, I had told her I was searching for a way to contextualize Janette's historical involvement with missions during the colonial era that was fair to her historical circumstances. I called it "an ethical portrait." Professor X seemed not to understand what I meant by this, and I barely did myself. Maybe frustrated with me, she blurted out, "Well, what are you afraid people are going to say? That she was racist? Well, she was." (By default, because she was a white missionary in colonized Africa.)

As I drove down Woodward Avenue, trying to find Grand River but really studying the people dotting the landscape, I shouted back to Professor X's voice in my head, "No, that framework won't work." I was noticing black and white people talking with one another in small, dispersed clumps. I had never seen this before: blacks and whites talking together in Detroit. But then again, I hadn't taken a really good look at Detroit. While witnessing these scenes, seemingly modeled for me like some kind of overly optimistic live-museum exhibit, I thought of Janette's love for the Angolan children whom she taught, and I felt admittedly proud of her that she attempted to cross racial boundaries at all, considering how difficult it remained in our own allegedly "civil" society. Witnessing the fragile landscape of cross-racial communication outside my car window, it also felt dangerous to bully those who have attempted to transcend racial barriers, if imperfectly, considering our sorry lack of models for doing so in contemporary life.

I was lost. The Mapquest map with the twenty-first-century directions had slid off the passenger seat onto the floor of my car, which left the map from 1919 on the seat next to me. Using this historical map as my guide, thinking about Professor X's comments, I tried to examine this location inside myself as it applied to my interpretation of the world outside my car. Could I see past the former, inside me, to recognize the latter, the ones outside? Detroit's? Janette's?

With this historical map leading my journey, I remembered Anne McClintock's association between maps and colonialism in her book Imperial Leather, "The map is a technology of knowledge that professes to capture the truth about a place in pure, scientific form, operating under the guise of scientific exactitude and promising to retrieve and reproduce nature exactly as it is" (28–29). Thinking about historicizing as a type of colonizing because we frame the past with alleged "scientific exactitude" invariably judging other cultures in the past with our own cultural biases, I considered reversing this process so the map from 1919 was leading me rather than me making judgments about it, the past, Janette, and her location. Perhaps, I thought, Janette's historical and political location, as with the location of 221 Avery, was unknowable, lost, on a map I could no longer read because the landmarks have been removed, and I was blinded by the new structures in their stead. Nevertheless crumbling, they are in my way of seeing. I would *never find* the historical Janette.

I thought more about McClintock's book, the relationship she draws between the Victorians' obsession with cleanliness and their racism. I applied this connection to my distaste for the crumbling Detroit landscape, *my* inherited Victorian desire for cleanliness. Yes, I did want to clean up Detroit. I did want it to stop crumbling, put a picket fence around it even. Maybe, according to Professor X, I was to apply this discovered desire for cleanliness in myself to Janette, to assume that Janette's desire to Christianize the world was an extension of a racist Victorian ideology, that because she invalidated the culture of Others in Africa, she assumed her culture superior (McClintock 226). But, I protested, she lived in Africa *for sixty years; she wrote and spoke the African language.* How could I possibly assume that I, pasting my present onto her past, would be able to transcend *my* historical location to understand hers? I did not want to be arrogant. I did not want to know. I wanted to not know. I wanted to be a student of this past. I drove, and I shouted at this past and Detroit for being an eyesore. While shouting at it, I actually began to like what it was teaching me . . . that it was crumbly and messy. No, it told me, I could not see this bygone history because history moved; it crumbled; it was *unmappable*.

The 1919 map did not lead me to Avery Street but, rather, took me on an enormous loop where I found myself about two blocks east of the library, where I had started.

I drove home on Jefferson Avenue to Grosse Pointe reminded of the scene from Joseph Heller's *Catch-22* when the main character, Yossarian, was walking through the ruins of Rome after World War II. Yossarian figured that when you added up all of the good people and the bad people "and then subtracted you might be left with only the children, and perhaps with Albert Einstein and an old violinist and sculptor somewhere" (512). I wanted to put Janette on an island with the children, Albert Einstein, the old violinist, and the sculptor, an island of sacred space where there were no boundaries like the ones I was forced to create with my words.

Liz, my friend from high school and college who is also from Grosse Pointe, was home from New York City visiting her family, and she said she'd help me find Avery Street later that weekend. I realized that the map I had gotten of the Turkey Trot 10K route I had run at Thanksgiving the day before in Detroit (was Detroit calling my name or what?) was virtually identical to the one from 1919 that I had "researched" at the library, only Avery was covered up with some directions about the race. The contemporary map had some key additions such as the location of new highways dividing Grand River Avenue in half. With the map from 1919, the Turkey Trot map, the Mapquest directions, and Liz as navigator (also key), we found Avery Street.

Avery Street was nothing like we had expected. Nearly all of the homes on the street were completely rehabbed, and most of the old Victorian homes were fantastically done up with newly painted trim. We drove through the street and were amazed because we had never seen homes being rehabbed in Detroit. There was a plaque on the street. Avery Street was in a historical neighborhood! We hadn't known there were historical neighborhoods in Detroit.

Next, I took Liz to the Detroit Historical Society, and we looked at the old photographs of Detroit that were on sale in the bookstore. As we drove down Woodward, Liz shouted out that she saw the old Central High School. It was on the next street, Cass, and she pointed to it. She had seen a photo of it at the store. "That was Janette's high school," I exclaimed. We turned around and drove past it to see that this old high school is now one of the main buildings for Wayne State University. It, too, had a plaque. This was really getting bizarre. The whole place, Detroit, was falling apart, but practically every building where Janette had been was either being rebuilt or was intact. My sacred-space theme was in jeopardy. Detroit, of all places, was not cooperating. Or was it trying to tell me something?

The day after Christmas, Liz and I were both home again, and Liz agreed to return to Detroit with me to take pictures, particularly of Avery Street. Still trying to work the sacred-pace theme, perhaps conceding to a very abstracted Professor X, I was playing with the idea of critiquing some of the gentrification going on in Detroit, the rehabilitation of a few old buildings into luxury townhomes, as evidence of some citizens' embracement of a cleansed history. I had no idea how it was actually going to fit with Janette's life or really had to do with anything. I was just trying to get started.

As I stood poised to take a photo of Avery Street, a middle-aged, white woman getting out of her car asked me quite abruptly why I was taking pictures of her neighborhood. I told her quickly about my project, and then she invited me into her house. She told me a little bit about the neighborhood, how the houses had been built at the turn of the century, starting around 1890 or so, but most people who had lived there had left after the 1967 Detroit riot. Other people had started to move back to the neighborhood and were restoring the homes. The woman's name was Mary. Mary wrestled with some papers in her office, trying to get me names of people who still lived in the neighborhood and had lived there for years, even before the addresses changed. They could maybe help me locate 221 Avery with its new address.

Mary's house looked absolutely beautiful. She had obviously put a lot of work into restoring her home and was rightfully proud of it. The dark woodwork in the foyer was polished and gorgeous, and she had furnished the living room with antiques. I did the squinting thing like I did outside the Wayne County Courthouse, imagining Janette on Avery Street, in the past.

When I got back in the car, with the names of Mary's neighbors, Liz said that she and my brother, Brendan, who was also with us, had been talking about how weird it was that I was researching a woman who lived a hundred years ago, and here she lived in a historical neighborhood. Avery, she said, was like a movie set for my story. The whole critique of gentrification in Detroit had started to depress me. Mary's house was cool, and now Mary, too, was part of my story. Still and again geography, material space, was challenging me furthermore to examine my own prejudices about it and—by default—Janette. Janette's historical subjectivity was not cowering beneath a crumbling building in shame and apology, nor was it behind a gate. It was standing tall and proud like a newly painted and varnished Victorian home! How confusing.

I sighed and said, "I've been thinking the exact same thing."

June 2000

A few months later, I was back in Michigan and had set aside two weeks to read through Janette's papers in Ann Arbor, commuting each day from my parent's house in Grosse Pointe. That week in the archives I found a photo of 221 Avery pasted into Janette's 1901 diary. Of course, I then headed to Avery that Saturday to try to track down the real house—*again*. (I had also lost the piece of paper with Mary's neighbors' names.)

It was a gorgeous June day, following two weeks of rather depressing weather, too nice to ponder the politics of location as I drove into Detroit. Janette's diary photo showed that 221 Avery was on a corner, which narrowed the candidates. As had been my habit as a researcher, I began taking pictures of a corner house on Avery Street that had some of the trim and windows that resembled details of the house in the 1901 picture. This corner house looked abandoned—not typical of Avery Street homes, but typical of the scene I had expected to find at Thanksgiving.

While I photographed 221 Avery, a young-looking black man came out of his house, which was across the street, and asked me why I was taking pictures. I showed him the picture from Janette's diary. We agreed that it was a terrible picture because it was so blurry. The man said he was upset about the current condition of 221 Avery. The owner didn't care about it and was using it to store junk. The owner had several other houses in Detroit, all junk heaps. He pointed out that all the windows had been taken out of the house. He wanted to buy the house, but the owner had quoted him a ridiculous price. We studied the 1901 picture and then the house. A few of the details added up: the itty-bitty 1901 trees, for example, seemed to be in the same spot as the very tall, mature, and leafy 2001 trees. "It could be the same house," I said, "if they've moved the sidewalks."

The man said that, in fact, at one point, they had widened the streets and maybe then moved the sidewalks. He said that the man who lived behind 221 Avery, Leroy, would know about the house because his aunt was the original owner (this didn't quite add up with Janette's story unless Leroy was very old, the aunt was his great-aunt, and the Millers rented the house from her at the turn of the century: possible). I smiled then, knowing how many places the Millers actually lived in Detroit, how much more I needed to research about other aspects of the story, like the history of colonialism in Africa as it related to Angola, for example. But I liked coming to Avery Street. I met people there. They were nice.

The man and I shook hands then, finally, and introduced ourselves. His name was Jeffrey. The neighborhood was called Woodbridge.

A Week or So Later

On the way back to my parents' house from Ann Arbor that day and after two full weeks in the archives reading Janette's diaries and her papers, I was particularly energized by the new impressions about early-twentieth-century Detroit and colonized Angola that I had gotten from Janette's texts. It was a very hot day, and I did not have air conditioning in my car. Nevertheless, and even when stalled for quite some time in traffic during Detroit's rush hour, I remained in a good mood. When stopped, I could look up at the highway exit signs that led to the streets like "Warren" and "Grand River," streets in Detroit I hadn't spent a lot of time on in my youth, although they were not far from my then-home. Janette's diary, along with my several journeys to Detroit to try to "visit" her on Avery, had taught me to think about these streets with curiosity and in an intimate way. Long ago, Janette had traveled these streets, "Warren Avenue" and "Grand River Avenue," on the streetcar, to work, to church, and to visit friends and family. I yearned to get on these streets, thereby cutting through my fear of this place previously connoting poverty and blight, also a "black" place. I deemed it once again ironic, if sadly humorous, that the texts of a white woman who had lived in Detroit nearly one hundred years before had made me particularly curious about these streets. As a practiced vulnerable observer at this point, I was closely attuned to these thoughts and emotions when in Detroit—a city with lessons for me.

My radio blared classic rock. I looked around at my compatriots stopped in traffic, drawn especially to the other poor souls like myself without air conditioning; they, like me, were dripping with sweat, wiping their brows. I suddenly felt a strong kinship with my fellow Detroiters, all of them—the sweaty folks in old cars like me, the cooled Ford execs in their air-conditioned SUVS, the workmen in their vans on their way to and from the next job.

I shortly discovered what had been holding us up. There had been an accident; it looked like someone was hurt and still in his car, a Corvette. Was the car locked?

Three cars' worth of drivers had apparently pulled over and were consorting—
the motley crew consisted of a white, wealthy-looking elderly couple heading,
I guessed, to the opera; a younger, white couple dressed casually in jeans; and
two young, black men wearing backward baseball caps. I had never seen such a
diverse arrangement of people like this gathered together in one spot, let alone
in the Detroit Metro area. Moreover, their gathering was tight and intent; their
body language connoted intimacy. I imagined these individuals genuinely connected to one another by "accident" and despite the socioeconomic and racial
barriers that would normally prohibit cross-race, cross-class encounters, if ever
a cooperative and intimate conversation.

In her book, Nedra Reynolds asks us to consider the importance of location,
the way texts are invariably embedded in place: "New maps of writing . . . will
devote a layer to the where of writing—not just the place where the writing occurs, but the sense of place and space that readers and writers bring with them to
the intellectual work of writing, to navigating, arranging and remembering, and
composing" (176). Indeed, when engaged with Janette's texts, I was drawn into
the space of their composition. Sure, these texts were written long ago. They were
in the library an hour away. But some of these texts, "Warren," "Grand River,"
were ubiquitous, contemporary, prevailing texts. These texts were *outside my car
window.* These texts, "Warren," "Grand River," signified real streets but were also
pulling me into an ideological place, to ideas. This place as a composition of sorts
linked the past and the present; it linked me to the Janette Miller of yore, the
physical woman who existed in the past, and the one I continually reimagined in
the ever-evolving present. The place linked me with Others—my fellow drivers,
the accident crew, the hurt driver, and unknown inhabitants of contemporary
Warren and Grand River avenues, who lived off the highway where Janette once
took the streetcar. The method of reading the landscape while also listening to my
emotions was almost a habit of mind at this point as I had fully began to associate
the historical Janette with the present landscape. Detroit/Janette was trying to
tell me something. Still. Again!

Right there, stopped in traffic, when "imagining a communion" between the
streets of historical and contemporary Detroit and "imagining a communion"
among those stopped at the accident, I conceived of a new framework for understanding and articulating the spirit of Janette Miller's texts—a main theme. Yes,
I would entitle my project "Imagined Communions." Janette's texts enabled my
felt and genuine connection with the Detroit area and the people who lived in its
environs, past and present. Janette's texts compelled me to question narratives
of racial separation. At once and finally, I abandoned a framework of analysis
connoting loss and alienation apart from a world that might misunderstand or

abuse it, the sacred-space theme; *I was to think of her texts as mapped onto and into the world, working in and on this world.*

That was the beginning. In my research about Janette Miller, I have employed the metaphor of imagined communions as an attempt to make meaning of the many genres of texts Janette produced along with the shifting contexts influencing and allowing their production. I use the concept of imagined communions to represent the relationship I recognize between Janette and myself as fellow diarists and to make visible the relationship that researchers might imagine between themselves and their historical research subjects. I use imagined communions to theorize the motivations behind Janette's diary texts: her desire to commune with others, particularly with her mother, thus drawing attention to the social functions of private texts and the intimacy between mother and daughter encouraged by nine-teenth-century, middle-class, American values. I use the concept to describe the turn-of-the-century women's missionary movement and its participants' drive to create relationships that transcend national boundaries. I argue that Janette's missionary newsletters, the several manifestations of her missionary administrations, and her various writings from Africa were products of this desire to promote harmony between cultures under the rubric of Christian conversion.

Using the landscape and my emotions in concert and while reading both material archives and supplementary reading, the more positive framing of Janette's work as a missionary "imagined communions" versus the more critical "sacred space" framing felt right to me and more ethically sound as I pulled together my data and began to write. However, it wasn't until a few years later that I would encounter scholars in general interested in similar work and also concerned with complicating the role of historical Western women missionaries who worked in what we might now call third-world countries. For example, scholars Sarah Robbins and Ann Pullen have been studying the life and writing of missionary Nellie Arnott, Janette's co-worker in Angola. In their work, they highlight the agency Arnott gained via this missionary work and her lifetime relationship with her Angolan constituents whom she taught while a missionary. During the "Competing Kingdom: Women, Mission, and Empire, 1812–1938" conference Pullen and I attended, scholars across the disciplines presented papers that collectively argued for more and better study of women's historical missionary work. Robbins's, too, has been inspired to theorize about methods and the emotions and, in relationship with her work with Arnott's writing, to consider "the interplay between a 'body' of archival artifacts, the absent 'body' of the original author, and the 'body' of the researcher, who not only assembles evidence but also composes identities." I have shown that this happened to me. The historical Janette Miller and the landscape that came to represent her "used" me in order that I might assemble and "compose" her identity for contemporary audiences and convincing me also not to edit out the spirit—so to speak—of her project.

I have also shown that these methods were grounded in more traditional scholarly activities. I "read" the landscape and assessed my emotions while perusing and synthesizing other data—including paper archives with "facts" and the ideas of others who also had "facts." Some readers might think that I have nevertheless deviated too far from the facts even when consulting them. I have also shared details of my personal and interior life. Some readers might find my sharing of this information irrelevant, unscholarly, or even unprofessional. However, describing our emotional attachments with our subjects, showing how our subjects can be guides, foregrounding the role of emotion in research, even when our subjects are dead, and being vulnerable observers in the first place do not mean that we write hagiography, engage in solipsism, or embellish data with "fiction." On the contrary, the more I listened to my intuition and synthesized what I was learning with issues related to my identity, the better I could think about what I read and saw. Realizing, acknowledging, synthesizing, and applying my feelings about Janette Miller to what I was learning about her in the archives and elsewhere also made the project worthwhile in itself and not just for what it was going to get me—a degree, a job, a publication.

The reinvestigation and reassertion of researchers' emotional attachments to their research subjects as discussed by Bizzell and Royster and outlined here also has an ironic connection to the turn-of-the-century, evangelical, feminine world views that Janette Miller embraced. These world views in their ideal manifestations emphasized women's connection and cooperation with other women for the sake of explicit feminine causes such as the care and education of children. The instinct to create communions between emotion, personal experience and epistemological systems might furthermore indicate a need to rearticulate linkages between belief and knowledge making, links made taboo in a twentieth-century academy that privileged scientific and empirical claims over emotional and personal ones.

Works Cited

Behar, Ruth. *The Vulnerable Observer: Anthropology That Breaks Your Heart*. Boston: Beacon, 1996.

Bizzell, Patricia. "Feminist Methods of Research in the History of Rhetoric: What Difference Do They Make?" *Rhetoric Society Quarterly* 30 (2000): 5–17.

Culley, Margo. Introduction. *One Day at a Time: The Diary Literature of American Women from 1764 to the Present*. Ed. Margo Culley. New York: Feminist, 1985. 3–26.

Gere, Anne Ruggles. "Articles of Faith." *College English* 64 (2001): 46–47.

Heller, Joseph. *Catch-22*. 4th ed. New York: Knopf, 1995.

Hunter, James Davidson. *American Evangelism: Conservative Religion and the Quandary of Modernity*. New Brunswick, NJ: Rutgers UP, 1983.

Hunter, Jane. *How Young Ladies Became Girls: The Victorian Origins of American Girl-hood*. New Haven, CT: Yale UP, 2002.

Kirsch, Gesa. "Innovative Research in the Study of Women's Literacy." Conference on College Composition and Communication. Palmer House Hilton, Chicago. 20–23 Mar. 2002.

McClintock, Anne. *Imperial Leather: Race, Gender and Sexuality in the Colonial Contest*. New York: Routledge, 1995.

Miller, Janette. Papers of Janette Miller, Congregationalist missionary to Angola. Boxes 1 and 2. Bentley Historical Library, University of Michigan, Ann Arbor.

Reynolds, Nedra. *Geographies of Writing: Inhabiting Space and Encountering Difference*. Urbana: U of Illinois P, 2003.

Robbins, Sarah. "Mapping the Composition of an African Missionary's Identity." Conference on Composition and Communication. Hilton New York, New York. 21–24 Mar. 2007.

Royster, Jacqueline Jones. *Traces of a Stream: Literacy and Social Change among African American Women*. Pittsburgh, PA: U of Pittsburgh P, 2000.

Sutherland, Christine Mason. "Feminist Historiography: Feminist Methods in Rhetoric." *Rhetoric Society Quarterly* 32 (2002): 109–22.

INTERVIEW: KATHRYN FITZGERALD—
"I'M OPEN TO WHATEVER I DISCOVER"

Kathryn Fitzgerald's work examines the teaching of composition in the late-nineteenth-century normal schools, and her publications include the 2002 Braddock Award–winning essay, "A Rediscovered Tradition: European Pedagogy and Composition in Nineteenth-Century Midwestern Normal Schools." Here, Fitzgerald discusses her serendipitous discovery of graduation essays in the University Archives of the University of Wisconsin–Platteville. In her response to this interview, Fitzgerald suggested that her "research projects aren't all that planned. The drawback to that is I have trouble getting them funded. The plus is I'm open to whatever I discover."

My archival work has focused on the teaching of composition in normal schools at the turn of the twentieth century. For a compositionist, this topic is doubly fascinating—not only did I expect to learn about what composition consisted of at the normal schools but how normal school instructors conceptualized teaching writing.

In the archives at the University of Wisconsin–Platteville, I discovered a couple of intriguing collections but was not sure that either had any significance outside my own quirky interest. One was a set of grammar and composition tests from a normal-school course, and the other was a class set of papers written not for a composition course but for a graduation exercise. Both were boxes simply filed with the university's artifacts on its own history. I read through both, attempting to apply any theoretical lens that might help me see significance in the papers. The set of papers for the graduation exercise was definitely more interesting, being about topics as diverse as the banking system of nineteenth-century Wisconsin to the life of the homesteader.

This discovery was definitely more of a "That's funny" than a "Eureka." "That's funny" suggests this is something of interest that's going to take a lot more thought. I didn't see the potential in the set of papers as long as I read them as individual, isolated products. But when I started thinking about them as a group in a particular context—the fiftieth anniversary of Wisconsin's statehood, occurring a few years after Frederick Jackson Turner, the historian and Wisconsin native, had declared the "closing of the frontier," I began to see the papers as writing the identity of the society emerging from the frontier, its values, its silences, its conflicts. The recognition was gradual. The resulting article was eventually published in *College English*.

INTERVIEW: KENNETH LINDBLOM—
SPINNING GOLD FROM OLD STRAW

Kenneth Lindblom's archival work centers on the Illinois State University Archives in Normal, Illinois. Lindblom believes the value of these relatively untouched university archives is owing, in large part, to elitist assumptions about which academic materials should be preserved. Lindblom's narrative reveals some of the pleasures of archival studies for scholars in composition-rhetoric.

The archival studies I have undertaken have been limited largely to one archive: the Illinois State University Archives in Normal, Illinois. Several decades ago, the material that was considered most precious was taken from the ISU archive and delivered to an archive at the University of Illinois–Urbana-Champaign. Left behind were the documents most specific to ISU's institutional history and other materials not considered to be of major historical interest. No rhetoric/composition historian would be surprised to find that a great deal of interesting material for our field is in the "less important" pile.

The sort of documents I have found of interest are largely handwritten notes of faculty and committee meetings; published school policies, courses of study, and plans; and handwritten correspondence. I have also found photos of the people whose work I am most interested in, and I have found useful some public records regarding specific points I require confirmed from private documents. I have also used some student papers and student newspapers from the ISU Archives.

As one might infer from the removal of the most-important documents to another archive, the ISU archives are not kept in the highest-quality environment possible. The materials that are there are kept in good condition and are "cataloged" all but entirely due to the efforts of the University Archivist, Dr. JoAnne Rayfield, an emeritus professor of history. Elsewhere, I have surmised that a normal school was not expected to attract the sort of historical attention major research universities were *always* expected to attract from future historians. This status has had two fortunate results: the archives have been allowed to accumulate with little organization (few hands have touched the material), and the archive is almost entirely unexplored, making it an exciting place to work.

In the year 2000, I worked for many weeks in the ISU archive, examining and transcribing documents and having hired two research assistants to go through specific boxes of material I had selected for study in consultation with the university archivist. I was interested in the history of writing instruction, broadly defined, at ISU. To my knowledge, no one, with the exception of Sandra Harmon, a practicing archival historian in the History Department at ISU, had ever examined anything regarding the teaching of writing at ISU, thus much of the early activities of my archival project were simply intended to get a sense of what might exist in this largely unexplored archive.

In hindsight, it was also clear that the university archivist was also getting to know me and my interests as a historian. As I studied and transcribed documents in the public area of the archive, Rayfield would produce from the caverns of the archive itself dusty envelopes and boxes and ask if she should add them to my truck of materials. Selection was required, as even with two research assistants, one lifetime would not be enough to explore all the information I was offered. As I accepted and rejected materials, the archivist improved her "acceptance" rate with me. I believe finding me materials that would excite my enthusiasm became part of her project. After a time, I realized I was most interested in the earliest days of the university, founded in 1857, and I became an expert on the policies and conditions of the school at the time, having read all the official documents and later historical accounts of that period.

The day Rayfield brought me a cache of over a dozen letters written by an ISU student to members of her family from the period of 1857 to 1860, we struck gold. The letters include in-depth discussion of the material conditions of the school and detailed descriptions of teachers and class work, all from the perspective of one, thoughtful student. I still remember Rayfield bringing me the manila folder and saying, "I don't know if this might be something of interest." Paper-clipped to the folder was a note stating that the letters had been sold to the archives in 1930 by the granddaughter of the author of the letters. One quick look inside, and I knew I had a great project.

"Striking gold" in an archive is not only a matter of luckily finding a previously unknown text that one simply discovers like a chunk of shiny metal. It is a matter of having created the conditions in which one might find old straw out of which one might spin historical gold. In thinking about the role of serendipity, I am reminded of Thomas Jefferson's oft-quoted statement about luck: "I am a great believer in luck, and I find the harder I work, the more I have of it." The long essay that resulted from my "gold strike" resulted from the efforts of the author of the letters, her mother, and then her children, who saved the letters for over six decades, her granddaughter's sale of the letters (the timing of which makes one think it resulted from hardship during the Great Depression), the archivist who bought and preserved the letters, and Rayfield, who produced the letters at the right moment. In addition, I had prepared myself by learning all I could about the historical context of local writing instruction at ISU and writing instruction more broadly. When I saw that this student's letters contained detailed information about teachers and classes, I knew it could be used to confirm or confront the officialized narratives available in other university sources and other historical accounts of the university's beginnings.

I believe the best way to remain open to new archival discoveries is to keep oneself from assuming a position too early in the process of study. One should determine a context for study—for example, I was interested in examining the teaching of writing in ISU from 1857 to 1875—but one should not go into an archive with too-specific a thesis in mind. At least not at first. When I first explored the ISU archives, I had no particular set of expectations of what I would find. If I did have such expectations, I would have tried to hold them in abeyance until I had learned enough to make a thesis based on the information I had found rather than on any prior expectations. At later stages of archival work, the historian's perspective is enormously important. A good historian can breathe new life into dead documents, making them useful again for a new audience with new purposes.

INTERVIEW: LINDAL BUCHANAN—
MAKING FORTUNATE CONNECTIONS

In her recent book *Regendering Delivery: The Fifth Canon and Antebellum Women Rhetors* (2005), Lindal Buchanan examines the careers of early-nineteenth-century women rhetors and argues that the fifth canon of rhetoric should be revised to include not only traditional considerations of voice, gesture, and movement but also the full web of social influences within which the rhetor performs both a single speech act and an entire career. In her fifth chapter, Buchanan examines the collaborative work that made antebellum women's rhetorical performances possible, helping these women rhetors fulfill family obligations and conform to social expectations. In the narrative that follows, Buchanan also reflects on the importance of collaboration for novice archival scholars by illustrating how her early forays into historical scholarship were supported by expert researchers in the field.

My research is largely historical and centers on women's rhetoric. Primary research materials typically include letters, journals, speeches, debates, newspaper articles, and textbooks; secondary materials include biographies, scholarly treatises, and social-movement or historical overviews. For the most part, I have borrowed texts (whether actual books or microfilm) from my own library or others; I have also accessed sources online.

To describe my own encounters with serendipity in the research process, in graduate school, I began researching a seminar paper on the writing/rhetorical process of woman's rights rhetors Elizabeth Cady Stanton and Susan B. Anthony. As I read the two women's letters, I realized the many ways in which Cady Stanton's motherhood imposed severe restraints upon her ability to research, compose, and deliver speeches, restraints that I identified strongly with as a mother and graduate student raising a child on her own. As I learned the ways in which Anthony's freedom and flexibility as a single woman allowed the pair to negotiate Cady Stanton's professional and parental responsibilities, I found myself thinking of the many ways in which I collaborated with other women in order to combine both my academic and family obligations (e.g., attending night classes while providing care for my daughter). This sense of identification with the plight and compensating strategies of Cady Stanton led me to explore antebellum women's rhetorical collaboration as a means of negotiating private and public conflicts. This investigation eventually developed into a dissertation project and my first book, *Regendering Delivery: The Fifth Canon and Antebellum Women Rhetors*.

However, when I first saw the connections between maternity and collaboration, I was intrigued but didn't know whether I had found a viable research topic or not. I searched scholarly research in rhetoric, composition, history, and women's studies, and although I found articles and books on gender in these disciplines, there was little to nothing about marital/maternal status and rhetorical collaboration, the focused topic of interest to me.

At this point, I had the good fortune to meet Carol Mattingly, an accomplished scholar in nineteenth-century women's rhetoric at a nearby university. I e-mailed her, describing my interest in the intersection of motherhood and rhetorical production regarding Cady Stanton and Anthony and asking whether this topic had been examined as I wasn't finding any research on it. She responded that nineteenth-century researchers "kinda-sorta" knew about maternity's impact on Cady Stanton's rhetoric, but that no one, to her knowledge, had looked closely at the matter to date. She encouraged me to dive in, and I proceeded to do just that.

My point here is that novices need feedback and guidance from experts to know a researchable topic when they find one. Today, as a result of this experience, I'm far more confident about my ability to find gaps in rhetorical scholarship and viable research topics. That said, I'll always be indebted and grateful to Carol for helping me through the process the first time.

To illustrate how that process works now, I began researching Sarah Siddons, a late-eighteenth-century British actress who appeared as a model of rhetorical delivery in such texts as Gilbert Austin's *Chironomia* (1806) and Henry Siddons's *Practical Illustrations of Rhetorical Gesture and Action* (1807). Initially, I simply wanted to know who she was and how she came to be used as an exemplar in these texts. However, as I read about her, I discovered that Siddons routinely performed throughout her pregnancies, literally continuing to appear onstage until the onset of labor pains. This surprised me as it ran counter to my assumption that public pregnancy was strongly discouraged until some time in the twentieth century. So, I went "wandering" and began to read about other seventeenth- and eighteenth-century British actresses and learned that many of them also performed throughout their pregnancies. Eventually, I became curious about nineteenth-century British actresses as well and found a new pattern. Many of these women retired from the stage upon marriage; those who continued acting handled pregnancy far more discreetly than their seventeenth- and eighteenth-century predecessors (at least that's my impression at this stage of research). In the end, I wrote two essays—one on Sarah Siddons and her place in rhetorical history and one on the ways in which social context determines the forms of pregnancy deemed [in]acceptable in public spaces.

In closing, I'd say that I've learned to pay attention to those moments during research when I come upon information that makes me think "That's odd" or "That's interesting." I try to follow up on such leads, reading further to see where they lead. Sometimes, I encounter a dead end, but sometimes I find a new research topic or discover new ways of looking at an old one.

KEEPING THE CONVERSATION GOING: THE ARCHIVE THRIVES ON INTERVIEWS AND ORAL HISTORY

Brad E. Lucas and Margaret M. Strain

The academic origins of oral history share notable similarities with writing studies. Both emerged from the shadows of institutionally established fields, and both gave voice to the inarticulate while forging new ways to think about researchers and the people they study. Both are interdisciplinary, and each gained disciplinary credibility toward the end of the twentieth century. Writing in 1996, Ronald Grele could say, "Within the academic historical profession the status of oral history has never been higher. . . . Issues raised by oral historians are more and more discussed within the profession . . . because they raise fundamental questions about historical practice in general" ("Directions" 71). However, the relationship between history and oral history was not always so sanguine: Some historians defined historical research as empirical, scientific scholarship but cast oral history as "supplement[al]," subordinate to written evidence ("Directions" 65). "The oral historian," observes Grele, "was akin to the archivist. He or she was a collector who made materials available to others who produced histories. The goal was to produce ideologically neutral documents and leave the interpretation to others" ("Directions" 65). Oral historians also faced charges—not without merit—that their work was flawed in terms of subjectivity, reliability, and validity. Debates about these issues have been addressed, if not fully resolved, by theoretical work (e.g., narrative analysis; speech act theory; and feminist theory) and articulated standards for practice (see Mishler; Fry; Lance). Fortunately, attitudes about the purpose of archival documents have broadened as well. Briefly, this chapter recounts how oral historians and composition scholars working with oral histories have responded to these challenges—and how these issues might inform one's

research. Then, the chapter outlines the methodological processes and considerations at stake (practical, ethical, and rhetorical) that govern data collection,
transcription, editing, publication, and preservation. Throughout, the aim is to
show how archival recordings must be approached with attention not only to
their *use* but also to the *processes of their creation*.

Perhaps one of the most frequent criticisms of oral interviewing is its subjectivity. How can we trust the narrative account of a single individual, with
its attendant biases? How are we to reconcile the presence of the interviewer?
Underpinning this claim is the lingering presumption that "pure" history is compiled from traditional *print* sources: diaries, letters, autobiographies, census polls,
church records, and the like. These primary sources are considered, by some, to
possess "truer" evidentiary value (i.e., more objective) than ephemeral speech.
Of course, the argument about the preference for written over spoken sources is
an old one—at least as old as Plato, who argues for the primacy of speech on the
grounds that the interlocutors in a dialogue can immediately register one another's
responses, clarify ambiguity, and attend to important nonverbal cues (*Phaedrus*
165–66). Writing, he holds, is more suspect than speech because of its distance in
time and place from the event. Compared to the immediacy of live conversation,
in which questions and answers create a cumulative dynamic, questions put to a
written text resound with a static sameness. William Moss identifies the paradox
of trusting a written text *because* it is an abstract record, rather than a real-time
oral exchange between speakers, arguing that this "inverse relation [between
evidence and abstraction] . . . is crucial to understanding the value of oral history"
(108). Print documents (the letter, the diary, the census poll) are constructions,
products of a writer's selective choices, one who may not be disinterested in representing events. As Gary Y. Okihiro reminds us, "historical explanations are really
only propositions placed within a general interpretive framework postulated by a
historian" (210). They are *a*—not *the*—narrative plausibly presented, but they are
narratives nonetheless. In some cases, the written document may have originated
from an oral source (Hoffman 87). Thus, oral evidence should be given the same
consideration and attention as print texts.

It is not a question, then, of privileging one form of evidence over another.
It is a question of accountability. Do oral artifacts hold up to standards of reliability and validity? Alice Hoffman defines reliability "as the consistency with
which an individual will tell the same story about the same events on a number
of different occasions. Validity refers to the degree of conformity between the
reports of the event and the event itself as recorded by other primary source
material" (89). The interview can, in fact, be the arbiter of reliability and validity,
given that the well-trained interviewer is in a unique position to produce the best
record possible—by questioning participants to reveal inconsistencies, gaps, and

silences to produce a more candid view than some written records can supply. In some instances, though, assessing an oral narrative for its reliability or validity is impossible due to idiosyncratic archived material or an absence of corroborative primary evidence. Rather than a stumbling block, such situations can open the door for new research and enable greater circumspection of existing resources. Whenever possible, the researcher should contextualize such sources, providing the social, cultural, economic, and material conditions that gave rise to the creation of the testimony and the rationale for its current use. This step allows a researcher to employ the primary source in fairness to his or her subject and maintain the integrity of the research. At the same time, not all experiences are created equal, nor are they replicable.

For the interviewer, the potential for distraction cannot be denied, yet the interviewer's presence is one of the genre's benefits: unlike the (sometimes) absent author(s) of print artifacts, the interviewer's identity is usually verifiable. Even more, the interviewer witnesses the very nonverbal responses of the interviewee that enhance the authenticity of an oral account. And some of the same arguments about the subjectivity of oral testimony are relevant to discussions about print-based historical evidence. That interview participants will report what they find interesting and significant—or elaborate on details to which they possess a strong affective response—is no less true of the historian who relies on written primary sources. Acts of editing, selection, distortion, and omission are integral to all data collection activities. Each type requires rhetorical scrutiny. For example, strategies for prompting memory (which we discuss later in this chapter) can trigger three stages of memory: registration, retention, and recall (Menninger 69). We initially *register* lived experience and *retain* some of those experiences over time. *Recall* is commonly thought to corrode over time as the present becomes more distant from the time of the initial experience, but as Gerald Nelms suggests, it is likely that recall, or "recollection, tempered by time, may in fact produce a less biased account and that it may even reveal a deception in a transactional record" (375). In other words, old memories may be more valuable because they are distant from the concerns of the present or the immediate past.

We agree with Nelms and other scholars who recognize the richness of oral evidence for historiographic work, arguing for the complexity and texture it can bring to previous accounts: (1) by "produc[ing] new information and new directions for research," (2) preserving "historical data that might otherwise be lost," (3) permitting historians "to explore the motivations, feelings and values of informants," and (4) providing a "mode of communication" for marginalized voices (Nelms 368–69). Offering a means of knowledge making that is on par with written primary sources, oral evidence should be used in research projects accordingly. Archival researchers should assess reliability, validity, and the rhetorical situation in which the interview was conducted. However, oral evidence should not be treated with undue suspicion simply because it was generated through a human voice, rather than a human hand.

To be sure, oral interviews are not new to our field. They comprise an integral part of much research: cognitive, medical, historical, and qualitative (e.g., case and longitudinal studies, ethnographies, focus groups). In addition, oral narratives are among the holdings of several archival depositories—textbooks (University of New Hampshire), personal papers (University of Rhode Island), writing centers (University of Louisville), and most recently, the Rhetoric and Composition Sound Archives (Texas Christian University) as well as many other smaller collections throughout the country. In a race against time and human longevity, many scholars have used interview methodologies to collect the memories of individuals whose experiences chronicle what we know of our disciplinary past. Due to the delicate and ephemeral nature of many recordings, the collection and preservation of these oral resources are pressing needs for the field's research future. Consequently, the practical and theoretical underpinnings of how one organizes, executes, and represents oral interviews are important to the seasoned and novice researcher alike. These considerations are significant not only because they affect the production of contemporary scholarship but also because others will one day rely upon the choices we have made about access to records, research tools, and interpretation of data (Brereton 575). Thus, we aim to ensure that archival researchers can benefit from *generating* recorded interviews; scholars can conduct oral histories to ensure that the dynamics of voice, narrative, and unwritten history are recorded to supplement print and other, more static archival forms. Our primary goal, though, is to prepare researchers to use archival recordings with a different sensibility than they might bring to print texts. To understand the best way to use oral recordings, researchers should know the processes that go into their production. To help contextualize oral recordings, this chapter provides an overview of the interview dynamic as well as the production, performance, and editing processes that go into archived oral recordings.

At first, the in-depth oral interview can appear deceptively simple: One person questions another person, and the answers are recorded as primary research data. A researcher can then simply quote material from a print transcription of the recording, just like any other printed text. The archival researcher should know, however, that as an organic form, the interview requires—in ways a print text does not—attention to its temporal, *kairotic* influences. The conception, planning, and implementation of effective interviews require extensive consideration and thoughtful, mindful decisions. Archival researchers will need to evaluate the larger context—the rhetorical situation—surrounding the interview to understand not only the interviewee's answers but also the questions provided by the interviewer. The next section discusses the practical components that inform the creation and use of an oral interview, noting theoretical, ethical, legal, and rhetorical considerations as we go.[1]

The Interview Participants

Archival researchers should consider how interviewees were selected and for what reason. Were the interviewees chosen because they are instrumental or high-profile figures, everyday people, or somewhere in between? For some projects, the selection may be obvious and apparent, in that a researcher will target a particular subject population for interviews. In other situations, though, a researcher may have had only a general population in mind and may have not known where to begin. Some interviewers refer to key figures as "gatekeepers," the people who—by the very act of granting the interview—lend a researcher a cultural credibility useful for recruiting other subjects. A department chair, a senior scholar, a long-time teacher, or simply a well-known and well-respected community member can open the doors for others to agree to interviews. Similarly, in "snowball sampling" recruitment, one interviewee is asked to provide contact information for other potential interviewees, growing the interviewer's subject pool just as a rolled snowball accumulates mass. In all such cases, the chronological sequence of interviews is important. For archival researchers, knowing the "why" of selection can inform analysis of the recording.

In the 1970s, historians showed a renewed interest in writing histories from an everyday perspective, spurring years of debate among oral historians who argued whether such history was as important as the emphasis on interviewing "elites" (Ritchie 5). While some researchers might be tempted to recruit only "important" or key figures, many scholars seek out "everyday" people who might not have played direct roles in vital decisions but can provide valuable perspectives that would not otherwise be available. In other words, some of the most useful resources might come from the most unlikely of interviewees: researchers should not discount an interview just because it involves lesser-known or peripheral individuals. Instead, consider *why* they were selected as interview subjects and what perspective they bring to one's research.

Another important source of information for the archival researcher is the correspondence associated with the interview. Typically, subjects are invited to be interviewed, and such queries can reveal the purpose of the study, the time requirements, and other logistical information. Such correspondence can provide valuable context to understand the interview. Researchers also must provide full disclosure about the uses of a recorded oral interview: Participants must be informed that their words may appear in conference presentations or scholarly or popular publications. For interviews included in an oral-history archive, interviewees understand that they will be generating material that will be accessible to others, and they have the right to limit that material's use. A Deed of Gift form (or other contract) is usually part of this process, in that interviewer and interviewee must sign a legal release of the material to the archive, enabling the material to be used for research (see appendix for Deed of Gift form, http://www.rcsa.tcu.edu/RCSA-deed-of-gift.pdf). If interviews have restrictions that prevent or limit use, this information should be included with the recordings. As with any other archival research, a researcher will want to check the availability of the recordings; if the researcher cannot find such information, he or she should contact an archivist for assistance.

Institutional Constraints

As many researchers know, interviews conducted by any member of a higher education institution (faculty, staff, or student) must be approved by an institutional review board (IRB) before any recordings can begin (see P. V. Anderson). The approval process is important because many IRBs will not even consider research that has already been conducted. Because oral histories often include references to people who are still living, both the generation and use of materials requires special awareness from researchers. Federal regulations provide guidance to IRBs around the country, but specific practices differ from campus to campus. It is beyond the scope of this chapter to address the range of issues surrounding IRB oversight and approval, but one thing is clear: Interviews *conducted for* research must go through IRB approval before they can be *used for* research. Although this process might appear to be simply a matter for field researchers, the IRB paper trail can be quite useful (if available). The IRB requires that an interviewer describes, in detail, how the research will be carried out: the project's aims; the type of people who will be invited to participate (and how they will be recruited); how and where the interviews will be conducted; whether and how the interviews will be recorded, transcribed, and stored; and whether the materials will be used in presentations and publications. Again, these supporting materials can provide rich context for understanding the conditions surrounding the interview, which ultimately impact what is recorded.

An interesting wrinkle has developed in recent years, though, in that the federal government's definition of oral history—research conducted for other researchers—has a unique status for IRB approval. According to Michael Carome, the associate director for regulatory affairs of the U.S. Office for Human Research Protection (OHRP), "oral history interviewing activities, in general, are not designed to contribute to generalizable knowledge and therefore do not involve research as defined by Department of Health and Human Services (HHS) regulations at 45 CFR 46.102 (d) and do not need to be reviewed by an institutional review board (IRB)" (qtd. in Shopes and Ritchie; see also "Oral History

Excluded"). In other words, *oral history interviewing is considered to be a method for generating primary material for others to use, not a method of research itself.* The differences might appear puzzling at first glance, but it all comes down to design. If the interviews are planned and shaped only for one research project, they are considered research and need IRB approval. If the interviews are planned solely to generate primary materials for archival storage and possible use by research-ers, then the interviews are considered oral history. Thus, it is possible that the interviews available for one's research were created for one purpose: to provide archival material for others to use.

Whenever possible, archival researchers should seek out the motives for gener-ating the materials. Doing so will provide context for interpreting the recordings and may reveal details that are not apparent simply through listening. Ultimately, the sponsoring institution or organization determines how recorded materials in an archive can be used. In general, most recordings are available because they were gifted to the archive, making the materials part of the public domain. In any case, though, researchers should discuss the recordings and their origins with the archivist to ensure that the materials can be used for scholarly research.

The Scene for the Interview

As with any historical research, preparation is key. Most researchers who conduct interviews know that prior to an oral interview, diligent preliminary work is needed to yield important contextual information about people—their work, their communities, and their environment. Interview preparation is a sign of respect for the interviewee, and an informed researcher can hone productive questions that focus exclusively on gathering material that is not otherwise available. When using an archived recording for research, listen carefully for clues that reveal whether the interviewer did his or her homework—after all, an interviewee may be less likely to share information with someone who did not take time to learn about the interviewee's public self.

In addition, whenever possible, consider where the interview took place. As one sociologist argues, the interview location is an important variable in the research equation, impacting the research findings and influencing the cultural product that emerges from the interview (Herzog 25). It may not seem like a significant variable, but place is crucial for the dynamic of the interview: It determines and shapes the encounter, impacting the interviewee's comfort level and allowing him or her to be interviewed without feeling interrogated (Adler and Adler 528; Berg 99–100). When participants and researchers do not share equal power in terms of status, education, or other forms of influence, the choice of location is particularly important because it can account for the lack of equity between participants (Seidman 40). Some researchers suggest that the content or subject matter should determine the interview location; others say that the interviewee should set the time and place (see Adler and Adler; Warren). All of these place-based variables might be useful to consider in archival work, revealing nuances and inflections that might otherwise be lost in an approach that simply aims to find quotable material.

Another important aspect of using oral interviews is the method by which the information is recorded, presented, and made available to the researcher. While some interviewers insist that written notes are sufficient to conduct useful interviews, most researchers opt for the ease and fidelity of recording technology. Of course, surreptitious recordings are prohibited—and usually illegal. Interviewees should *always* be informed that they are being recorded. Too often, though, the problem with audio recordings has less to do with the equipment than the environmental factors—the ambient noise—that can interfere with a recording. The presence of wind, machinery, neighboring conversations, background music, and any other unwanted sound can render some recordings difficult and, at times, useless.

For many researchers, inexpensive equipment was sufficient for an audible interview, but the clarity and longevity of the recording makes a difference in the archives. For years, the standard medium was magnetic audiocassette tape, but digital recorders are used more widely now. Digital recordings, however, carry many of the same risks: Recordings can be erased, damaged, or rendered useless. Advances in voice-recognition software offer tempting tools for researchers who want to automatically transcribe a digitally recorded interview, but to date the technology is still not reliable or time-efficient—and material in an archive may reflect the errors of the software (homonyms, misinterpretations of words, and so on). Although audio formats are constantly changing, digital recordings offer the promise of easier transfers across media, but there is still much debate about the range of necessary or ideal recording standards.[2] Suffice it to say that recorded interviews may appear in an archive in a variety of forms—and those forms are constantly changing. An archivist will be the best guide for assistance with unusual or out-of-date formats.

In most cases, both interview questions and answers are audible because researchers take care to reduce conditions for ambient noise. They also take basic precautions to ensure that precious interview time is not wasted. Interviewers are encouraged to have fully charged batteries and test their equipment before each session to ensure that work is not lost, but best practices are not always followed. Do not be surprised if a recording ends in midsentence due to a lack of power or other malfunction. Also, all too often, a recording will capture the voice of only one individual, so if only one person's voice is audible, the microphones might be to blame. Some researchers use a second recorder as a backup, just in case the primary recorder malfunctions; be sure to use the best recording available—and not the low-end backup recording.

Occasionally, oral-history researchers employ follow-up interviews (perhaps via e-mail or mail) designed to extend or clarify a point of conversation. Interview participants may also have supplied the interviewer with related support materials or identified related print texts during the exchange (e.g., essay, personal papers, letters, and the like). These ancillary sources can be useful forms of cross-referencing data and place the interview within a broader, potentially richer context.

Finally, researchers using archived interview resources may find themselves facing many, many hours of listening, viewing, and notetaking. Most recording devices include time counters that will allow the researcher to stop and resume work without difficulty. Furthermore, some archives provide users with a subject index, organizational outline, or links (if it is an online document) to help researchers access and retrieve particular moments within a larger document. An archivist may also be aware of additional cataloging and finding aids to help the researcher navigate through the material.

The Interview Dynamic

Another consideration for working with archived recordings is the interview dynamic itself. Throughout the process of staging the interview, most interviewers aim to develop a rapport with the participant: establishing empathy, identification, and a mutual sense of understanding. From the tone used at first contact to the way nonverbal behaviors are displayed, the interview can be greatly enhanced or diminished based on the interviewer's relationship with the interviewee. As Alessandro Portelli writes, "The interviewees are always, though perhaps unobtrusively, studying the interviewers who 'study' them" (70). We know from empirical studies of interview dynamics that participants assess one another's personalities, and participants construct and perform a particular version of themselves in relation to the subject matter (see Barrick, Patton, and Haugland; Paunonen, Jackson, and Oberman; Rapley; and Dingwall). In short, the interview dynamic is highly performative and deeply interpersonal, relying on a keen sense of *ethos* and *pathos* for all persons involved.

Using material from an oral interview requires that the researcher fully understand this dynamic, not simply skim through a transcript until he or she finds what might be useful. Because interviews are rarely linear and often recursive, similar content will show up at various points in the recording, so any utterances need to be considered in the larger context of the conversation. In addition, listening to the dynamic of question and response may reveal inflections, hesitant pauses, and long silences that can be useful for determining which questions are difficult or burdensome to answer. Finally, reconstructing a sense of the relationship between interviewer and interviewee may help reveal participants' motives—which can help the researcher determine how the speakers might have shaped and influenced each other's comments.

Consequently, the preparation and posing of questions is crucial for understanding the rhetorical dimensions of interviewing. After all, the interviewer's arrangement and delivery of questions can drastically affect the interview. In addition to a large cache of prepared questions, savvy researchers will prepare an "interview guide," a set of questions organized into the imagined shape of the conversation in terms of topical progression. If such a guide is available in the archive, it can be a key indicator of the interviewer's aims—and suggest how they were or were not realized in the actual interview. However, there is some danger in giving the guide too much significance, simply because the dialogic energy of the interview will be lost if an interviewer insists on rigidly following a progression of topics. Oral historian Donald A. Ritchie explains, "An interviewer must always be prepared to abandon carefully prepared questions and follow the interviewee down unexpected paths, always helping the interviewee by questioning, guiding, coaxing, and challenging" (9). In other words, an oral interview should be allowed to generate material as well as the means for its creation. As Nelms has it, the dynamic falls into the first canon of rhetoric: "interviewer and the informant of an oral history interview . . . collaborate in the discovery or creation of historical meaning. Together, they participate in what rhetoricians call *invention*" (378).

All in all, the relationship between interviewer and interviewee is mutually developed and sustained, and the dynamic of questions and answers is vital to study throughout the interview text. After all, shouldn't an archival researcher know where the conversation began, what was generated during the exchanges, and how the conversation is situated in the larger narratives of the community?[3]

Questions and the Canons

The archival researcher should also consider the formation and structure of the questions and their impact on the resulting discussion. In general, interview questions should be open ended and followed with additional queries about the answers. The interview should not simply be a series of interrogatories but instead should serve as an opportunity to ground the dialogue in the context of prior research. Charles T. Morrisey offers oral historians a two-sentence format for questions: *stating the problem*, followed by *posing the question* ("Two-Sentence"). In other words, the desired end is a reciprocal dynamic: The interviewer states something he or she knows before asking the interviewee for something more. For example, an interview with a prolific researcher might involve a question set up like this: "I see that from 1987 to 1989 you didn't attend any conferences but published a book and three journal articles. Since you already had tenure, what was motivating your research at that time?" For archival researchers, assessing the quality and nature of the questions in the interview might provide a clearer sense of *how* and *why* the answers were generated. In other words, the answers you see might simply be a result of the *way* the questions were asked.

But archival researchers should remember that asking good questions is only part of the dynamic. The best questions often come from the best listening practices—focusing not only on what is said but what is not. Kathryn Anderson and Dana C. Jack remind oral historians:

> [W]e need to refine our methods for probing more deeply by listening to the levels on which the narrator responds to the original questions. To do so, we need to listen critically to our interviews, to our responses as well as to our questions. We need to hear what women implied, suggested, and started to say but didn't. We need to interpret their pauses and, when it happens, their unwillingness or inability to respond. (163)

For interviewers, attentive planning of questions and focused listening are sufficient for good interviews, given that no one particular approach will work in all situations. Every interview is highly dependent on the situation, the relations between participants, and their position in relation to the material (see Rapley). In short, every interview carries with it a particular rhetorical situation with a particular exigence, and archival researchers should pay careful attention to the not-said, the silences, the half starts, the suggestions, and the implications that arise from both sides of the interview.

In rhetorical terms, the five canons all come into play with the oral interview. The generating of questions and the collaborative "conversational narrative" require invention processes, and the interview guide is a practice of arrangement (as is transcription and editing, which we address shortly). Style is developed, managed, and performed throughout the dynamic, from the establishment of rapport to the vocalization of questions and answers—the rhetorical delivery for both parties. Of course, one of the most compelling issues surrounding oral interviewing is the element of memory. The veracity of memories is a subject of regular debate, particularly regarding events deep in an individual's past, yet even memories are prepared and performed for an interview. Given the purpose of the interview and time between scheduling and the interview itself, both parties have time to prepare for the performance and develop means for remembering their plans. However, the dialogic nature of the oral interview strives not just to elicit memories that have been rehearsed over the years but to stimulate recall—to prompt new memories and reveal old ones.

Examining oral interviews in an archive requires attention to the rhetorical dynamics of the interview, but such dynamics are far-reaching and differ from discipline to discipline. And some approaches have been found to be more effective than others, especially when memory is involved. The founders of cognitive interviewing, for example, contend that four mnemonic approaches enhance recall. First, interviewees "reinstate" the surrounding context of an event by articulating not only their mental state but also their physical surroundings. Second, interviewees catalog or report everything that they can remember, no matter how small or ostensibly insignificant. Third, interviewees recall an event in a temporal order that is not chronological, perhaps by starting with the ending. Finally, interviewees recall the event from the perspective of another observer. Such approaches have been shown to be quite effective in eliciting correct information (see Geiselman, Fisher, MacKinnon, and Holland; Köhnken, Milne, Memon, and Bull). In sum, effectively understanding interviews conducted by researchers in other fields may require a subsequent researcher to do some research about their interviewing methodology.

However, if the nature of the interview is historical, even regarding recent history, bear in mind that subjects may have distorted memories of events. Among oral historians, for example, it is a commonplace that interviews reveal the present recollection of the past, not pristine information about the past. When it comes to eliciting memories, interviewers can consider material devices as well as the process of raising questions or asking for response. Some interviewers have used old photographs, tools, or costumes to prompt memories and encourage participants, and other forms of such "material probes" can trigger responses in interviewees that simple questions cannot (see Modell and Brodsky; De Leon and Cohen). The materiality of place can itself be important, as some researchers encourage interviews to be conducted on site, in situ, or via a "walkabout" through the place of the event; time lines, maps, diagrams, and other visual renderings can also be fruitful (Slim, Thompson, Bennett, and Cross 120–25). Information about such prompts should also be considered as the archival researcher works with the oral interviews.

Finally, because so much information is generated during an interview, researchers often write supplemental materials (notes or even recordings) for themselves during the course of an interview or afterwards. Such materials, if available, may reveal ideas, insights, or regrets from the experience—before the immediacy of the interview is lost. An archival researcher should examine such documents, if at all possible, or inquire about their existence, or even may wish to follow similar practices. That is, he or she might take notes not only on the content of what is said but on his or her general impressions of the interview itself.

Representing the Recording, Creating a Text

Because most archival researchers work with printed materials, issues of textual creation and composition are rarely addressed, but this may be changing. For example, in Patricia Donahue and Gretchen Flesher Moon's collection, *Local Histories: Reading the Archives of Composition*, several archival projects interrogate the conditions under which a few texts may have been created. In general, though, most researchers assume the document appears in a form approved by the author(s). However, researchers interested in working with archived recordings must be particularly aware of the issues that arise when an interview moves from oral into printed form. It is a process of translation, one that takes readers further away from the raw interview as the transcript becomes more "readable" through each stage of editing. For some researchers, the initial transcription must aim for verbatim representation, documenting every audible false start and phrase. Other scholars, however, edit the utterances with a heavy hand, rearranging sections to accommodate the conversational place holders (e.g., "like," "umm," "yes") and associative jumps in recall, to construct a coherent line of conversation or meet the constraints imposed by genre or publishing conventions. The original interview and its edited version(s) may be vastly different texts.

Ideally, archival scholars should work with the original recording *and* any transcriptions or edited texts, keeping in mind that the grammatical tools of transcription can be wielded for powerful interpretive bias. Ostensibly, punctuation and other textual manipulations facilitate readers' comprehension, syntactically and semantically. Such changes also function coincidently with the central aim of the transcriptionist-editor: to capture typographically the voices in the interview with their cadences, intonations, inflections, and rhythms. The differences in pacing signaled by a dash, ellipsis, or period are subtle but significant because ultimately the editor is trying to convey not only the content of the speech but also the persona of the speaker. As part of ethical practice, interviewers usually give preliminary transcripts to the interviewee for the process of "audit review," allowing the interviewee to make corrections, emendations, or changes to reflect accurately his or her spoken performance. When available, these audit-review texts can help to explain an interviewee's delayed response, a pause, or period of silence recorded on tape—and its representation in print. An interviewee may edit heavily the responses, retract lengthy passages, or add material that substantially changes the original meaning of the conversation. Many people have never seen a verbatim transcript of their spoken words before, and they may find the transcript embarrassing (especially in the presence of fellow scholars in language and literacy). Archival researchers may be surprised to see how unreadable verbatim transcripts are—even from the most erudite of interviewees. More important, researchers should study closely the permutations of the interview as it moves from audio recording to print text.

Issues of representation apply not only to the interviewee but to the interviewer as well. What is his or her place in the transcription? Many scholars see the interviewer's role as subordinate and subsequently minimize the interviewer's presence in the text (see Baum). But the interviewer is always already an audience, the voice to which the other responds, and no amount of editing can completely efface the position of the interviewer and the exchange of voices—any more than the interviewer can be removed from the scene of the dialogue. In some collections, archival researchers may find that neither of the recorded voices is transcribed; only an index is created to guide researchers through the content. This situation arises because some oral-history collections have moved away from verbatim transcripts and tedious audit-edit review processes, opting instead for the more spare (and economical) practice of providing only finding aids and indexes that allow researchers to locate the material—and lets the researcher decide if it is worth transcribing for use. Even so, however extensive an index might be, it still serves as an interpretive filter that may obscure content valuable for one's particular research agenda. Such practices, in effect, force researchers into the more valid practice of listening carefully and determining how best to represent the voices in print. Before incorporating excerpts from sound recordings into published work, researchers should listen multiple times to every statement used to ensure that their written transcription is both an *accurate* transcription and an *honest* interpretation. Just as with printed texts, omissions and emendations must be documented and explained for audiences that do not have access to the original data.

As we hoped to have illustrated, interviewers makes purposeful decisions at every level of their research process: sometimes based upon their own judgments, sometimes in collaboration with their interview subjects, and sometimes determined by the constraints of the genre of the finished projects. These decisions—both practical and rhetorical—have important implications for the quality of archives we enjoy and their usefulness as historical data. As composition and rhetoric increasingly relies upon archival collections, scholars will need the methodological tools as well as the ability to evaluate resources, weigh conflicting narrative accounts, and appreciate the strengths and limitations of oral evidence.

Oral archives abound in many university libraries, historical societies, and online journals and databases. Because of the delicate medium on which earlier interviews were stored, some oral recordings are housed in special collections, museums, or even music libraries. Others, sadly, are stowed away in file cabinets and storage closets, often because someone had the foresight to record the interviews but did not have the opportunity or awareness to place the recordings in more secure or accessible storage. Finding oral recording collections, then, may require a bit of archival detective work. Searching through finding aids—and having conversations with archivists—can allow a researcher to find recordings that have rarely (if ever) been used. Within our field, collections like the Rhetoric and Composition Sound Archives (RCSA) and the Oral History Archive of the Writing Centers Research Project (WCRP) can serve as starting points for archival research. The RCSA offers a bibliography of published print and online interviews; links to online databases, oral-history listservs, digital libraries, and other oral-history archives; and a list of its holdings with a form for submitting new oral interviews.[4] The Oral History Archive, a facet of the much-larger WCRP, features interviews with individuals associated with the founding and development of writing centers and provides an interview list of scholars they plan to add to their collection.

On a broader scale, the international reach of the Oral History Association makes it a centralized organization for resources and professional contacts, and new initiatives like StoryCorps° aim to promote the recordings of everyday people and their stories.[5] Of course, digital technology has allowed oral—and now video—recordings to be shared around the world, and online resources provide a wealth of support materials for starting an oral history project. For example, the American Memory project (http://memory.loc.gov), an archival initiative sponsored by the U.S. Library of Congress, has gathered an amazing array of life histories online and in print/audio collections like *American Life Histories, Manuscripts from the Federal Writers' Project, 1936–1940* and *Born in Slavery: Slave Narratives from the Federal Writers' Project, 1936–1938.* Regional and state oral-history associations, as well as historical societies, are also rich avenues to explore in the pursuit of archived recordings and interdisciplinary fieldwork.

We take such pleasure in interviewing and sound recordings because they allow researchers to listen closely to the voices from the past, and we hope that more scholars begin to incorporate oral interviews in their own historical work. After all, in the words of David Silverman, we have become "the interview society," a social and epistemological phenomenon that is simply part of our modern existence (see also Atkinson and Silverman; Gubrium and Holstein; Holstein and Gubrium; and Kvale). For those of us in rhetoric and composition, this pronouncement resonates with special meaning. We turn to oral-history and interview scholarship to preserve and access our past and generate future knowledge; to understand the inextricable links among oral, written, and visual literacies; and to engage in research practices that do justice to those with whom we work. We hope this essay is part of an ongoing conversation toward these ends—an open answer to researchers' questions that can generate more.

Appendix

RCSA

The Rhetoric and Composition Sound Archives
c/o Brad Lucas, Box 297270, TCU, Fort Worth, TX 76129

DEED OF GIFT

❏ RECORDED INTERVIEW	❏ RECORDED SPEECH, TALK, OR LECTURE
Name of Interviewer: _____	Speech, Talk, or Lecture by: _____
Name of Interviewee: _____	Date (or Estimated Date) of Speech, Talk, or Lecture: _____
Date (or Estimated Date) of Interview: _____	Place of Speech, Talk, or Lecture: _____
Number, Type of Media: _____	Number, Type of Media: _____

- As a permanent gift for scholarly and educational use, I assign the recorded materials described above to the Rhetoric and Composition Sound Archives (RCSA).

- I own these materials and have authority to assign my rights, title, and interest in them to RCSA. These materials are free from encumbrances and restrictions. I have not assigned these materials or my rights to them to anyone else.

- Subject to any restrictions filled in below, I assign to RCSA all of the rights I have in these materials, including legal title, intellectual property rights, and literary rights. I also assign to RCSA all my rights, title, and interest in copyright in these materials, including the exclusive rights of reformatting and digitizing, reproduction, distribution, preparation of derivative works (*e.g.*, streaming digital audio, transcripts), public performance, and display in any media and languages, worldwide. I understand that these materials may be used for research (such as dissertations, scholarly journal articles, conference presentations, *etc.*) and may be quoted from or published in various forms. I assign copyright interest to RCSA with the understanding that I keep the right to full personal use of these materials in original work of my own creation.

  Restrictions: _____

  _____

- Subject to any restrictions filled in below, I agree that RCSA may dispose, in a manner it deems appropriate, of any of these materials that, in RCSA's judgment, have no permanent scholarly value.

  Restrictions: _____

  _____

Interviewer Signature:

_____

Date: _____

Interviewee Signature:

_____

Date: _____

Speaker or Lecturer Signature:

_____

Date: _____

Notes

1. For some scholars, conducting interviews is simply a means to inform a particular research agenda, a "qualitative research interview," rather than a more public, archival document like an oral history. However, scholars who appreciate the methodological complexity of interviews and oral history understand that such practices can serve both ends: Many research interviews can ultimately become part of an archive for other researchers to use.

2. Library and government resources often provide best practices in recording standards. The National Archives and Records Administration provides information, as does the Library of Congress's National Recording Preservation Board, established in 2000—a telling sign of the emerging attention to audio archives.

3. Recognizing the rhetorical complexities of the interview situation, some scholars avoid the term *interview* altogether. For example, Grele calls oral-history interviews "conversational narratives," joint activities that bring together an interviewer and interviewee to mutually construct knowledge. *Envelopes* 135.

4. Currently housed at Texas Christian University in Fort Worth, Texas, the RCSA was established in 2004 as a vehicle for collecting extant oral recordings for an archive and promoting the practice of oral history and interviews. According to its mission statement, "The Rhetoric and Composition Sound Archives is a national organization dedicated to the collection, production, and preservation of audio, visual, and print interviews that document the history of rhetoric and composition studies." For more details, visit the RCSA at http://www.rcsa.tcu.edu.

5. A nonprofit project started in 2003, StoryCorps® is a nationwide oral history project that aims "to honor and celebrate one another's lives through listening . . . recording the stories of our lives with the people we care about, we experience our history, hopes, and humanity." The "largest oral history project of its kind," StoryCorps® is regularly featured on National Public Radio, and its recordings are housed in the Library of Congress. For more details, visit http://www.storycorps.net.

Works Cited

Adler, Patricia A., and Peter Adler. "The Reluctant Respondent." *Handbook of Interview Research: Context and Method.* Ed. Jaber F. Gubrium and James A. Holstein. Thousand Oaks, CA: Sage, 2002. 515–35.

Anderson, Kathryn, and Dana C. Jack. "Learning to Listen: Interview Techniques and Analyses." *The Oral History Reader.* Ed. Robert Perks and Alistair Thomson. New York: Routledge, 1998. 157–71.

Anderson, Paul V. "Ethics, Institutional Review Boards, and the Involvement of Human Participants in Composition Research." Ed. Peter Mortensen and Gesa E. Kirsch. *Ethics and Representation in Qualitative Studies of Literacy.* Urbana, IL: NCTE, 1996. 260–85.

Atkinson, Paul, and David Silverman. "Kundera's Immortality: The Interview Society and the Invention of Self." *Qualitative Inquiry* 3 (1997): 304–25.

Barrick, Murray R., Gregory K. Patton, and Shanna N. Haugland. "Accuracy of Interviewer Judgments of Job Applicant Personality Traits." *Personnel Psychology* 53 (2000): 925–51.

Baum, Willa K. *Transcribing and Editing Oral History.* Nashville, TN: Amer. Assoc. for State and Local History, 1991.

Berg, Bruce L. *Qualitative Research Methods for the Social Sciences*. Boston: Allyn & Bacon, 2001.

Brereton, John C. "Rethinking Our Archive: A Beginning." *College English* 61 (1999): 574–76.

De Leon, Jason Patrick, and Jeffrey H. Cohen. "Object and Walking Probes in Ethnographic Interviewing." *Field Methods* 17.2 (2005): 200–204.

Dingwall, Robert. "Accounts, Interviews, and Observations." *Context and Method in Qualitative Research*. Ed. Gale Miller and Dingwall. Thousand Oaks, CA: Sage, 1997. 51–65.

Donahue, Patricia, and Gretchen Flesher Moon, eds. *Local Histories: Reading the Archives of Composition*. Pittsburgh, PA: U of Pittsburgh P, 2007.

Dunaway, David K., and Willa K. Baum, eds. *Oral History: An Interdisciplinary Anthology*. 2nd ed. Walnut Creek, CA: Alta Mira, 1996.

Fry, Amelia. "Reflections on Ethics." Dunaway and Baum 161–72.

Geiselman, Edward, Ronald P. Fisher, David P. MacKinnon, and Heidi L. Holland. "Enhancement of Eyewitness Memory with the Cognitive Interview." *American Journal of Psychology* 99 (1986): 385–401.

Grele, Ronald. "Directions for Oral History in the United States." Dunaway and Baum 62–84.

———. *Envelopes of Sound: The Art of Oral History*. 1975. 2nd ed. Chicago: Precedent, 1985.

Gubrium, Jaber F., and James A. Holstein. *Handbook of Interview Research: Context and Method*. Thousand Oaks, CA: Sage, 2002.

Herzog, Hanna. "On Home Turf: Interview Location and Its Social Meaning." *Qualitative Sociology* 28.1 (2005): 25–47.

Hill, Michael. *Archival Strategies and Techniques*. Newbury Park, CA: Sage, 1993.

Hoffman, Alice. "Reliability and Validity in Oral History." Dunaway and Baum 87–93.

Holstein, James A., and Jaber F. Gubrium. *The Active Interview*. Thousand Oaks, CA: Sage, 1995.

Köhnken, Gunter, Rebecca Milne, Amina Memon, and Ray Bull. "The Cognitive Interview: A Meta-analysis." *Psychology, Crime, and Law* 5 (1999): 3–28.

Kvale, Steinar. *InterViews—an Introduction to Qualitative Research Interviewing*. Thousand Oaks, CA: Sage, 1996.

Lance, David. "Oral History Project Design." Dunaway and Baum 135–42.

Library of Congress. American Memory Collections. *American Life Histories, Manuscripts from the Federal Writers' Project, 1936–1940*. <http://memory.loc.gov/ammem/wpaintro/wpahome.html>. 4 Sept. 2007.

———. *Born in Slavery: Slave Narratives from the Federal Writers' Project, 1936–1938*. <http://lcweb2.1oc.gov/ammem/snhtml/snhome.html>. 4 Sept. 2007.

Menninger, Robert. "Some Psychological Factors Involved in Oral History Interviewing." *Oral History Review* 3 (1975): 68–75.

Mishler, Elliot G. *Storylines: Craftartists' Narratives of Identity*. Cambridge, MA: Harvard UP, 1999.

Modell, Judith, and Charlee Brodsky. "Envisioning Homestead: Using Photographs in Interviewing (Homestead, Pennsylvania)." *Interactive Oral History Interviewing*. Ed. Eva McMahan and Kim Lacy Rogers. Hillsdale, NJ: Erlbaum, 1994. 107–40.

Morrisey, Charles T. "The Two-Sentence Format as an Interviewing Technique in Oral History Fieldwork." *Oral History Review* 15 (1987): 43–53.

Moss, William. "Oral History: An Appreciation." Dunaway and Baum 107–20.

Nelms, Gerald. "The Case for Oral Evidence in Composition Historiography." *Written Communication* 9.3 (1992): 356–84.

Okhiro, Gary Y. "Oral History and the Writing of Ethnic History." Dunaway and Baum 199–214.

"Oral History Archive, The." The Writing Centers Research Project. <http://coldfusion.louisville.edu/webs/a-s/wcrp/oral.cfm>. 3 Nov. 2007.

"Oral History Excluded from IRB Review." Oral History Association. <http://omega.dickinson.edu/organizations/oha/org_irb.html>. 12 June 2007.

Paunonen, Sampo V., Douglas N. Jackson, and Steven M. Oberman. "Personnel Selection Decisions: Effects of Applicant Personality and the Letter of Reference." *Organizational Behavior and Human Decision Processes* 40 (1987): 96–114.

Plato. *Phaedrus. The Rhetorical Tradition: Readings from Classical Times to the Present.* Ed. Patricia Bizzell and Bruce Herzberg. 2nd ed. Boston: Bedford, 2001. 138–68.

Portelli, Alessandro. "What Makes Oral History Different?" *The Oral History Reader.* Ed. Robert Perks and Alistair Thomson. New York: Routledge, 1998. 63–74.

Rapley, Timothy John. "The Art(fulness) of Open-Ended Interviewing: Some Considerations on Analyzing Interviews." *Qualitative Research* 1 (2001): 303–23.

Rhetoric and Composition Sound Archives. <http://www.rcsa.tcu.edu/index.html>. 1 Nov. 2007.

Ritchie, Donald A. *Doing Oral History.* New York: Twayne, 1995.

Seidman, Irving E. *Interviewing as Qualitative Research.* New York: Teachers College P, 1991.

Shopes, Linda, and Don Ritchie. Interview with Dr. Michael Carome. 7 Jan. 2004. Excerpt printed in "An Update on the Exclusion of Oral History from IRB Review." Oral History Association. <http://omega.dickinson.edu/organizations/oha/org_irbupdate.html>. 12 June 2007.

Silverman, David. *Qualitative Research: Theory, Methods and Practice.* London: Sage, 1997.

Slim, Hugo, Paul Thompson, Olivia Bennett, and Nigel Cross. "Ways of Listening." *The Oral History Reader.* Ed. Robert Perks and Alistair Thomson. New York: Routledge, 1998. 114–25.

StoryCorps. <http://www.storycorps.net>. 4 Sept. 2007.

Warren, Carol A. B. "Qualitative Interviewing." *Handbook of Interview Research: Context and Method.* Ed. James A. Holstein and Jaber F. Gubrium. Thousand Oaks, Ca: Sage, 2002. 83–101.

DEEP SEA DIVING: BUILDING AN ARCHIVE AS THE BASIS FOR COMPOSITION STUDIES RESEARCH

Lynn Z. Bloom

Full fathom five thy father lies;
Of his bones are coral made:
Those are the pearls that were his eyes:
Nothing of him that doth fade,
But doth suffer a sea-change
Into something rich and strange.
                    —*Shakespeare, The Tempest*

Deep Sea Diving: The Metaphor and the Practice

Shakespeare's lines in the epigraph perfectly capture the nature of archival retrieval. The deep sea diver, a.k.a. the archivist, is looking for buried treasure. At "full fathom five"—or even deeper—lie the coral and the pearls and whatever else may have survived life's tempests. These relics, shards, fragments constitute the body of evidence necessary for the research at hand. Much has been lost, forgotten, completely washed away. The rest is in danger of disappearing. Everything that survives has suffered "a sea-change" and as a consequence of the catalytic action of time, has become transfigured "into something rich and strange," more valuable and more beautiful than it was in its original incarnation. It is up to the archivist to search out these materials, convey them to the surface, pluck the valuable materials from the detritus, enriched and enhanced by juxtaposition with other materials in the collection.

Before I drown you in this metaphor, let me extract a few more observations from it. I didn't set out to be an archivist, but once I was immersed in my research,

I had no choice but to plunge into the deep. Before I could study the primary texts, I had to locate them, and this meant a quest for books scattered far and wide. Fortunately, daily exercise for thirty years (no heavy lifting but a lot of walking and swimming) had provided the stamina and the energy for this deep sea diving, an undertaking not for the faint of heart. Nevertheless, I did not do this in isolation; the diver needs a team to provide reinforcement: extra hands, clear vision, backup when the search seems hopeless or just plain exhausting.

Research Issue: To Discover the Essay Canon

Canon theory, jump-started by Barbara Herrnstein Smith's incisive "Contingencies of Value" in 1983, was pervasive in the early to mid-1990s, when I began my study. Canons abounded. Harold Bloom (to whom I am not now nor have I ever been related) weighed in with *The Western Canon* in 1994—perhaps a response to Paul Lauter's manifesto in *Canons and Contexts* (1991) on how he and others were intent on making the literary canon hospitable to women and minority authors. Alan Golding (1995) and Jed Rasula (1996) anatomized the processes and products of canon formation in poetry. Ning Yu and I discovered the critical canon of American autobiography (1994). But essays, the most pervasive form of prose writing in the country, the genre dearest to my heart as a writing teacher and emerging essayist myself, never surfaced in the critical literature, although from 1986 on some of the best were collected in *The Best American Essay* series, edited by Robert Atwan.

So my study began with the question, "Is there a canon of contemporary American essays?" "If there is a canon of contemporary American essays, what essays constitute this canon?" and "Where are they reprinted?" For to attain canonical status, a work of literature in any genre, no matter what its original place of publication—newspaper, little magazine, or mass market, book—has to be reprinted widely, in many places, and read often, over an extended period of time. Little did I know at the outset that to answer these seemingly simple questions with hard evidence, rather than simply flipping through the essay anthologies in my office for an impressionistic look at what was hot at the moment, would necessitate a year of planning, followed by three years of searching for the raw materials that would provide the body of solid evidence necessary to yield accurate results. The only place essays are routinely reprinted, I discovered, is in Readers (capitalized to distinguish this term from the book's human reader), the anthologies intended for Freshman Composition. Consequently, I had to find the Readers; those that I could locate and examine hands-on would be the pearls of this study.

By then, the refined research question had become, "What essays by what authors did American college students read in Freshman Composition from 1946 to 1996?" This period spans the fifty years from the GI Bill to widespread Internet and photocopying capability that allows teachers to abandon textbooks and compile their own individual course packets of readings, inaccessible to researchers. It took about a year (this was before the Internet enabled such sleuthing to be conducted in nanoseconds, rather than months) to identify the titles of all the Readers that were published during this fifty-year span, 1,750 Readers containing a total of 113,250 essays. These were impossible numbers to deal with and would have given undue weight to volumes with limited use and consequently little influence. I had to figure out how to identify a meaningful segment of this amorphous universe.

Research Method

A comprehensive and significant sample would be more appropriate for this investigation, weighted to give priority to the most widely used works (think *Norton Reader*, the uber book). So I defined a canonical Reader as one published in four or more editions during that time period, 58 titles in 325 volumes—about 20 percent of the total number. My research assistant had identified the titles and obtained photocopies of nearly all the tables of contents—when possible, from the publishers, but publishers keep very little. Their mergers, acquisitions, and general tidiness work against comprehensive holdings. My secretary compiled these titles in spreadsheets that could be organized and accessed by essay author, essay title, original place of essay publication (not always apparent from the textbooks' tables of contents), anthology author, anthology title, publisher, publication date, and edition.

My research also required hands-on examination of the texts themselves. Without looking at the actual books, it would have been impossible to obtain any of the following information so crucial to my study.

- What was the exact essay being included? Excerpts from a given author's work often appeared under multiple titles, many supplied by the textbook editors; did these titles refer to the same piece or to different ones? Cases in point are from Maya Angelou's *I Know Why the Caged Bird Sings*, excerpts from which are variously titled "The Fight," "Momma, the Dentist, and Me," and "Momma's Private Victory"; and from Richard Wright's *Black Boy*, "The Library Card," "My First Lesson in How to Live as a Negro," and "The Power of Books." Not a single one of these titles appears in the original autobiographies.
- The nature of editorial meddling, in addition to providing alternative, unauthorized essay titles. Which texts were intact, which weren't? If they were excerpted (often without ellipses, as a comparison with the original source would reveal), what was omitted? And why? The resultant excerpted texts

enabled us to see, as well, which pieces later editors copied from existing text-books (nearly all)—in effect, stealing their predecessors' editorial work—and which were copied from the original source (scarcely any).

- The pedagogical rationale for including a particular essay, as defined by the apparatus—headnotes, study questions, instructor's guides. This material also provided valuable evidence for interpreting the values, biases of editors, publishers, the temper of the times. For example, up until the mid-1990s, the biographical information in textbooks seldom identified authors such as Richard Rodriguez or Gloria Anzaldúa as gay, even when their sexual orientation was the subject of the anthologized piece. That this practice has changed in the past decade reflects changes in society at large.

- The book's overarching pedagogical rationale, determined from all of the above, introductory essays, advice on how (rarely why) to read and how (and sometimes why) to write.

The Task before the Task: Finding the Readers

We knew exactly what to look for, the textbooks and—if in separate volumes—the instructor's manuals (mostly missing, these are a truly fugitive genre—write one at your peril!). If these could have been augmented by a collection of syllabi based on these books, to indicate which essays were actually taught, my understanding of an essay's canonicity might have been corroborated by direct means rather than by inference from the fact that certain authors, certain essays are reprinted in edition after edition of these bestselling, widely used books, and that certain questions, certain writing assignments appear year after year in these compilations. But before teachers started putting them online, syllabi were even harder to find than textbooks, and I got nowhere with online pleas. Lost, trashed, forgotten—where are the syllabi of yesteryear? But even if I had found some, there is no indication that they'd have been representative of the instruction of the millions of students exposed to these textbooks—and to try to find fugitive syllabi would have extended the research by another decade.

Next, we had to find the books themselves. Had a comprehensive archive of twentieth-century textbooks been available, this would have been easy. But when I began this research in 1995, there was no such collection, and finding the books was problematic. Even today, the existing archives—the National Archive of Rhetoric and Composition physically located at the universities of New Hampshire and of Rhode Island—contains random and isolated volumes; many are missing entirely. When searching the NACR online catalog for books in multiple editions, I've found that Lee Jacobus's *World of Ideas*, first published in 1983 and currently in its seventh edition (2006), is represented only by the third edition (1990). *The*

Norton Reader, now in twelve editions, is represented by the first edition (1965), second (1969), third (1973), fourth (1977), and seventh (1988) editions. Holdings of *Decker's Patterns of Exposition*, currently in its seventeenth edition, are more robust and include the first (1966), fourth through thirteenth (from 1974 to 1992) and fifteenth (1998) editions—but not the others. My own *Essay Connection*, published since 1984 and now in the ninth edition, is not there at all, alas—but it will arrive in my forthcoming donation of all the archival materials I've collected. The NACR collection appears—as is typical of low-budget collections and/or those furnished entirely with donations—to have been acquired on an ad hoc basis rather than systematically. Although a comprehensive collection would be the most useful, a partial collection is better than none.[1] (For a discussion of further difficulties of making such a collection related to the ephemeral nature of the works themselves, editorial indifference, limitations of money and space, and donor disappearance, see this chapter's appendix, "Problems of Textbook Collection.")

In the absence of a textbook archive, I had to build my own. To thoroughly investigate textbook publication, dissemination, and storage required enormous amounts of time and effort. Fortunately, the terms of my endowed professorship at the University of Connecticut, made possible by the Aetna Foundation, plus a research grant from National Council of Teachers of English (NCTE), provided the funding for the necessary research and secretarial assistance and travel. I estimate that constructing this archive and database took fifteen hundred to eighteen hundred hours total—a process far too labor intensive for an article and far too costly (upward of $50,000 in salaries, exclusive of fringe benefits) but appropriate for the series of essays (including this one) and the works-in-process that this collection supports.

Operative Principles: Building an Archive

The archive had to be comprehensive, systematically determined, and collected as efficiently and inexpensively as possible. I consulted library personnel about how to do this and got good answers on possible sites of collections and key words to scan bibliographies for. However, because I was an inadvertent archivist—my primary focus was always on the research questions rather than on the collecting—I never used the *A* word, and it did not occur to me to seek advice from a professional archivist. Today, my first act would be to brainstorm with an archivist or one who has worked extensively in comparable archives—especially to find fruitful Web links. I would also learn the fundamental rules and procedures of systematic collection building.

I didn't realize until analyzing the subject in this very essay that if I had conceived of the project as "creating an archive" rather than "finding textbooks," I would have felt free to ask all the living textbook authors and editors to donate complete runs of their books to this project. Whereas I had scruples about asking authors I didn't know to give their works to me personally, I would easily have so-licited everyone's contributions to an archive. I do not believe, however, that most graduate education in the humanities or most postgraduate research is oriented toward archive building, even if one is in fact using archival material. Trained to value professional expertise and to suspect amateur interlopers, most scholars do not give themselves license to poach on another's credentialed territory, even when they understand the terrain very well. Thus, professional archivists need to raise clients' awareness, not only of possible uses of the existing collections but also of how to add to these. Archivists can also help to spread the A word by encouraging scholars to consider the materials they generate or acquire as archives-in-progress rather than simply as random collections.

In my own case, the number of books I acquired had to reach a critical mass before I could think of the assemblage as an *archive* rather than as a *collection*. The nature of a critical mass depends on its context and its potential yield of results. In my own research, *critical mass* meant a large enough number of textbooks to provide empirical verification that a given essay was reprinted often enough over the span of fifty years to be canonical—one hundred reprints extrapolated from a 20 percent sample of all books published during this period. Hence, my quest, as described above in "Research Method," for all the textbooks published in four or more editions during that time period.

I acquired books in a number of different ways:

- Fortunately, *e-mail listservs* of rhetoric/composition organizations, such as writing program administrators, were of great help in spreading the call for the identified books to specifically targeted audiences. As books trickled in, we could adapt the requests to fill in the gaps.
- I augmented the listserv requests with *pleas at professional meetings* and a couple of *ads in professional journals. Letters* and *phone calls* to faculty friends who were textbook editors themselves elicited additional volumes, both as gifts and as loans.
- *Faculty inertia* contributed more to the discovery of elusive textbooks than any other single means. Here's why. Book samples arrive on faculty shelves. Those that survive the grasp of used book dealers may lurk in faculty of-fices for decades, unacknowledged, uncared for until the faculty member moves or retires, whereupon the books are simply thrown out. Buttonholing retiring colleagues and *offering to help them clean out their offices* yielded a surprising number of books.
- *Direct pursuit.* Sending a research assistant to other college libraries and writing directors' offices or composition studies collections tracked down other fugitive volumes.

- *Online library catalogues* would today be of great help in locating books for interlibrary loan and would probably make the process much faster—and, thus, cheaper—than was possible in the mid-1990s.

Results

The Compilation of an Archive

This search took three years, even though—sigh—it receives a only couple of sentences in the publications derived from it. My secretary could compile the computerized database as the books came in, adding new information with each new volume, but I needed to wait the entire three years until the data were compiled before I could begin to interpret it. Data compilation was a painstaking, seemingly never-ending process, involving continuous checking and rechecking of information against the books themselves. Perhaps it always is. Scientists might expect this, but this sort of large-scale data-driven analysis of literary texts and textbooks is uncommon in composition and rhetoric research. The establishment of an archive should make it easier to do and thus facilitate its being done more often. Research reports depersonalize this process and scarcely refer to its boring, monotonous, repetitive nature; the need to revive the compilers' flagging morale at intervals; the importance of camaraderie on the trek up the Mount Everest of data. We discount these at our peril.

The search yielded 175 actual books in hand and the tables of contents of all but one of the 325 requisite canonical volumes. With money enough and time, many of the remaining outstanding books could probably be located, but to do so is not cost-effective for me to pursue. These canonical volumes, a 20 percent sample of all the Readers published in the United States from 1946 to 1996, contain approximately twenty-one thousand reprintings of some eight thousand different essay titles by 4,246 different authors. My research team compiled the titles in a database, which can be made available online or on CD, and can be sorted in various ways identified above. I have defined the canonical essayists as authors whose works have been reprinted twenty or more times during this fifty-year period (since I'm using a 20 percent sample, in actuality the minimum number of reprints for canonical authors would probably be a hundred). Thus, I've used viability—rather than, say, supreme quality—as the major criterion for determining pedagogical canonicity. That only 175 authors have emerged as canonical may seem a surprisingly small number, but it's on par with the numbers of poets derived from the canonical theoretical explanation of canon formation in poetry (see Rasula; and Golding). And it's comparable to the percentage of canonical autobiographers derived from my own prior research in canonical autobiography (Bloom and Yu).

Research Yield

This archive provides innumerable possibilities for research, actual and potential. It has enabled me to determine the influence of these canonical textbooks in general and the essay canon in particular on the values, virtues, and limitations of twentieth-century composition pedagogy in "The Essay Canon" (1999), the stakeout article for an entire book on the canonical essays of freshman composition. These textbooks, in fact, provide a compendium of readings of fifty years of American culture in the second half of the twentieth century, the years in which most people teaching composition today came of age. Thus, they offer a window on American values—aesthetic, literary, political, psychological, sociological, religious, economic—and evidence through texts and apparatus alike as to how these changed over time. Adding to the textbooks themselves are four Readers based on the canon research that I edited or coedited: *The St. Martin's Custom Reader* (2001), *The Arlington Reader: Canons and Contexts* (2003, 2nd ed. 2008, 3rd ed. forthcoming), *The Brief Arlington Reader* (2004), and *The Essay Connection*, sixth (2001) through ninth (2010) editions.

Other of my research publications and conference presentations based on this textbook archive include a further examination of the enduring essay canon in "Essays with Legs" (2007), and analyses of the textbook material for the following issues:

- *class*—"The Ineluctable Elitism of Essays and Why They Prevail in First-Year Composition Courses" (2007)
- *gender*—"Women Writers in the Center: Canonical Women Essayists" (2006)
- *authorial presence*—"The Essayist In—and Behind—the Essay: Vested Writers, Invested Readers"(2004)
- *pedagogy*—"Good Enough Writing" (2006)
- *anthology compilation*—"Once More to the Essay: The Essay Canon and Composition Textbooks" (2000)
- *archival possibilities*—"Stalking the Wild Archive" (2007) and "Deep Sea Diving" (2010), which you are reading here

There are more to come.

Archival Gift

What has become an archive for my own research in the past decade will in time become a gift to the profession. To supply new answers for new questions that others will ask, I will make the database available online and on CD for future researchers and donate all the 175 to 200 books collected and auxiliary materials (including photocopies of the tables of contents of all 325 books) to the National Archives of Composition and Rhetoric when my own research is completed.

Research Potential for Others

Research potential, like beauty, is in the eye of the beholder. A single researcher, or team, does not have world enough and time to explore all the possibilities embedded in the primary materials. Some topics to pursue, buried in plain sight in my textbook archive, include the following:

- the evolution of a political or topical issue (feminism, ecology, civil liberties) over a twenty-five- or fifty-year period, as represented in selected canonical Readers
- the rise and fall of particular authors (Emerson, Mailer, Woolf)
- the emergence of women, African American, and other ethnic authors
- readers and political correctness
- changes in pedagogy—advice on reading or writing—in a single Reader or between two or more different types of Readers
- reasons for the pervasive persistence of modes-of-discourse Readers (despite long-term discrediting of the "modes" approach in teaching)
- changes in headnote composition—such as disclosure of sensitive biographical information (sexual preference, for instance), discussion of political issues
- changes in Readers' levels of difficulty and assumptions about student readers
- use (or avoidance) of research on rhetorical theory and composition studies
- book design—uses of color, illustrations, white space, and more
- embedded conflicts between marketing considerations and best-practices pedagogy

Each of these topics—of the many awaiting exploration—embeds possibilities for original research, discovery, controversy, and genuine additions to our understanding of the vast swath of humanistic writing to which virtually all first-year college students in America are exposed. This archive, like all, is at your service.

Appendix: Problems of Textbook Collection

Apparently, myself now excepted, nobody loves or systematically keeps large numbers of textbooks from the past half century. Why?

The ephemeral nature of the works themselves. In the sink-or-swim ocean of composition textbook publishing, 80 percent of books published in first editions are not revised and republished. Too often, they are adopted only by their author or the author's school. They sink like stones. In recent years, as we know, in order to try to starve the used-book market, publishers pressure the surviving authors to revise their books on a three-year cycle, whether or not changes in the discipline warrant this. There is little incentive for anyone, except the authors themselves, to keep the out-of-date volumes.

Editorial indifference. Publishers treat textbooks as commodities, rather than works of literature or repositories of pedagogical theory and lore; like cars, new models quickly become obsolete and are junked. Thus, even publishers don't keep copies of old volumes, that is, editions of books they themselves have published earlier than the previous edition or two, either. Unless they are bound with the textbook, instructor's guides are even more quickly expendable, sometimes disappearing while the work to which they refer is still in print. (Often, now, instructor's guides are available only online, presumably for the life of the edition to which they pertain.) This practice is exacerbated by publishers' mergers and frequent changes of editors, whose successors have little or no investment—emotional or economic—in their predecessors' projects.

Limitations of money. As a matter of policy and economy, libraries rarely buy or keep textbooks, especially older editions. Why invest in works doomed to obsolescence? Textbooks lose their transience when they assume historical interest as part of a pedagogical collection, but it takes specialist scholars in the field to recognize the latent worth of such a compilation.

Limitations of space. Storage space is always limited in libraries, offices, and businesses; space costs money, and collections of obsolete textbooks are not seen as having high historical or research value by people outside certain areas of composition studies and rhetoric. Even the cognoscenti have to weed (a lovely biblio-agrarian term) their collections or be buried by the annual harvest of publishers' samples.

Limitations of time. Strike while the donor is alive! In the final analysis, even pack-rat faculty clearing out their offices upon retirement are likely to discard their treasure trove. That is the time for the collector to pounce. Prospective collectors, perhaps in conjunction with their libraries, should keep track of the whereabouts—and health—of the profession's elders. Libraries at the author's home and school should not take for granted that they will be the recipients of the author's work, either upon retirement or death; suitors should anticipate the inevitable, woo the prospective donor, and obtain an agreement to acquire the goodies at the appropriate time.

Every archive needs an advocate who can ensure uninterrupted institutional commitment of personnel, space, and funds to maintain any archive, of whatever size. And every archive needs an archival advocate, to scold, nag, lobby, and otherwise keep the collection visible and alive.

Note

1. Researchers—and, I assume, archivists—always think that more is better and that the whole is better than the sum of its parts. The current platinum standard for archival collections in the United States is the Harry Ransom Humanities Research Center at the University of Texas, Austin. Begun in 1956, the Ransom Center since 1988 has been directed by Thomas F. Stanley, who with annual multimillion dollar funding, "has attracted a great deal of notoriety through eye-popping acquisitions (including the papers of Isaac Bashevis Singer, Norman Mailer, David Mamet, and the Watergate-related papers of Carl Bernstein and Bob Woodward)"—for $5 million (Bryne A10). For a dazzling list of holdings ranging from Woody Allen, Lord Byron, e. e. cummings, T. S. Eliot, George Eliot, and James Joyce to David O. Selznick, John Steinbeck, Dylan Thomas, Walt Whitman, W. B. Yeats, and Florenz Ziegfeld, see http://www.hrc.utexas.edu/research/fa/#.

Works Cited

Atwan, Robert, ed. *The Best American Essays*. Boston: Houghton, 1986.

Bloom, Harold. *The Western Canon: The Books and School of the Ages*. New York: Harcourt, 1994.

Bloom, Lynn Z. "The Essay Canon" *College English* 61.4 (1999): 401–30.

——, ed. *The Essay Connection: Readings for Writers*. Boston: Houghton, 6th ed., 2001; 7th ed., 2003; 8th ed., 2006. 9th ed. Cengage, 2010.

——. "The Essayist In—and Behind—the Essay: Vested Writers, Invested Readers." *The Private, the Public, and the Published: Reconciling Private Lives and Public Rhetoric*. Ed. Barbara Couture and Thomas Kent. Logan: Utah State UP, 2004. 94–111.

——. "Essays with Legs." NonfictionNow Conference. University of Iowa, Iowa City. Nov. 2007.

——. "Good Enough Writing." *What Is 'College Level' Writing?* Ed. Patrick Sullivan and Howard Tinberg. Urbana, IL: NCTE, 2006. 71–91.

——. "The Ineluctable Elitism of Essays and Why They Prevail in First-Year Composition Courses." *Open Words*. 1.2 (2007): 62–78.

——. "Once More to the Essay: The Essay Canon and Composition Textbooks." *symplokē* 8.1–2 (2000): 20–35. Rpt. in *On Anthologies: Politics and Pedagogy*. Ed. Jeffrey R. Di Leo. Lincoln: U of Nebraska P, 2004.

——. "Stalking the Wild Archive." College Conference on Composition and Communication. New York. March 2007.

——. "Women Writers in the Center. Canonical Women Essayists." College Conference on Composition and Communication. Chicago. March 2006.

Bloom, Lynn Z., and Louise Z. Smith, eds., with Ning Yu. *The Arlington Reader: Canons and Contexts*. New York: Bedford, 2003. 2nd ed., with Louise Z. Smith. New York: Bedford, 2008.

——, eds. *The Brief Arlington Reader: Canons and Contexts*. New York: Bedford, 2004.

——, eds. *The St. Martin's Custom Reader*. New York: Bedford, 2001.

Bloom, Lynn Z., and Ning Yu. "An American Autobiography: The Changing Critical Canon." *a/b: Auto/Biography Studies* 9.2 (1994): 167–80.

Byrne, Richard. "20 Years of Archival Ambition." *Chronicle of Higher Education*, 3 Aug. 2007, A:10–11.

Decker, Randall. *Decker's Patterns of Exposition*. Boston: Little, 1966; 4th ed., 1974; 5th ed., 1976; 6th ed., 1978; 7th ed., 1980; 8th ed., 1982.

Decker, Randall, and Robert Schwegler. *Decker's Patterns of Exposition.* Boston: Little, 9th ed., 1984; 10th ed., 1986. New York: Addison-Wesley, 11th ed., 1988; 12th ed., 1990; 13th ed., 1992; 15th ed., 1998.

Eastman, Arthur, et al., eds. *The Norton Reader.* New York: Norton, 1965; 2nd ed., 1969; 3rd ed., 1973; 4th ed., 1977; 7th ed. 1988.

Golding, Alan. *From Outlaw to Classic: Canons in American Poetry.* Madison: U of Wisconsin P, 1995.

Jacobus, Lee. *The World of Ideas.* New York: Bedford, 1983; 3rd ed., 1990; 7th ed., 2005.

Lauter, Paul. *Canons and Contexts.* New York: Oxford UP, 1991.

Rasula, Jed. *The American Poetry Wax Museum: Reality Effects, 1940–1990.* Urbana, IL: NCTE, 1996.

Schwegler, Robert. *Patterns of Exposition.* New York: Longman, 2003.

Smith, Barbara Herrnstein. "Contingencies of Value." *Critical Inquiry* 10.1 (1983): 1–35. Rpt. in Smith, *Contingencies of Value: Alternative Perspectives for Critical Theory.* Cambridge, MA: Harvard UP, 1988.

AUTOBIOGRAPHY OF AN ARCHIVIST

Nan Johnson

> There are several myths attending the archive. One is that it is
> unmediated, that objects located there might mean something
> outside of the framing of the archival impetus itself.
>
> —*Diana Taylor,* The Archive and the Repertoire:
> Performing Cultural Memory in America

In the mid-1980s, I was a young assistant professor with no training in historical research whatsoever who had set for herself the task of writing a project entitled "Nineteenth-century Rhetoric in North America." I was working in the Department of English at the University of British Columbia teaching the history and theory of rhetoric, composition, and argument courses. Nothing I was doing professionally and nothing I had done up that time, including writing a dissertation, had prepared me to do historical research. When I look back on it, I am surprised I ever came up with anything, so haphazard was my lurching after method. I certainly did not know that archival research, acts of collecting, and "framing" historical evidence would transform my understanding of historiography and my definition of what it means to account for the history of rhetorical practices as cultural phenomena.

Like most English studies folks, I had been trained in close reading. As I cast about for a sense of historical method, my first hunch was that my colleagues in the "old" periods like medieval and Renaissance must know *something* about historical research. I sought them out in their offices, cornering them with what must have seemed the most obvious question of all time: "I want to trace the development of nineteenth-century rhetoric, what do I do first?" Lucky for me they had an answer: "Identify archives where there are holdings that would help you, go there, study the texts, start gathering evidence." At the same time, I knew that Andrea Lunsford (my colleague at UBC at the time) and Winifred Horner (the first history of rhetoric scholar I met) had been doing historical research on Scottish rhetoric. These good women had even *traveled to Scotland* to gather editions of texts and study archival material.

Pointed in the direction of archives and gathering primary texts by good advice and example, I filled out my first grant proposal requesting travel money for archival research. Startled to actually get the money, I traveled to the British Library, the Bodleian Library at Oxford University, rare-book collections at Cambridge University, the Canadian National Archives in Ottawa, and Robarts Library at the University of Toronto. I imposed on the patience of archivists and research librarians as I learned by trial and error how to identify sources and to record and copy what seemed important. I found, as most archival scholars do, that there is a great deal of serendipity in archival research. Sometimes I found what I thought I was looking for, sometimes I did not; sometimes I found something else instead and that lead me to material I never expected. As time went on, I would come to have a high regard for the discovery of the *unexpected*; so often evidence I had not anticipated would lead me to knowledge I had not envisioned.

In the early days, I was unconscious of all this as an intellectual process. In addition to traveling to archives, I also consulted archives at a distance, becoming a familiar face to our interlibrary-loan librarian and staff as I sent for college catalogues and nineteenth-century American textbooks and materials I could not find in Canada. I began to write, relying on piles of note cards, photocopies of textbooks and dissertations, a fledgling collection of hardcopies of nineteenth-century rhetoric texts, and manila folders galore packed with secondary articles on nineteenth-century rhetoric. I plunged into writing *Nineteenth-Century Rhetoric in North America* with the illusion of the innocent: I thought I had located, studied, copied, and collected enough data.

About two-thirds the way through and writing under a preliminary contract from Southern Illinois University Press, a creeping sense of panic started to come over me. I realized I did *not* have enough material to finish the book. I had ended up writing an account that lead to a final chapter that I could not document. (Anyone else had *this* experience?) *Now*, I know that this kind of gap is actually a wondrous opportunity for intellectual and archival invention. *Then*, all I knew was that I wanted to finish the book with a discussion of how the formal discipline of rhetoric supported the cultural agenda for liberal education in North America, and it looked to me like I did not have the primary materials to do it. "Not a whole other round of archival research," I moaned. Desperate and racing for the tape of a submission deadline, I culled through my piles and folders and library of texts just in case I had missed something! This was the moment that without consciousness of my method, I visited the archive of my own for the first time.

Within the archive I already had, I was intrigued to find that I had more than enough material to pursue the argument I wanted to make in what became the last chapter in *Nineteenth-Century Rhetoric in North America*, "Habits of Eloquence" (173–226). Packed into small, Girl Scout cookie–size cardboard boxes arranged across the old couch in my cramped study, tucked into folders in my two rolling files, embedded in stacks of already much-beloved old textbooks, I located evidence I did not realize I had already collected: speeches by key educators addressing the importance of rhetoric in a liberal education; essays by similar figures published in nineteenth-century education periodicals; arguments for the benefits of rhetorical study in the introductions of textbooks by Samuel P. Newman, Alexander Bain, and John Franklin Genung; and annotations in college catalogues explaining the intended outcomes of rhetoric classes. The recognition that I had the evidence I needed in my own untidy collection of research materials, not yet an "archive" in my own thinking, was a key moment in my life as a writer of archival histories. This was the first time it occurred to me that there was reason and rhyme in what and how material gets collected that was not always immediately clear.

As I did my archival research for my first project, the acts of "framing" that shape how an archive becomes an archive and the configuration of the knowledge it represents observed by Diana Taylor were well underway in my process. I can see, looking back, that as I researched, identified, studied, found, made choices, and followed leads, I was giving contour, weight, direction, and angle to the materials I collected. Those configuring choices affected the substance of the historical narrative I ended up writing. Perhaps, the surprise that I had material I did not really remember collecting was just a *forgetting* of methodological choices I had already made. I do not think this process is as simple as saying one finds the evidence in an archive that one is looking for. It feels messier than that: more creative, more intellectually intuitive, more metonymic. I understand what Taylor means by "framing" and by likening the archival process to an inexplicable dance between what we go to find and what is there to recognize. This sounds a bit like comparing the archival experience to making art.

The autobiography of my life as a collector and archivist picks up again after my first project was published. After writing my narrative about nineteenth-century academic rhetoric, I seemed to have material "left over." After moving to take job at Ohio State University, I unpacked my materials for the completed project thinking I would store what I had already used. (Interestingly, it never occurred to me to actually dispose of any of these materials.) Instead, I found myself trying to make sense of these leftovers. Upon closer inspection, I could see that I had collected a greater range of rhetoric texts than I treated in my discussion of academic rhetorical theory and practices. In the leftovers were assorted letter-writing manuals, elocution texts, rhetoric reciters, and reading anthologies. I had not used this historical material because in my original mindset, these texts represented popular rhetorical education, and that fell outside the territory I had charted for myself in the first book. Actually, these leftovers comprised a "collection within the larger collection." In the terms I would use now, I had compiled an "archive within an archive," and that newly recognized material would point the way toward a new historical project. The leftovers, appropriately recognized and framed as new evidence, were pointing toward another narrative waiting to be written. As it turned out, at the very next Conference on College Composition and Communication, I presented a paper on popular rhetorical education in nineteenth-century America. It was at this time that I also began working on the parlor rhetoric concept that would coanchor my second project, *Gender and Rhetorical Space in American Life: 1866–1910* (2002). I never did store any material. I was thinking like an archivist even then.

There is an important postscript to this moment in my story when I first recategorized leftover material as part of the archival core for a new inquiry. As amazing as it is to me now, twenty years ago I was aware of but not focused on the gender and class politics of rhetorical education, or so I thought. Interestingly, the unpacking and pretense at organizing storage revealed yet another set of leftovers, yet another collection within the collection. I had also collected material on nineteenth-century attitudes toward women's education, curriculum information from women's colleges, and flagged passages or references to women in the textbooks or documents already in the archive. It would take much more time before the force of this second collection within the collection would reveal the connection between parlor rhetoric and gendered rhetorical space that emerged later as the dual focus of my second project.

The years unfolded in a crowded and intense way. Persistently in a back corner of my scholarly mind, the project yoking popular rhetoric, gender, and rhetorical space slowly developed. The most tangible fact that this project was being nurtured somewhere in my mind was that I continued to collect historical materials. Only now, I collected in categories. My archival method had evolved definitively; earlier, I stumbled unknowingly into collecting in categories I had framed without noticing it. Now, I quite consciously collected in particular genres, primarily letter-writing manuals, elocution texts, parlor rhetoric manuals, and anthologies of readings for performance. The archive was filling up with popular rhetoric handbooks. At the same time but still less intensely, I began to amass more material on nineteenth-century cultural attitudes toward women's rhetorical education and any gendered rhetoric materials I came across. As I sought out rhetoric manuals marketed to the general public, I found texts like *The Ellen Terry's Ladies Reciter* (1884), a volume compiled in the name of that great lady of the Shakespearean theater and claiming to be a "Proper book to put into the hands of schoolgirls, sweethearts, wives and daughters "(iv). This cross-over text that was both popular and gendered was interesting. "Where there was one manual like this, there must be another," I reasoned. From then on, I was on the lookout for rhetoric manuals that were aimed at one gender or the other, and I found several. Through incremental recalibrations of what I sought and what I collected, the gap closed slowly between the popular rhetoric collection and the gender and rhetoric collection within my ever-expanding archive.

At this point in my story, collecting archival material had become a heuristic act. Collecting had become as important to my ability to imagine a historical problem as the close study of texts, background reading, or the review of existing scholarship. The determinate dialectic between the material and the intellectual imagination blended the roles of collector and archivist irrevocably, making the act of collecting historical material an inquiry laden with tendency. It might seem too simple to say that acts of collecting and the formation of the collection epistemologically constructed the argument I would eventually make about the gendered struggle in American culture over rhetorical space. Yet, the historical evidence, continually shaped by framed collecting, would eventually provide an intellectual hologram for the project, an insight hovering above the archive waiting to be seen.

Through tumultuous and challenging times in my life, I never stopped collecting. Every antique mall, antiquarian bookstore, and second-hand whatnot shop in my path was an opportunity to look for books and any trace of the popular uses of rhetoric. While others on the tour of William T. Sherman's boyhood home in Lancaster, Ohio, were listening attentively to the tour guide describe the famous general's early life, I was leaning as close as possible to the only bookcase in the historic residence to see if a copy of Ebenezer Porter's *Rhetorical Reader* (1848) or Albert Cogswell's *Gentlemen's Perfect Letter Writer* (1877) might be spied through the smoky-glass case supposedly holding Sherman's original library. Somewhat like a dedicated birder, I diligently recorded such sightings in small, unexpected archives: historic residences, historical societies, even the "libraries" of old inns claiming to have historical relevance. I carefully filed my notes as if I were adding the literal texts to my archive. The imperative of collecting was by now a constant intellectual habit.

One cold, snowy day (possibly 1996), a huge billboard advertising the antique mall that "had everything" enticed me off Interstate 71 despite worsening blizzard conditions. I drove away an hour later with a copy of *The American Orator* (1901), a parlor rhetoric text that included photographs I would later use in *Gender*

and Rhetorical Space to illustrate the limitations of "feminine" rhetorical performances. I had no idea that winter day exactly how *The American Orator* would
figure in my developing theory of gendered rhetorical space; I was only exalted
to have "new stuff" in my hands. Smiling all the way up the icy on-ramp headed
south to Columbus, I bore the volume home in triumph. Collecting efforts like
these, too numerous to count, sustained an enterprise of scholarly research even
when few words got down on the page. My sense of the domain and ideology of
parlor rhetoric deepened as my archive of popular treatises grew, and folders
bulged with copies of elocution manuals and letter-writing guides. Collecting
was thinking: thinking was collecting.

My new collections of letter writing texts, elocution texts, and popular rhetoric
manuals expanded the original pile of leftovers into a substantial new wing of
my archive. Instead of a half-dozen examples of these genres of texts, I had accumulated dozens. The depth and range of these new collections now extended
my holdings in nineteenth-century rhetoric materials beyond that of many formal
archives and rare-book rooms. I was visiting my own archive more often.

While I never missed the opportunity to collect popular manuals or what struck
me as gendered materials, I still had not made the intellectual connection between
my interest in how rhetorical pedagogy was marketed to the general public and
the gendered bias I had identified in parlor rhetorics like *The American Orator*.
Had I forgotten once again why I was identifying the sources I was so assiduously
compiling? What was I missing? Why weren't the collections fitting together?

I was determined to figure out the Big Picture of my developing argument.
What *had* I collected? What could it tell me? I took everything out of the archive
shelves and made piles on the floor, one pile for each genre I had been collecting:
a pile of elocution manuals, a pile of letter-writing texts, a pile of parlor rhetoric
texts, a pile of encyclopedias that treated letter writing, a small stack of conduct
manuals that included advice on letters. I set up all these collections in stacks in a
wide circle, like the outside rim of a large wheel. I made signs for each stack with
black magic marker on yellow, lined paper: Elocution! Letter Writing! Encyclopedias! Conduct Manuals! Parlor Rhetoric! I stared and stared, around the rim
of signs, around the wheel of stacks. With astonishment, I realized there was no
center to my wheel. All the stacks seemed to be pointing inward to something.
What was it? I placed a blank sheet of yellow paper in the center. What was the
stack that was not there? What was the hub of the wheel? I stood in the center
of the wheel on the blank paper and turned slowly, looking at all the stacks of
books and signs on the rim and then, quite simply, I saw it. I realized with a rush
of adrenalin that all the stacks represented historical evidence of the same phenomena: *types of rhetorical pedagogy that inscribe women into gendered rhetorical
spaces!* There was the argument for the whole book right on the floor, all points

on the wheel pointing to the center: gendered rhetorical space. I made the sign immediately and placed it in the center of the wheel.

The wheel experiment revealed that the coherent argument linking popular rhetorical education to gendered rhetorical roles was in the material of the archive all along, embedded in the hardback copies and the aging, brown pages, in the framing, in the forgotten rationale for collecting. I left the wheel on the floor for a couple of days. Finally, I had to move the material out of harm's way so I made a sketch of it with the center now filled in, "Gendered Rhetorical Space," and taped it to the wall above my computer under the title "Archival Wheel."

I looked at all the "collections" in my archive with new eyes. Traces of gendered formulations of rhetorical behavior seemed to be everywhere! I felt very much like a kid who had been looking at one of those playful drawings of the farm-yard with the tricky direction: "Find the light bulb in the farmyard." Of course, once one *sees* the light bulb skillfully sketched into the top of the barn door, one simply can not *stop* seeing it! In exactly this way, I saw the whole archive anew with just that kind of "oh, my gosh" clarity. The Archival Wheel was a dramatic example of the heuristic force of the archival, and it set me on yet another phase of collecting as invention.

The recognition of the intellectual architecture of the Archival Wheel created new archival impulses and shifted my methods of collecting evidence. The wheel had revealed an interrelated system of prescriptive rhetorical treatises working in concert to constrain women's rhetorical choices and spaces. That system was obviously a dynamic one, one sustained by cultural energy and discourses. What were the cultural conditions and values that set this system in motion and sus-tained it? How could I trace the everyday influence of that system? To answer these questions, I started collecting a greater range of cultural materials. Hoping to be able to document the ubiquitous nature of cultural discourses converging upon rhetorical practices and space as a sites for limiting women's choices, I kept the image of the archival wheel constantly in mind.

Locating books long out of circulation but still in the stacks across the river in the repository of the OSU Library, I recalled, examined, and copied dozens of collections of the "masterpieces" of American oratory published in the late nineteenth and early twentieth centuries. This material allowed me to track the extent to which women speakers were written out of the canon of American public speaking. I added extensive holdings in periodical literature to the archive, collecting issues of *Godey's Lady's Book, Peterson's Ladies National Magazine, The Ladies Repository, The Ladies Companion, Educational Review, The Atlantic Monthly,* and *Scribner's Monthly* that focused on the topics of women's education and women's roles. Biographical and autobiographical accounts of the careers of "famous" American women such as Mary Earhart's *Eminent Women of the Age*

(1868) and Mary A. Livermore's *The Story of My Life or the Sunshine and Shadow of Seventy Years* (1897) started appearing on the archive shelves as I concentrated on collecting evidence of how women who did achieve prominence as public speakers handled the cultural pressure to conform to traditional roles.

The collection of such texts took me well beyond the arc of the archive I compiled during my earlier work on nineteenth-century academic rhetoric. Although I did collect supporting cultural materials for that study, those materials were generically traditional: rhetoric treatises and discussions of the role of rhetoric in education. In collecting an archive for the developing project on gender and rhetorical space, I had already exceeded the perimeters of that original archival impulse by extending generic categories of "rhetorical text'" to include sources of rhetorical instruction published under other generic headings such as "parlor entertainment" and "conduct." With the goal of accounting for nature and effects of multiple venues of prescriptive rhetorical education in cultural motion (the archival wheel), I now focused even more attention on collecting cultural materials that charted a new rubric for *where* evidence of rhetorical theory and practices could be located. Inevitably, my definitions of what can be called "the rhetorical" shifted as well.

I now knew that the sources of gendered rhetorical education were multiple, formal, informal, academic, popular, blatant, and subtle. Intensifying my search for cultural evidence of the problem of rhetorical education and gendered rhetorical space, I began to collect artifacts of material culture, a category of evidence that I could not have imagined seeking as a novice archivist.

In *Gender and Rhetorical Space*, I used several illustrations to convey the embodied rhetorical limitations that nineteenth-century middle-class women were encouraged to see as virtues. Prominent among these illustrations was "Dear Millie," a drawing from the front cover of a nineteenth-century advertising circular that would become the featured visual in the chapter on letter writing. More important, "Dear Millie" became the prototype for the kind of artifact of material culture that would become increasingly important to my research and to the configuration of the archive:

> On the cover of *The Shelby Dry Goods Herald*, a sales catalogue published locally in Shelby, Ohio in 1883, a fashionably dressed, middle-class young woman holds up a letter in one hand and an envelope in the other as if she had just opened a letter that had brought her good news. Simulated handwriting on the letter and envelope lends realism to this engraved line-drawing in which the smiling woman looks directly out into the reader's eyes. The drawing fills most of the space of this 8-by-11 catalog bearing the title *The Shelby Dry Goods Herald*. (Johnson 77)

Figure 19. "Dear Millie," *Shelby Dry Goods Herald*, 1883.

I found Millie smiling from the cover of *The Shelby Dry Goods Herald* in a box of ephemera on the counter of one of my favorite used-book shops three blocks from my house. I stopped in to see if I could find yet *another* nineteenth-century encyclopedia. Amusing myself with some desultory browsing, I flipped through a box of odds and ends, something I did not usually do. Ephemera had not yet gotten my collecting attention. When I saw Millie, I knew at first sight that the troublesome letter-writing chapter I had been struggling with had just fallen into place and that my archival process had changed permanently.

Call it luck? I called it fate. Collecting "Dear Millie" was a turning point in my archivist autobiography. Sightings of rhetoric texts in the bookcases of facsimile nineteenth-century libraries and homes and imagining parlor rhetoric texts as common "sideboard" texts in American homes had come close to conjuring the reality of use I so wanted to understand about the place of rhetoric in American life. Holding the tattered catalogue cover of *The Shelby Dry Goods Herald* in my hands and looking at Millie waving her opened letter, I grasped for the first time the complete ordinariness and power of rhetorical protocol in the lives of the women I was studying.

"Dear Millie" revealed the synergy between rhetorical forms and the material texture of everyday life; that revelation now shapes how I recognize and collect artifacts of rhetorical culture. This has become my guiding question: *What does this everyday artifact tell us about how rhetorical genres and values are put in place and upheld?* By deploying this question, a wider arc of cultural inscriptions dictating whose words matter in American culture has become obvious. I continue to look for nineteenth-century materials but have extended my collecting to twentieth-century artifacts that will allow me to continue to explore the complex rhetorical problem of whose words are valued in American culture and why. Recent additions to the archive reveal evidence of the inscription of rhetorical culture by everyday materials: a 1901 postcard photograph of President William McKinley addressing a large crowd at the Pan American Exposition bearing the caption, "The last words of President McKinley's address, Pan American Exposition"; a copy of the *Banner Program* Chautauqua (1912), emblazoned with the Chautauqua goals, "Recreation, Education, Development, Free Speech, Honest Convictions"; *My Hero Book* (1947), an elementary schoolbook highlighting the lives of "Great Men," which provides the full text of "The Gettysburg Address" as the first selection (Diemer 7); and an issue of *National Geographic* (August 1965) covering the career and funeral of Winston Churchill and commemorating Churchill's death with a tear-out, plastic LP recording of Churchill's speeches capturing "the sound of living history" (199). Ephemera, schoolbooks, magazines, records, and more are quickly filling new cardboard boxes in the archive and messily piling up in stacks that are slipping onto the floor. My life as an archivist thus far encourages me to anticipate that another Archival Wheel might soon be forming!

Works Cited

American Orator, The. Chicago: Kulman, 1901.

Banner Program. Chautauqua, 2–8 Sept. 1912. Redpath-Vawter Chautauqua System. Odessa, MO.

Cogswell, Albert. *The Gentlemen's Perfect Letter Writer.* New York: Cogswell, 1877.

Diemer, George W., ed. *My Hero Book: Book Five.* The How and Why Library Series. Cleveland, OH: Bullard, 1947.

Earhart, Mary. *Eminent Women of the Age: Being Narratives of the Lives and Deeds of the Most Prominent Women of this Generation.* Hartford, CT: Betts, 1868.

The Ellen Terry Ladies' Reciter. N.p.: Hurst, 1884.

Johnson, Nan. *Gender and Rhetorical Space in American Life, 1866–1910.* Carbondale: Southern Illinois UP, 2002.

———. *Nineteenth-Century Rhetoric in North America.* Carbondale: Southern Illinois UP, 1991.

Livermore, Mary A. *The Story of My Life, or the Sunshine and Shadow of Seventy Years.* Hartford, CT: Worthington, 1897.

National Geographic Magazine 28, 1965, 153–225.

Porter, Ebenezer. *The Rhetorical Reader.* New York: Newman, 1848.

The Shelby Dry Goods Herald. Advertisement. Knisely. Fall and Winter 1883.

Taylor, Diana. *The Archive and the Repertoire: Performing Cultural Memory in America*: Durham, NC: Duke UP, 2003.

CONTRIBUTORS

INDEX

CONTRIBUTORS

Linda S. Bergmann is an associate professor of English at Purdue University and the director of the Purdue Writing Lab. She has started several WAC programs and directed writing centers at three universities. Her teaching experience includes undergraduate courses in composition, literature, pedagogy, and literacy and graduate seminars in writing program administration. She has published more than fifteen articles and chapters and coedited *Composition and/or Literature: The End(s) of Education* (2006). She is currently completing a textbook on undergraduate research writing for Longman.

Lynn Z. Bloom is Board of Trustees Distinguished Professor and Aetna Chair of Writing at the University of Connecticut. She has published numerous creative nonfiction/academic essays, including "(Im)Patient," which was named Best American Essay of 2005, and "Writing and Cooking, Cooking and Writing," both included in *The Seven Deadly Virtues and Other Lively Essays* (2008), *Doctor Spock: Biography of a Conservative Radical* (1972), *Writers without Borders: Writing and Teaching Writing in Troubled Times* (2008), and twenty-three other books. A book-length version of "The Essay Canon" (*College English*, 1999) is in progress, analyzing the fall and rise of the ubiquitous and now-hot genre—the essay—(after a century of second-class citizenship) that is the foundational material for 150 years of composition teaching and creative nonfiction. The archive discussed in this essay forms the research basis of this book and of its overview essay.

Jessica Enoch is an assistant professor of English at the University of Pittsburgh, where she teaches courses in composition and rhetoric, public writing, literacy, and feminist rhetorics and pedagogies. Her book *Refiguring Rhetorical Education: Women Teaching African American, Native American, and Chicano/a Students, 1865–1911* was published in 2008. Her work has also appeared in *College English, College Composition and Communication, Rhetoric Society Quarterly*, and *Composition Studies*.

Lynée Lewis Gaillet is an associate professor of English at Georgia State University, where she teaches a wide range of rhetoric/composition courses. She is a past president of the Coalition of Women Scholars in the History of Rhetoric and Composition and a past executive director of the South Atlantic Modern Language Association. Gaillet is an editor of *Scottish Rhetoric and Its Influences, Stories of Mentoring: Theory* *and Praxis* (with Michelle Eble) and the revised edition of *The Present State of Scholarship in Historical Rhetoric* (with Winifred Bryan Horner).

Cheryl Glenn is Liberal Arts Research Professor of English and Women's Studies and a codirector of the Center for Democratic Deliberation at the Pennsylvania State University. She has been chair of the Conference on College Composition and Communication. Her many scholarly publications include *Rhetoric Retold: Regendering the Tradition from Antiquity through the Renaissance* (best book/honorable mention from the Society for the Study of Early Modern Women), *Unspoken: A Rhetoric of Silence Choice* (outstanding academic title), *Rhetorical Education in America*, *The St. Martin's Guide to Teaching Writing*, *The Writer's Harbrace Handbook*, *Making Sense: A Real-World Rhetorical Reader*, and *The Harbrace Guide for College Writers*. Glenn's rhetorical scholarship has earned her three fellowships from the National Endowment for the Humanities, the Richard Braddock Best Article of the Year Award from *College Composition and Communication*, and an Outstanding Article Award (shared) from *Rhetoric Review*.

Tarez Samra Graban is an assistant professor of English at Indiana University, where she teaches rhetoric, writing, and public discourse and works with graduate students who are interested in historical traces of humor, genre, and other evolving concepts in the field. Graban's interest in archival theory and practice is twofold: to develop research methodologies for rhetoric and discourse studies and to develop pedagogies for bringing undergraduates into the archives to do original work. Her articles have appeared in *Rhetorica*, *College Composition and Communication*, *WPA: Writing Program Administration*, and *Writing on the Edge*.

Nan Johnson is a professor of English at the Ohio State University. She teaches courses in the history of rhetoric, composition theory and pedagogy, rhetorical criticism, feminist rhetoric, historiography in rhetoric and composition studies, and writing. She is the author of *Nineteenth-Century Rhetoric in North America* (1991) and *Gender and Rhetorical Space in American Life, 1866–1910* (2002). After thirty years in the field of rhetoric and composition, Johnson says she would rather be working in this discipline than doing anything else.

Barbara L'Eplattenier is an associate professor in the Department of Rhetoric and Writing at the University of Arkansas–Little Rock. With Lisa S. Mastrangelo, she coedited *Historical Studies in Writing Program Administration: Individuals, Community and the Formation of a Discipline*, which won the 2004 WPA Best Book of the Year award. Her research interests focus on archival history and methods, grant writing and persuasion, and gender/queer studies. In 2007, she cohosted the Sixth Feminisms and Rhetorics Conference in Little Rock, Arkansas.

Neal Lerner is the director of training in communication instruction for the Program in Writing and Humanistic Studies at the Massachusetts Institute of Technology. He is the author of *The Idea of a Writing Laboratory* (2009), coauthor (with Mya Poe and Jennifer Craig) of *Learning to Communicate in Science and Engineering: Case Studies from MIT*, and coauthor (with Paula Gillespie) of *The Longman Guide to Peer Tutoring*, second edition (2004). Additional publications have appeared in

College Composition and Communication, College English, Writing Center Journal, Written Communication, Composition Studies, IEEE Transactions on Professional Communication, and the *Journal of Technical Writing and Communication,* as well as in edited collections. His current research is a history and contemporary classroom study of teaching high-school English in Holyoke, Massachusetts.

Brad E. Lucas is an associate professor and chair of the Department of English at Texas Christian University. He is a codirector of the Rhetoric and Composition Sound Archives, the editor of *Composition Studies,* and the author of *Radicals, Rhetoric, and the War: The University of Nevada in the Wake of Kent State* (2006). His work has also appeared in *Rhetoric Review, Issues in Writing,* and *Kairos: A Journal of Rhetoric, Technology, and Pedagogy.*

Margaret J. Marshall is an associate professor of English at the University of Miami, Florida, where she teaches courses in composition, rhetoric, and gender. Marshall's scholarship centers on rhetorics of educational discourse, both historical and current. Her books, *Contesting Cultural Rhetorics: Public Discourse and Education, 1890–1900* (1995) and *Response to Reform: Composition and the Professionalization of Teaching* (2004), trace historical remnants in current discussions of literacy, writing instruction, and the preparation of teachers. She has also written a composition textbook, *Composing Inquiry: Methods and Readings for Investigation and Writing* (2009), coedited the proceedings for the Reinvention Center's 2006 National Conference, and contributed essays to *The Politics of Writing Centers* (2001), *Pedagogy, CCC, English Education, AERJ,* and the *Iowa Journal of Rhetoric.* The essay for this collection derives from an ongoing project examining public discussions of education and race.

Thomas Masters taught composition, literature, speech, and media studies from 1969 to 2003 for the Leyden High Schools, Franklin Park, Illinois, where he also was instrumental in curriculum design, school reform, and teacher leadership. He has taught media courses at Lewis University and rhetoric at both the University of Illinois–Urbana and at the University of Illinois–Chicago, where he served as assistant director of the writing center. At UIC, he completed a PhD in language, literacy, and rhetoric (1989). The University of Pittsburgh Series in Composition, Literacy, and Rhetoric published his *Practicing Writing: The Postwar Discourse of Freshman English* (2004). Since 2003, he has taught in the Multicultural Urban Educator program of DePaul University's School of Education; directed the Midwest chapter of Education and Unity, a consortium of students, parents, teachers, community stakeholders, school administrators, and professors who promote educational renewal; and has been editorial director for New City Press, Hyde Park, New York.

Lisa S. Mastrangelo is a professor of English and the coordinator of women's studies at the College of Saint Elizabeth, in Morristown, New Jersey. She is the coeditor, with Barbara L'Eplattenier, of *Historical Studies of Writing Program Administration: Individuals, Communities, and the Formation of a Discipline,* which won the 2004 WPA Best Book of the Year award. Her work has appeared in journals such as *Composition Studies* and *Rhetoric Review.*

Sammie L. Morris is the head of Archives and Special Collections and an associate professor of library science at Purdue University. Morris graduated from the University of Texas–Austin with a master of library and information science degree, specializing in archival enterprise. Her undergraduate degree is in English literature from the Louisiana Scholars' College at Northwestern University. She is certified by the Academy of Certified Archivists and is a past president of the Society of Indiana Archivists. Sammie is also an active member of the Society of American Archivists and the Midwest Archives Conference. She serves on the Indiana State Historic Records Advisory Board and offers instruction to graduate and undergraduate students at Purdue University on archival theory and practice. Sammie's research interests include preservation and digitization of archives, best practices for the archives profession, methods for improving access to archives, and the history of the archives profession. Her writings have appeared in many of the nation's top archives journals.

Lori Ostergaard is an assistant professor of writing and rhetoric at Oakland University whose archival research explores the composition scholarship and practices of early-twentieth-century normal-college faculty and high-school teachers in the Midwest. She coedited the essay collection *Transforming English Studies: New Voices in an Emerging Genre* (2009) with Jeff Ludwig and Jim Nugent.

Alexis E. Ramsey is an assistant professor of rhetoric at Eckerd College, where she is also the coordinator of the writing portfolio. She teaches courses in analytic and persuasive writing and environmental writing. Her areas of interest include research methodologies, particularly archival research, digital archives, WAC/WID, and environmental rhetoric. Her most recent publication appeared in *FormaMente: International Research Journal of Digital Future*.

Kelly Ritter is an associate professor of English and the director of composition at the University of North Carolina–Greensboro. Her articles and essays have appeared in *College English, College Composition and Communication, Rhetoric Review*, and *WPA: Writing Program Administration*, among others. Her book is *Before Shaughnessy: Basic Writing at Yale and Harvard, 1920–1960* (2009).

Liz Rohan is an associate professor of composition and rhetoric at the University of Michigan–Dearborn, where she teaches writing and related courses. She has published several articles in journals such as *Rhetoric Review, Pedagogy, Computers and Composition, Auto/bio*, and *Kairos*, a few of which won best-article or research awards. With Gesa Kirsch, she edited the essay collection *Beyond the Archives: Research as a Lived Process* (2008).

Shirley K Rose is a professor of English and director of writing programs at Arizona State University. Formerly at Purdue University, where she worked with colleagues from literature, American studies, and history to develop graduate and undergraduate courses in archival research, theory, and practice, she won a Provost's Study in a Second Discipline Fellowship to study archival practices with Sammie Morris, head of Purdue Archives and Special Collections. Rose is a past president of the Council of Writing Program Administrators and has published work in historical studies of writing program administration. She is currently editing, with Irwin Weiser, a collection of scholarship on issues of community engagement for writing programs and regularly teaches a seminar in writing program administration.

Wendy B. Sharer is an associate professor of English at East Carolina University, where she also serves as director of composition. Her books include *Vote & Voice: Women's Organizations and Political Literacy, 1915–1930* (2004), *1977: A Cultural Moment in Composition* (2008, coauthored with Brent Henze and Jack Selzer), and *Rhetorical Education in America* (2004, coedited with Cheryl Glenn and Margaret Lyday).

Margaret M. Strain is the director of graduate studies and an associate professor of English at the University of Dayton, where she teaches courses in writing, composition theory, and histories of rhetoric. She is also a codirector of the Rhetoric and Composition Sound Archives and a coeditor of interviews for *Kairos: A Journal of Rhetoric, Technology, and Pedagogy*. Her work on composition historiography, feminist pedagogy, and disciplinary uses of oral history has appeared in *JAC*, *Rhetoric Society Quarterly*, *Writing on the Edge*, and edited collections. Her current research focuses on the rhetorical role of the Gaelic language to mediate Catholic Anglican relations in nineteenth-century Ireland.

Katherine E. Tirabassi is an assistant professor of English at Keene State College in Keene, New Hampshire, where she teaches composition and literacy theory, creative nonfiction, and professional writing. She earned her doctorate in rhetoric/composition from the University of New Hampshire (2007), and her dissertation, "Revisiting the 'Current-Traditional Era': Innovations in Writing Instruction at the University of New Hampshire, 1940–1949" received the CCCC James Berlin Memorial Outstanding Dissertation Award in 2008. She is currently the chair of the Northeast Writing Center Association and has cowritten chapters in edited collections on writing center and library collaborations and graduate students in the writing center. Her research interests include historical/archival research, composition theory, ethnographic research, and writing center/writing across the curriculum theory and practice.

Chris Warnick is an assistant professor of English at the College of Charleston, where he also directs Writer's Group, a writer's studio for first-year composition students. After completing his dissertation on undergraduate personal writing from the 1960s and 1970s, his research has focused on workshopping student writing and on the use of countercultural writers in the composition classroom during the 1970s. He is currently working on a project tracing the history and genealogy of cultural-studies-based writing textbooks.

Elizabeth Yakel is an associate professor at the University of Michigan School of Information in the Archives and Records Management and Preservation of Information specializations. Her major research interest is access to primary sources and user-based evaluation in archives and special collections. Recently, she has been investigating how social computing and Web 2.0 applications affect access to archives and connect communities to collections. Her research has been supported by the National Historical Publications and Records Commission, the Institute for

Museum and Library Services, and the Andrew W. Mellon Foundation, and she has published numerous articles in such publications as *Archival Science* and *American Archivist*. Yakel is also active in the Society of American Archivists, where she served on the governing council (1992–95) and was elected a fellow in 1999.

Helena Zinkham is the acting chief of the Prints and Photographs Division at the Library of Congress, which cares for fourteen million pictures spanning the 1500s to the present. Her work with visual collections began at the Maryland Historical Society library in 1977. Her publications include *A Guide to Print, Photograph, Architecture, and Ephemera Collections at the New-York Historical Society* (1998) and chapters on reading and describing photographs for *Photographs: Archival Care and Management* (2006). As a librarian, she also enjoys teaching cataloging and visual literacy at the Rare Book School.

INDEX

All numbers in bold type refer to pages with illustrations.

SHARP (Society of the History of Authorship, Reading, and Publishing), 103
Sherman, William T., 294
Siddons, Henry, 254
Siddons, Sarah, 254–55
significance, historical, 207
Silverman, David, 273
Slomba, Elizabeth, 20, 178n1
society, interview, 273
Society of American Archivists, 53
socioeconomic and racial barriers, 244
Special Collections. *See* archives
standard icon for manuscripts, 104
Stanton, Elizabeth Cady, 211, 253
Steedman, Carol, 1
Stewart, Cora Wilson, 46
StoryCorps, 273, 275n5
storytelling, 36, 38
strategic responses to audience and situation, 213–14
Stukel, James, 199
subjectivity, historical, 242
successive segmentation, 113–14. *See also* online research, search strategy
surrogate researcher, 146
synonym generation. *See* online research, search strategy

taxonomical framework, 212–17
Tayler, Diana, 290, 292
terministic screens, 199–200
Thesaurus for Graphic Materials, 127
Tillotson, Marcia, 220, 222, 222–30
Tirabassi, Katherine E., 20, 178n1, 178n2
transference, 221
Truth, Sojourner, 119, **121**

United States Indian School (Carlisle, Pennsylvania), 123, **124**, 153

unprocessed collections. *See* hidden collections
usable past, 25
OHRP (U.S. Office for Human Research Protection), 264

visual literacy, 120, 127, 128, 129. *See also* photographs
visual propaganda, 124
vulnerable observer, 234, 239, 246. *See also* archival research, emotional response to

Waters, Donald J., 83
WCRP (Oral History Archive of the Writing Centers Research Project), 273
Web, deep, 102, 113, 123, 124, 175. *See also* online research
Wells, Susan, 188
Wikipedia, 122
Willard, Frances, 214
Windels, Holmstedt, 18
women, absence of, in archival records, 187–88
women in composition, 187
"Women's History Archives," 94
"Women's History Resources in the Library of Congress Prints and Photographs Division," 126
WorldCat Registry, 103, 104, **105–9**, 111, 116, 140. *See also* online research
writing as valuable artifact, 179n3

Yahoo, 113, 122, 123. *See also* online research, search engines
Young, Richard, 59

Zenger, Amy, 20, 178n1
Zotero, 117